Praise for *Reading Nahum–Malachi*

Steven Tuell has written a lucid, concise, and informative commentary on the last six books of the Book of the Twelve Prophets. His commentary addresses historical, compositional, and theological issues in a manner that will be especially accessible for undergraduate and seminary students in Christian colleges, universities, and theological seminaries.

—Marvin A. Sweeney
Claremont School of Theology and
Academy for Jewish Religion

Steven Tuell has addressed his considerable skill as a good reader of texts to the much neglected six "minor" prophets who close the Christian Old Testament. By his alert, steady attentiveness he shows why these neglected books merit attention, and why the neglect of them is a misfortune. Tuell's reading is fresh, reliable, and suggestive. His commentary will be, in time to come, a substantial reference point for our continuing work and study.

—Walter Brueggemann
Columbia Theological Seminary

With admirable clarity and characteristically well-informed insight, Steven Tuell's exegesis engages the historical particularity of the final six witnesses collected into the prophetical "Book of the Twelve." Citing Sirach 49:10 as his mandate, he is also keenly attentive to the ways these individual voices contribute to the theological vitality of the book as a whole. In short, readers will appreciate that he achieves the balance he sets as his interpretative goal.

—S. Dean McBride, Jr.
Professor Emeritus of Biblical Hebrew and
Old Testament Interpretation
Union Presbyterian Seminary
Richmond, Virginia

This well-written book by a leading scholar in prophetic literature is a welcome addition to the literature on the minor prophets. Both graduate students and pastors, especially, will appreciate the erudite discussions of issues of transmission, translation, and structure, coupled with a keen theological sense of how these texts speak to the world today.

—Corrine Carvalho
Professor of Theology
University of St. Thomas

READING NAHUM–MALACHI

Smyth & Helwys Publishing, Inc.
6316 Peake Road
Macon, Georgia 31210-3960
1-800-747-3016

Library of Congress Cataloging-in-Publication Data

Names: Tuell, Steven Shawn.
Title: Reading Nahum-Malachi : a literary and theological commentary / by Steven Tuell.
Description: Macon, GA : Smyth & Helwys Publishing, 2016. | Includes bibliographical references and index.
Identifiers: LCCN 2015037348 | ISBN 9781573128483 (pbk. : alk. paper)
Subjects: LCSH: Bible. Minor Prophets--Commentaries.
Classification: LCC BS1560 .T84 2015 | DDC 224/.907--dc23
LC record available at http://lccn.loc.gov/2015037348

Reading Nahum–Malachi

A Literary and Theological Commentary

Steven Tuell

Also by Steven Tuell

Ezekiel
(Understanding the Bible Commentary)

Constituting the Community: Studies on the Polity of Ancient Israel in Honor of S. Dean McBride, Jr. (co-edited with John T. Strong)

1 and 2 Chronicles
(Interpretation)

The Law of the Temple in Ezekiel 40–48

Contents

Abbreviations

AB	Anchor Bible
ABD	*Anchor Bible Dictionary*. Ed. David Noel Freedman. 6 vols. New York, 1992
ACCS	Ancient Christian Commentary on Scripture. Downers Grove, IL: Intervarsity
ANET	*Ancient Near Eastern Texts Relating to the Old Testament.* Ed. J. B. Pritchard. 3rd ed. Princeton, 1969
ANETS	Ancient Near Eastern Texts and Studies
AOAT	Alter Orient und Altes Testament
AOTC	Abingdon Old Testament Commentaries
BAR	*Biblical Archaeology Review*
BASOR	*Bulletin of the American Schools of Oriental Research*
BBB	Bonner biblische Beiträge
BETL	Bibliotheca ephemeridum theologicarum lovaniensum
BibOr	Biblica et orientalia
BibS(N)	Biblische Studien (Neukirchen, 1951–)

B-TS Biblische-Theologische Studien

BZAW Beihefte zur Zeitschrift für die alttestimentliche Wissenschaft

CBQ *Catholic Biblical Quarterly.*

CFTL Clark's Foreign Theological Library

CHJ *Cambridge History of Judaism.* Ed. W. D. Davies and Louis Finkelstein. Cambridge, 1984-

ConBOT Coniecta biblica: Old Testament Series

CahRB Cahiers de la Revue Biblique

CTA *Corpus des tablettes en cuneiforms alphabétiques découvertes à Ras Shamra-Ugarit de 1929 à 1939.* Ed. A. Herdner. Mission de Ras Shamra 10. Paris, 1963

DDD *Dictionary of Deities and Demons in the Bible.* Ed. K. van der Toorn, B. Becking, and P.W. van der Horst. Leiden, 1995

DJD Discoveries in the Judean Desert

EncJud *Encyclopedia Judaica.* 16 vols. Jerusalem, 1972

FOTL Forms of Prophetic Literature

HALOT Koehler, L., W. Baumgartner, and J. J. Stamm, *The Hebrew and Aramaic Lexicon of the Old Testament.* Trans. and ed. M. E. W. J. Richardson. 4 vols. Leiden, 1994–1999

HBC *HarperCollins Bible Commentary.* Ed. J. L. Mays et al. 2d. ed. San Francisco, 2000

HBD *HarperCollins Bible Dictionary.* Ed. P. J. Achtemeier et al. 2d. ed. San Francisco, 1996

HCOT Historical Commentary on the Old Testament

HSB	*HarperCollins Study Bible*, Rev. ed. Ed. H.W. Attridge et al. San Francisco, 2006
HSM	Harvard Semitic Monographs
HTKAT	Herders theologischer Kommentar zum Alten Testament
HTR	*Harvard Theological Review*
HUCA	*Hebrew Union College Annual*
IBC	Interpretation: A Bible Commentary for Teaching and Preaching
IBT	Interpreting Biblical Texts
IDBSup	*Interpreter's Dictionary of the Bible: Supplementary Volume.* Ed. Keith Crim. Nashville, 1976
IEJ	*Israel Exploration Journal*
Int	*Interpretation*
IRUSC	Interpretation, Resources for the Use of Scripture in the Church
JAOS	*Journal of the American Oriental Society*
JBL	*Journal of Biblical Literature*
JETS	*Journal of the Evangelical Theological Society*
JHebS	*Journal of Hebrew Scriptures*
JJS	*Journal of Jewish Studies*
JR	*Journal of Religion*
JSB	*The Jewish Study Bible.* Eds. Adele Berlin and Marc Zvi Brettler. New York: Oxford, 2004

JSOTSup	Journal for the Study of the Old Testament: Supplement Series
KAT	Kommentar zum Alten Testament
LHB/OTS	Library of Hebrew Bible/Old Testament Studies
LPT	Library of Protestant Thought
LXX	The Septuagint
MT	The Masoretic text of the Hebrew Bible
NCBC	New Century Bible Commentary
NIB	*The New Interpreter's Bible.* Nashville: Abingdon, 1994-2002
NIBCOT	New International Bible Commentary on the Old Testament
NIBD	*The New Interpreter's Dictionary of the Bible.* Nashville: Abingdon, 2006-2009
NICOT	New International Commentary on the Old Testament
OTE	*Old Testament Essays*
OTL	Old Testament Library
SHBC	Smyth & Helwys Bible Commentary
SBLDS	Society of Biblical Literature Dissertation Series
SBLSymS	Society of Biblical Literature Symposium Series
TCS	Texts from Cuneiform Sources
Tg. Neb.	*Targum Nebi'im*
Tg. Ket.	*Targum Kethubim*
TLZ	*Theologische Literaturzeitung*

UBC Understanding the Bible Commentary

VAB Voderasiaische Bibliothek

VT *Vetus Testamentum*

VTSup Supplements to Vetus Testamentum

WBC Word Bible Commentary

WMANT Wissenschaftliche Monographien zum Alten und Neuen Testament

ZAW *Zeitschrift für die alttestamentliche Wissenschaft*

Preface

In my first position out of graduate school, at Erskine College in Due West, South Carolina, among the first new friends my wife, Wendy, and I made were Melanie Nogalski in the Admissions Office and her husband Jim—a newly-minted PhD like me, who was looking for someone with whom to read Hebrew. Our friendship has continued to the present day. Jim Nogalski is one of a few biblical scholars who have revolutionized our discipline. Whether or not one is convinced by his thesis that the Book of the Twelve must be read *as* a book, no one who works with the Twelve today can fail to reckon with his insightful and erudite work. Jim's influence is apparent throughout this volume, and while in many places I depart from his construal of the Twelve, his insights have been foundational to my own reading of these intriguing, challenging, and most definitely *not* "minor" prophets.

It was through Jim that I came know Mark Biddle, editor of this series. I am grateful for Mark's careful reading and insight, as well as for his patience. I am thankful not only to Mark and to Jim but also to all my colleagues in Lemadim Olam—Bill Bellinger, Corri Carvalho, Jerome Creach, Nancy Declaisse-Walford, Clint McCann, Pam Scalise, John Strong, Jim Watts, and particularly Stephen Cook, for his insights into Haggai and Zechariah. Thanks are owed, too, to the participants in and organizers of the SBL seminar "Formation of the Book of the Twelve," particularly to Paul Redditt. Their invitation to me in 2000 to present a paper on Haggai–Zechariah and Ezekiel marked my first official foray into scholarship on the Twelve.

I am grateful to President Bill Carl, to Dean Barry Jackson, and to the Board of Directors of Pittsburgh Theological Seminary for granting me sabbatical leave to work on this project. Thanks are owed to the hard-working staff of the Barbour Library, and to my administrative assistant Kathy Anderson, now enjoying her well-earned retirement. Thanks to my faculty colleagues at PTS, particularly to Hebrew Bible colleagues Jerome Creach and Ron Tappy, to Edith Humphrey and Dale Allison, for insights into the history of the interpretation of the Twelve, and to my colleague emeritus Don Gowan, for his wonderful work on Habakkuk. The students in my course on the Book of the Twelve at PTS have, as is ever the case, taught me at least as much as I taught them; thanks are particularly owed to Nicole Carlin, who showed me that God's love is mentioned in Zephaniah as well as in Hosea and Malachi, causing me to rethink my approach to these books.

Several churches have given me the opportunity to preach and to teach on the Twelve: thank you to the pastors and congregations of Grace Presbyterian in Butler, Pennsylvania; Fox Chapel Presbyterian in Pittsburgh, PA; First Presbyterian in Monaca, PA; Oakmont Presbyterian in Oakmont, PA; to Westminster Presbyterian in Pittsburgh, PA; to my home church, St. Paul's United Methodist in Allison Park, PA; and to my pastor and friend Ron Hoellein. I was also privileged to explore these books with the good folk attending Family Week at the United Methodist Camp and Retreat Center at Jumonville, PA, and with the clergy and laity of Lake Erie Presbytery at their Big Event.

For their unfailing love, prayers, and acceptance, I thank my parents, Bernard and Mary Tuell, who introduced me to the Bible; my sons Sean, Anthony, and Mark; and particularly my wife, Wendy: *z'ot dodi wezo't re'i.*

Introduction

The six books covered in this volume, Nahum, Habakkuk, Zephaniah, Haggai, Zechariah, and Malachi, are the latter half of a collection of twelve short prophetic books grouped together in the Bible, sometimes called the "Minor Prophets." These six books severally span the period from the end of the Assyrian empire in the seventh century BCE to the fall of the Neo-Babylonian Empire and the emergence of Persia in the fifth century BCE. Zephaniah is set in the reign of Josiah, the last truly independent king of Judah, who ruled in the time of Assyria's decline. Nahum describes the fall of Nineveh, Assyria's capital, with fiendish glee. The rise of Babylon in the wake of Assyria's collapse, and the tragic consequences of this development for Judah, unfold in Habakkuk. Haggai, Zechariah, and (presumably) Malachi are set in the Persian period, after the Babylonian exile. While the settings of Zephaniah, Haggai, and Zechariah are explicitly stated in their superscriptions (Zeph 1:1; Hag 1:1; Zech 1:1), however, the historical contexts of the other three are not specifically defined. Content would seem to point to the above-proposed setting for Nahum and for Habakkuk, but the date and setting of Malachi are less certain.

The composition history of these books raises further questions. While it is commonly accepted that the hymns that open Nahum (Nah 1:2-11) and close Habakkuk (Hab 3:1-19) may have been added to those books, the motivation for that expansion calls for consideration. Indeed, some scholars have argued that Malachi is entirely a redactional product, having been broken off from the series of oracles that concludes the canonical form of Zechariah (Zech 9–14; so Petersen 1995), perhaps in order to yield the number twelve. The purpose of Zechariah 9–14 (generally regarded as a late addition to the text) requires exploration, as does the effect of these chapters on the book of Zechariah in its final form.

As interesting as a book-by-book reading of Nahum–Malachi may be, however, these books also have a collective identity. A better designation for the "Minor" Prophets is their ancient designation, the Book of the Twelve. Scholarship on the Book of the Twelve has in recent years increasingly turned toward seeing this entire corpus *as* a book: an intentional, unified whole rather than a mere collection (e.g., House 1990, Nogalski 1993 and 2011, Jones 1995, Schart 1998, Redditt 2008). Redactional links among our six books are particularly evident in Haggai 1–Zechariah 8, which was clearly edited as a single book, but one may identify other common features. Further, through views explicitly offered in pre-critical writings, through the implicit clues to ancient readings found in the Masoretic notes related to the Twelve, and through the ordering of the books in the canon, we may discover evidence of how ancient readers approached these texts.

The Book of the Twelve

In his *City of God* (18:29), Augustine writes of "the book of the twelve prophets, who are called the minor from the brevity of their writings, as compared with those who are called the greater [*maiores*] prophets because they published larger volumes." For Augustine, the distinction of the "Minor" Prophets from the "Major" ones was a matter of length only, not of significance. Unfortunately, one cannot say the same for the contemporary church. Students in my course on the Prophets—seminarians, most of whom have grown up in the church—have often told me that they had never before read from or heard a sermon preached on the "Minor" Prophets, let alone studied them. I have even heard those stirring words of Amos, "Let justice roll down like waters" (Amos 5:24), attributed to Martin Luther King, Jr.—who of course *said* them but knew full well when he did so that he was quoting Scripture! This obscurity extends particularly to Nahum through Malachi. The Revised Common Lectionary, for example, offers no readings from Nahum, only one each from Habakkuk (1:1-4; 2:1-4), Haggai (1:15b–2:9) and Zechariah (9:9-12), and only two each from Zephaniah (1:7, 2-18 and 3:14-20) and Malachi (3:1-4 and 4:1-2a).

If the Twelve have often been absent from the Christian pulpit, they have not, thankfully, been missing from biblical scholarship. Interpreters have largely forgotten Augustine's conception of the shorter prophetic books from Hosea to Malachi as a single Book of the Twelve Prophets (*libro duodecim prophetarum*) until relatively recently, however. From the Enlightenment to the late twentieth century, commentators (with rare exceptions: e.g., Budde 1921; Wolfe 1933) tended to treat the Twelve as distinct and separate books rather than as a single corpus. For example, Conrad von Orelli, although recognizing that ancient canon lists regard the Twelve as a single book (Orelli 1893, 1–2), said that they "are found united, just because of their smallness"

(Orelli 1893, 1). Similarly, although commentaries have tended to group members of the Twelve together in their treatment, such groupings have been largely incidental: matters of convenience rather than intention. Scholars have rarely paid attention to interrelationships among the books in such collections (e.g., Achtemeier 1986 and 1996; Limburg 1988; Floyd 2000).

This was certainly not the case among pre-modern interpreters. Sirach 49:10 reads, "May the bones of the Twelve Prophets send forth new life from where they lie, for they comforted the people of Jacob and delivered them with confident hope"—indicating not only that the Twelve were understood as a single, corporate entity but also that, at least in ben Sirach's view, the theme of the Book of the Twelve is a comforting word of hope and deliverance, a proposal we will test in this commentary. In the Jewish apocalypse 4 Ezra 14:44-48, ninety-four books are transcribed from the heroic scribe's ecstatic dictation: seventy secret books and twenty-four books that are to be made public—that is, the books of Jewish Scripture (for the twenty-four-book canon, see also *b. B. Bat.* 14b and *Gos. Thom.* 52). This number clearly assumes that the Twelve count as a single book (note that Samuel, Kings, Chronicles, and Ezra–Nehemiah are all single books in the Hebrew Bible; their division can be traced to the Septuagint [abbreviated LXX], a translation of the Jewish Scriptures into Greek from the third to second centuries BCE).

Josephus, on the other hand, speaks of twenty-two authoritative books (*Con. Ap.* 1.38-40), of which thirteen, written by *hoi meta Mousen prophetai* ("the prophets after Moses") tell of events *apo de tes Mouseos teleutes mechri tes Artaxerxou* ("from the death of Moses to the reign of Artaxerxes"): presumably, the Former Prophets (Joshua, Judges, Samuel, and Kings) plus the other "historical" books (Ruth, Esther, Chronicles, and Ezra–Nehemiah) and the Latter Prophets (Isaiah, Jeremiah, Ezekiel, the Twelve, and Daniel, whom Josephus evidently regarded as a prophet, although the Jewish canon places his book among the *Kethubim*, or Writings; so Koch 1987, 241). Bishop Melito of Sardis (late second century), whose reckoning of the Jewish canon numbers either twenty-six (if, as he states, Samuel–Kings count as four books and Chronicles as two) or twenty-two books (if Kings and Chronicles each count as a single book; note that Melito also substitutes Wisdom for Esther, and that he evidently combines Lamentations and Jeremiah), also regards the Twelve as one book (*ton dodeka en monobiblo*; cited in Eusebius, *Hist. eccl.* 4.26.14). In his famous Easter letter of 365 CE (*Epis.* 39.4), Athanasius follows Josephus in reckoning the Old Testament as containing twenty-two books, a number that he relates to the Hebrew alphabet (a tradition going back to Origen's day, cf. Christensen 1986, 37–38). Athanasius's canon is much like Melito's, save that he does not include Wisdom (he does, however, include both the Letter of Jeremiah and Baruch, combining these, along with Lamentations, with the book of Jeremiah) and that he counts two books of Kings (Samuel and Kings); he too regards the Twelve as a single book. We could cite numerous other examples from early Christian literature, but we will conclude with Jerome, whose preface to the books of Kings also lays out a twenty-two-book canon related to the alphabet. Jerome arrives at that number by combining Ruth with Judges and Lamentations with Jeremiah; he too assumes that the Twelve constitute a single book (*liber duodecim Prophetarum*). Although there was considerable debate in antiquity surrounding how to number the canon, then, the Twelve were consistently reckoned as a single book.

The medieval Jewish scribes (called Masoretes) responsible for the Hebrew text on which our Old Testament is based (called the Masoretic Text, or MT), also regarded the Twelve as a single book, or at any rate as belonging to a single scroll. In addition to the notes at the end of each of the twelve books counting the number of verses, there is a note following Malachi referring to the Twelve as a whole (compare the similar note at the end of the Torah, the five books traditionally attributed to Moses). Further, in contrast to Isaiah, Jeremiah, and Ezekiel, the Masoretes do not mark the middle verse of each book in the Twelve, but rather mark the middle of the Twelve as a whole (see the marginal note on Mic 3:12 in the MT). In the Talmud, Judaism's authoritative compendium of the teaching of the rabbis, *b. Baba Bathra* presents the Twelve as a unit even more forcefully. According to the sages (*b. B. Bat.* 13b), scribes are to leave four lines between each book of the *Nebi'im* (that is, the Prophets), and even between each book of the Torah; however, for the Twelve, only three lines are to be left between each book. *B. Baba Bathra* 14b gives the reason for this distinction: the Book of the Twelve is a single book, following Jeremiah, Ezekiel, and Isaiah. Similarly, *b. Baba Bathra* 13b speaks of the "eight prophets": clearly Joshua, Judges, Samuel, Kings (the Former Prophets), Isaiah, Jeremiah, Ezekiel, and the Twelve (the Latter Prophets; cf. Jerome, *Incip. Prol. Lib. Reg.*, who also counts eight prophetic books). *B. Baba Bathra* 15a attributes the authorship of the Book of the Twelve (together with Ezekiel, Daniel, and Esther) to *'anshey keneset haggedolah* ("the men of the Great Assembly"), suggesting, again, that the rabbis regarded the Book of the Twelve as a unified composition.

Of course, it is one thing to say that the Twelve are to be read together, as one book; a different kind of question is, what *sort* of book? It is possible to emphasize the unity of the Book of the Twelve to the exclusion of the evidence within it for the complex history of this composite work (e.g., House 1990 and Christensen 2009). As Ehud ben Zvi in particular has shown, such a reading fails to account for the distinctive character of the individual works within the Twelve, or for the independent consideration of these books in ancient tradition (for example, the *pesharim* [that is, commentaries] on Nahum and Habakkuk from Qumran; cf. ben Zvi 1996, 131–33; Pajunen and von Weissenberg, 2015). Clearly, the Book of the Twelve is not a book in the way that Esther is a book, or even that Ezekiel is: it does not have the commonality of plot, style, and theme we would expect of a single author or group of authors, writing at a particular time and in a particular context. Nonetheless, the Twelve may well be a book in the way that Proverbs and Psalms are books: that is, a collection of originally independent units intentionally arranged to form a novel whole. More to the point, the Book of the Twelve is a book in the way that the Book of Isaiah is a book. Indeed, the impetus behind the editing and arrangement of the disparate material in the Isaianic anthology (incorporating the eighth century material contained in Isa 1–39, the exilic material in 40-55, commonly called "Deutero-Isaiah," the postexilic material in 56–66, commonly called "Trito-Isaiah," and the "Isaianic apocalypse" in 24–27) may well also have produced the Book of the Twelve (Steck 1991).

Broadly speaking, contemporary biblical studies approach texts in two ways. One approach, called "diachronic reading," attempts to place the text in its proper context in the history and culture of ancient Israel, and to read it from that perspective. Another, called "synchronic reading," looks at the text as a whole, in its final form. This commentary will attempt to maintain a balance between diachronic readings, regarding each of the six books we will study in their historical and social settings, and synchronic readings, regarding their interrelationship and their canonical function in the Twelve as a whole.

The Canonical Order and Placement of Nahum–Malachi

Although the order of the first six books in the Twelve varies considerably, particularly when the LXX and the MT are compared, the order of the last six is remarkably stable. Not only do the MT and the LXX agree in this arrangement, but so do the first century CE versions of the Twelve found at Nahal Hever (8HevXIIgr) and Wadi Murabba'at (MurXII), and the order witnessed in the *Lives of the Prophets* 11–16 and 5 Ezra 1:39-40 (second or third century CE). In the Talmud, *b. Baba Bathra* 14b (which also identifies the Twelve as a single book) affirms that the Book of the Twelve opens with Hosea and closes with Haggai, Zechariah, and Malachi. The exceptions are the clearly idiosyncratic list in *The Martyrdom and Ascension of Isaiah* 4:22, which places Nahum prior to Jonah and Obadiah, and Zephaniah between Haggai and Zechariah, and 4QXIIa, a fragmentary text from Qumran that apparently places Jonah after Malachi (but cf. Pajunen and von Weissenberg, 2015, who argue that Jonah did not come immediately after Mal on this scroll). Where the fragments of the Twelve from Cave 4 at Qumran preserve a sequence (the end of one book followed by the beginning of another), however, they generally support the MT: 4QXIIa apparently has Malachi following Zechariah (questioned by Pajunen and von Weissenberg, 2015, 737–38), although Jonah comes after Malachi; 4QXIIb has Haggai following Zephaniah; and 4QXIIg has Obadiah following Amos, as well as Habakkuk following Nahum. This suggests that among the 4QXII fragments, only Jonah may be out of place according to the MT sequence—perhaps placed last in 4QXIIa in accordance with its late composition rather than its eighth-century setting (cf. 2 Kgs 14:25).

In short, the sequence Nahum, Habakkuk, Zephaniah, Haggai, Zechariah, Malachi is broadly attested and evidently very old. These six seem to be arranged in chronological order—except for Zephaniah. According to its superscription, Zephaniah is set "in the days of King Josiah son of Amon of Judah" (Zeph 1:1). The scathing judgments against Jerusalem's ruling class that follow, however, say nothing of Josiah's reforms (2 Kgs 22:1–23:25) begun in the eighteenth year of his reign, when the king was twenty-six (approximately 622 BCE). It seems probable, then, that Zephaniah must date before the reform to the years of Josiah's minority. Neither Nahum nor Habakkuk is dated (in sharp contrast to Haggai and Zechariah, where dates figure prominently); however, we can infer dating from their content. Nahum gloatingly describes the sack of Nineveh, capital of the Assyrian Empire, by the alliance of Nabopolassar of Babylon and Cyaxeres of Media, in 612 BCE. Yet the prophet shows no awareness of the tragic end of Josiah's reign in 609 BCE, when the king died in battle at Megiddo while vainly attempting to stop Pharaoh Necho II's march through his kingdom. Habakkuk describes the rise of the Neo-Babylonian Empire and the ravages carried out by this empire in Judah, suggesting a date well after Josiah's death, probably during the revolt of Jehoiakim. By rights, then, Zephaniah ought to precede both Nahum and Habakkuk.

On the other hand, Nahum and Habakkuk appear to have been edited together (cf. Schart 1998, 246–51; Fabry 2006, 100–101). Nahum opens with a psalm: an acrostic poem praising God the divine warrior for God's justice (Nah 1:2-11). Habakkuk *concludes* with a psalm describing God as a warrior (Hab 3:1-19), defiantly proclaiming God's righteousness in the face of tragedy: a necessary affirmation, as the remainder of the book questions God's justice in light of the suffering brought on by the Babylonian invasion (e.g., Hab 1:2-4, 12-13). Nahum and Habakkuk, then, are sandwiched between two psalms. The content and character of these psalms will be discussed further in context. For now, it is sufficient to note that the pairing created by this editorial process both affirms God's judgment through historical processes and critiques an overly simplistic identification of God's activity with those processes—or at any rate, with our understanding of them.

The image of the end both joins Nahum and Habakkuk in theme and also ties them to their context. The psalm that opens Nahum speaks of God bringing "a full end" (Heb., *kalah*) to the wicked (Nah 1:8-9), a theme that sounds again in Zephaniah 1:18 with reference to the day of the LORD visited upon Jerusalem. Habakkuk too is given a vision that "speaks of the end [*qets*], and does not lie" (Hab 2:3). The noun *qets* ("end") appears in the Twelve only here and in Amos 8:2, where it speaks of the end of the northern kingdom. These links, as we will discuss below, strongly suggest that the end revealed to Habakkuk is not, as some have suggested, the end of Babylonian oppression, but rather the end of *Jerusalem* (compare Ezek 7:1-9, which also uses *qets* in this way). But read in the context of the Twelve, this emphasis on last things becomes, in the words of Brevard Childs, "a dramatic illustration of the eschatological triumph of God" (Childs 1978, 51).

The placement of this pair of prophets prior to Zephaniah is perhaps best explained by postulating, with Nogalski and others, an earlier collection, a "book of the Four" (Albertz 2003) consisting of Hosea, Amos, Micah, and Zephaniah (Nogalski 1993a, 278–80 and Schart 1998; compare, for example, Zeph 1:1 with Hos 1:1 and Mic 1:1). Nahum and Habakkuk have been incorporated into this older collection by insertion. That they were inserted prior to Zephaniah, rather than being appended after it, is best explained by considering the redactional technique by which Haggai and Zechariah have been combined as a single book. The date formulae that structure this compound work (Hag 1:1, 15; 2:1, 10, 20; Zech 1:1, 7; 7:1) are sequential, with the exception of Zechariah 1:1, which predates Haggai 2:10 and 20. Seth Sykes proposes that these overlapping dates "reinforce a thematic connection between the two prophetic texts"; in this way, the overlap contributes to the unity of Haggai–Zechariah as a "unified, whole utterance" (Sykes 2002, 27). Similarly, by inserting Nahum–Habakkuk prior to Zephaniah, the redactors of the Twelve have reinforced the unity of the whole through overlapping dates.

Malachi, like Nahum and Habakkuk, is undated. Nonetheless, the witness of every attestation of the order of the Twelve apart from 4QXIIa supports the placement of Malachi at the end of the Twelve, and hence the implication that it is to be read in the same postexilic context as Haggai–Zechariah. The evidence of Malachi's incorporation into the Twelve also supports this placement. The LORD's love for Israel is an important theme in Hosea, as 3:1 in particular demonstrates (cf. also 11:1 and 14:5 [4]; note that the verse numbers in the Hebrew text sometimes differ from those in the Christian Old Testament; where this difference occurs anywhere in the biblical texts we cite, this commentary will give the Hebrew citation first, followed by the OT numbering in brackets or parentheses). Malachi 1:2 and 2:11 also mention the LORD's love for Israel. No other prophet among the Twelve mentions this theme (but cf. Zeph 3:17). John D. W. Watts has argued therefore that Hosea 1–3 and Malachi form a literary frame around the Twelve (Watts 2000b, 212). Further, the prophecies of Nahum (1:1), Habakkuk (1:1), and Malachi (1:1) are each designated as a *massa'* ("oracle"; cf. also the use of this term in Zech 9–14, at 9:1 and 12:1), so that this designation both opens and closes the latter half of the Twelve. Combined with internal evidence implying a Persian Period dating (e.g., the anti-priestly stance of Mal 2:1-3; cf. Isa 65:5; 66:3), this evidence for the placement of Malachi makes its dating somewhat after the time of Haggai and Zechariah more likely.

The Plan for this Commentary

This commentary will treat the last six books of the Twelve in sequence, in their canonical order. In general, this study will stay with the MT whenever possible, although it will consult older Hebrew manuscripts where available and the ancient versions (especially the LXX and the *Targum of the Prophets* [*Tg. Neb.*], a translation of the Prophets into Aramaic for use in the synagogue) to ensure the best reading. Unless otherwise noted, English translations will come from the NRSV.

The Masoretic scribes have divided the text into subunits, either by adding a space between sections within a line (called a break *setumah*), or by starting the next section on a new line, skipping a line if necessary (break *petukhah*). While we might postulate that there was at one point a difference in significance between these two divisions (perhaps *petukhah* indicated a major break, *setumah* a minor), there does not appear to be any such distinction in the Masoretic text as we have it. The Qumran texts show that this is an ancient, pre-Masoretic system, which gives us a window into the logic of ancient readings. While the Masoretic divisions will not always be followed, they will inform our determination of the units within these six books.

Each treatment will begin with an introduction to the book. The introduction will open with an essay on reading that particular prophet, focusing on theological issues, themes, or problems raised by that book. It will then proceed to a discussion of the authorship, date, and setting of the book, followed by an analysis of its structure. Next, the commentary will discuss the role of the particular prophetic book under consideration within the Book of the Twelve by considering its the relationship to another book or unit within the Twelve that particularly illumines its final form. Only after this introduction will the discussion turn to a unit-by-unit consideration of the book in question.

Nahum

Reading Nahum

No selections from Nahum appear in the Common Lectionary, but that is scarcely surprising. Nahum is a difficult and disturbing book, which gloats over the collapse of Assyria's capital Nineveh (2:1-14 [1:15–2:13]), describing the fall of the city through a mock dirge (3:1-19). Even more troubling, however, particularly to modern readers, is the imagery used to depict this fall: Nahum describes Nineveh as a woman, so that its siege becomes a mugging and its fall a rape (3:5-6). Poetically, Nahum is a masterpiece: even in English translation, its vivid imagery and striking use of language and rhythm come through:

> The crack of whip and rumble of wheel,
> galloping horses and bounding chariot!
> Horsemen charging,
> flashing sword and glittering spear. (3:2-3a)

However, appreciating the poetic artistry of Nahum is not unlike appreciating the grandeur of Albert Speer's architecture in the official buildings of Nazi Germany, or the cinematic breakthroughs and innovations achieved by D. W. Griffiths in his horrifically racist film *The Birth of a Nation.* Whatever the artistic value of the work, its intent cannot help coloring its appreciation.

Of course, Speer's architecture and Griffith's cinematography both manifest the culture of the powerful. Nahum represents the voice of the powerless: one must read this book in a colonial context, with tiny Judah struggling under the heel of its Assyrian oppressors. As John Goldingay observes, "Nahum is divinely-inspired resistance literature" (Goldingay 2009, 18). Wilhelm Wessels, viewing Nahum from a South African context, describes the extreme language of this book as theological and poetic "'overstatement' of expression" that both "served as an outlet for suppressed or cropped-up emotions" of an oppressed people and also imaginatively created "a world free from the domination of the cruel Assyrians, stripped of their power"; it is not to be taken literally "as a call to violence or a legitimation of violence" (Wessels 1998, 625). Clearly, one must read and use Nahum with care: to apply such literature directly and uncritically to the context of comparative power and privilege enjoyed by most of us in the modern, post-industrial West would be a serious mistake. Nevertheless, while knowledge of Nahum's historical context may explain the book's violent, hateful content, it surely does not excuse it (as Wessels recognizes; cf. 1998, 615, 627). Judaism and Christianity alike teach that we need to expect better, of ourselves and of our God. The two great questions about Nahum for any person of faith, then, are what is this book is doing in the canon and, since it *is* in the canon, how can it be read. There is little realistic hope of answering the first question: one might as well wonder what Jude is doing in the canon, or the Song of Songs. The canonizing process itself has provided guidance toward answering the second, however (cf. Childs 1979, 443–46).

How can we read Nahum? The process of incorporating Nahum into the Book of the Twelve has given Nahum's oracles against Nineveh a poetic preface that places Assyria's fall in a theological context. The opening psalm (1:2-11) affirms that God is a God of justice who punishes the wicked and the oppressor: "The LORD is slow to anger but great in power, and the LORD will by no means clear the guilty" (1:3). Nineveh's destruction, then, is not the capricious act of a violent deity. Next, a transitional section leading into Nahum's oracles against Nineveh (1:12-14) ascribes Judah's oppression at Nineveh's hands to God: "Although I have afflicted you, I will afflict you no more" (1:12). Implicitly, the God of justice who now judges Assyria had formerly used that nation to punish Judah for its own faithlessness and injustice. In its incorporation into the Twelve, editors have paired Nahum with Habakkuk, which is also called an "oracle" (Heb., *massa'*; compare Nah 1:1 and Hab 1:1) and which *ends* with a psalm (Hab 3:1-19). Habakkuk poignantly describes the ambiguity of God's will manifest in history (1:12-17) and also addresses Judah's own acts of injustice and oppression (Hab 1:2-4). This canonical context prevents the careful and caring reader from an uncritical embrace of Nahum's simplistic, black and white ideology.

The reflections of John Wesley offer a devotional approach to Nahum. In his seminal tract, *A Plain Account of Christian Perfection*, Wesley writes, "We ought quietly to suffer whatever befals [sic] us, to bear the defects of others and our own, to confess them to God in secret prayer, or with groans which cannot be uttered" (Wesley 1777, 130). As theologian Marjorie Suchocki observes, Wesley extraordinarily calls us to "confess the sins of others as though they are our own" (Suchocki 2008). This, I propose, is another way that we may appropriate Nahum as Christian Scripture. The perspective of this book is, sadly, not strange to us. We can surely recognize in ourselves the delight in the misfortunes of others, and the desire for vengeance, that Nahum expresses. Indeed, Scripture often confronts these emotions directly and honestly (e.g., Jer 11:20; Pss 3:7; 104:35; 137:8-9). Recognizing the presence and power of these emotions before God in prayer provides catharsis: the spleen vented, the poison drawn, we are freed to live our lives in joy, not anger; in love, not hatred. Reading Nahum, then, provides the opportunity for the recognition of these same dark emotions in ourselves and in our world—a recognition that ought to lead us not to jingoism and the pursuit of vengeance but to earnest repentance and the pursuit of peace. It also calls us to confess these sins and pray for the redemption of a world still in thrall to violence and retribution.

Authorship, Date, and Setting

The name "Nahum" apparently derives from the verb *nakham*, meaning "comfort," although that has doubtful significance as regards the message of this book. We have no reason to think that this name is a pseudonym (*contra* Spronk 1997, 33) or an artificial construct (in contrast to Malachi, which is almost certainly not an actual name), although it may be a contraction of a fuller, theophoric (that is, containing the name of a god) name such as Nehemiah ("the LORD comforts," derived from the same root). Nahum is said to come from Elkosh (1:1), a place name found nowhere else (*Tg. Neb.* intriguingly turns this into a family name, "the house of Qoshi"). It is possible that "Elkosh" contains the name of the Edomite god Qaush, in which case a location in southeastern Judah near the border with Edom is likely (Roberts 1991, 41). This, however, is conjecture.

As neither the superscription nor the headings of any of the oracles in this book give dates, the only guidance to the dating of Nahum comes from its content. The detailed depiction of the fall of Thebes to the Assyrians in 3:8-10 makes plain not only that Nahum was written subsequent to that event in 663 BCE, but also that the book has been written close enough to that event for it to serve, as it does here, as a vivid example: what the Assyrians did to Thebes is now done to their own great city, Nineveh. Indeed, some scholars date the composition of Nahum, in part or in whole, to the mid-seventh century BCE, soon after the fall of Thebes (e.g., Spronk 1997; Roberts 1991; Fabry [2006, 88] holds that 3:8-17 is the oldest part of the book). This is certainly possible; the anger and hatred this book expresses speak either to the immediate experience of Assyrian oppression or to the fresh memory of that experience. However, one might question whether the gloating, mocking tone of 3:1-7, or 3:18-19, would have been possible in a time of Assyrian strength. It makes more sense to date this poetry closer to the time of Nineveh's destruction, when Assyria was in decline, or even shortly after the city's fall in 612 BCE (Sweeney 2000, 422). Yet it is difficult to account either for the use of Thebes as an example or for the intensity of emotion in this poetry if the book as a whole is dated long after Assyria's fall (as, e.g., Christensen 2009, 56).

That said, there are also ample reasons for thinking that Nahum is not a literary unit dating to the seventh century. The psalm that opens this book (1:2-11) is based on an acrostic poem, only the first half of which has been used (1:2-8; see the discussion of this passage below in context). It is possible that Nahum himself could have incorporated a preexisting psalm into his book (so Roberts 1991, 48); however, Nineveh is not mentioned in this psalm, and further, the emphasis on divine justice and forbearance in 1:2-11 is missing from the oracles in 2:1(1:15)–3:19. Nor is Nineveh mentioned in 1:12-14, a transitional unit dissimilar from the oracles both formally and theologically. It seems most likely, then, that Nahum as we have it is a composite work. The most likely occasion for the expansion of the original oracles seems to be the incorporation of Nahum into the Book of the Twelve, in perhaps the fourth century BCE.

Nineveh

The area that would become the city of Nineveh was occupied from the late Neolithic Era (c. 5000 BCE) and became part of the newly emergent kingdom of Assyria early in the second millennium BCE. By the Middle Assyrian period (1200–750 BCE), Nineveh had become a significant town. The northernmost of the two major overland trade roads linking Mesopotamia to the Mediterranean began in Nineveh, making the city important for trade from early on. But the road from Nineveh was also the route used by the Assyrian military for raids on the lands of the seacoast. In the reign of Sennacherib (704–681 BCE), Nineveh became not only the royal residence but also the sole capital of the Assyrian empire. From a town two miles in circumference, Nineveh grew to a city eight miles around, its outskirts spanning the Tigris: not quite a "three days walk across," perhaps (cf. Jonah 3:3), but still a city of appreciable size! Two massive walls now fortified the city, the inner one featuring fifteen gates, while a sophisticated system of water channels made Nineveh lush, a city of gardens. The jewel of the city, however, was the king's "Palace without a Rival" constructed on a terrace built over a minor tributary of the Tigris, atop a seventy-five-foot high platform (Roux 1980, 298; Negev et al. 1986, 283). Sennacherib says of this great structure:

> Beams of cedar . . . I stretched across their roofs. Great door-leaves of cypress, whose odour [sic] is pleasant as they are opened and closed, I bound with a band of shining copper and set them in their doors. A portico patterned after a Hittite palace . . . I constructed inside for my lordly pleasure. (*ARAB* 2.366, cited in Roux 1980, 298)

Assyrian culture seemed to reach its height under Ashurbanipal (668–631 BCE), grandson of Sennacherib, whose library of 25,000 tablets remains the greatest store of knowledge about ancient Mesopotamian history, religion, art, and politics known. In truth, however, Assyria's collapse was already underway; scarcely a generation after Nineveh reached its pinnacle of beauty and importance, the Assyrian empire was no more, and the city lay in shambles. Repeated rebellions severely weakened the empire. Then, in 616 BCE, the alliance of Nabopolassar of Babylon and Cyaxeres of Media tore Assyria apart. By 612 BCE Nineveh had fallen, and by 610 BCE the remnants of Assyria's leadership had been rousted out of their last refuge in Haran. By the mid-fourth century, Nineveh was a forgotten, insignificant ruin. Herodotus, in his discussion of the conquest of Mesopotamia, passes it by with scarcely a mention (*Hist.* 1.178:1).

Structure

The Masoretes divide Nahum into four parts: 1:1-11 (break *setumah*), 1:12-14 (break *petukhah*), 2:1-14 ([1:15–2:13] break *setumah*), and 3:1-19. As will be seen below, these divisions broadly coincide with units many modern interpreters recognize. The book opens with a brief superscription (1:1). A broken acrostic psalm follows (1:2-11), setting this entire book in the context of divine justice. Then, following the messenger formula (1:12), comes the meat of the book. After an introduction (1:12-14), two poetic oracles lay out Nahum's message against Nineveh. The first oracle (2:1-14 [1:15–2:13]) targets Nineveh for destruction, setting Israel free from Assyria's oppression. The second oracle (3:1-19) is a mock dirge that celebrates, rather than laments, the fall of Nineveh and its king: "Then all who see you will shrink from you and say, 'Nineveh is devastated; who will bemoan her?' Where shall I seek comforters for you?" (Nah 3:7).

Nahum and Jonah

In the narrative flow of the Twelve, the depictions of Nineveh in Nahum and in Jonah stand curiously at odds—a tension heightened in the LXX order, where Jonah immediately precedes Nahum. In Nahum, Nineveh is unreservedly evil, bound for a well-deserved destruction. By contrast, Jonah depicts Nineveh as an example of earnest, indeed extravagant, repentance (Jonah 3:5-9). Of course, one solution to this tension is historical. The oracles of Nahum were written in the white heat of hatred for an oppressor whose atrocities were still fresh. Jonah was written much later, in the period after the exile, at a sufficient remove that it was possible to use Israel's ancient enemy as a type for the repentance of the nations.

The canonical structure of the Twelve, however, invites us to read Jonah *before* Nahum. The logic for the placement of Jonah in the first half of the Twelve, prior to Micah in the MT, may likewise be "historical": placing this book in the mid-eighth century context of "Jonah son of Amittai, the prophet," who is cited in Second Kings 14:25 as a source for its account of the expansion of the northern border of Israel under Jeroboam II. Furthermore, Jonah's mission to Nineveh would make no sense after the destruction of the city imagined so avidly in Nahum. Still, the narrative logic of the Twelve compels further consideration of this question. What happened to Nineveh between Jonah and Nahum? *Tg. Neb.* immediately addresses this problem in the first verse of Nahum:

> The oracle of the cup of the curse Nineveh was to drink. In former times, Jonah son of Amittai, the prophet from Gath Hepher, prophesied against her, and she repented from her sins, but then, when she sinned again (Aramaic *de'osephath lemikhye*), Nahum of the house of Qoshi prophesied against her again (Aramaic *tab*; the same root is used to describe Nineveh's repentance [*wetabath*]), as is written in this book (Nah 1:1; author's translation).

So too Theodoret of Cyrus (fifth century CE), noting the patience of God (Nah 1:3), says "you Ninevites are witnesses to this, practicing repentance and finding salvation, and then guilty of extreme wickedness and for a time not paying the penalty for it" (Hill 2006, 179; cf. also 177–78). One solution to this puzzle, then, is that Nineveh, after having repented, fell once more into sinfulness. Another would be to question whether Nineveh ever really repented at all. The Mishnah (the compendium of rabbinic wisdom which, together with its commentary called the Gemara, makes up the Talmud) lifts up Nineveh as an example of sincere repentance, an impression that the

Babylonian Talmud intensifies (*b. Taan.* 16a; cf. Ego 2003, 159). In contrast, the Jerusalem Talmud questions the sincerity of Nineveh's repentance in the first place (*y. Taan.* 65b; cf. Ego 2003, 161–62). By either reading, the message of the Twelve to its readers is, "Do not take God's forgiveness for granted." Although the LORD is "a gracious God and merciful, slow to anger, and abounding in steadfast love, and ready to relent from punishing" (Jonah 4:2; cf. Exod 34:6-7 and Nah 1:3), it is disastrous to presume upon the LORD's grace.

While the implicit narrative arc of Jonah and Nahum applies this lesson to foreign Nineveh, Nahum's fellow *massa'* Habakkuk applies the lesson learned quite specifically to Jerusalem, condemned for injustice and oppression—as does Zephaniah. Indeed, the *massa'* of Malachi will similarly hold Judah's priests and people accountable for their hypocrisy. A Christian reader may recall the stern warning against casual repentance in Hebrews 6:4-6: "For it is impossible to restore again to repentance those who have once been enlightened, and have tasted the heavenly gift, and have shared in the Holy Spirit, and have tasted the goodness of the word of God and the powers of the age to come, and then have fallen away" (cf. also Heb 10:26-27 and 1 John 3:6-9). As Nahum's opening psalm grimly declares, "no adversary will rise up twice" (Nah 1:9).

Commentary

Superscription (1:1)

The book of Nahum opens with the phrase *massa' Nineweh,* commonly rendered, as in the NRSV, "An oracle concerning Nineveh." After the explicit mention of Nineveh here in the book's opening, the city is not named again until the two oracles (2:8[7]; 3:7). Scripture mentions Nineveh by name only seventeen times. Genesis 10:11-12 describes Nineveh as one of the first cities in the world, founded by Nimrod, the world's first king. In 2 Kings 19:36//Isaiah 37:37, Nineveh is the place to which Sennacherib returns after his armies withdraw from the siege of Jerusalem. Otherwise, the city is mentioned only in Jonah (nine times, in 1:2; 3:2-7; 4:11), Nahum (three times: 1:1; 2:8[7]; 3:7), and Zephaniah 2:13. Given the importance of Nineveh as the capital of the Assyrian empire, and hence as the center of the power that was Israel's great oppressor through the eighth and seventh centuries, it is surprising that Scripture mentions the city so rarely. Perhaps this absence is deliberate—the willful refusal to grant a memorial to a cruel oppressor: "Your name shall be perpetuated no longer" (Nah 1:14).

In the superscriptions of Nahum, Habakkuk, and Malachi, the NRSV translates the word *massa'* as "oracle" (so too the old NIV; NIV 2011 has "prophecy," while NJPS has "pronouncement"). However, it often designates a load to be carried (thirty-five times; e.g., Num 4:15-49, where *massa'* refers to sacred objects distributed among assigned Levitical clans when the tabernacle is shifted), hence the KJV reading, "The burden of Nineveh" (Nah 1:1). The term can also be a proper name (Gen 25:14//1 Chr 1:30, and probably Prov 30:1; 31:1, although NRSV reads "oracle" here). The Hebrew Bible uses *massa'* twenty-seven times with reference to a prophetic pronouncement, mostly in Isaiah (ten times) and Jeremiah (eight times). The eight occurrences in Jeremiah, however, are clustered in a single passage (23:33-40) punning on the dual meaning of *massa'* (23:33). When Jeremiah's audience asks for a *massa'* ("oracle"), he is to reply, "You are the burden [*massa'*], and I will cast you off, says the LORD." Jeremiah's editors, who did not get the pun, have added a midrash (a rabbinic term for application or interpretation) rejecting the use of the term *massa'* in Israel (23:34-40; cf. Perdue and Wilson 2006, 1042). The occurrences of *massa'* in Isaiah come primarily in the oracles against the nations in Isaiah 13–23 (13:1; 14:28; 15:1; 17:1; 19:1; 21:1, 11, 13; 22:1; 23:1; cf. also 30:6, where the *massa'* is directed against Egypt). In the prophets apart from Isaiah and Jeremiah, *massa'* appears once in Ezekiel (12:10, in an oracle pronouncing doom on the prince in Jerusalem) and five times in the Book of the Twelve (always, as in Isaiah, as a heading; cf. Nah 1:1; Hab 1:1; Zech 9:1; 12:1; Mal 1:1). The remaining three instances of *massa'* as a prophetic pronouncement are 2 Kings 9:25 (for Joram's destruction), 2 Chronicles 24:27 (for the many pronouncements of doom against Joash), and Lamentations 2:14 (for false oracles giving hope).

Floyd (2000 and 2002), following Weis (1992, 28–29), proposes that when used for a prophetic speech, *massa'* designates a literary genre (that is, a type of discourse) involving "prophetic reinterpretation of a previous revelation" (Floyd 2002, 409–10); Nahum, Habakkuk, Malachi, and Zechariah 9–14, then, are all exemplars of this prophetic genre. This proposal seems needlessly complex, however, since in most places where *massa'* refers to a prophetic pronouncement, it plainly designates a judgment oracle (cf. Achtemeier 1986, 7, who renders *massa'* in Nah 1:1 as "*threatening word*" [emphasis hers]). Indeed, the two apparent exceptions prove the rule. In Jeremiah 23:33, the prophet's audience likely asks for a word condemning Babylon (like Hananiah of Gibeon's oracle in Jer 28:1-4), but ironically receives instead personal condemnation. Similarly, although Lamentations 2:14 uses *massa'* for oracles that had offered false hope to Jerusalem, that need not mean that these were oracles of salvation; the false oracles could also have offered hope by predicting doom for Jerusalem's enemies. The *massa'* of Nahum, as we will see, is certainly all about judgment. As Nahum's prophecy is directed against Nineveh, the capital city of the Assyrians, Isaiah's oracles against foreign nations likely influenced the use of *massa'* as a title for Nahum's book (so too Goldingay 2009, 7).

The superscription further identifies this book as *sepher khazon*: "the book of the vision" of Nahum (1:1). This is the only book in the Hebrew Bible that identifies itself in its title *as* a book (though this designation does appear within biblical books, with reference to the book itself or to some section within it; e.g. Deut 17:18; 31:24-26; Isa 30:8; Jer 25:13; 30:2; 36:2, 32; Ezek 2:9). Given Nahum's literary character, it is certainly an appropriate designation. Only Isaiah and Obadiah are also called "visions" (Heb., *khazon*; Isa 1:1; Obad 1:1; but cf. Hab 2:2). Still, the concept of vision characterizes Judean prophecy: Ezekiel sees "visions of God" (*mar'ot 'elohim*; Ezek 1:1); Habakkuk sees the oracle (Hab 1:1); and Micah and Amos curiously "see" the word of the LORD (Amos 1:1; Mic 1:1). In contrast, revelation comes to the Israelite Hosea through the ear, not the eye: "The word of the LORD" comes to him (Hos 1:1), rather than a vision. The same is true of other prophets related theologically and ideologically to the northern, Levitical ideals given fullest expression in the book of Deuteronomy: thus, Jeremiah (1:1-2, 9-10) and Zephaniah (1:1) also receive the word (and, as noted above, Amos and Micah "see" the word). In time, the idea of revelation by the word prevailed over the vision, as the title *nabi'* ("prophet"; literally, "one called") prevailed over the title *khozeh* ("visionary"). Therefore, the postexilic prophets Haggai, Zechariah, and Malachi all receive the word of the LORD (cf. Hag 1:1; Zech 1:1; Mal 1:1), as do Jonah (1:1) and Joel (1:1).

Framing Psalm: The LORD Goes to War (1:2-11)

Nahum begins with a psalm praising God the divine warrior for God's justice (Nah 1:2-11). A certain Pastor Frohnmeyer of Würtemberg (cited in Delitzsch 1873, 11) first noted the acrostic features of this poem. Unlike the acrostics with which we are familiar in English literature, where the first letters of successive lines spell out words or phrases (a technique also found in ancient Babylonian poetry; cf. Soll 1992, 58–59), Hebrew acrostics use all the letters of the alphabet in successive lines (Pss 9–10; 25; 34; 111; 112; 145; Prov 31:10-31; cf. also Sir 51:13-30, of which vv. 13-19 have been recovered in Hebrew from Qumran [11QPsa coll. XXI]) or stanzas (Pss 37; 119; Lam 1; 2; 3; 4).

In Nahum 1:2-11, however, the acrostic is incomplete. The sequence *'aleph* (v. 2a), *beth* (v. 3b), *gimel* (v. 4a) is clear (although with the interposition of vv. 2b-3a between the *'aleph* and *beth* lines), but there is no *daleth* line (v. 4b begins instead with *'aleph*). Then, while the *he* and *waw* lines follow in sequence (v. 5a and b), the *zayin* line requires one to read not the initial word, but the second word in the line (v. 6a). The *kheth* (v. 6b) and *teth* (v. 7a) lines again are clear. A *yod* line is probable: although v. 7b begins with a *waw* (the Hebrew conjunction), it is easy to imagine the addition of this letter by a scribe; removing the extraneous conjunction yields a line beginning with *yada'* (literally, "he knows . . ."; cf. Nogalski 1993b, 104). The sequence ends in v. 8 with *kaph*: the first two words of this verse likely belong to the previous stanza (cf. NRSV, and the discussion below), so that the new line begins with *kalah* ("a full end"). After this, the acrostic sequence disappears, only halfway through the Hebrew alphabet. As a result, some interpreters deny that there is an acrostic here at all (e.g., Floyd 1994). Nonetheless, as G. B. Gray observed in 1898, it is difficult to imagine how the alphabetic sequence that we can clearly see could have emerged by chance (cited in Renz 2009, 8). Others attempt to emend the text so as at least partially to restore the acrostic (cf. the discussion in Renz 2009, 8–9)—although with no clear text-critical explanation as to how the alphabetic sequence could have become obscured (so Floyd 1994, 424–26).

This leaves two possibilities. First, Nahum or his editors could have deliberately composed the text as it is, as a broken acrostic (e.g., Renz 2009, 21–22). This is of course possible, but it would be without precedent in biblical literature. While the biblical acrostics sometimes vary from our expected alphabetical order (note that the inversion of *'ayin* and *pe* in Lam 2; 3; 4 and Ps 10 is also found in some ancient alphabet lists; e.g., the tenth-century BCE Tel Zayit Inscription [Tappy et al. 2006]) or creatively toy with that order (e.g., Ps 34 skips *waw* and adds an additional *pe* at the end, so that while the twenty-two lines are preserved, the initial, middle, and final letters of the acrostic spell out *'aleph*; cf. Soll 1992, 59), the point of the form remains completion. This is apparent even in the partial acrostic in Psalms 9–10 (a single psalm in the LXX and the Latin Vulgate), for while the middle of the acrostic is lost, the beginning and end of the alphabet are represented, making it most likely that the original poem was damaged or altered in the course of its editing and transmission (as the division of this poem into two psalms in the MT, reflected in our Old Testament, already may indicate). The only genuine parallel to the partial acrostic of Nahum 1 extant is 11QPs[a]155 (also called Syriac Psalm III, as a medieval version of the poem survives in Syriac), an acrostic psalm that ends with *pe*. Although the bottom of the scroll from cave 11 at Qumran is damaged and the ending of the psalm is lost, Patrick Skehan concluded through comparison with other columns on the scroll that on the undamaged original, this Hebrew version of the psalm was no longer than the extant Syriac version (Skehan 1965, 1).

Skehan argues that this psalm is complete as it is, and was intended to be a partial acrostic (Skehan 1965, 4–5). Still, absence of evidence is not evidence of absence; the Hebrew and Syriac versions of this psalm could both be fragments of an original, complete acrostic poem.

This brings us to the second possibility: that Nahum 1:2-11 represents an original acrostic psalm reshaped for use as the introduction to Nahum. Several features point to the expansion of the poem in its present form. For example, as we noted above, there is an insertion between the *'aleph* and *beth* lines (1:2-3) drawn from Exodus 34:6-7 (Renz 2009, 10), a passage to which Jonah 4:2 also alludes. The effect of its inclusion here is to soften the wrath of the divine warrior by emphasizing God's patience—and also, incidentally, to pick up on the delay of punishment expressed at the conclusion of Micah, the preceding book in the MT order of the Twelve (Mic 7:18-20; so Nogalski 1993a, 106–107). Another clear indication of expansion is 1:9-11. Some interpreters conclude the opening psalm at v. 8, as the acrostic elements appear only in the first eight verses (e.g., Brown 1996, 70–71; Fabry 2006, 91–92, 94). In addition, the form of the poetry changes in vv. 9-11, from two lines to the verse to three. Yet vv. 9-11 explicitly continue the thought expressed in the acrostic, to the point of continuing the vocabulary (the use of *kalah* in 1:8 and 9) and imagery (the reference back to the fire imagery of 1:6 in 1:10b) of that poem. That these verses begin and end with plotting against the LORD (1:9 and 11 both use the verb *khashab* ["plan, plot"], although in v. 9 with the preposition *'el* and in v. 11 with *'al*) likely indicates that they constitute a unit added to the original psalm (*contra* Fabry 2007, 90–91, 94, who holds that while 1:9-2:1 is later than the original oracles, it predates the addition of the acrostic). In the text as it now stands, however, these verses complete the poem and lead into the introduction to Nahum's oracles that follows.

In its final form, Nahum 1:2-11 serves to place Nahum's naïve assertions regarding Nineveh's fall on a theological base. In context, the enemy condemned as the LORD's adversary (Nah 1:8-9), who "plots evil against the LORD" (Nah 1:11), must be read as Nineveh or its king. This poem does not name Nineveh, however; instead, like many poems in the Psalter, it identifies the enemy from whom deliverance is sought in broad, stereotypical terms. This lack of specificity, added to the incomplete character of the acrostic in Nahum 1:2-10 and the signs of expansion within the poem, all suggest that Nahum's editors are using a selected portion from a larger work. Further, as the discussion of this poem will show, there are clear parallels between 1:2-11 and Habakkuk 3:1-19, so that these two hymns frame Nahum and Habakkuk, prompting us to read them together (so Schart 1997, 244; Fabry

2006, 100). In short, it seems likely that the editors chose the psalm in Nahum 1 to introduce this book, and edited and reworked it with an eye both to its place in the final form of Nahum and to Nahum's position in the Twelve.

The opening verse of the poem identifies the LORD as "[a] jealous and avenging God," who "is avenging and wrathful" (1:2). The Hebrew adjective *qanno'* (rendered "jealous" in the NRSV) appears only here and in Joshua 24:19, which also describes the LORD as *'El qanno'*: "a jealous God." The reader may recall that the Ten Commandments forbid the worship of idols "for I the LORD your God am a jealous God [Heb., *'El qanna'*], punishing children for the iniquity of parents, to the third and fourth generation of those who reject me, but showing steadfast love to the thousandth generation of those who love me and keep my commandments" (Exod 20:5-6// Deut 5:9-10). Like the related, and slightly more common, adjective *qanna'* (cf. also Exod 34:14; Deut 4:24; 6:15), *qanno'* expresses divine zeal and passion, for good and for ill (note that the NJPS renders the first line of Nah 1:2 as "The LORD is a passionate, avenging God."). Deuteronomy 4:24 puts it well: "the LORD your God is a devouring fire"!

The depiction of God as an avenger (Heb., *noqem*) in Nahum 1:2 is also distinctive; indeed, this verb occurs nowhere else in the Twelve. Apart from the specific context of family honor (cf. the various references to the *go'el haddam* ["avenger of blood"] in Num 35 and Deut 19, and the cities of refuge from the avenger in Josh 20; note that the LORD appears as *go'el* in Exod 6:6; Jer 31:11; 50:34; Mic 4:10; Pss 19:14; 107:2; and 18 times in Isa 40–66 [15 times in 40–55]), Torah rules out vengeance in the human world, at least among the people Israel (Lev 19:18, although cf. Exod 20:21-22, where a slave beaten to death by a master is to be avenged). Thus, Saul is condemned for seeking vengeance (1 Sam 14:24), while David is commended for leaving vengeance to God (1 Sam 24:12). However, vengeance against foreign oppressors is a different matter (Josh 10:13; Esth 8:13; Jer 50:15)! Indeed, God too can be said to take such vengeance on behalf of God's own (Gen 4:15, 24; Deut 32:43; Ezek 25:12, 15), or for God's own honor (Jer 46:10). A particularly intriguing parallel to Nahum 1:2 is Jeremiah 51:36, which like our poem alludes to the exodus (cf. Nah 1:4). Often in Scripture, however, *naqam* ("take vengeance") expresses God's vengeance against a sinful and rebellious Israel, carried out in defense of the helpless, and on behalf of God's own covenant and name (Lev 26:25; Isa 1:24; Jer 5:9, 29//9:9; 15:15; Ezek 24:8). So, while the passionate, avenging God of the psalm seems at first perfectly consonant with the message of Nahum's oracles against Nineveh

(2:1[1:15]–3:19), this language also introduces a note of ambiguity lacking in those poems.

Nahum 1:2b-3 further qualifies this depiction of divine passion, wrath, and vengeance. While affirming that "the LORD takes vengeance on his adversaries and rages against his enemies," this insert qualifies the divine rage and vengeance: "The LORD is slow to anger but great in power, / and the LORD will by no means clear the guilty" (Nah 1:3). The poem here quotes from the divine self-affirmation on Sinai in Exodus 34:6-7. This passage is quoted throughout Scripture, usually with a decided accent on God's grace and forgiveness (e.g., Pss 86:15; 103:8; 145:8; Neh 9:17; Joel 2:13; Jonah 4:2). In Nahum, however, the recollection of this passage serves to qualify divine wrath and judgment, not to turn it aside; indeed, God's rage and vengeance poured out on Nineveh is the point of this book. It is certainly significant that in Nahum an assertion of God's might follows the statement of God's patience ("slow to anger *but great in power*," Nah 1:3; emphasis mine), rather than, as in Exodus, a statement of God's grace (Exod 34:6: "slow to anger, *and abounding in steadfast love and faithfulness*," emphasis mine). Further, unlike the citations of Exodus 34:6-7 listed above, Nahum 1:3 emphasizes the inevitability of divine punishment by quoting Exodus 34:7: "the LORD will by no means clear the guilty" (Heb., *wenaqqeh lo' yinaqqeh*; cf. Num 14:18; Jer 30:11//46:28). Nineveh's destruction is assured, not as the act of an unpredictably passionate, wrathful deity but rather as the measured response of a just God. Jonah 4:2 quotes this same passage with reference to Nineveh, although there concerning Nineveh's salvation, not its destruction (Timmer 2010). Indeed, where Nahum alters the reference to God's steadfast love and quotes the line referring to punishment, Jonah does the opposite, describing God as "ready to relent from punishing" (Heb., *wenikham 'al-hara'ah*; likely using *nakham* ["relent"] to pun with *naqah* ["declare innocent"]). This may well reflect Jonah's use of Nahum.

In Nahum 1:2-11, the passionate, wrathful, avenging God is revealed through the storm: "His way is in whirlwind and storm, / and the clouds are the dust of his feet (1:3b)." The idea of God manifest in the storm (called a "storm theophany") appears throughout the Hebrew Bible and is very old. Some of the most ancient texts in Scripture picture the LORD appearing in the storm, wielding wind, thunder, and lightning as weapons (cf. Exod 15:1-18; Judg 5:1-31; Ps 29). This image draws on the ancient myth of the creator god as a warrior who defeats the monster of chaos, identified with the wild, raging waters of the sea or the flood, and establishes order (e.g., Pss 74:12-17; 104:1-9; Isa 51:9-11; Hab 3:8-10). The storm theophany can depict God coming to deliver God's own (in addition to the ancient texts cited above, cf. Ps 18 and Hab 3:12-15). However, it also shows God coming against God's people in judgment (e.g., Amos 1:2; Mic 1:2-7; Zeph 1:2-9) and, particularly, can signal the day of the LORD, when God's just reign must at last be recognized by all (e.g., Joel 2:2; Amos 5:18-20). Since Scripture uses the image of God coming in the storm with particular reference to the LORD's deliverance of Israel from slavery in Egypt (Exod 15:1-18) and to the revelation of the LORD on Sinai (Exod 20:16-19), later texts can use the image to allude to those events as well, so that the storm theophany becomes an affirming expression of divine presence (e.g., Ezek 1:4-28; cf. Tuell 2009, 12).

The language of Nahum's psalm is typical in many respects. The warrior God manifest in the storm "rebukes the sea and makes it dry" (1:4), recalling the victory of the creator over unruly water. Tertullian (*Anti-Marcion* 4.20) found in this passage (as well as in Hab 3:10) a prophecy of Jesus walking on the water (Matt 14:22-23//Mark 6:45-52//John 6:16-21) and stilling the storm (Matt 8:23-27//Mark 4:35-41//Luke 8:22-25), texts that likewise assert God's control over chaos. For Nahum's editors, however, this image would surely call to mind the exodus out of Egypt (Exod 14:21; 15:8; cf. Isa 51:9-11)—in context, a particularly potent parallel for God's deliverance of Judah from Assyrian oppression. This exodus allusion provides a link backwards to Micah, whose language of deliverance also recalls the exodus (Mic 7:15), and forward to Habakkuk, where the psalm concluding that book also alludes to God's deliverance at the Reed Sea (cf. Hab 3:8-15). To a modern reader, the imagery of 1:5-6 doubtless sounds more like an earthquake or volcano than a thunderstorm; however, such language does accompany the storm theophany elsewhere in Scripture—particularly in Habakkuk 3:6, 10 (cf. Judg 5:4-5; Ps 18:7-15; and the curious "anti-theophany" in 1 Kgs 19:11-13). In most ancient songs of the divine warrior, God marches into battle out of the *south*—that is, from the region of Sinai (cf. Deut 33:2-3; Judg 5:4-5; Hab 3:3, 7) or Zion (cf. Amos 1:2). In contrast, here God's wrath is manifest in the *north*: "Bashan and Carmel wither, / and the bloom of Lebanon fades (1:4b)."

While Bashan, Carmel, and Lebanon are all in northern Palestine, we need not infer from this a northern setting for our poem. Psalm 29, an ancient song that also sets forth a storm theophany, similarly describes the force of the storm evident in the forests and pastures of the north (Ps 29:5-6, 9), so this picturesque language could be traditional. This line breaks the acrostic pattern, however, suggesting that it is an insertion from the poem's editors (taking the place of the original *daleth* line). Furthermore, while the English translation of the NRSV masks this, the line begins and ends with the same word, *'umlal* (translated "wither" and "fades"), suggesting that this line is an intact unit inserted into the preexisting poem. Bashan, Carmel, and Lebanon appear together in the same verse in only one other place in Scripture: in Isaiah 33:9, part of a liturgy that also depicts God going to war against Assyria. The connection is further strengthened by the use in both contexts of the verb *'amal* ("languish") and by similar imagery (in Nah 1:4b, "the bloom of Lebanon fades"; in Isa 33:9, Bashan and Carmel "shake off their leaves"; note, too, the brush fire imagery of Isa 33:10 and Nah 1:10), making it likely that the editors of Nahum are aware of Isaiah's liturgy, and deliberately recall it here (Spronk 1991, 41). Nahum's first oracle (Nah 2:3[2]) again lifts the hope that Assyria's conquest of the north (cf. 2 Kgs 17:5-41) would be undone, which is another theme shared with Micah's closing chapter: "Shepherd your people with your staff . . . let them feed in Bashan and Gilead as in the days of old" (Mic 7:14; so Nogalski 1993a, 158–59 and 1993b, 107–109; cf. Ezek 37:15-28).

In 1:7 the psalm shifts abruptly from the violent depiction of God's passion ("His wrath is poured out like fire, and by him the rocks are broken in pieces") to an account of God's providential care: "The LORD is good, a stronghold in the day of trouble." The God of the storm is, of course, present in the midst of the storm: indeed, God's goodness and security are manifest to the faithful *particularly* in hard times. The reader may recall Psalm 46:2(1): "God is our refuge and strength, a very present help in trouble."

The next line, however, is difficult. In Hebrew, 1:7b is only three words long, far shorter than any other line in this poem: *weyode'a khose bo* (mechanistically, "he knows those who take refuge in him"). The verb *yada'* ("know") has more to do with experience, indeed with relationship, than with what modern Western readers would call "knowledge." A good translation, then, requires something stronger than "know"; for example, the NJPS has "he is mindful of those who seek refuge in Him." The NRSV "protect," however, is based on the further assumption that the first two words of the following verse (Heb., *ubsheteph 'ober*: that is, "and in/with a flood overflowing") belong to this line: so "he protects those who take refuge in him, even in a rushing flood" (1:7b-8a). This course, also proposed by the editors of the BHS (the standard critical edition of the Hebrew Bible), has the additional advantage that the next line then begins with *kaph*, and so continues the acrostic pattern. Many read *ubsheteph 'ober* with the following verse, so that the flood becomes the means by which God brings "a full end" to the adversary (so NJPS, NIV and KJV, cf. Christensen 2009, 196–98). This solution, however, requires us to accept the anomalously short line in v. 7b and to break the acrostic sequence sooner than need be. Others propose that due to poor transmission, something is missing from the text (for example, Roberts 1991, 45 suggests that the divine name is missing from the beginning of v. 7b and that the latter half of v. 8a has dropped out altogether). Nevertheless, neither the LXX nor the *Tg. Neb.* supports the emendation of the passage; rather, they represent separate attempts to come to terms with the text before us. Given the text as we have it, then, it seems best (with NRSV and BHS) to read the opening words of v. 8 as the conclusion to v. 7b, so that the overwhelming flood becomes the very place of God's presence with those who seek refuge in the LORD, to comfort and to deliver (as in Hab 3:16-19; cf. Ps 46:2-4[1-3]; Jonah 2:1-9). Given that Isaiah had compared the oncoming hordes of Assyria to the waters of the Euphrates in flood (Isa 8:5-8), it is certainly appropriate that in Nahum Judah experiences God's judgment on Nineveh as deliverance in the midst of the flood. The reader may again recall the Gospel accounts of Jesus calming the storm, and gospel hymns such as Charles Tindley's "Stand By Me":

> When the storm of life is raging,
> Stand by me.
> When the storm of life is raging,
> Stand by me.
> When the world is tossing me
> Like a ship upon the sea,
> Thou who rulest wind and water,
> Stand by me.

Nahum's psalm, too, affirms that in the midst of chaos and trouble, the LORD is present as a stronghold and a deliverer.

After this brief interlude of reassurance offered to God's faithful, the mood of the psalm shifts again with the following line, back to the conviction that God's enemies are doomed: "He will make a full end of his adversaries, / and will pursue his enemies into darkness" (Nah 1:8). This again is a difficult line. Where the NRSV reads "his adversaries," the MT has *maqomah* ("her place"). The NJPS follows the MT, as do the KJV and NIV (though the editors of the NIV have chosen to read "Nineveh" in brackets, understanding *maqomah* as a reference to that city). LXX, however, has *tous epegeiromenous* ("the ones who rise up"), and Aquila (a second century CE Greek translator of Jewish Scripture) reads *apo anistamenon* ("from those who rise up"). *Targum Nebi'im* has *'im 'amemaya' deqamu* ("with the people who stand"). These translations presuppose a text different from the one before us, reading not *maqomah* ("her place"), but *beqamayw* ("with those who rise up [against] him"; note that while Aquila seems to presuppose a consonantal text very like ours, he pronounces it as *miqqamayw*, "from those who rise up against him"). This is an easily understandable scribal error, as the initial *beth* and *mem* are similar, and confusions of final *he*, *waw*, and *yod* are common. Given the agreement among the versions, it seems best to emend the text here, with the NRSV (and the NJPS footnote), and read "his adversaries." In context, the difference may not seem that great: after all, in either case, the clear referent is Nineveh. The distinction is worth preserving, however. While the MT assumes continuity between the poem and the oracles (the "her" in "her place" being the city of Nineveh, feminine in Hebrew; cf. 3:4-6), the best reading of this verse keeps that relationship ambiguous. Apart from the superscription, the enemy is not identified as Nineveh until Nahum's first oracle (2:9[8]).

The final clause too is difficult: *we'oyebayw yeradeph-khoshek* (mechanistically, "and his enemies he will pursue—darkness" [?]). Both the LXX (*kai tous ethrous autou dioxetai skotos*) and the Vulgate (*et inimicos eius persequentur tenebrae*) reproduce the Hebrew sequence word for word—although in those versions, *darkness* becomes the subject of the verb (cf. the KJV "and darkness shall pursue his enemies"). This is not an impossible rendering of the Hebrew, but the *maqqeph* (a Hebrew mark used rather like a hyphen) linking the verb to the noun *khoshek* ("darkness") in the MT makes this reading unlikely: darkness is not pursuing here, but rather has something to do with the pursuit (grammatically, "darkness" is an adverbial accusative). A meaningful English translation requires us to supply a linking word between the verb and the noun. *Targum Nebi'im* has "his enemies he will hand over to Gehenna [Aramaic *legehinam*]," providing both a preposition and an interpretation for the Hebrew *khoshek*. Similarly Theodoret of Cyrus writes, "he will consign to ruin and unending darkness those rashly opposing him" (Hill 2006, 180; for the biblical texts used by Theodoret, cf. the notes in Hill 2006, 3–7). The NRSV, NIV, NJPS, and most commentators (e.g., Roberts 1991, 45; Spronk 1997, 51; Christensen 2009, 200) likewise read that the LORD will pursue his enemies "into darkness." In the Hebrew, however, the relationship of *khoshek* to the verb remains ambiguous.

Perhaps, like the "overwhelming flood" of the previous line, the darkness here speaks to the *setting* of God's action (grammatically speaking, reading *khoshek* as an adverbial accusative of manner rather than place). God will pursue and destroy God's enemies *in* darkness, or darkly, that is, on the day of the LORD, famously described as "darkness, not light, and gloom with no brightness in it" (Amos 5:20; cf. 5:18) and as "a day of darkness and gloom, a day of clouds and thick darkness" (Joel 2:2; cf. 2:31 and Zeph 1:15).

Similarly, Ezekiel 34:12 describes the day that God the divine shepherd seeks out and rescues God's flock as "a day of clouds and thick darkness" (*yom 'anan we'arpel*, as in Joel 2:2 and Zeph 1:15; cf. Tuell 2009, 238). The day of the Lord is a major recurring theme in the Book of the Twelve (e.g., Rendtorff 2000; Nogalski 2003), so allusion to it here would not be surprising. The point is that the fall of Nineveh assures—and in context prefigures—God's ultimate victory over evil and injustice. Archbishop Desmond Tutu heartily concurs with the Twelve when he affirms, "The texture of our universe is one where there is no question at all but that good and laughter and justice will prevail. In the end, the perpetrators of injustice or oppression, the ones who strut the stage of the world often seemingly unbeatable—there is no doubt at all that they will bite the dust" (Perry 2010).

In the final movement of our poem (1:9-11), the Lord addresses the enemy directly:

> Why do you [masculine plural] plot against the Lord? . . .
> From you [feminine] one has gone out
> who plots evil against the Lord,
> who counsels wickedness [masculine, again] (Nah 1:9, 11).

The unnamed plotters are masculine, but the psalm also addresses the nation or city from which the plotter comes (*mimmek* ["from you"] in v. 11; such nouns are feminine in Hebrew). In context, the place is Nineveh, and the plotters are Assyria's kings (cf. Nah 1:13-14). Yet, consistent with the pattern in the poem thus far, the enemy remains unidentified, so that the language is applicable to any circumstance of rebellion against God (cf. García-Treto 1996, 604; Sweeney's proposal [2000, 431–35] that the feminine singular pronoun in 1:11, like those in 2:1[1:15], refers to Judah seems forced). The schemes of the unnamed enemy, however, are in vain; the Lord "will make an end; no adversary will rise up twice" (Nah 1:9).

The reader may recall Psalm 2, where in response to the vain plotting of "the kings of the earth" (Ps 2:2), the Lord laughs them to scorn, warning them to submit to divine authority, "or he will be angry, and you will perish in the way" (Ps 2:11). As we have seen, v. 9 picks up the language of v. 8, continuing the theme of God completely destroying (i.e., making a "full end" of) God's adversaries. Indeed, the grammar of this verse (a participle is used) could suggest incipient action: after long exercising divine patience (cf. 1:3), God is now ready to act at once against God's enemies. The clause *lo-taqum pa'amayim tsarah* ("no adversary will rise up twice," 1:9) also expresses this theme of divine forbearance now at an end. The abstract noun *tsarah* (read as "trouble" by the NIV, and "affliction" by the KJV) is best understood, through comparison with the ancient Ugaritic (the language of old Canaan) word *tsrt*, as "hostility"; here it is "used concretely as a substitute or synonym for 'adversary, enemy'" (Roberts 1991, 46; cf. Ps 54:9[7]), as the NRSV and NJPS rightly read. Now that God has decided to act, the enemy is doomed. No more second chances will be given!

The juxtaposition of images in Nahum 1:10, which describes the fate of the enemy, seems odd to us: "Like thorns they are entangled, / like drunkards they are drunk; / they are consumed like dry straw." What does drunkenness have to do with thorns? When we listen to the sound of the first two lines, understanding the love of Hebrew writers for assonance and puns, the association makes better sense (poetically, if not rationally): *ky 'ad-sirim sebukim ukesab'am sebu'im.* Roberts understands the first two lines of this three-line verse as a depiction of the threat posed by the adversary: "Though God's enemies present a formidable front like a thicket of interwoven thorns, and though their warriors are stout, well-provisioned, and well-liquored . . . they will be devoured like dried-up stubble" (Roberts 1991, 46). Proverbs 26:9 also combines the two images ("Like a thornbush brandished by the hand of a drunkard is a proverb in the mouth of a fool"), although using different Hebrew words for "thorn" and "drunkard" than are used in Nahum 1:10. This suggests the possibility that the drunk in the brier patch may have been a traditional commonplace—like the drunk in the gutter in our culture. Elsewhere, Scripture presents drunkenness as a shameful condition rather than a threatening one (for other instances of the Hebrew verb *saba'*, cf. Deut 21:20; Isa 56:12; Ezek 23:42; Prov 23:20-21). Indeed, Nahum's second oracle (Nah 3:11) uses the shame of drunkenness as a metaphor for the shame of military defeat. Habakkuk condemns Babylon because "you make your neighbors drink, pouring out your wrath until they are drunk" (Hab 2:15; see the discussion of this passage below, in context). In consequence, judgment will come to Babylon: "Drink yourself, and stagger! The cup in the LORD's right hand will come around to you, and shame will come upon your glory" (Hab 2:16; for the LORD's cup of wrath, cf. Isa 51:17-23; Jer 25:15-29; 49:12; 51:7; Ezek 23:32-34). Likely, then, drunkenness in Nahum 1:10 symbolizes imminent defeat and shame (so Christensen 2009, 208–209, 369–71), making it more likely that the thorn bush image, too, represents entanglement and helplessness. Like passed-out drunks hopelessly caught in a thorn bush, unable to escape an approaching brushfire, the enemies of the LORD can offer no resistance to the doom that is coming.

Introduction: Judah Set Free (1:12-14)

These verses take the reader from Nahum's poetic preface (1:2-11) to the prophet's oracles against Nineveh (2-3 [1:15–3:19]). Therefore, some scholars combine this unit with the preceding psalm (Robertson 1990, 43; Brown 1996, 72–73), while others preface it to the following oracle (Floyd 2000, 3). Nonetheless, its important role as the transition from the framing psalm, which speaks generally of God's judgment against God's enemies, to Nahum's oracles, which speak specifically of the LORD's devastation of Nineveh, justifies its separate treatment (cf. Christensen 2009, 248–49).

The unit begins with a formula often found in prophetic books: "Thus says the LORD" (1:12a). This expression is commonly called the messenger formula because of its parallels with the language used by royal messengers in the ancient Near East. Such messengers would preface their speeches with the name of their sovereign, and then deliver their message in first person, as though the king were actually speaking (e.g., the speech of the Rabshakeh in 2 Kgs 18:19-35//Isa 36:1-20//2 Chr 32:9-15). By analogy, then, the prophet appears to function like a messenger sent to Israel from the divine court, speaking on God's behalf (Holladay 1970, 31–33).

While we can describe the messenger formula as a typical feature of prophetic literature generally, it is not evenly distributed among the prophetic books. The Book of the Twelve uses the messenger formula 44 times; by comparison, the formula occurs 40 times in Isaiah, 153 times in Jeremiah, and 125 times in Ezekiel. Within the Twelve, the messenger formula does not appear at all in Hosea or Joel, but occurs 14 times in Amos, once in Obadiah (Obad 1), not at all in Jonah, and twice in Micah (Mic 2:3; 3:5). In the six books with which our study is concerned, the messenger formula appears once in Nahum (1:12), not at all in Habakkuk or Zephaniah, five times in Haggai (Hag 1:2, 5, 7; 2:6, 11), 20 times in Zechariah (though only once [Zech 11:4] in 9–14), and once in Malachi (Mal 1:4).

Taking the greatly differing lengths of these books into consideration, the messenger formula appears most often, and with a roughly comparable frequency, in Jeremiah, Ezekiel, Amos, Haggai, and Zechariah. Since these books represent three distinct periods in Israel's history (the eighth, sixth, and fifth centuries BCE), and at least two theological traditions (Amos and Jeremiah alike could be described as "Deuteronomic," while Ezekiel and Haggai–Zech 1–8 are both "Priestly"), the messenger formula is plainly not restricted to any single period in history or stream of tradition. We can reach no conclusions regarding the date or the theology of Nahum 1:12-14 based on this formula alone.

Nevertheless, the content of this unit reveals a theological subtlety and sophistication missing from the following chapters. The LORD declares, "Though I have afflicted you, I will afflict you no more" (1:12). That is, Assyria's oppression had been God's doing, presumably permitted due to Israel's sin. This is a consistent theme in the prophets concerned with Assyria's rule (e.g., Isa 10:5; Hos 11:5-7; Amos 7:10-17; Mic 3:9-12), but it does not arise in either of the two oracles that represent the bulk of Nahum. There, Judah is the innocent victim of Assyrian oppression, and Assyria is the evil empire. Most likely, then, this transitional unit, like the opening psalm, derives from the final redaction of the book and its incorporation into the Twelve.

The first line of 1:12 is difficult: *'im-shelemim weken rabbiym weken nagozzu we'abar* (mechanistically, "if full and therefore many, even so they will be cut off, and [it] will pass") could describe the days of trouble now past (so NJPS) or the enemy about to be overthrown (so NRSV, NIV). The versions introduce an additional level of complexity, as both the LXX and Syriac have instead a statement about God ruling over many waters, evidently assuming something like *moshel mayim rabbim.* It is easy to imagine scribal error yielding something like the MT out of this hypothetical reconstruction, which is also broadly supported by context (cf. the references to the flood in 1:4, 8, and in 2:9[8]) and by the occurrence of the expression *mayim rabbim* ("many waters") elsewhere in Scripture (e.g., 2 Sam 22:17; Isa 17:13; Ezek 27:26; Hab 3:15; Ps 29:3; Song 8:7). Still, the more difficult reading in the MT is to be preferred. Indeed, Spronk (1997, 59) and Christensen (2009, xxii) note that in the MT of 1:12, the first letters of the words in the first clause spell *'ashur*, that is, Assyria (although since the word is always spelled elsewhere with two *shins* [*'ashshur*], this may be a coincidence). At any rate, this clause probably depicts the imminent end of the enemy, despite their apparent strength. "The LORD declares to Judah, / And now I will break off his yoke from you / and snap the bonds that bind you" (Nah 1:13). The reader may be reminded of the famous confrontation between Jeremiah and Hananiah of Gibeon (Jer 27–28; note that *mot*, the word for "yoke" used in Nah 1:13, is not used in the Jeremiah passage, which uses *motah* and *'ol* [though *mot* and *motah* are clearly related]). There, Jeremiah declares that the LORD has imposed the yoke of Babylon upon Judah and its allies, while Hananiah falsely asserts, "Thus says the LORD of hosts, the God of Israel: I have broken the yoke of the king of Babylon" (Jer 28:2). This parallel underlines the twofold character of the yoke metaphor as expressing both a bondage from which deliverance is sought and a burden imposed by the LORD that must be borne obediently. Indeed, the yoke can be a positive image of service. Christian readers may think of Jesus saying, "Take my yoke upon you, and learn from me; for I am gentle and humble in heart, and you will find rest for your souls. For my yoke is easy, and my burden is light" (Matt 11:29-30). Similarly, in the Mishnah, Rabbi Joshua ben Korhah declares that by praying the Shema (a very important Jewish prayer opening with Deut 6:4-9, so called after its first word in Hebrew, *shema'* ["Hear!"]), one first takes up "the yoke of the kingdom of heaven" (*'ol malkut shamayim*), and then "the yoke of the commandments" (*'ol mitswot*; *b. Ber.* 13a). Submission to God's yoke is the duty, and the joy, of the faithful. But according to Nahum 1:12-14, one burden God had formerly imposed upon Judah is about to be lifted forever. The LORD will break Assyria's yoke.

In 1:14, the LORD once more addresses the enemy, who formerly had been permitted to oppress God's people. The male pronouns for the oppressor in this verse as in the previous one ("his yoke") indicate that the enemy is not Nineveh or Assyria generally, but Assyria's ruler (so Sweeney 2000, 432)—although the enemy is not yet explicitly named. In three sweeping declarations of judgment, God thoroughly undoes the power of this oppressor. First, God robs him of his descendants: there will be no seed to preserve the name and identity of the king into future generations. Second, the idols of the enemy are "cut off," that is, destroyed (Heb., *karat*). This destruction is in keeping with the instructions in Deuteronomy 12:2-3 regarding idols; ancient Near Eastern practice instead involved the gods being taken captive and their images placed in the temple of the conqueror (recall the captivity of the ark in 1 Sam 4–6). Third, the king is condemned to death, to be buried without name, without remembrance, without gods, and without honor. In sharp contrast to Assyria's apparent power and glory ("Though they are at full strength and many," Nah 1:12), God declares of the enemy, *qallota* (literally, "you are light"; Nah 1:14). Assyria's ruler is a lightweight, incapable of any action at all apart from God's empowerment, which God has now withdrawn. The NRSV captures the point well: "you are worthless."

First Oracle: The Fall of Nineveh (Nah 2:1-14 [1:15–2:13])

Some interpreters treat Nahum 2–3 (1:15–3:19) as a unit (e.g., García-Treto 1996, 596; Spronk 1997, 5), which is certainly defensible. These chapters constitute the meat of the book and are clearly interrelated—perhaps even intertwined (cf. Nogalski 1993b, 114, 123; Christensen 2009, 42–43). Nevertheless, the different styles of the two oracles confirm the wisdom of the Masoretic scribes in treating them as distinct units. While the first oracle depicts Nineveh's fall through the straightforward description of a military assault, metaphor predominates in the second oracle, particularly the metaphors of the city as a woman (3:4-13), its guards as locusts (3:15b-17), and its rulers as shepherds (3:18-19). There are of course exceptions: 2:12-14 (11-13) uses the metaphor of the lion to depict the end of Assyria's royal line, while 3:1-3 presents a vigorous, straightforward description of the assault. Still, the overall character of each oracle is sufficiently distinctive to warrant their separate treatment.

As the differing chapter divisions in the MT and the Christian Old Testament indicate, the tradition is a bit uncertain as to where the first oracle begins. Some scholars (e.g., Sweeney 2000, 434; Roberts 1991, 54) see 2:1(1:15) as the conclusion of the preceding unit. However, the opening words of this verse describe the approach of a herald: "Look! On the mountains the feet of one / who brings good tidings, / who proclaims peace!" (Nah 2:1[1:15]). As Roberts acknowledges, "the announcement of the herald bringing good news could be seen as the introduction of a new oracle" (Roberts 199, 54; cf. Floyd 2000, 55). While "peace" may seem an odd appellation for the violence and devastation the following verses depict, *shalom* ("peace") means not the absence of conflict but the *presence* of health, vitality, and wholeness (as the use of the adjective *shalem* for the "full strength" of the enemy in 1:12 demonstrates). For Nahum, the *shalom* of oppressed Judah is only possible with the end of its oppressor, namely, with the fall of Nineveh and the end of the Assyrian empire. So too, in Isaiah 2:2-4//Micah 4:1-3 the nations can "beat their swords into plowshares" (Isa 2:4//Mic 4:3) only after they surrender to the LORD's ways and judgments (Isa 2:3-4//Mic 4:2-3), while in Isaiah 61:2 "the year of the LORD's favor" is also "the day of vengeance [*naqam* (!); cf. Nah 1:2] of our God." Peace without justice is no peace at all. Notably, when Jesus reads from Isaiah 61:1-2 in the Nazareth synagogue, he pointedly drops the last line (Luke 4:18-19)—not because he sides with the oppressors (Romans, in first-century Palestine) but because he brings new life to everyone, Jew and Gentile, oppressed and oppressor, alike (Luke 4:25-27; cf. Isa 66:18-23; Jonah 3; Zech 14:16-21). As Habakkuk learns, *shalom* can be sought and found *despite* oppressive circumstances (Hab 3:17-19). Faithful living may require us to stand like Nahum against the prevailing culture; as Haggai and Zechariah demonstrate, however, it may also involve working within that culture.

Undoubtedly Nahum 2:1(1:15) is related to Isaiah 52:7, "How beautiful upon the mountains are the feet of the messenger who announces peace" (cf. also Eph 6:15). It could be that Nahum depends on Deutero-Isaiah, so that 2:1 (1:15) becomes part of the postexilic editing of this book (so Nogalski 1993b, 97–98). In contrast, it is also possible that Deutero-Isaiah depends on Nahum here. The anonymous prophet of the exile, one could argue, applies to the end of Babylon and the *shalom* of the exiles, an image used by Nahum for the end of Nineveh and the *shalom* of Judah (so Spronk 1997, 61; Sweeney 2000, 435; Goldingay 2009, 30). The next line of 2:1 (1:15), which explicitly addresses Judah, may resolve the issue:

> Celebrate your festivals, O Judah,
> fulfill your vows,
> for never again shall the wicked invade you;
> they are utterly cut off.

In the broader context of the Twelve, this statement becomes an end-time promise of Judah's final liberation connected to the day of the LORD. In its immediate context in Nahum, however, the reference must be to the time after Nineveh's fall. The tremendous optimism of this acclamation makes its date unmistakable, for within three years of the fall of Nineveh, Judah *would* be invaded—first by Egypt, then, with devastating consequences, by Babylon. Surely, then, these words could not have been spoken at any time long after Nineveh met its end; they belong to the poem in its original setting. Nahum expresses the naïve hope that the fall of Nineveh means freedom from oppression—a hope Habakkuk will see dashed to pieces by the rise of Babylon (cf. Hab 1:5-17).

There is an abrupt shift of addressee in 2:2(1) from Judah to Nineveh: "A shatterer has come up against you." We have already seen such sharp transitions within units in this book (cf. 1:8-9, 13-14), so this need not signal a new section. What is good news for God's people can only be bad news for their oppressors! The MT has "scatterer" (Heb., *mephits*) rather than "shatterer," a reading followed by *Tg. Neb.*; the LXX oddly has *emphuson eis prosopon sou* ("one who breathes in your face," a reading that prompted Theodoret of Cyrus [Hill 2006, 182] to find here a foreshadowing of the giving of the Spirit in John 20:22). There is ancient precedent for the divine warrior scattering (Heb., verb *puts*) the enemy (Num 10:35; Ps 68:2; for the LORD scattering Israel, cf. Jer 18:17), so many interpreters argue for staying with the MT here (e.g., Roberts 1991, 56; Sweeney 2000, 437; O'Brien 2004, 45–46). Yet, in the context, which refers to the breaching of Nineveh's walls (cf. 2:1[2], "Guard the ramparts; watch the road"), it is best, with the NRSV and JPSV, to emend the MT to *mapets* (a participle of *patsats*, "shatter," rather than *puts*, "scatter). Similarly, Ezekiel 9:2 calls the weapon wielded by the angels who come to destroy sinful Jerusalem *keli mapatso* ("his implement of shattering"; NRSV reads "his weapon for slaughter"). This term also appears in Jeremiah 51:20 with reference to the LORD's war club.

Thus, while human troops assail Nineveh, there is no doubt that God is the power behind the assault.

Nahum 2:3(2) reads the assault on Nineveh as a restoration of all Israel, including the former northern kingdom ("the majesty of Jacob, as well as the majesty of Israel"), despite its former devastation. The NRSV encloses this verse in parentheses, suggesting that it is not intrinsically connected to its context, an assessment shared by many interpreters (e.g., Roberts 1991, 64–65; García-Treto 1996, 609; Nogalski [1993b, 113–14] sees all of 2:1-3 [1:15-2] as an insertion). The statement of God's restoration of Israel in this verse seems at odds with the mainstream of this poem, which concerns Nineveh and depicts human agents (2:14[13] is likely an expansion; see the discussion of this passage below). Still, as we have seen, "the shatterer" in 2:2(1) is the LORD, so the statement of divine action in this verse is not out of place. In the opening poem, however, the interest in the restoration of the north occurs in a line that breaks the acrostic pattern, and is most likely an insertion (cf. 1:4b). Most probably, then, this verse too has been added by Nahum's editors.

The lines that follow describe the assault on Nineveh in vigorous, straightforward poetry:

> The shields of his warriors are red;
> his soldiers are clothed in crimson.
> The metal on the chariots flashes
> on the day when he musters them (2:3[4]).

The red shields and clothing of the attacking troops may mean that their shields are stained and their garments soaked with blood (so Goldingay 2009, 34; cf. Isa 63:1-6; Rev 19:13). But since Ezekiel 23:14 describes the Chaldean troops depicted on Assyrian reliefs as "portrayed in vermilion" (cf. Tuell 2009, 154, 157–58), this may simply mean that the Babylonian uniforms are red (so Achtemeier 1986, 20; Spronk 1997, 89). The foot soldiers attack supported by the cavalry. The mention of the chariots in 2:4-5 (3-4) makes it likely that the NRSV "chargers" is correct (following LXX and Syriac, and cf. the NJPS footnote; the MT *wehabberoshim* ["and the cypresses"] is most likely a scribal error for *wehapperashim* ["and the horsemen"], but cf. KJV, NIV, and Roberts 1991, 58). The word *sokek* in 2:6 (5), which occurs only here, is probably related to the verb *sakak* ("cover, screen"). The NRSV translates *sokek* with the unusual word "mantelet," a screen protecting soldiers from enemy fire. Given the depiction in this verse of the troops stumbling hastily toward the wall and the statement in the following verse, "The river gates are opened, the palace trembles" (Heb., *namog*: literally, "melts"; used elsewhere in circumstances of terror, cf. Exod 15:15; Josh 2:9, 24; Isa 14:31; Jer 49:23), it seems most likely that *sokek* describes a siege engine, a wheeled shelter affixed to a battering ram used to breach Nineveh's walls (so JPSV; Roberts 1991, 59; Spronk 1997, 94; for depictions of these rams in action from the Lachish Relief, cf. Ussishkin 1982, 73–75, 82–83, 84, 100, 106, and the description and reconstruction on 101).

Once its walls are breached and its gates are forced open, the city is overwhelmed. "It is decreed that the city [literally, "she"; *Tg. Neb.* understands this to mean the queen, but the city itself is likely intended] go into exile" (2:8[7]; cf. 3:10). The first word in this verse, Hebrew *hutstsab* ("it is established"), is unusual. *Targum Nebi'im* apparently reads *hatstsab* (*tsiba'* in Aramaic), that is, the queen's litter; the LXX has "the foundation was exposed" (reading *gulletah* as "uncovered"; see the discussion of the verb *galah* in 3:5, below). A long-standing tradition (for example, the medieval Jewish commentators Rashi, Ibn Ezra, and Kimchi) holds that Huzzab is the name of the Assyrian queen (cf. KJV, NJPS, and the discussion in Christensen 2009, 287–91) and that she is the one being exiled. The NRSV is correct to stay with the MT and to translate *hutstsab* as a form of the verb *natsab* ("stand, establish") with an indefinite subject (so Christensen 2009, 287; cf. also NIV). The point is the unavoidable *fact* of this exile: Nineveh's doom stands, fixed and irrevocable. The fate the Assyrians had imposed upon the Israelites is now imposed upon them.

Nahum 2:9 (8) is, apart from the superscription, the first mention of Nineveh in this book: "Nineveh is like a pool / whose waters run away." This line is difficult to interpret. The MT has "like a pool of water, she is from days [past]" (cf. NJPS, KJV). The NRSV "whose waters have run away" follows the LXX, which may reflect the claim of Greek historian Diodorus Siculus regarding Nineveh's siege and fall. He writes that Arabaces the Mede besieged Nineveh for two years. Then, in the third year, a flood destroyed the city's fortifications, and, his defeat imminent, Assyria's king committed suicide by setting fire to his own palace (Diodorus Siculus, *Bib. hist.* 2.26-27). Certainly, this would fit with the constant imagery of water and flood in this book. Indeed, the NJPS for 2:7(6) reads, "The floodgates are opened, / And the palace is deluged" (cf. Roberts 1991, 59–60). Ezekiel 31:10-14, however, attributes the fall of Assyria to the Babylonians rather than the Medes (cf. Tuell 2009, 215–16), while according to the Babylonian Chronicle (Oppenheim 1969, 304–305), the city fell to the Babylonians and Medes in concert. Further, archaeological investigation confirms that fire, not flood, destroyed Nineveh (Sweeney 2000, 436). Since Nineveh was built along, and even *over*, the Tigris and its tributaries, and was famous for its channels and well-watered gardens, the use of water imagery in association with the city is easy to understand. Nahum here provides a literary figure for Nineveh, not a factual description of its fall (as NJPS recognizes; cf. also Spronk 1997, 99–100). After long years of resting cool and undisturbed, like a pool of placid water, Nineveh has at last experienced the turmoil it had inflicted on other cities of the ancient world.

Nahum depicts the fall of Nineveh in a series of vivid scenes, from the piteous image of weeping slave women "moaning like doves and beating their breasts" (2:8[7]) to the panicked flight of its defenders ("'Halt! Halt!'—but no one turns back," 2:9[8]) to the looting of its treasures (2:10[9]). In 2:11(10), the despair and horror of Nineveh's population finds potent expression:

> Devastation, desolation, and destruction!
> Hearts faint and knees tremble,
> all loins quake,
> all faces grow pale!

The alliterative "Doom, desolation, and destruction!" translates the Hebrew *buqah umebuqah umebullaqah*, capturing a sense of Nahum's poetry. All of these forms occur only here (although their derivation from known roots makes their meaning clear), and all sound very like another Hebrew word, *baqia'*, referring to breached, ruined city walls (cf. Isa 22:9; Amos 6:11). The expression *qibbetsu pa'rur*, rendered "grow pale" in the NRSV, appears elsewhere only in Joel 2:6, which likely depends on its use in Nahum; its meaning is uncertain. The Masoretic scribes suggest ignoring the *'aleph* and reading *parur*, meaning "pot"; *Tg. Neb.* and LXX also pursue this course, comparing the faces of Nineveh's population to a burned pot (hence the KJV "gather blackness"). *HALOT* (2000, 909) proposes that *pa'rur* means "heat," which could suggest either faces turning red with agitation or heat being drawn *from* the faces, turning them pale (so NRSV, NJPS, NIV). Whatever this expression means, it obviously conveys extreme emotion, whether fear or anger or dismay.

In 2:12-13 (11-12), the oracle abruptly shifts from straightforward description to metaphor. Suddenly, instead of soldiers and slave women, advancing chariots and fleeing citizens, the poet speaks of lions:

> What became of the lions' den,
> the cave of the young lions,
> where the lion goes,
> and the lion's cubs, with no one to disturb them?

We should note that the MT and LXX alike have "pasture" rather than "cave" here (cf. JPSV). The NRSV emends the Hebrew *mir'eh* ("pasture") to *me'arah* ("cave"), which preserves the parallel with "den" in the first line and, furthermore, makes better sense. We do not usually think of lions as having a pasture! Nineveh had been a lion's den where the great cats could be at ease and from which they could go forth to ravage the world. The poet says that, horrific as those days of predation had been (the den is filled with "prey" and "torn flesh," 2:13[12]), they are now over: "The lion has torn enough for his whelps / and strangled prey for his lionesses" (2:13[12]). The destruction of the lion's den marks the end of the lion's depredations.

While Assyria itself may be the lion in this metaphor (so O'Brien 2004, 45), it is more likely that the lion is the king, and by extension the royal line (with, e.g., Roberts 1991, 67; Spronk 1997, 104–106; García-Treto 1996, 612). From the reign of Shalmanesar III (859–824 BCE) in Assyria's Middle Period to the last days of Ashur-etel-ilani (627–612 BCE), king of Assyria when Nineveh fell, the royal seal of Assyria featured the king battling with a rampant lion (Dick 2006, 246). Assyrian reliefs place the king hunting the lion alongside depictions of his military victories (Dick 2006, 260). The lion hunt defines the king, not only as the shepherd who defends his people from the beasts of the wilderness (cf. Nah 3:18-19) but also as the lion itself. The king identifies with his prey (Dick 2006, 244). Similarly, the Hebrew Bible associates the lion with the royal line of Judah. In Jacob's deathbed blessing on his son Judah, the patriarch declares,

> Judah is a lion's whelp;
> from the prey, my son, you have gone up.
> He crouches down, he stretches out like a lion,
> like a lioness—who dares rouse him up? (Gen 49:9).

Solomon's throne made this lion motif concrete. Its armrests were two ivory lions overlaid with gold, and twelve other lions stood along the steps leading up to the throne (1 Kgs 10:18-20//2 Chr 9:17-19). A particularly intriguing parallel to Nahum 2:12-13 (11-12) is Ezekiel 19:1-9, which likewise takes the royal lion metaphor in unexpected directions. Granting to Judah's royal house its identification with the lion, the prophet asks what happens to lions in civilized realms. They are, of course, hunted down, trapped in pits, locked in cages, or killed (Ezek 19:4, 8-9)! While this is the implicit fate of Assyria's royal house in Nahum 2:12-13 (11-12) as well, the following verse makes that fate explicit.

The last verse of this oracle is prose, not poetry, and unpacks the metaphorical language of 2:12-13 (11-12): "See, I am against you, says the LORD of hosts, and I will burn your chariots in smoke, and the sword shall devour your young lions; I will cut off your prey from the earth, and the voice of your messengers shall be heard no more" (2:14[13]). *Targum Nebi'im* consistently demonstrates this prosaic tendency. Significantly, in 2:12-13 (11-12), *Tg. Neb.* renders "lion" as "the king," "lionesses" as "his wives," and "whelps" as "his sons," while in 2:14 (13) it has *shiltonak* ("your rulers") for MT *kephirayik* ("your young lions"). It seems most likely that 2:14 (13) similarly represents the later interpretation of Nahum's oracle, probably by the editor responsible for this book in its final form (cf. Nogalski 1993b, 117); indeed, this verse quotes from the second oracle ("See, I am against you, says the LORD of hosts," 3:5; see the discussion of this phrase below). Nonetheless, in the book as it stands, this explicit prose interpretation of the lion metaphor neatly concludes the first oracle. The end of Nineveh means the end of Assyria and its royal line.

Second Oracle: No Mourners for Nineveh (3:1-19)

Nahum 3:1-19 brings together numerous styles and forms (cf. Nogalski 1993b, 117; Floyd 2000, 61–64); indeed many scholars (e.g., Roberts 1991, 76–77; Sweeney 2000, 447) identify the last two verses as a separate oracle directed against the king rather than the city. The abrupt shift in the middle of 3:15 could indicate an expansion of the original oracle, with vv. 15b-17 linked to its context by the catchword *yelek* ("locust"). If so, however, we have no way of knowing whether that expansion was made by Nahum himself, by someone else in the course of the transmission of Nahum's oracles, or by the editors of the Twelve in the assembly of the book in its final form. In the book as it stands, 3:1-19 is a mock dirge for slain Nineveh—a taunt hurled at the stricken city that now experiences the humiliation and suffering it had so often and for so long imposed upon other cities.

Nahum's second oracle opens with a mocking call to mourn the city whose fall the first oracle (2:1-14 [1:15–2:13]) has described: "Ah, City of bloodshed, utterly deceitful" (3:1). This oracle could be called a taunt song, since the prophets use the opening exclamation (Heb., *hoi*) to preface a taunt or threat (e.g., Isa 1:4; Jer 22:13; Ezek 13:3, 18; Amos 5:18; and the five "woes" in Hab 2; compare Luke 6:24-26), but *hoi* is often used as an exclamation of grief (e.g., 1 Kgs 13:30; Jer 22:18). Hence the KJV renders "Woe to the bloody city." The ironic search for mourners in 3:7 also indicates that this oracle is a lament, albeit a satirical one (cf. Isaiah's parable concerning the king of Babylon in Isa 14:3-23; and the lament over Tyre in Ezek

27:1-36). In contrast, St. John Chrysostom takes Nahum's invitation to mourn seriously:

> Let us mourn with Nahum . . . . Let us not weep for him who is already dead, but let us weep for the rapacious man, the grasping, the covetous, the insatiable. Why should we mourn for the dead, in whose case it is impossible henceforth to effect anything? Let us mourn for these who are capable even of change. . . . May it come to pass that both they may be freed from their malady, and that none of us may ever fall into it. (*Hom. Jn 11:41-42*)

The characterization of Nineveh as *'ir damim* (NRSV "City of bloodshed," although the KJV "bloody city" is preferable) underlines both the violence and the ritual defilement (cf. Lev 12:4; 17:10-14) of this foreign capital. It is quite likely that this passage has influenced Habakkuk 2:12, where the identification of the "bloody city" is uncertain (perhaps Babylon; perhaps Jerusalem). But the influence of this language is particularly apparent in Ezekiel (cf. 7:23, 9:9, and especially 22:2, 3 and 24:6, 9), where *Jerusalem* is the bloody city.

Nahum's artistry is evident in the double-intentional language of this verse. Nineveh has long been a "bloody" city in a metaphorical sense, as a perpetrator of violence. Now, however, Nineveh is *literally* bloody; blood flows from the bodies of the slain heaped in its streets (Nah 3:3). Further, Nineveh is "full of booty—no end to the plunder" (3:1). The wording is unusual; *pereq* appears elsewhere only in Obadiah 14, where it refers to a parting of ways or crossroads; in Nahum, it seems to refer to a divided portion or a piece torn away (cf. Sweeney 2000, 442; Christensen 2009, 336; the NRSV "booty" follows *Tg. Neb.*; LXX has *adikias* [unrighteousness]). The word translated "plunder" in the NRSV, Hebrew *tareph*, would be better rendered "prey" (indeed, the NIV reads "victims"!). This imagery, then, recalls the description in Nahum 2:13 (12) (the preceding verse if, as we have proposed, 2:14 [13] is an insertion) of Nineveh as a lion's den, filled with prey (*tareph* appears in both verses) and torn flesh (cf. García-Treto 1996, 613). Now, however, Nineveh has *become* prey. Its own treasures are looted (cf. Nah 2:9); its own citizens are slaughtered.

Much like the first oracle, Nahum 3:2-3 presents a straightforward, vigorous depiction of the sacking of Nineveh by enemy troops, in the same chopped, staccato rhythm:

> The crack of whip and rumble of wheel,
> galloping horses and bounding chariot!

Horsemen charging,
flashing sword and glittering spear (3:2-3a).

But after describing the corpses heaped in Nineveh's streets, the poet moves on to a metaphorical depiction of this disaster as the rape of Nineveh (3:4-7).

This second oracle represents both Nineveh (3:4-7) and Thebes (3:8-9) as women—a fairly common notion in the ancient Near East. In Canaan and Phoenicia, a city could be personified as a goddess, the consort of the city's patron god (cf. Fitzgerald 1972, 406–15). Cities in Mesopotamia were regarded as masculine rather than feminine, but the patron goddess of a city could still be identified with the city itself (cf. Biddle 1991, 175–79). Similarly, Scripture can personify a city (usually Jerusalem), or the people of God themselves, as a woman wedded to the LORD (e.g., Hos 2:16-18; Jer 2:1-2; cf. the NT portrayal of the church as the bride of Christ in Eph 5:22-32; Rev 19:6-9; 21:9-27). Still, the prophets generally use this metaphor negatively, not positively. If Israel is wedded to the LORD, then religious faithlessness, through idolatry, and political faithlessness, through foreign alliances, become adultery (Fitzgerald 1972, 404–405; e.g., Hos 2:4-14, Jer 3:1-10; 31:32, and especially Ezek 16 and 23). Also, as Nahum 3:4-7 brutally demonstrates, if the city or the nation is a woman, then its conquest becomes a rape (cf. Isa 47:3; Lam 1:8; Hos 2:9-10; Ezek 16:36-37; 23:10, 29).

The depiction of Nineveh as "the prostitute, gracefully alluring" (3:4) sounds unnervingly like a rapist's claim that his victim was "asking for it." Little wonder that many feminist readers regard passages such as this as pornography (e.g., Setel 1985; Van Dijk-Hemmes 1993; cf. Patton 2000, 222–26; O'Brien 2004, 53). In pornography, female sexuality is objectified and "depicted as negative" (Setel 1985, 87); that is, as "impure, eroticized and in need of control" (Patton 2000, 224). Setel finds this pornographic objectification particularly in the prophets, for whom "objectified female sexuality" becomes "a symbol of evil" (Setel 1985, 86). Sure enough, the portrayal of Nineveh as a prostitute (the Hebrew *zonah*, as O'Brien [2004, 51] notes, can refer to "any promiscuous woman" [cf. Deut 23:18]; indeed, "any woman who does not meet societal expectations of sexual conduct"; cf. also Goldingay 2009, 38) is consistent with other prophetic denunciations of cities or nations personified as women. But when the prophets use *zonah* (and the related terms *zanah*, "commit fornication"; *zenut* and *zenunim*, "fornication") for Israel (e.g., Hos 1:2; 4:13-15; Jer 2:20; 3:3), Judah (e.g., Jer 3:8-10), Jerusalem (e.g., Isa 1:21, Ezek 16:30, 31, 33, 35; 23:44), or Samaria (e.g., Ezek 23:44; Mic 1:7), they relate the term particularly to the marriage metaphor. Each of these could be regarded symbolically as God's spouse, so that adultery becomes a metaphor for spiritual and political faithlessness (cf. O'Brien 2004, 51). Passages such as Ezekiel 16 and 23, for all their graphic offensiveness, do not function as pornography (*contra* Van Dijk-Hemmes 1993, 173), since rather than gazing pruriently from a distance, the reader is compelled to identify with the victims in these accounts (cf. Smith-Christopher 2005, 145-46; Tuell 2009, 153–54). Of course, Nineveh, as a foreign city, could scarcely be accused of being unfaithful to the LORD (as O'Brien [2004, 53] observes; however, cf. Isa 23:15-17, where Tyre is compared to a prostitute). Nor is there any attempt to identify with the victim here—far from it! Apart from mockery and insult, then, what might be the point of such language in Nahum?

A clue may be found in the further characterization of Nineveh as ". . . mistress of sorcery, / who enslaves nations through her debaucheries, / and peoples through her sorcery" (3:4). This combination of sexual rapacity and supernatural power sounds like a description of the goddess Ishtar, the embodiment of female sexuality in Mesopotamia. Ishtar's association with the planet Venus, which is both the morning and the evening star, indicates her duality. As the embodiment of wifely virtues, she represents "safe" sex and fertility; however, she also represents dangerous passions, and so embodies prostitution and warfare. Nineveh was associated with Ishtar from ancient times. Indeed, the preface to the Code of Hammurabi identifies Nineveh as the site of a temple to Inanna, the ancient Sumerian name for the goddess (Meek 1969, 165). In the fourteenth century BCE, during a period of Hurrian dominance in the region, King Tushratta twice sent the image of the "Ishtar of Nineveh" to Egypt, to heal his in-law, Pharaoh Amenophis III (Kamrat 2007, 271)—showing not only the antiquity of Ishtar's connection to Nineveh but also the association of the goddess with magic. Perhaps, then, Nahum here identifies the city with its patron goddess (cf. García-Treto 1996, 614; Christensen 2009, 348; Goldingay 2009, 43).

Whatever the intent of Nahum's language regarding Nineveh as prostitute and sorceress, his identification of the city as a woman leads directly into the depiction of Nineveh's fall as a rape:

> I am against you,
> says the LORD of hosts,
> and will lift up your skirts over your face;
> and I will let nations look on your nakedness
> and kingdoms on your shame (Nah 3:5).

The divine title "LORD of hosts" (Heb., *Yhwh tseba'oth*) is very old. Indeed, Frank Moore Cross proposes that *Yhwh*, the sacred Name of God (rendered in most English translations as "the LORD") derives from this title. According to Cross, *Yhwh tseba'oth* is a sentence name, like those ascribed to gods and goddesses in old Canaanite poems (Cross 1973, 66–67). In the sentence *Yhwh tseba'oth*, *yhwh* is the verb—a causative form of *hayah*, the Hebrew verb of being—so that the sentence reads, "he creates the (divine) hosts" (Cross 1973, 65). God was worshiped as *Yhwh tseba'oth* particularly in association with the ark of the covenant (cf. 1 Sam 4:4; 2 Sam 6:2//1 Chr 13:6; Isa 37:16), and so with Zion and the Jerusalem temple (e.g., Isa 18:7; 24:23; 25:6; 31:4-5). The distribution of this title among the prophetic books is intriguing. While the divine name *Yhwh tseba'oth* appears sixty-two times in Isaiah and seventy-seven times in Jeremiah (in the form *Yhwh 'elohe tseba'oth* ["the LORD, the God of hosts"], the name also appears in Jer 5:14; 15:16; 35:17; 38:17; 44:7), it does not appear at all in Ezekiel; most likely it has been polemically excluded from that book due to Ezekiel's low view of Jerusalem's political and religious establishment (so Tuell 2009, 137; cf. Mettinger 1982, 11, 109–13; note that Ezekiel also never uses the word "Zion"). In the Book of the Twelve, the title appears in Amos in the form *Yhwh 'elohe tseba'oth* ("the LORD, the God of hosts," Amos 4:13; 5:14-16, 27; 6:8; cf. also 2 Sam 5:10; 12 Kgs 19:10, 14; Pss 59:6[5]; 80:5[4], 20[19]; 84:9[8]; 89:9[8]; for "God of hosts" alone, cf. Ps 80:8[7], 15[14]); Micah 4:4 and all six of the books with which we are concerned use "the LORD of hosts" (Nah 2:14; 3:5; Hab 2:13; Zeph 2:9-10; 14 times in Haggai; 53 times in Zechariah; and 24 times in Malachi). We will discuss the significance of the disproportionate use of this title in the last three books of the Twelve in context. For now, it is enough to note that, consistent with its Zion associations, Judean prophets tend to use the title "LORD of hosts."

The LORD of hosts not only pronounces judgment upon Nineveh ("I am against you") but also enacts that judgment by pulling Nineveh's skirts up over her head (MT uses the verb *galah*, "strip, uncover"), so that the nations may "look on [her] nakedness" (3:5). The Hebrew word *ma'ar* ("nakedness") occurs only here and in 1 Kings 7:36 (in a description of the intricately wrought wheeled stands for the basins used by the priests in the temple precincts, on which every bare space [*ma'ar*] was filled with carvings). It is evidently related, however, to *'erwah* (usually translated "nakedness"), a word consistently used in the Hebrew Bible for shameful exposure or activity (e.g., Exod 20:26; Deut 24:1). The term *'erwah* appears most often in the Leviticus Holiness Code (specifically, in Lev 18:6-19 and 20:11, 17-21, where *'erwah* occurs 32 times). There, to "uncover [someone's] nakedness" (verb *galah* with *'erwah*) is to engage in shameful, defiling sexual intercourse, particularly incest or sexual relations with a menstruating woman (cf. Ezek 16:37-41; 22:10, 18, and perhaps Gen 9:20-27). Elsewhere, the expression "uncover (someone's) nakedness" refers to the metaphorical rape of cities personified as women, not only Samaria (Ezek 23:10; cf. Hos 2:11-12 [9-10]) and Jerusalem (Ezek 16:36-37; 23:29; cf. Lam 1:8) but also Babylon (Isa 47:3). Likely, this is the intent in Nahum 3:4-7 as well (cf. O'Brien 2004, 52).

More is going on here than the metaphorical depiction of Nineveh's fall. For as long as humans have taken up weapons against one another, rape has been the inevitable accompaniment of war. Certainly, Nahum knew of women brutalized by Assyrian troops in their numerous Palestinian campaigns (depicted, e.g., in Isa 3:16–4:1 and Amos 7:16-17). Nor, unfortunately, was violence against women in wartime restricted to Israel's enemies. Deuteronomy 20:14 declares the women of a defeated enemy to be legitimate spoils of war (although Deut 21:10-14 requires soldiers to marry women taken in battle, and forbids their sale as slaves). What Nahum says was done to Nineveh metaphorically would have been the actual experience of the women of Nineveh once the walls were breached and the soldiers poured in.

As a war crime, rape reflects the "engendering" of warfare, with the masculine conquerors triumphant over a humiliated, feminized enemy (Smith-Christopher 2005, 152–53); but stripping and ritual humiliation would not have been restricted to the female population of the city. Numerous ancient Near Eastern inscriptions and reliefs depict male prisoners of war marching into captivity, stripped naked and bound so that they cannot cover themselves. Isaiah 20:4 describes how the Assyrians forcibly stripped Egyptian and Ethiopian prisoners of war, marching them into captivity naked from the waist down in order to humiliate them (cf. Floyd 2000, 70; Sweeney 2000, 443). Isaiah 7:20 describes another aspect of this humiliation. The beards and pubic hair of the prisoners would be shaved (cf. 2 Sam 10:4; Ezek 5:1-17), a symbolic emasculation that, once more, fits into the engendering of war (cf. 3:13, "Look at your troops: they are women in your midst"). The verb used for the LORD's action against Nineveh in Nahum 3:5 (*galah,* "to strip") can also mean "exile" (cf. 2:8[7]; 3:10). Daniel Smith-Christopher proposes that this usage came about "because of the Neo-Assyrian and Neo-Babylonian practice of stripping and humiliating captive males" (Smith-Christopher 2005, 154). When Nahum depicts Nineveh as stripped and humiliated, then, he is pronouncing upon that city the fate that Assyria had brought to Samaria, to Thebes, and to countless others. Indeed, should we be tempted to regard ourselves as morally superior to Nahum and his ancient counterparts, the shameful photographs from America's recent war in Iraq, of prisoners at Abu Ghraib stripped naked and forced into humiliating poses, tragically demonstrate that these attitudes are with us still.

This language is, without question, deeply disturbing and offensive. How is a person of faith to read these words? Wessels notes that Nahum's language is the purposefully extreme expression of an oppressed people's anger and frustration and is not to be taken literally as legitimating violence (Wessel 1998, 625). Still, words undoubtedly have power; it would be disingenuous to suggest otherwise. Elizabeth Achtemeier wrote that the book of Nahum is "not about human vengeance and hatred and military conquest—but a book about God" (Achtemeier 1986, 5; so too Robertson 1990, 80). Certainly, God is the actor in this book, particularly when one reads it through the interpretive lens offered by its framing psalm and introduction (1:2-14); indeed, Achtemeier called this poem the "theological key" to Nahum (Achtemeier 1986, 6). Still, Nahum 3:4-7 is disturbing not only for the violence against women it portrays and so may legitimate, but also precisely *because of* its theological implications. In this metaphor, God becomes a rapist.

It is vital for the faithful reader to remember that Nahum's language is metaphorical, not literal. Christian readers will recall that the New Testament compares Jesus to a thief (Matt 24:43//Luke 12:39; 1 Thess 5:2, 4; 2 Pet 3:10; Rev 3:3; 16:15), and that Jesus' parables compare God to an unjust judge (Luke 18:1-8) and a cruel master (Matt 25:14-30//Luke 19:11-27). Those descriptions, of course, are not literal either, but metaphors, intended to shock us into unexpected insights concerning God and the world. Nahum's prophecy powerfully expresses God's wrath against a brutal oppressor, a word our world still needs to hear. The great Jewish philosopher and theologian Abraham Heschel cautioned against the modern tendency to confuse love with sentimentality. He wrote,

> Since justice is [God's] nature, love, which would disregard the evil deeds of man, would contradict His nature. Because of His concern for man, His justice is tempered with mercy. Divine anger is not the antithesis of love, but its counterpart, a help to justice as demanded by true love. (1962, 77)

Inasmuch as Nahum's metaphor communicates this message, it remains effective. However, as Patton observes regarding all metaphorical language, "at some point the metaphor will fail" (Patton 2000, 228). Just as Nineveh is not literally the goddess Ishtar, "gracefully alluring, mistress of sorcery" (3:4), so God is not literally the male *Yhwh tseba'oth* who assaults and humiliates the goddess.

Julia O'Brien calls for a "balanced ethical response to the book of Nahum" that affirms God's judgment but also denies "any response to evil—including the reader's own—that perpetuates the very ideology of brutality that it seeks to oppose" (O'Brien 2004, 57). The challenge for the reader is to hear Nahum's language not only in its social and historical context as resistance literature but also in its literary and theological context, within the Book of the Twelve and within Scripture as a whole. The pairing of Nahum with Habakkuk serves as a corrective to a too-literal interpretation of historical circumstances as acts of God. So too, contrasts with Jonah and with Zechariah 9–14 call into question Nahum's exclusive assumptions, implying that God ultimately intends salvation for the nations as well as for Israel. Finally, Hosea calls the aggressively male depiction of *Yhwh tseba'oth* in Nahum into question. Here the LORD, depicted as Israel's mother (Hos 11:1-4), declares, "I am God, and no man" (Hos 11:9; "man" is preferable to the NRSV "mortal," as the Hebrew is *'ish*, not the generic *'adam*). The faith would be ill served by a reading that expels Nahum from the canon on the spurious grounds of our alleged moral or religious superiority. We need to hear this ancient text and to be challenged by it. However, it also will not do to smooth over the offense of this text. Otherwise, we may find ourselves worshiping an idol made in our own violent, self-serving image.

Nahum 3:8-10 describes the fall of a great city of Egypt—personified, like Nineveh, as a woman. Nahum uses the city's Egyptian name, No-amon (cf. Jer 46:25, which has "Amon-No"; Ezek 30:14-16 has simply "No," although in 30:15 *khamon No* ["the hordes of Thebes"] puns on Amon-No). Although ancient interpreters sometimes misidentified No-Amon as Alexandria (cf. *Tg. Neb.* and Vulgate), the NRSV and NIV rightly recognize it as Thebes (note that NJPS, like the KJV, stays with the Egyptian name here). Thebes was one of the great cities of ancient Egypt; indeed, it served as Egypt's capital for much of the second and first millennia BCE, making its comparison to the Assyrian capital Nineveh ("Are you better than Thebes?" 3:8) particularly apt. Like Nineveh, Thebes was associated with a great river (the Nile), which served as part of its defenses ("her rampart a sea, water her wall," 3:8). Also like Nineveh, Thebes had been the center of a great empire, able to call upon allies and mercenaries for its defense (3:9; for Ethiopia [Cush], Put, and Libya as Egyptian allies, cf. Tuell 2009, 210, 223, on Ezek 30:5; compare Jer 46:9, where the trio is Cush, Put, and Lud [Lydia], and see also Ezek 27:10; 38:5). But despite its strength, Thebes could not stand: "Yet she became an exile [*gam-hi' laggolah*], / she went into captivity" (3:10).

When Thebes fell to Assyria in 663 BCE, it experienced all the atrocities that befall a conquered city (3:10). Its leaders were humiliated, bound, and divided by lot into groups to be imprisoned or killed (or perhaps, divided among the soldiers as slaves [so Spronk 1997, 131; Christensen 2009, 360]; cf. Joel 3:3 [4:3]; Obad 11). Its children were brutally slaughtered, "dashed into pieces at the head of every street" (3:10; cf. 2 Kgs 8:12; Isa 13:16; Hos 10:14; 14:1 [13:16]; Ps 137:9).

In 3:11-15a, Nahum declares that Nineveh will fall just as Thebes had fallen. Like Thebes, Nineveh will "be drunken" (for drunkenness as a metaphor for military defeat, cf. the discussion of Nah 1:10 above, and of Hab 2:15-16 below). The fortresses defending Nineveh will fall like ripe figs into the mouths of their attackers (3:12). No resistance will be possible. Nineveh's troops "are women" (Heb., has *'ammek nashim*, "your *people* [are] women"; Floyd [2000, 74] argues that this refers to the surviving population, as most of the men have been killed) and its gates will not hold (3:13). Nahum 3:14-15a, which returns to the straightforward language of 3:1-3, describes the attempts of the city to prepare for the coming siege:

> Draw water for the siege,
> strengthen your forts;
> trample the clay,
> tread the mortar,
> take hold of the brick mold! (3:14).

But all of these preparations are doomed to failure. In this poem, the fire of the brick kiln leads inexorably to the devouring flames of the burning city; the sword "will devour you like the locust" (3:15a).

The locust image calls to mind the book of Joel, where the metaphor of the locust plague is also used for invading armies; indeed, apart from Joel 1:4; 2:25 and Nahum 3:15-16, the term *yeleq* ("creeping locust") appears only in Jeremiah 51:4, 27 and Psalm 105:34. Nogalski proposes a complex history for 3:15-17, arguing that while the Joel-influenced phrases using *yeleq* in 3:15 and 16 belong to the final editing of the book, the bulk of this material entered the book before its incorporation into the Twelve (1993b, 124–27). Alternatively, the use of the locust metaphor in 3:15a may have prompted the expansion in 3:15b-17. Whatever redactional process led to the text before us, it is clear that the locust metaphor in 3:15b-17 works differently than the metaphor in 3:15a, being based not on the locust's rapacity (the sword devouring "like a locust") but on the numbers and speed of the locust swarm (cf. Nogalski 1993b, 120–21). Although Nineveh has multiplied its merchants to "more than the stars of the heavens" (a measure of the city's wealth), although its scribes are "like swarms of locusts" (a measure of Nineveh's legendary status as a center of learning), and although its defenders too are "like grasshoppers," none of this will save the city. Just as the locust "sheds its skin and flies away" (3:16), so Nineveh's purveyors of wealth and wisdom, as well as its defenders, will fly away to parts unknown (3:16).

Like Nahum's first oracle (cf. 2:12-14 [11-13]), the second oracle ends with a royal metaphor. But this time, it is the image of the king as shepherd (3:17-18). Like the lion metaphor, the shepherd metaphor was common in the ancient Near East and is very old, going back to the ancient Sumerian king lists (Oppenheim 1969, 265–66). Hammurabi, founder of the first great Babylonian empire in the eighteenth century BCE, had written, "Hammurabi, the shepherd, called by Enlil am I; the one who makes affluence and plenty abound" (Meek 1969, 164). The title was used by the Assyrian kings as well: Adad-nirari III (810–723 BCE) is described as "(a king) whose shepherding they [i.e., the gods] made as agreeable to the people of Assyria as (is the smell of) the Plant of Life" (Oppenheim 1968, 281), and Esarhaddon (680–669 BCE) is called "the true shepherd, favorite of the gods" (Oppenheim 1968, 289). The expression was still in use at the rise of the Neo-Babylonian Empire—both Nabopolassar (626–605 BCE) and Nebuchadnezzar (605–562 BCE) were called "shepherds" (Odell 2005, 432). The Hebrew Bible amply attests to the use of the shepherd metaphor for Israel's rulers (cf. 2 Sam 5:2; Jer 3:15; Ezek 34:1-10; Mic 5:1-5a; Zech 10:2-3; for the LORD as shepherd, cf. Ps 23; Ezek 34:11-16), an idea that lies back of the New Testament image of Jesus as the Good Shepherd (John 10). The point of the metaphor is that the king cares for his people as a shepherd tends the flock. But this is not the case for Nineveh:

> Your shepherds are asleep,
> O king of Assyria;
> your nobles slumber.
> Your people are scattered on the mountains
> with no one to gather them (3:18).

The image of leaderless people "scattered on the mountains" recalls the oracle of Micaiah ben Imlah concerning the death of Ahab: "I saw all Israel scattered on the mountains, like sheep that have no shepherd" (1 Kgs 22:17//2 Chr 18:16). The "lost sheep" metaphor is used by Ezekiel to represent the Babylonian exiles (Ezek 34:6), and it figures in the depictions of the lost in the New Testament (Matt 9:36//Mark 6:34; for God searching for the lost sheep, cf. Matt 18:12-14; Luke 15:1-7). But of course, in Nahum the point is not the salvation of a leaderless people, but their destruction. Just as the "lost tribes" of Israel were scattered by the Assyrian exile and vanished from history, so Nineveh is doomed to dissolution.

Assyria's royal line has been mortally wounded and will never recover (3:19). The image of the "incurable wound" (*nakhal* with *makkah*) is adopted powerfully by Jeremiah, who uses this image for Jerusalem (Jer 10:19 for Zion's pain [note the scattering of shepherds' flock in 10:21] and 30:12 for God's diagnosis, leading to restoration; cf. also Jer 8:22)—much as Ezekiel adopts the "bloody city" as an image for Jerusalem (cf. the discussion of Nah 3:1, above). In the prophetic canon, then, the images Nahum projects outward, onto Judah's enemy, come to be applied inwardly, to Jerusalem itself. But in Nahum, Judah has been the innocent victim of Assyrian oppression—an oppression now ended. The expression "clap the hand" (verb *taqah* with *kaph*, meaning "palm") can designate sealing a deal, much like a handshake (Prov 6:1; 17:18; 22:26). It also denotes rejoicing (Ps 47:1), however, as does the similar expression *naqah* with *kaph* (2 Kgs 11:2)—although the latter construction is used in Ezekiel to signify the beginning or the end of an act of judgment (Ezek 6:11; 21:14, 17; 22:13). The clapping of "All who hear the news about you" most likely involves the second option, as if the nations were applauding Nineveh's fall (cf. Spronk 1997, 116). Yet, it may mean, as it does in Ezekiel, that justice has been served.

Intriguingly, Nahum ends with a rhetorical question: "For who has ever escaped your endless cruelty?" (3:19; Spronk [1997, 144] regards this as a later addition). In light of Nahum's oracles, this question opens into praise, for Nineveh's fall has ended Assyria's previously ubiquitous oppression. Habakkuk, however, will *begin* with a rhetorical question:

> O LORD, how long shall I cry for help,
> and you will not listen?
> Or cry to you "Violence!"
> and you will not save? (Hab 1:2).

Evidently, Assyria's fall did not mean the end of violence and oppression after all.

Habakkuk

One of my favorite plays is *The Fantasticks*, a two-act musical fairy tale. In the first act, two best friends, pretending to be bitter enemies, forbid their children (a son and a daughter) to see one another. Sure enough, just as the friends had planned, the boy and girl fall in love. Next, the fathers stage a phony kidnapping, with the boy "rescuing" the girl and so winning her father's "grudging" approval. As the first act curtain closes, the cast is frozen in a smiling, hugging tableau: happy ending! In fact, when I first saw this play, I turned to my wife Wendy and asked, "What could possibly happen now?" Act two begins with the characters still frozen in their happy-ending poses. But they cannot hold the pose for long. Soon the group hug breaks apart. The best friends discover, now that they are in-laws, a dozen little things they cannot stand about one another. The boy and the girl lose their infatuation and break up. In short, life goes on. Like *The Fantasticks*, Habakkuk reminds us that, contrary to Nahum's naïve expectations, there are no closing act curtains in life or in history. Habakkuk is about what happens *after* Nahum's "happy ending."

Reading Habakkuk

On September 11, 2001, I was teaching at Randolph-Macon College in Ashland, Virginia, just north of Richmond. I remember the shock and horror that seized our little college town as news trickled in that Tuesday morning. First, we learned of a bizarre and horrible accident involving a plane colliding with one of the Twin Towers of the World Trade Center. Then swiftly came the unthinkable revelation that this was *not* an accident but a terrorist attack, involving *two* airliners deliberately targeted on the Towers. We later learned that another plane had been targeted on the Pentagon, and that still another, intended to crash into either the Capitol or the White House, was forced down near Shanksville, Pennsylvania, by its heroic passengers and crew—saving the lives of others at the cost of their own. Many in our community had family and friends who worked in the Pentagon, or lived and worked nearby; others either were from New York themselves or had family or friends in the city, some of whom worked at the World Trade Center. So this attack hit home for us: we felt that *we* had been assaulted, directly and personally.

On Thursday of that week, the Ashland community held a memorial service on our town square. I was among those asked to speak. As I wrestled with what word to bring, indeed with *how* to speak a word of the Lord to this horrible event, I was led to the book of Habakkuk. Here was a prophet who knew what it was like to lose family and friends to a remorseless enemy. The shock and horror we felt, Habakkuk also knew. In the poem concluding this book, I found words that spoke to my own anger, grief, and desire for vengeance:

> I hear, and I tremble within;
> my lips quiver at the sound.
> Rottenness enters into my bones,
> and my steps tremble beneath me.
> I wait quietly for the day of calamity
> to come upon the people who attack us (Hab 3:16).

Yet on that grim day, this prophet also pointed us toward the wisdom we needed to look beyond our shock and anger, to defy the apparent meaninglessness of the moment and refuse to surrender to despair:

> Though the fig tree does not blossom,
> and no fruit is on the vines;
> though the produce of the olive fails
> and the fields yield no food;
> though the flock is cut off from the fold
> and there is no herd in the stalls,
> yet I will rejoice in the LORD;
> I will exult in the God of my salvation (Hab 3:18).

The stark honesty of Habakkuk's struggle with doubt and uncertainty in the face of suffering may take us aback. Certainly, in the history of the interpretation of this book, many have rushed to the prophet's defense. Theodoret of Cyrus, for example, insists that the prophet merely "adopted the attitude" of the doubter, "putting the question as though anxious in his own case to learn the reason for what happens" (Hill 2006, 191). Since this is an oracle (Hab 1:1) delivered "under the influence of the Spirit," the apparent anguish of the prophet's cry ("O LORD, how long shall I cry for help, and you will not listen?" Hab 1:2) cannot be real: "it is obvious that, instead of suffering that fate personally, he is exposing the plight of those so disposed and applying the remedy" (Hill 2006, 192).

Surely this defense is unnecessary. People of God in all times and places have known that faith and doubt are not opposites: indeed, deep faith and profound doubt can occupy the same heart. Long after John Wesley's vaunted Aldersgate experience, when his heart was "strangely warmed" and he knew the assurance that Christ "had taken away my sins, even mine" (Outler 1964, 66), he wrote in a letter to his brother Charles, "[I do not love God. I never did]. Therefore [I never] believed, in the Christian sense of the word. Therefore [I am only an] honest heathen, a proselyte of the Temple" (Outler 1964, 81; note that the portions in brackets were written in Wesley's private shorthand). Yet in that same letter, Wesley affirmed, "I find rather an increase than a decrease of zeal for the whole work of God and every part of it," and urges his brother, "O insist everywhere on *full* redemption, receivable by *faith alone*; consequently, to be looked for *now*" (Outler 1964, 82). So too, after the death of Mother Teresa, famed for her life of selfless service to the poorest of the poor in Calcutta's slums, letters written to her confessors and superiors were published that revealed the depth of her personal struggles with doubt, darkness, and fear:

> Please pray for me—the longing for God is terribly painful and yet the darkness is becoming greater. What contradiction there is in my soul.—The pain within is so great—that I really don't feel anything for all the publicity and the talk of the people. Please ask Our Lady to be my Mother in this darkness. (Mother Teresa 2007, 174)

This should be no surprise to followers of the crucified Lord, who cried out from the cross, "My God, My God, why have you forsaken me?" (Mark 15:34//Matt 27:45). Indeed, Mother Teresa could write, "I have come to love the darkness.—For I believe now that it is a part, a very, very small part of Jesus' darkness & pain on earth" (2007, 214).

Habakkuk (both the prophet and the book) unflinchingly recognizes that sometimes the worst thing that can happen, happens. Sometimes the hurricane moves inland. Sometimes the cancer comes back. Sometimes those we love do not get better, do not come home safely—or do not love us back. Yet, as Donald Gowan ruefully observes, "Christian worship tends to be all triumph, all good news (even the confession of sin is not a very awesome experience because we know the assurance of pardon is coming; it's printed in the bulletin). And what does that say to those who, at the moment, know nothing of triumph?" (Gowan 1976, 38). When tragedy strikes, we have no use for Pollyanna optimism, for shallow, saccharine assurances that all will be well. Habakkuk recognizes our need to see God in the midst of doubt, struggle, loss, and pain, and affirms God's presence even there—indeed, especially there.

Authorship, Date, and Setting

The name "Habakkuk" itself is intriguing, not so much for its meaning (*habaqquq* refers to an aromatic garden plant; a related Arabic word denotes the herb basil) as for its derivation: Habakkuk is not a Hebrew, but an Akkadian name (so Gowan 1976, 13). It may not be surprising that an educated, cultured Judean would have an Akkadian name: after all, Akkadian had been the language of Mesopotamia since the third millennium BCE. Nevertheless, it is certainly ironic, as Habakkuk witnesses the threatening rise of Akkadian-speaking Babylon (1:5-17).

This Babylonian connection is also apparent in *Bel and the Dragon*, a delightful pair of legends tacked onto the end of Daniel in the LXX in which Habakkuk too appears; indeed, a superscription in the LXX (not found in Theodotion, whose text of Daniel was the one used by the early church [Smith-Christopher 1996, 156]) attributes this text to "the prophet Habakkuk, son of Jesse, of the tribe of Levi." In the second of these stories, Daniel slays a "dragon" by feeding the creature cakes of "pitch, fat, and hair" (*Bel* 27). The humiliated priests, who had worshiped the reptile as a god, force the king to throw Daniel into a den of lions (*Bel* 31-32; cf. Dan 6:8-25 [7-24]). Though starved, the lions refuse to eat the prophet; but after six days, Daniel is hungry. Therefore, the angel of the LORD appears to Habakkuk (Greek *Ambakoum*, also used in the LXX of Hab 1:1 for the name of the prophet). The Greek *angelos Kuriou* ("angel of the LORD") is used in the LXX for *mal'ak Yhwh*, the angel of the LORD's presence (e.g., Gen 22:11; Exod 3:20; Num 22:22-27). In Daniel, the angel of the LORD only appears in the Greek additions to the book, and in the prophets, is found only in Isa 37:36//2 Kgs 19:35 and in Zech 1:11-12; 3:1, 5, 6; 12:8 (in Hag 1:13 and Mal 2:7, *mal'ak Yhwh* refers to a human messenger). This angel appears to Habakkuk in Judea, as he is taking bread and stew to reapers in the field. After directing him to take the food instead to Daniel in Babylon (*Bel* 33-34), the angel seizes Habakkuk by the hair (cf. Ezek 8:3; Theodotion notes that Habakkuk was transported "by the power of the spirit," as in Ezek 2:3; 3:24; 8:3; 11:1, 24; 37:1), and carries him to Babylon (*Bel* 36). Once he has delivered the food to Daniel, the angel returns Habakkuk to Judea (*Bel* 39). This strange account demonstrates that for the Greek-speaking Jews who told this story, Habakkuk was, like Ezekiel and Daniel, a figure related to the Babylonian exile.

The book of Habakkuk itself says nothing explicit of the prophet's time or place: as with Nahum, one must deduce these from the book's content. The mention of the Chaldeans and the devastation they have wrought throughout the world (Hab 1:6; cf. vv. 5-11 and 14-17), however, confirms our impressions from the prophet's name and from the setting of *Bel and the Dragon.* Although "Chaldeans" (Heb., *Kashdim*) can be used broadly for the people of Mesopotamia (cf. "Ur of the Chaldeans" in Gen 11:28, 31; 15:7), it is usually and particularly applied to the Babylonians (e.g., the numerous references in 2 Kgs 24–25).

The *Pesher* Habakkuk from Qumran

The textual finds from Qumran—the so called "Dead Sea Scrolls"—are a boon to scholars working in nearly every book of the Bible; we have already referred to the fragments of the Book of the Twelve from Cave Four. However, the Qumran finds have particular significance for students of the book of Habakkuk. One of the nearly intact scrolls uncovered in Cave One is a study (called a *pesher*, or "interpretation") of Habakkuk, designated 1QpHab. This *pesher*, dating from the late first century BCE, reads the book as a prophecy concerning the Qumran community: it interprets passages from Habakkuk 1–2 as relating to incidents in their communal life, and particularly to the life of their founder, the Teacher of Righteousness. Still, the extensive quotes from the first two chapters of Habakkuk strewn through this *pesher* provide our oldest and best witness to the Hebrew text of this book.

The Rise of the Neo-Babylonian Empire and Fall of Judah

For Nahum, the fall of Nineveh meant the end of oppression and the beginning of a new age of freedom for Judah, "for never again shall the wicked invade you" (Nah 2:1 [1:15]). In truth, however, the fall of Nineveh set in motion a series of events that led to Judah's decline and fall. After Nineveh fell in 612 BCE, the Babylonians pursued the remnants of Assyria's leadership to Haran. By 609 BCE, Assyria was no more, but this futile, last-ditch stand at Haran had fatal consequences for Judah.

Egypt propped up Assyria in its final hours. Although Assyria and Egypt had long been bitter rivals, that rivalry was settled when the Assyrians invaded Egypt and sacked Thebes in 663 BCE (cf. Nah 3:8-10). Psammetichus I (664–610 BCE), an Assyrian protégé, founded the Saite Dynasty, which unified Egypt and sponsored a cultural renaissance. By the end of his reign, with Philistia under his thumb, Psammetichus controlled much of the Mediterranean coast. His successor Necho II (610–595 BCE) remained an Assyrian ally. Thus, when in 610 BCE Ashur-ubalit II, last of Assyria's kings, was forced to abandon Haran as well, Necho marched north to his aid—a march that took Pharaoh's armies through the kingdom of Judah. When Josiah (640–609 BCE) intervened, intercepting the Egyptians at the plains of Megiddo, his army was defeated, and the Judean king was killed (2 Kgs 23:29-30//2 Chr 35:20-27). Necho II, whose troops now occupied Palestine, deposed Josiah's successor Jehoahaz, deporting him to Egypt (2 Kgs 23:34-35//2 Chr 36:1-4; Jer 22:10-12) and appointed a new king of his own choosing: Jehoahaz's older brother Jehoiakim (609–598 BCE). Jehoiakim swore loyalty to Pharaoh and became an Egyptian vassal.

Egypt's claim to Palestine did not stand unchallenged, however. The victorious Babylonians also laid claim to these former Assyrian possessions. Nebuchadnezzar (605–562 BCE; he is called "Nebuchadrezzar" in Ezekiel and Jeremiah, a form closer to the Akkadian *Nabu-kudurri-utsur*), son of Nineveh's conqueror Nabopolassar, defeated the Egyptian army at Carchemish in 605 BCE, forcing the Egyptians to withdraw from Palestine (Horn and McCarter 1999, 193; cf. 2 Kgs 24:7; Jer 46:2-12). Jehoiakim then shifted loyalties, becoming a Babylonian vassal. Nevertheless, once Nebuchadnezzar's forces withdrew, Jehoiakim attempted to revolt, seeking allies among the minor kingdoms in the region. This revolt proved disastrous: Nebuchadnezzar devastated Judah and placed Jerusalem under siege. The city escaped destruction when Jehoiachin, Jehoiakim's son and successor, surrendered it to the Babylonians in 597 BCE. Afterward, Jehoiachin was taken away into exile, together with seven thousand soldiers, a thousand skilled laborers, the king's officials, and "the elite of the land" (2 Kgs 24:15-16).

Nebuchadnezzar installed Jehoiachin's brother Zedekiah (597–587/6 BCE) as king (with 1 Chr 3:16 and 2 Chr 36:10; 2 Kgs 24:17 claims that Zedekiah was Jehoiachin's uncle, but Chronicles seems to have access to authentic Judean sources here; cf. Tuell 2001, 25–26). Zedekiah too swore fealty to Babylon—at first. Early in his fourth year (594/3 BCE), however, Zedekiah made an alliance with Pharaoh Psammeticus II (594–588 BCE). Jeremiah 27:3 mentions the kings of Edom, Moab, Ammon, and Tyre as participants in a conference in Jerusalem at which they discussed an alliance in rebellion against Babylon, doubtless supported by Egypt.

When Zedekiah actually launched his revolt, Nebuchadnezzar responded in force. Once more, Judah was devastated, and by 588/587 BCE (cf. 2 Kgs 25:1//Jer 52:4; Ezek 24:1), Jerusalem was again under siege. This time there would be no reprieve. Although Zedekiah's Egyptian ally Hophra (589–570 BCE), successor to Psammeticus II, did succeed for a brief time in lifting the siege of Jerusalem, his intervention ultimately failed; Nebuchadnezzar's armies returned to Jerusalem to finish their conquest (Jer 37:5-10). In 587/586 BCE, Jerusalem fell. The Babylonians destroyed the temple and the palace. The Holy Ark, footstool of the LORD of Hosts, disappeared. Zedekiah saw his sons put to death before his eyes; then, his eyes were put out so that the last thing he ever saw was the death of his sons, and he went away in chains to Babylon. A king in David's line would never again sit on a throne in Jerusalem. Further, the Babylonians continued their policy of deportation, removing a large part of the population to scattered sites throughout Mesopotamia. For any traditionally minded Judean, it was the end of the world. Like the prophecies of Jeremiah and Ezekiel, then, Habakkuk's words are set in this time of national tragedy.

Dating Habakkuk

As with Nahum, however, a different question relates to the composition history of this book: was Habakkuk indeed composed as a unit late in the seventh century BCE when it is set? While one can read the book as a unit on a superficial level, close reading swiftly reveals problems with the assumption of simple authorial unity. The opening verses of Habakkuk read much like the outcry and complaint that typically open prayers for help in the Psalter (so Gowan 1976, 21–23; e.g., Ps 13:2-3 [1-2]; 22:2-3 [1-2]; 130:1-2). Habakkuk cries out of a situation of violence and injustice from which God is apparently absent (1:2-4). The natural assumption of the reader is that the prophet is speaking of his own community here. The description of Babylon's rise in 1:5-11 then seems to be a response to the complaint: God has raised up Babylon to punish the evil and injustice bewailed by the prophet (cf. Hab 1:12). However, the "you" addressed in these verses is not the prophet but the community; the second-person verbs and pronouns in this passage are plural. In 1:12, another complaint begins, raised on the community's behalf and directed now at Babylon, which indiscriminately and mercilessly destroys righteous and wicked alike.

The prophet resolves to "stand at my watchpost" (2:1) until God responds to this complaint. The LORD responds with a vision that "speaks of the end, and does not lie. / If it seems to tarry, wait for it; / it will surely come, it will not delay" (Hab 2:3). What does this vision mean? Is it Babylon whose inevitable end is declared, or is it Jerusalem? The statement in 2:5c ("They gather nations for themselves, and collect all peoples as their own") certainly addresses Babylon, but fits oddly into its context; 2:4-5b deals generally with wealth and arrogance in wisdom language (cf. Prov 30:15-16). The five woes that follow do not clarify matters. In the first woe, 2:8 deals directly with

Babylon, which has "plundered many nations," but 2:6-7 are concerned with wealth taken not through plunder but through abusive lending practices (so too Nogalski 1993b, 130). The second and third woes (2:9-11 and 12-14) also appear to address the leaders of Jerusalem (but cf. 2:10b, which has Babylon in view); in contrast, the fourth woe (2:15-17) clearly addresses the Babylonian conquerors. The fifth woe, against idolatry, in 2:19 could appropriately be addressed against Babylonian practice (cf. Isa 40:18-20 and 44:9-20, particularly 44:9-10, to which the insert at Hab 2:18 certainly alludes), but similar condemnations of idolatry in Judah are certainly not lacking in Scripture! Gowan proposes that this uncertainty is deliberate: the woes have "purposely been expressed in general terms which could apply again and again to tyranny in many forms" (Gowan 1976, 57; cf. also Goldingay 2009, 50). However, the woes are characterized less by ambiguity than by tension between isolated lines referring to Babylon and the oracles in which they appear. These verses give the overall impression that editors have reworked words originally addressed to Judah to address Babylon.

In Habakkuk 3 as well, close reading prevents us from regarding this concluding psalm as a simple unit. While 3:3-15 is a theophanic hymn, vv. 2 and 16-19 redirect the tone and tenor of the poem so that it becomes a prayer for help. In short, the general impression is not one of unity but of development throughout, and tension within, the book of Habakkuk.

Bernhard Duhm dated Habakkuk to the Greek period, so that the threat it describes comes from the Seleucids; indeed, he emended the Hebrew *Kashdim* ("Chaldeans") in 1:6 to *Kittim*, a term used in Genesis 10:4 to refer to people from the Aegean (1 Macc 1:1 identifies Kittim as the birthplace of Alexander the Great; cf. Duhm 1906, 19–21). Curiously, 1QpHab, a text not yet known in Duhm's time, also identifies the enemy as the Kittim; yet the quote from Habakkuk 1:6 in this *pesher* still reads *Kashdim* (cf. 1QpHab 2.11-12). No one today follows Duhm, either in his dating of Habakkuk or in his emendation of 1:6. Still, Duhm's late dating (and correspondingly his proposed emendation) grew out of his sensitivity to genuine conflicts within Habakkuk (so Nogalski 1993b, 135 n. 21). In contrast, William Foxwell Albright saw "no valid reason why the book should not be treated as a substantial unit and dated between 605 and 589 B.C." (Albright 1950, 2). Albright nonetheless held that Habakkuk "was not an original spirit but that he possessed a considerable amount of literary appreciation," so that his book is composed using earlier material—indeed, according to Albright, the psalm in Habakkuk 3 derives from no fewer than four separate sources (Albright 1950, 8–9)! Similarly, Theodore Hiebert proposes that Habakkuk's closing poem is a very old hymn celebrating the victory of the divine warrior, comparable in age as in content to such ancient songs as Exodus 15:1-18 or Judges 5:1-31 (Hiebert 1986, 119); the editors, he proposes, have added this hymn to Habakkuk (Hiebert 1986, 137–39; 1996, 652–55). Jörg Jeremias identifies a seventh-century core in Habakkuk; however, he regards 1:5-11 and 14-17 as belonging to later redactors that he designates as *Unheilspropheten* ("prophets of calamity"), whose work dates from the time of the exile (Jeremias 1970, 109). Michael Floyd envisages an original prophecy of Habakkuk in the late seventh century predicting Babylon's rise (1:5-11), which prompted concern when Babylon proved cruel and unjust. He proposes that this later reflection on the prophecy, attributable either to Habakkuk himself or to editors writing in his name, occurred late in the exile in the context of Persia's rise and internal Babylonian conflicts, which enabled "Habakkuk" to declare God's imminent judgment on Babylon (Floyd 2000, 87). Jim Nogalski, due particularly to the common pattern of usage and vocabulary in Habakkuk 1:5-11 and Nahum 3 (Nogalski 1993b, 147–49), assigns all the Babylonian material to the editors who incorporated Habakkuk into the Twelve. Of course, this also removes the reason for proposing a late seventh century setting for the original material, which Nogalski sees as likely postexilic in origin (Nogalski 1993b, 152–53).

How is a reader to respond to these varying perspectives on the date of this book? One might say that this entire discussion is moot: whether Habakkuk dates in fact to the late seventh century or not, its canonical form and setting invite us to read it in that context. The book grounds its ultimate message of triumph over despair in a concrete historical experience of despair, namely the Babylonian destruction of Judah and the consequent exile (cf. O'Brien 2004, 60). Similarly, Psalm titles sometimes set their poems in the context of events from David's life, thereby grounding the general language of the psalm in a concrete life circumstance (e.g., Pss 34; 51). Still, it would be a mistake either naively to assume a Babylonian setting for the entire composition or cynically to surrender the attempt to understand the text's history. Either approach short-circuits the interpretive process, an important part of which is the struggle to see this text in the historical context out of which it emerges.

While Habakkuk has evidently undergone substantial revision in the course of its transmission, we have no reason to question the legitimacy of its original setting in the late seventh century BCE. While Nogalski has successfully demonstrated that the editing of this book emphasizes that Babylonian setting, elements in Nogalski's "Babylonian layer" resist late dating. In particular, the shock and surprise at Babylon's rise evident in 1:5-6 ("Be astonished! Be astounded!") and the vain hope for deliverance in 1:12 ("We shall not die") ring true; it is difficult to imagine that these pain-filled, poignant words do not come from the time of Babylon's rise and Judah's fall. Similarly, while Hiebert and others have demonstrated the original independence of the framing psalm in Habakkuk 3, we need not assign its insertion into the book to Habakkuk's editors. Indeed, the expansion of this poem at 3:2, 16-19 fits the perspective of the original book, which expressed more ambivalence about divine action than Habakkuk's later editors (and indeed, many of its later interpreters) found comfortable! In the final form of Habakkuk, the editors who incorporated this book into the Twelve have simplified and clarified its focus, particularly by modifying the woes in chapter 2 so that they focus not inwardly, on Judah, but outwardly, on Babylon. In so doing, they have implicitly shifted the import of Habakkuk's vision of the end (2:1-5) from Jerusalem's certain fall to Babylon's inevitable destruction as a harbinger of the day of the LORD.

The horror that Habakkuk expresses so poignantly could describe Judah's experience during any of the Babylonian invasions. However, Habakkuk speaks not only of the threat posed by Babylon, but also of that threat coming as a surprise:

> Look at the nations, and see!
> Be astonished! Be astounded!
> For a work is being done in your days
> that you would not believe if you were told (Hab 1:5).

This suggests that Habakkuk's prophecy opens in the time of Jehoiakim's revolt when Judah first experienced a Babylonian invasion (with, e.g., Rudolph 1975, 194; Andersen 2001, 27).

Structure

Most modern interpreters of Habakkuk (e.g., Rudolph 1975; Gowan 1976; Achtemeier 1986; Nogalski 1993b) see the book as falling into three parts following its superscription (1:1): a dialogue between the prophet and the LORD (1:2-2:5; note that Gowan 1976, 19, 22 and Richards 2006, 1256 place 2:5 at the beginning of the woes, rather than at the end of the dialogue), a list of five woes (2:6-20), and the concluding psalm (3:1-19). Others see the book as falling into two parts, chapters 1–2 (the dialogue between Habakkuk and the LORD, or Habakkuk's *massa*) and chapter 3 (Habakkuk's prayer; so Sweeney 2000, 457; Andersen 2001, 14). Yet the Masoretic paragraphing breaks the text up differently. The scribes understand Habakkuk 1 as a unit: the first break (*setumah*) comes at 1:17. In the MT, the dialogue between the prophet and God in 1:2-17 sets forth an inquiry into God's justice, leading into, though structurally distinct from, God's response to Habakkuk's cry (2:1-8 in the MT).

The Masoretes' treatment of the second chapter is more difficult to understand. They divide this chapter into six parts, indicated by paragraph breaks at vv. 8 (break *petukhah*), 11 (break *petukhah*), 14 (break *setumah*), 17 (break *setumah*), 18 (break *setumah*), and 20 (break *petukhah*). Reading 2:1-8 as a unit seems odd to a modern reader. Habakkuk 2:1-5 certainly seems to stand as a unit consisting of Habakkuk's fervent declaration that he will stand at his post until God answers him (2:1), and God's grim reply (2:2-5). Habakkuk 2:6a ("Shall not everyone taunt such people and, with mocking riddles, say about them . . .") then introduces the five woes that follow, each introduced by *hoi* (cf. the discussion of Nah 3:1, above): 2:6b-8, 9-11, 12-14, 15-17, 19. The Masoretic paragraphing, however, reads the first woe together with the opening unit. This calls our attention to the link between the woes and Habakkuk's vision of the end in a way that the modern approach, reading 2:1-5 with the preceding section rather than as the beginning of the material that follows, does not. Indeed, as we will see, the woes issue forth from Habakkuk's vision. The breaks at vv. 11, 14, and 17 recognize the second, third, and fourth woes as individual units, while the break at 2:18 calls our attention to this verse: a late insertion that, violating the pattern, relates to the following, fifth woe (2:19). The five woes in turn conclude with 2:20, which leads into the framing psalm (see the discussion of Nah 1:2-11 above, and the discussion of Nahum and Habakkuk read together below) that follows.

The psalm in Habakkuk 3 is a clear unit, marked off by a title much like those found in the book of Psalms (3:1) and by a closing dedication, again reflecting Psalm titles (3:19). The Masoretes divide this poem into three parts marked by paragraph breaks at vv. 7 (break *setumah*) and 13 (break *petukhah*). Here, we can understand the reason for their divisions, even if we do not agree with them: 3:8 begins a speech addressed to the Lord, while 3:13 contains the expression *selah*, a common interlude marker in the Psalms (although the Masoretes do not treat the other incidents of *selah*, at 3:3 and 9, as section markers).

Perhaps the simplest way to think of Habakkuk's structure is in three parts, corresponding to its chapter divisions (so Floyd 2000, 81–82; O'Brien 2004, 59; and cf. Roberts 1991, 82, who includes 2:1 in his first part). Duane Christensen's analysis of the structure of combined Nahum and Habakkuk supports such a division. Read together, these books form a chiasm, centered on Habakkuk 1 (cf. Christensen 1996, 732):

A Hymn of theophany (Nah 1)
  B Taunt song against Nineveh (Nah 2–3)
    C The problem of theodicy (Hab 1)
  B' Taunt song against the "wicked one" (Hab 2)
A' Hymn of theophany (Hab 3)

"Theodicy" refers to God's justice and to the attempt to vindicate God's justice in the face of suffering and evil. The dialogue in Habakkuk 1 is not a theodicy: no solution to the problem of evil is even attempted (so Gowan 1976, 9–10). Nevertheless, this chapter certainly may be described as struggling with the question of theodicy, as it raises the fundamental question of the place of evil in a world created by a just and caring God (cf. Hab 1:12-13). This commentary will approach Habakkuk as divided into the superscription (1:1), the theodicy dialogue (1:2-17), the woes (2:1-20), and the framing psalm (3:1-19).

Habakkuk and Nahum

As has already been observed (see the discussions above in the Introduction and the Nahum commentary), we are intended to read Nahum and Habakkuk together. Psalms frame these books (Nah 1:2-11; Hab 3:1-19). Nahum is described as both an "oracle" (*massa'*) and a "vision" (*khazon*), while Habakkuk is "The oracle [*massa'*] that the prophet Habakkuk saw [*khazah*]." The two books also share important themes: each is directed against a foreign power (Assyria and Babylon), and each speaks of the end (the end of Assyria in Nah 1:8-9, and the end of Jerusalem/Babylon in Hab 2:3).

Other commonalities relate to the likely social position of the two prophets. Donald Gowan proposes that Habakkuk was a professional prophet and finds evidence for this not only in the book's title (Habakkuk is one of only three prophets expressly identified *as* a prophet in the title of his book; cf. Hab 1:1; 3:1, and compare Hag 1:1 and Zech 1:1) but also in the close connections between the language of Habakkuk and the wisdom traditions emerging from Israel's educated upper class (Gowan 1976, 13–15). Jeremias identifies both Nahum and Habakkuk as *Kultprophetie* ("cult prophecy") related to the Jerusalem temple liturgy (cf. Jeremias 1970, 67–69 and Wilson 1980, 276–79). In his anthropological study of prophecy, Robert Wilson describes such figures, working closely with the central religious and political authorities of their cultures, as "central intermediaries," who are "primarily responsible for maintaining their societies and for promoting community welfare" (Wilson 1980, 83–84). Indeed, Schart characterizes both Nahum and Habakkuk as *Heilsprophetie* ("salvation prophecy"), as in his view, neither book offers a critique of Israel (Schart 1998, 246; cf. also O'Brien 2004, 64): a claim that we will challenge in our discussion of Habakkuk.

The interweaving of the two books is a bit astonishing, however, given their sharply contrasting character. Nahum had expressed the naïve hope that the end of Assyria meant the end of Judah's oppression: "never again shall the wicked invade you" (Nah 2:1[1:15]). In contrast, Habakkuk is grimly aware that politics, like nature, abhors a vacuum. The removal of Assyria only clears the way for the rise of a new oppressor: the resurgent Babylonian empire. When we read Nahum in the light of Habakkuk, then, we see how shortsighted Nahum's naiveté and cultural chauvinism are. Christensen's chiastic rendering of Nahum and Habakkuk read together, which places Habakkuk 1 at the center of this composite text, also has theological implications. If indeed "[t]he problem of theodicy" (Christensen 1996, 732) is the heart of Nahum-Habakkuk, then the text itself calls into question the simple equation of historical process and divine will found particularly in Nahum 2–3. The canonical context cautions the reader against too ready an embrace of Nahum's ideology.

At the same time, the canon also invites us to read Habakkuk in the light of Nahum. This certainly seems to have been the intention of Habakkuk's editors, who redirect the message of judgment in this book from Judah to Babylon, heightening the parallel with Nahum's message of judgment against Nineveh. Likely it is more difficult for us today to embrace (with Nahum) the possibility of God acting in history than it is for us to see (with Habakkuk) the problems such a concept raises. Yet our faith is grounded in the notion of the God who acts: who liberates Israel from bondage, who speaks through the prophets, and who enters history as one of us in the person of Jesus of Nazareth. Further, we are invited and encouraged, if not *commanded*, to lift our needs and concerns to God in prayer—a pointless exercise, if God does not, cannot, or will not act in the world. As Karl Barth wrote regarding prayer,

> Let us approach the subject from the given fact that God answers. God is not deaf, but listens; more than that, he acts. God does not act in the same way whether we pray or not. Prayer exerts an influence upon God's action, even upon his existence. That is what the word "answer" means. (Barth 2002, 13)

In our jaded and cynical age, it may be more important for us to read Habakkuk in the light of Nahum than vice versa.

Commentary

Superscription (1:1)

Like Nahum, Habakkuk begins by identifying this book as an "oracle" (Heb., *massa'*, see the discussion of Nah 1:1, above). If, as we saw in Nahum, a *massa'* is a prophecy of judgment, then the next question must concern the identity of the accused. The simple answer, derived from a reading of this book in its final form, is that Habakkuk is a judgment oracle against Babylon, just as Nahum's *massa'* targeted Nineveh. As we will see, however, a closer reading also reveals a considerable critique directed inwardly, against Judah.

Also like Nahum, Habakkuk's work is characterized as a vision: this is the "The oracle that the prophet Habakkuk *saw*" (Hab 1:1, emphasis mine; cf. 2:1-5). The verb used, *khazah*, can mean simply "see," though perhaps with an added emphasis on true perception (e.g., Exod 18:21). It refers particularly, however, to seeing a vision (e.g., Num 24:4, 16). As we have seen (cf. the discussion of Nah 1:1, above), prophets from the north and those associated with the northern Levitical traditions expressed particularly in Deuteronomy tend to hear the word rather than to see visions of God (cf. Hos 1:1; Mic 1:1; Jer 1:1). On the other hand, southern, particularly Jerusalemite traditions emphasize revelation of the eye rather than the ear (so Isa 1:1; 2:1; Ezek 1:1; Obad 1; Nah 1:1). The content of the book, which describes the emergence of Babylon as an imperial power and its military aggression into Judah, confirms the impression that Habakkuk was a Judean.

Intriguingly, the superscription expressly identifies Habakkuk as "the prophet" (Heb., *hannabi'*), an identification found also in the superscription to the framing psalm (3:1). *Targum Nebi'im* stresses this identification even more, introducing this book as "The prophecy the prophet Habakkuk prophesied"! The only other prophets identified as such in the titles of their books are Haggai and Zechariah. This identification could be another means by which the editors of the Twelve have explicitly structured the latter half of their book. However, it could also suggest a similar perspective on the part of the prophets themselves. Likely, Habakkuk, Haggai, and Zechariah were all what Robert Wilson has called "central intermediaries" (Wilson 1980, 83; 287–89), closely linked to the centers of power in their time and place (see the discussion of "Habakkuk and Nahum," above). Yet even if Habakkuk was a professional prophet (cf. Gowan 1976, 13–15, and the discussion above) with an official role in the palace, the temple, or both, it is nonetheless clear that his position served neither to blind him to injustice in his society nor to muzzle his response.

Theodicy Dialogue (1:2-17)

The Common Lectionary has only one reading from Habakkuk: 1:1-4; 2:1-4 is read in the Season after Pentecost, Year C (proper 26, and as an alternate reading on proper 22). This lectionary selection reflects a common view of Habakkuk's structure, which sees 2:1-4 in continuity with, and as the conclusion of, the dialogue in 1:1-17 (e.g., Nogalski 1993b, 127; Gowan 1976, 19). However, as we have seen, the MT breaks at the end of the first chapter, setting the dialogue apart from Habakkuk's vision. The resumption in 2:1 of the first person singular forms found in 1:2-4 also supports this structure. Finally, chapter 1 both begins (1:2) and ends (1:17) with questions directed to the Divine. This commentary will treat the debate on divine justice in Habakkuk 1 as a unit, apart from its resolution in chapter 2. Alternating human and divine perspectives clearly demarcate the three parts of this unit. Thus, 1:1-4 is a first-person cry and complaint from the prophet, 1:5-11 is a response from the LORD directed (as we will see) to the leaders of the community, and 1:12-17 is a second complaint, raised by the prophet on behalf of the community.

The language of Habakkuk 1:2-4 reflects clear links to wisdom traditions and to the central institutions of palace and temple. Habakkuk's "cry for help" uses a relatively rare Hebrew word, *shawah* (1:2). This term for "cry" appears only twenty-one times in Scripture, primarily in the Psalms (nine times) and Job (eight times; in contrast, Habakkuk's second term for "cry," *za'aq*, appears 74 times). The word *khamas* ("violence") appears six times in Habakkuk (1:2, 3, 9; 2:8, 17 [twice]), as often as in the far longer book of Ezekiel. Otherwise, as we might expect from the prophetic concern for opposing violence and injustice, the term is fairly evenly spread through the Latter Prophets (it is absent only from Hosea, Nahum, Haggai, and Zechariah). Outside of the prophets, *khamas* occurs particularly in the Psalms (14 times) and Proverbs (7 times; note that this term also appears twice in Job). In the Torah, *khamas* is the reason for Noah's flood in the priestly account (Gen 6:11, 13), and describes the sin of the northern tribes Simeon and Levi (Gen 49:5) in contrast to Judah's kingly dignity (Gen 49:8-12). Similarly, thirteen of the eighteen appearances of the term *madon* ("contention," Hab 1:3) are in Proverbs. The hypothesis that Habakkuk was a central intermediary, then, seems borne out by his vocabulary.

Habakkuk's complaint concerns not only the prevalence of violence and injustice but also particularly the impotence of the social institutions that ought to restrain the violent:

So the law becomes slack
and justice never prevails.
The wicked surround the righteous—
therefore judgment comes forth perverted (Hab 1:4).

The mention of *torah* (NRSV "law") here has prompted some to propose that this text must date to the postexilic period, when the Torah (that is, the first five books of Scripture in Jewish tradition) was complete, but there is no reason to think that this passage has the entire Torah as we have it in view. The expression, "the law becomes slack" (Heb., *taphug torah*), appears nowhere else. Indeed, apart from Habakkuk 1:4, the verb *pug* ("turn cold, grow weary, be comforted") appears only three times: in Genesis 45:26, for Jacob's response to the news that Joseph was alive (Heb., *wayyipag libbo*, rendered in JPSV as "His heart went numb" [cf. KJV]; NRSV reads, less literally and more prosaically, "he was stunned"), and in Psalm 38:9 ("I am utterly spent") and 77:3 ("My soul refuses to be comforted"). On the other hand, this expression is similar to Ezekiel 7:26: "instruction shall perish [Heb., *torah to'bad*] from the priest," suggesting that a similar context may be in view in Habakkuk. Zephaniah 3:4 declares that the priests of Jerusalem "have profaned what is sacred, they have done violence [a verbal form of *khamas*] to the law [Heb., *torah*]." Ezekiel 22:26, which quotes this passage from Zephaniah (cf. Duguid 1994, 72–75; Tuell 2009, 146–47), expands on it to condemn the priests for specific offenses: "they have made no distinction between the holy and the common, neither have they taught the difference between the unclean and the clean, and they have disregarded my sabbaths, so that I am profaned among them." Similarly, Hosea 4:6 condemns the priests of Israel, "since you have forgotten the law [Heb., *torah*] of your God." It is no wonder that Jeremiah condemns the complacency of those who blithely assume that "instruction shall not perish [*lo' to'bad torah*; cf. Ezek 7:6] from the priest, nor counsel from the wise, nor the word from the prophet" (Jer 18:18)! Scripture is clear regarding the fundamental responsibility of the priests to know, observe, and teach *torah* (e.g., Lev 10:10-11; Deut 33:8-10; 2 Kgs 17:27-28; 2 Chr 15:3; Ezek 44:23-24). Quite probably then, Habakkuk 1:4, like these other, similar passages from the prophets, condemns the priests for failing in that responsibility, thereby weakening the moral and spiritual influence of *torah*. The reference to judgment being "perverted" may also be a critique of the priests, to whom some traditions assign this responsibility (e.g., Exod 21:6; 22:7-8; Deut 21:1-5; but cf. Ezek 44:24). It is more likely, though, that Habakkuk has in mind other, secular judges (cf. Zeph 3:3) who have likewise failed in their responsibilities, to the detriment of the common people of Judah.

Habakkuk 1:5-11 seems to provide a response from the LORD to the injustice and violence bemoaned in 1:2-3, as well as to the failure of Judah's religious and secular leadership to address this crisis depicted in 1:4. Implicitly, God is "rousing the Chaldeans" (1:6) as a judgment and a punishment—a perspective found in the other prophets of the Neo-Babylonian period (e.g., Jer 25:8-11; Ezek 24:1-14; Isa 40:1-2), and reminiscent of the approach earlier taken to Assyria (e.g., Isa 10:5; Hos 11:5-7; Amos 7:10-17; Mic 3:9-12; cf. the discussion of Nah 1:12-14, above). These verses do not make this intention explicit, however; they deal rather with the Chaldeans' widespread conquests (1:6, 10-11) and bestial violence (1:7-9). Further, as was observed above, 1:5-11 addresses not the prophet who has raised the complaint but the community. The apparent misfit of this passage with its context has prompted some to see 1:5-11 as a later insertion (e.g., Nogalski 1993b, 146–53; Jeremias 1970, 109). Others propose that these verses state the problem to which Habakkuk is responding. Gowan notes ironically that in this passage "the Chaldeans are coming for *violence* (vs. 9); the very thing about which Habakkuk has been complaining, and so [God] seems to be warning that things are going to get worse and not better" (Gowan 1976, 35). Indeed, Gowan proposes that perhaps the entire first chapter is Habakkuk's complaint, prompted by the LORD's oracle concerning Babylon, and that the prophet quotes and responds to that oracle here:

> [F]or him, this created a serious theological problem because he saw that the wickedness which already troubled him would thereby be compounded. . . . In this case the oracle was never in any sense an answer to his dilemma, but was a part of the problem from the beginning. (Gowan 1976, 36)

Similarly Floyd, who defines "*massa'*" as a prophetic response to a previous prophecy (see the discussion of the term *massa'* in Nah 1:1, above), argues that Habakkuk's *massa'* (cf. 1:1) clearly fits that pattern: 1:5-11 is a "quotation of problematic prophecy" to which the prophet's complaint responds (Floyd 2000, 81).

However, the best reading of 1:5 supports the idea that 1:5-11 is a response to 1:2-4. The MT of 1:5 reads *re'u baggoyim*, translated by the NRSV as "Look at the nations" (cf. also *Tg. Neb.*, NIV, and NJPS). In contrast, the LXX reads "Behold, despisers" (Greek *idete, hoi kataphronetai*). Acts 13:41 quotes the LXX of Habakkuk 1:5 at the climax of Paul's sermon to the Jews of Antioch of Pisidia as a warning against "scoffers" who fail to recognize what God has done in Christ. The LXX translation assumes the Hebrew *bogedim* ("traitors, treacherous ones") rather than *baggoyim* ("at/among the nations") in this verse, a reading that actually appears in one Hebrew manuscript, and is also presupposed by the Syriac. While the quotation of Habakkuk 1:5 is missing from 1QpHab, the *pesher* on this verse says that it concerns *hbwgdym 'm 'ysh hkzb*: "the traitors with the Man of the Lie" (the chief adversary of the Teacher of Righteousness; cf. 1QpHab 2.1-2). We do best then to follow the LXX here, and emend *baggoyim* to *bogedim*. The reading yielded by this emendation explains why 1:5-11 addresses a plural audience rather than the prophet: this is Habakkuk's oracle, spoken by the prophet in the LORD's name to the traitors (*bogedim*) identified in his complaint, who render Torah impotent and pervert justice (1:2-4; cf. Isa 24:16; Jer 9:2; Prov 11:6; 13:2; 13:15). Habakkuk's editors have apparently reworked 1:5-11 with an eye toward Nahum 3 in a way that both fosters the link between the two books and intensifies the accusation against Babylon in Habakkuk (Nogalski 1993b, 147–49). Nevertheless, a core of this passage probably goes back to the original prophet and speaks out of a late seventh century BCE setting.

The surprise evidenced in 1:5-6 regarding the means of the LORD's correction—via a revived Babylonian empire—may seem strange to us in hindsight. Nevertheless, the story of Hezekiah's encounter with the envoys of Merodach-baladan (2 Kgs 20:12-19//Isa 39:1-8, cf. the cryptic account of this visit in 2 Chr 32:25-26, 31) also reflects Judah's ignorance of the dangerous potential Babylon contained. Merodach-baladan was a Babylonian leader who opposed Sargon II of Assyria (722–705 BCE). Until Sargon at last took the city, forcing Merodach-baladan to flee to Elam for refuge, he ruled Babylon independently for twelve years (721–709 BCE). Upon Sargon's death in 705 BCE, Merodach-baladan rebelled again, but by 703 he was defeated by the new Assyrian ruler Sennacherib (704–681 BCE), so that he died in exile. Still, a continuing series of Babylonian rebellions against Assyria, likely inspired by Merodach-baladan, culminated in Sennacherib's sack of Babylon in 689 BCE. Simmering resentment over this act would issue forth finally in Nabopolassar's rebellion, the destruction of Nineveh, and the end of Assyria's empire.

According to the biblical record, Merodach-baladan sent envoys to King Hezekiah of Judah (727–697 BCE; both Isa and 2 Chr follow 2 Kgs in placing this event late in Hezekiah's reign, so that it foreshadows the Babylonian conquest; however, any meeting with Merodach-baladan's envoys would have had to take place prior to Hezekiah's own failed revolt, and its consequences).

Hezekiah, who plainly did not regard Babylon as a potential threat, not only welcomed the envoys but also took them on a tour of his treasury, showing off all the riches of his kingdom. The prophet Isaiah, learning of this act of hubris, declared that Babylon would one day return to loot the treasuries of the king and the temple and to carry the people into exile (2 Kgs 20:16-18// Isa 39:5-7); Hezekiah responded, "Why not, if there will be peace and security in my days?" (2 Kgs 20:19//Isa 39:8).

In any case, while the expression of surprise in 1:5 may well reflect Judah's initial reaction to Babylon's rise, the oracle that unfolds in the following verses demonstrates knowledge of Babylon's considerable military triumphs:

> I am rousing the Chaldeans,
> that fierce and impetuous nation,
> who march through the breadth of the earth
> to seize dwellings not their own (Hab 1:6).

The description of Babylon as "fierce and impetuous" (Heb., *hammar wehannimhar*) recalls Zephaniah 1:14, which describes the day of the LORD as "bitter" (Heb., *mar*) and "hastening fast" (*maher*: a form of the verb rendered "impetuous" in the NRSV of Hab 1:6); these two words appear together only in Habakkuk 1:6 and Zephaniah 1:14. As the day of the LORD is a major theme of the Book of the Twelve in its final form, this description of Babylon in the language of Zephaniah 1:14 likely reflects the work of Habakkuk's editors. Similarly, the depiction of Babylon mocking kings and rulers and of its effortless triumph over "every fortress" (1:10-11) contrasts vividly with the impotence of Nineveh's kings and fortifications in Nahum 3, while using language and imagery found in that oracle (Nogalski 1993b, 148). Again, it appears most likely that this description reflects the editing of Habakkuk's prophecy.

The characterization of Babylon as a bestial predator in 1:8 recalls the depiction of Nineveh in Nahum as a lion's den (Nah 2:12[11]–3:3). It is unlikely, however, that this is an intentional parallel, as Habakkuk uses different beasts (leopards, wolves, and eagles rather than lions) and has a different focus (the leonine imagery in Nahum addresses Assyria's royal house; no such intention is evident in Hab 1:8). Leopards and wolves function elsewhere in Scripture as paradigmatic predators of the wild (for leopards, cf. Hos 13:7 and Song 4:8; for wolves, cf. Isa 65:25; for both leopards and wolves, cf. Isa 11:6 and Jer 5:6), but the only parallel for Habakkuk's comparison of the military prowess of an enemy with the leopard is Daniel 7:6, where the fourth beast is "like a leopard"; indeed, Habakkuk 1:8 may be the inspiration behind the depiction of the nations as beasts in Daniel's vision. Wolves elsewhere represent domestic, not foreign, adversaries: Zephaniah 3:3 refers not to a foreign enemy but to the judges of Jerusalem as "evening wolves" (par. Ezek 22:27), and in Genesis 49:27, "Benjamin is a ravenous wolf." In contrast, the eagle as a symbol of warlike ferocity (e.g., 2 Sam 1:23) represents Assyria in Hosea 8:1 and is used specifically for Babylon in a number of texts (in addition to Hab 1:8, cf. Deut 28:49; Jer 4:13; 48:40; 49:22; Ezek 17:3, 7; Lam 4:19; and perhaps Dan 7:4, where the first beast, likely representing Babylon, has "eagle's wings"). The representation of Assyria and Babylon as eagles may reflect the experience of exile: just as eagles snatch up and carry off their prey, so Assyria and Babylon carried their victims off to distant places (cf. Ezek 17:3, 7). If so, then this image in particular belongs to the later editing of the book.

The translation of 1:9 is difficult. The first problem this verse poses is the meaning of *megammat*, which occurs only here. The LXX *anthestekotas* ("resisting") assumes a different Hebrew word, perhaps *megorah*, from the verb *gur*, "to provoke or attack." Still, 1QpHab does not differ from the MT here, so we should stay with *megammat*. This word is likely related to the root *gamam*, having to do with abundance or completion (hence the word *gam*; "also, even," and cf. Isa 21:12, which Köhler-Baumgartner proposes should be read as "the night ends" rather than "also the night"; *HALOT* 2000, 197). As *megammat* parallels *kulloh* (literally, "all of it") from the first line of the verse ("They all come for violence [Heb., *khamas*; cf. 1:2-3]"), the point seems to be that the troops of Babylon are moving in concert (NRSV "with faces pressing"; NJPS "the thrust of their van"; NIV "their hordes advance").

The second problem in 1:9 is how to render the phrase *penehem qadimah* (literally, "their faces eastward [forward?]"). The NRSV and NJPS alike assume that this phrase has to do with Babylon's advance: hence, "with faces pressing forward" (NRSV) or "the thrust of their van is forward" (NJPS). The KJV and NIV follow *Tg. Neb.* and the Vulgate, which assume that *qadimah* here has to do with the hot east wind, blowing in from the desert. This interpretation also has the support of the Habakkuk *pesher* from Qumran, which interprets this verse as describing the "burning wrath and livid faces" (*khrn ʿp wzʿp ʿpym*; 1QpHab 3.12-13) of the Kittim. Finally, the otherwise obscure simile at the close of this verse, "they gather captives like sand," makes sense if the Babylonians are imagined as the desert wind (cf. also Hab 1:11, "Then they sweep by like the wind"). Whatever the meaning of this difficult verse, however, its reference to Babylonian captivity makes it most likely that 1:9 too belongs to the later editing of the book.

Habakkuk 1:7 says of the Babylonians, "their justice and dignity proceed from themselves." While contemporary Western readers may regard such self-sufficiency as a good thing, Scripture teaches that true justice and dignity derive not from us but from the LORD, who "loves righteousness and justice" (Ps 33:5; see also Job 37:23; Pss 36:6; 103:6; 106:3; Isa 5:16; 28:17; 33:5; Jer 4:2; 9:24; Mic 7:9). The word rendered "dignity" in the NRSV (*se'et*, related perhaps to the verb *nasa'*, meaning "raise up") occurs only five times in Scripture, apart from Habakkuk. Only one passage, Psalm 61:5 (4), uses the term positively for a human being, and even there, the psalmist speaks of enemies who plot to bring down "a person of prominence." Genesis 49:3 describes Jacob's firstborn Reuben as "excelling in rank" (*yeter se'et*), although it also condemns him as "unstable as water" (Gen 49:4). The three remaining occurrences of *se'et* are in Job (13:11; 31:23; 41:25), where the term refers to divine rather than human dignity. Indeed, it is intriguing to note that Leviticus uses an identical term, *se'et*, for the raised spots of leprosy (cf. Lev 13:2, 10, 19, 28, 43; 14:56)! Habakkuk will later assert concerning the proud, "Their spirit is not right within them" (Hab 2:4). Indeed, Scripture everywhere urges humility before God and others (e.g., Num 12:3; 2 Sam 22:28; 2 Chr 7:14; 1 Cor 1:26-31; Eph 5:21; Phil 2:3). As Habakkuk 1:11 asserts regarding Babylon, overweening self-esteem too readily becomes self-idolatry: "they transgress and become guilty; / their own might is their god!" The term translated "become guilty" in the NRSV (the verb *'asham*) occurs most often in priestly material (eleven times in Lev, twice in Num, four times in Ezek; though *'asham* does appear five times in Hosea). The language used of Babylon in 1:7 and 11b, much like the language of 1:1-4, reflects priestly and wisdom sources, suggesting that here too we may be dealing with Habakkuk rather than with an editor. That God should at the same time use Babylon to chastise Judah and condemn Babylon for its own injustice and hubris is not strange. Similar ambivalence is apparent in Isaiah regarding Assyria, also condemned for "arrogant boasting" and "haughty pride" (Isa 10:12): "For [the king of Assyria] says: / 'By the strength of my hand I have done it, / and by my wisdom, for I have understanding'" (Isa 10:13). God, however, declares that Assyria is nothing but a tool, wielded by the LORD for the LORD's own purposes (Isa 10:15). So too Ezekiel declares that once God has sheathed God's sword—that is, once Babylon has served its purpose—the sword will itself undergo judgment (Ezek 21:35-37 [30-32]):

> You shall be fuel for the fire,
> your blood shall enter the earth;

> You shall be remembered no more,
> for I the LORD have spoken (Ezek 21:37 [32]).

Similarly, though Habakkuk understands the reason for Babylon's assault on Judah, the violence of that assault nonetheless horrifies him, a horror made particularly evident in the second complaint (1:12-17).

Habakkuk 1:12-17 raises a complaint not about Judah but about Babylon. Nogalski sees this shift as indicative of Habakkuk's editing; he proposes that 1:12a, 13-14, an original wisdom speech directed generally against "the wicked" (1:13), has been expanded at 1:12b and 15-17 so that it is now a speech against Babylon (Nogalski 1993a, 143). Once more, however, the ambivalence in these verses is not unusual. Isaiah both refers to Assyria as a weapon in God's hand, wielded against Judah (cf. Isa 7:20; 10:5-6), and offers assurance that the judgment will be limited in scope: specifically, that Jerusalem will not fall (Isa 7-8; cf. Isa 2:2-4//Mic 4:1-3). Habakkuk, too, expresses hope that Babylon's depredations will be limited. He prays, "O LORD, you have marked them for judgment; / and you, O Rock, have established them for punishment" (1:12). Babylon has been marked "for judgment" and "for punishment" against Judah, not for its destruction. Surely, this prayer implies the hope that Judah, though chastened, will survive. Still, horrified by the vehemence of Babylon's assault, he fears for his people's safety—and, as it turns out, rightly so.

Habakkuk cries out, "Are you not from of old, O LORD my God, my Holy One?" (1:12). While God's action and faithfulness from ancient times are recognized throughout Scripture (for other places where God acts in or from *qedem* ["antiquity"], cf. Deut 33:27; Isa 45:21; 46:10; 51:9; Ps 44:2 [1]; 55:19; 77:6, 12 [5, 11]; Prov 8:22; Lam 2:17), the closest parallel to Habakkuk's words is Psalm 74:12-13:

> Yet God my King is from of old,
> working salvation in the earth.
> You divided the sea by your might;
> you broke the heads of the dragons in the waters.

As the psalm in Habakkuk 3 also describes the victory of the divine warrior over the waters of chaos (Hab 3:8; cf. Isa 51:9; Ps 77:16), this language in 1:12 is certainly suggestive: if the psalm reflects the piety of Habakkuk, its selection and inclusion in this book may be the work of the prophet rather than his editors.

Habakkuk addresses God intimately and personally, as "O LORD my God, my Holy One." God is addressed throughout the book of Isaiah as "the Holy One of Israel" (25 times; e.g., Isa 1:4; 41:14, 16; 60:9, 14), and so as "his [that is, Israel's] Holy One" (Isa 10:17; 49:7) and "your [plural] Holy One" (Isa 43:15), but Habakkuk 1:12 is the only place in Scripture where God is called "*my* Holy One." This first-person devotional language is reminiscent of the Psalms (e.g., Pss 3:4, 8 [3, 7]; 23:1; 71:3; 43:5; 91:2; 104:1, 33; 144:1-2). Habakkuk's cry comes from a personal relationship with God and the corresponding expectation that God will prove faithful.

Although the MT of 1:12 reads "we shall not die," the NRSV of this verse follows the Jewish tradition identifying this passage as one of the *Tiqqune Sopherim*, scribal emendations made to preserve divine honor, and so reads "You [i.e., God] shall not die" (cf. NJPS, NIV 2011, Gowan 1979, 30). Indeed, *Tg. Neb.* extends this verse into a meditation on God's eternity. However, nothing in the context of 1:12 relates to theological abstraction. Habakkuk does not question God's eternity (God is, after all, "from of old"), but God's justice (cf. 1:13). It is best then to stay with the MT and LXX, and read, "*We* shall not die" (cf. KJV and the old NIV). While 1:12a is missing from the Habakkuk *pesher*, 1QpHab 5.3, which interprets this verse, reads, "The interpretation of the word, which is: God will not destroy his people by the hand of the nations." Clearly, this *pesher* depends on the reading from the MT. Achtemeier, who also stays with the MT, sees this passage as an expression of confident faithfulness: God will preserve God's own (Achtemeier 1986, 39–40; so also Nogalski 1993b, 149, who accordingly assigns this statement to his "Babylonian layer"). Again, the context makes this reading difficult. In the next verse, the prophet asks, "Your eyes are too pure and you cannot look on wrongdoing; why do you look on the treacherous, and are silent when the wicked swallow those more righteous than they?" (Hab 1:13). The image of the wicked swallowing up the righteous may, like 1:2-4, involve a protest against homegrown injustice (cf. Pss 35:25; 124:3, Prov 1:12). A particularly interesting parallel, however, is Hosea 8:8, which refers to the Assyrian conquest of the northern kingdom: "Israel is swallowed up; now they are among the nations" (cf. Isa 49:19; Jer 51:34 and Lam 2:16, for Zion swallowed up by Babylon). Habakkuk, it seems, fears that Judah is now suffering the same fate. "We shall not die" is a cry of hopeful desperation: surely, surely we will not die; surely the God Habakkuk addresses as "my Holy One," who is faithful "from of old," will not permit the destruction of Judah! Nevertheless, of course, Judah was destroyed, and they *did* die.

Habakkuk 1:14-17 is an extended metaphor of conquest and exile: the people of Israel, indeed the nations of the world (1:17), are "like the fish of the sea" (1:14), and Babylon is the fisherman with his net, scooping them all up hand over fist, ruthlessly and indiscriminately. Intriguingly, Habakkuk's description of the world's peoples as seafood parallels "like the fish of the sea" with "like crawling things [Heb., *remes*] that have no ruler" (1:14). The noun *remes* appears seventeen times in the Hebrew Bible, primarily in the priestly accounts of the creation (Gen 1:24-26) and the flood (Gen 6:7, 20; 7:14, 23; 8:17, 19; 9:3). *Remes* also occurs in other texts influenced by the priestly creation account (Ezek 38:20; Hos 2:18; Pss 104:25; 148:10; note that Ezek 8:10 relates more directly to the laws of ritual uncleanness from Lev discussed below, and to Deut 4:18, which forbids idols made in "the likeness of anything that creeps [*kol-romes*] on the ground"). Of particular interest, given the wisdom influence evident in Habakkuk, is the description of Solomon's wisdom in 1 Kings 4:33: "he would speak of animals, and birds, and reptiles [Heb., *remes*], and fish." While the noun *remes* does not appear in Leviticus, a verbal form of the same root denotes a whole class of unclean animals: "You shall not defile yourselves with any swarming creature that moves [Heb., *haromes*] upon the earth" (Lev 11:44; note that Lev 11:46 cautions against "every living creature that moves [Heb., *haromeset*] through the waters"). Further definition of these creeping, crawling creatures appears in Leviticus 11:42: "Whatever moves on its belly, and whatever moves on all fours [i.e., crawls or creeps], or whatever has many feet." Water *remes* would include eels, crabs, clams, and snakes—broadly speaking, anything living in the water that is not a fish (i.e., does not have fins and scales; cf. Lev 11:9-12).

That clean and unclean alike are snatched up in the fisherman's net may remind Christian readers of Jesus' parable of the dragnet (Matt 13:47-50), where the sorting of the catch corresponds to the last judgment. In Habakkuk, this image of clean fish and unclean *remes* mixed together may relate to the experience of exile, where observance of the laws concerning ritual purity was impossible (cf. Ezek 4:9-17), and where loss of cultural and religious identity through absorption into the unclean nations—the fate suffered by the northern kingdom—was a serious risk. The statement that they "have no ruler" (Heb., *lo'-moshel bo*, 11:14; 1QpHab 5.13 reads *lmshl bw* ["to rule over them"], but as the following interpretation makes nothing of this reading and no other version presumes it, it is most likely a scribal error) may also relate to the experience of the exiles, as the destruction of Jerusalem meant the end of kingship (see the discussion of Jehoiachin and Zedekiah, Judah's last Davidic kings, above). Nevertheless, in biblical terms, this statement stands in sharp contrast to the priestly creation story, where humanity is charged with dominion over creation—expressly including "the fish of the sea" and "every creeping thing" (*kol-haremes*; cf. Gen 1:26-27). Though the term used for rule (Heb., *mashal*) in Habakkuk 1:14 does not appear in the Genesis passage, it refers to humanity's lordship over creation in Psalm 8:7 (6): "You have given them dominion over the works of your hands." In Habakkuk's allegory, where people are fish and "crawling things," Babylon plays the role of the human fisherman. Rather than exercising responsible stewardship over creation, the fisherman consumes all that he catches ("his portion is lavish, and his food is rich," Hab 1:16). Such gluttony is not only irresponsible, but also impious: "he sacrifices to his net / and makes offerings to his seine (1:16)." This is a restatement, in allegorical terms, of the Babylonian hubris described in 1:11, "their own might is their god" (cf. also 2:18-19). As 1:14-17 seems to presuppose the experience of exile, it likely derives from the editors. Still, in the text before us, Habakkuk's anguished question regarding God's justice in the face of the Babylonian assault remains; indeed, the experience of conquest and exile intensifies it. How can a just God permit such evil to continue? Or, in the story world of Habakkuk's allegory, "Is he then to keep on emptying his net, / and destroying nations without mercy?" (1:17).

The Woes (2:1-20)

In the MT, where the first chapter is set off as a unit, the next paragraph break comes after 2:1-8. As we have seen, this reading understands 2:1-5 not as the conclusion of the preceding unit but as the beginning of the following one. Accordingly, this commentary will treat the five woes in 2:6-20 as unpacking God's revelation to Habakkuk in 2:1-5 (so too Sweeney 2000, 469; Floyd 2000, 82–83).

In the final form of Habakkuk 1, the chapter ends with a question: will Babylon's depredations be permitted to continue? Even if this explicit question traces to Habakkuk's editors, the question of God's justice emerges unmistakably from this dialogue. Indeed, a reader of this book attentive to biblical parallels is bound to think of the book of Job (so too Gowan 1976, 27–28; O'Brien 2004, 80). Habakkuk, like Job (e.g., Job 9:4-12), does not question God's existence or God's sovereignty; indeed, for Habakkuk as for Job, it is his personal experience of God's goodness that throws the question of God's justice into such sharp relief (cf. Hab 1:12). Also like Job (e.g., Job 26:18-21), Habakkuk demands a personal encounter with the divine: "I will keep watch to see what he will say to me, / and what he will answer concerning my complaint" (Hab 2:1). Two terms denote the place where the prophet awaits God's reply. The first, rendered "watchpost" in the NRSV, is *mishmeret*, a term that frequently refers to cultic and ritual observance (e.g., Josh 22:3; Ezek 40:45-46), although the Hebrew Bible also uses it for a secular guard post (e.g., 2 Sam 20:34; Isa 21:8). The second is *matsor* (NRSV "rampart"), a term for a fortification related to Akkadian *maṣṣartu* and Aramaic *matsra'*, meaning "boundary." This term appears in the Hebrew Bible only four times apart from Habakkuk, all apparently late (Zech 9:3; Ps 60:11 [9]; 2 Chr 8:5; 11:5; cf. Nogalski 1993b, 153–54). A related term, *matsurah*, while primarily found in postexilic 2 Chronicles (cf. 2 Chr 11:10, 11, 23; 12:4; 14:5; 21:3), however, also appears in Isaiah 29:3 and Nahum 2:2 (1), both likely seventh-century texts. Perhaps, then, the use of *matsor* does not require a late dating for our passage (cf. also Jeremias 1970, 105–106 on the use of the Akkadian term in Assyrian military contexts).

In any case, it is likely that the image of the prophet taking a guard post on the city walls is intended metaphorically rather than literally (with Achtemeier 1986, 42). Hosea similarly states, "The prophet is a sentinel [Heb., *tsopheh*] for my God over Ephraim" (Hos 9:8; for the ordinary use of *tsopheh* for actual sentinels, cf., e.g., 2 Sam 13:34; 2 Kgs 9:17-18). Ezekiel too became a sentinel charged with warning Jerusalem of God's impending judgment (Ezek 3:17; 33:2, 6-7). In neither of those instances, it should be observed, does God give the prophetic sentinel any assurance of a good outcome; indeed, both Ezekiel and Hosea foresee destruction for their people. Further, Ezekiel is warned to expect rejection from his community (Ezek 3:18-21), while Hosea records that according to the people of Israel, "The prophet is a fool, the man of the spirit is mad" (Hos 9:7). We should not be surprised, then, should Habakkuk too receive bad news. Achtemeier, who rejects the parallel between Habakkuk and these other prophetic sentinels, proposes that Habakkuk's role is more like that described in Isaiah 62:6-7, although without the "persistent intercession before God" featured in that passage (Achtemeier 1986, 42). Nevertheless, it seems very possible that Habakkuk 2:1 has influenced this text from Trito-Isaiah, *particularly* as regards their persistence: the prophets

> shall never be silent.
> You who remind the LORD,
> take no rest,
> and give him no rest
> until he establishes Jerusalem (Isa 62:6-7).

Habakkuk too resolves to hold God accountable: "I will keep watch to see what he will say to me, and what he will answer concerning my complaint" (Hab 2:1).

The NRSV of 2:1b ("and what he will answer concerning my complaint") follows *Tg. Neb.* and the Syriac (cf. also NJPS). The MT and LXX have instead the first person, "what I will answer" (cf. KJV, NIV, Sweeney 2000, 470 and Floyd 2000, 83, who proposes that the psalm in Hab 3 constitutes Habakkuk's answer to God's revelation). 1QpHab is not helpful here, as the verse itself is missing, and the interpretation does not directly refer to it (cf. 1QpHab 6.14). The difference between *'ashib* ("I will answer") and *yashib* ("he will answer") is unlikely to be due to scribal error; it seems rather that either the prophet's response has been emended to the LORD's, or vice versa. The interpreter must decide which reading best explains the others; to this reader, it seems more likely that a passage compelling God's response to the prophet ("what he will answer") would have been softened into a statement requiring the prophet's response to God ("what I will answer") than the other way around. We must also ask which seems to be the best reading in context: is the concern of this verse how Habakkuk is to answer God, or how God will answer Habakkuk? The thrust of the entire passage argues for the latter. Job 23:4 uses *tokakhat*, the word rendered "complaint" in the NRSV of Habakkuk 2:1, for Job's "charge of malfeasance against God" (Vanderhooft 2010). Similarly, in Habakkuk 2:1, *tokakhat* refers back to the theodicy dialogue in the previous chapter; indeed, Sweeney suggests that reference is being made particularly to 1:12-17, "in which YHWH is explicitly named" (Sweeney 2000, 470). As George Adam Smith has written, "Habakkuk's task is God Himself, the effort to find what He means by permitting tyranny and wrong" (cited in Gowan 1976, 20).

In Habakkuk as in Job, God responds (Hab 2:2; cf. Job 38:1). For the first time in this book, the speaker is identified clearly and unambiguously: "Then the LORD answered me and said: Write the vision; make it plain on tablets" (2:2; cf. Gowan 1976, 26). The verb *ba'ar* ("make plain") appears elsewhere only in Deuteronomy, where it is found twice: in 1:5, which introduces the text of the *torah* as written out by Moses (although the NRSV has "Moses undertook to expound this law," both the introductory context of this verse and the use of *ba'ar* in Deut 27:8 suggest that writing rather than explication is intended), and in 27:8, where the text of Moses' *torah* is copied clearly onto standing stones at Ebal. Habakkuk 2:2 also refers to a clearly written text (with Haak 1992, 55), but the following phrase, *lema'an yaruts qore' bo* ("in order that one reading [aloud] in it may run"[?]), is anything but clear! 1QpHab 7.3 differs from the MT only in having a definite article ("*the* one who reads in it"); the LXX seems to assume this reading rather than the MT. The NIV, understanding the one who reads and runs to be a messenger, translates accordingly: "that a herald may run with it" (cf. Sweeney 2000,

471). Yet, as this phrase follows a statement that the message is to be written plainly, it makes sense that it should relate in some way to its ease of reading. The NRSV "so that a runner may read it" imagines that the message is posted publicly (like the stones at Ebal; cf. Deut 27:1-8), written in large, clear letters so that even someone running by would be able to read it. It is also possible, however, that the running in this passage is metaphorical rather than literal. *Targum Nebi'im,* influenced not only by the parallels for *ba'ar* but also by the reference to the tablets (Heb., *hallukhot*; cf. Exod 32:16; 34:1; Deut 9:17; 10:2-4), presumes that the message Habakkuk has been given relates to the Torah, and states that his message is for those "who hasten to become wise." The NJPS similarly understands this phrase to mean that the message can be read quickly: "Inscribe it on tablets, / So that it can be read easily."

Many interpreters have wondered about the unspecified content of Habakkuk's "vision for the appointed time" (2:3). The Habakkuk *pesher* shows that the Qumran community understood his vision to refer to the last days, "which will be beyond all that the prophets say" (1QpHab 7.12-13). In the New Testament, Hebrews 10:37 understands this passage to refer to Jesus' return: "For yet 'in a very little while, the one who is coming will come and will not delay.'" In traditional Jewish interpretation, Habakkuk's vision has been understood as a reference to the coming of the Messiah; the twelfth of the Rambam's Thirteen Principles of Judaism ("I believe that Messiah will come, and though he tarry, I will expect him daily") alludes to this passage, which states "if it seem to tarry, wait for it" (2:3). Similarly, Augustine (*Civ.* 18:31) writes that Habakkuk here predicted "the advent of Christ, who was to come." Gregory of Nazianzus, who is depicted together with Habakkuk in Orthodox iconography (Bucur and Mueller 2011, 88), understands Habakkuk's vision to be of the risen, victorious Christ, by which Christ proclaims, "Today salvation has come to the visible and to the invisible world. Christ is risen from the dead, rise all with Him!" (*Orat.* 45.1, cited in Bucur and Mueller 2011, 99). Such interpretations follow more easily from the LXX, which reads that the vision "will arise *in* the end" (Greek *anatelei eis peras*), than from the MT, which reads *weyapheakh laqqets*: that is, "it testifies, or witnesses, *to* the end" (cf. 1QpHab 7.6, which has *ypykh*, a slightly different form of the same verb). The NRSV, following the MT, reads, "it speaks of the end, and does not lie" (cf. also NIV; the NJPS has "a truthful witness for a time that will come," which seems more an interpretation than a translation). Our passage seems to assume that Habakkuk will live to see the fulfillment of his vision; after all, the prophet is told, "If it seems to tarry, wait for it; / it will surely come, it will not delay" (2:3).

On the other hand, as J. J. M. Roberts observes, the "foreshortening of prophetic expectations" (Roberts 1979, 249) is a common element in prophetic prediction (cf. the many New Testament texts predicting that the end of the world would come soon, e.g., Mark 13:30; 1 Cor 7:29-31; Rev 22:12, 20). Many interpreters would agree with the claim in the Habakkuk *pesher* from Qumran: "God told Habakkuk to write what was coming upon the last generation, but the fulfillment of the end he did not let him know" (1QpHab 7.1-2; e.g., Achtemeier 1986, 42–43; Robertson 1990, 171). Still, nothing in the context, or in the book so far, points us to the distant future; Habakkuk's complaint calls for a response in the here and now.

Some interpreters propose that the theophany in chapter 3 is Habakkuk's vision report (e.g., Sellin 1930, 405; Roberts 1991, 148–49; Vanderhooft 2010, citing Albright). This is an old idea: the Talmud (*b. Meg.* 31a) assigns both Ezekiel 1 and Habakkuk 3 for reading on Pentecost, suggesting that it understood them as related prophetic visions. Orthodox iconography shows Habakkuk receiving a vision of Christ glorified, depicted in ways reflecting Habakkuk's psalm (cf. Bucur and Mueller 2011, 88–90, 97–98, and the discussion of 3:2, below). Certainly, the first explicit reference one finds to the visionary "seeing" something comes in that poem (3:7). Yet, as we will see, the prophet refers to that theophany as a report he has *heard* rather than a vision he has seen (3:2, 16). Further, there is certainly evidence for "visions" whose content involves words rather than images. The prophet Amos is shown a basket of summer fruit (*qayits*) and told, "The end [*qets*] has come upon my people Israel" (Amos 8:1-2; note that this is, apart from Hab 2:3, the only occurrence of *qets* in the Book of the Twelve). His vision is not about *qayits* ("summer fruit"), of course, but about the word "*qayits*"—a punning reference to Israel's end (*qets*). So too, Jeremiah sees the branch of an almond tree (*shaqed*), and is told, "I am watching [*shoqed*] over my word to perform it" (Jer 1:11-12). Micah and Amos alike "see" the word of the LORD (Amos 1:1; Mic 1:1). Ezekiel sees (and swallows!) a scroll inscribed with the "words of lamentation and mourning and woe" that he is to bear (Ezek 2:10; cf. Ellen Davis 1989, 65–66: God's word "comes to Ezekiel already *as a text*" [emphasis hers]). Indeed, in the superscription to this book, Habakkuk sees the oracle (Hab 1:1). Perhaps, then, Habakkuk "sees" a word in 2:3 as well, which would explain why he is able to write his vision out so plainly and simply. Habakkuk's vision "speaks of the end, and does not lie" (Hab 2:3). Perhaps this is not an interpretation or a summary, but the vision itself: Habakkuk sees, and writes, *haqqets*: "the end."

The most natural assumption for a reader of the prophets would be that Habakkuk's vision of "the end" means the end for his people: for Judah and Jerusalem. Such is the case for Hosea and Ezekiel, both of whom, like Habakkuk, are metaphorical sentinels on the wall. Such is the case for Amos, who is also given a vision of *qets*—and again for Ezekiel, who in 7:1-9 (a complex poem that Eichrodt has called "a fugue . . . circling round in mighty sweeps, and again and again returning to the one theme," Eichrodt 1970, 101) sings repeatedly of Jerusalem, "An end has come, the end has come" (Ezek 7:2, 3, 6). Comparisons with Job are once more cogent: just as Job's encounter with the divine yields no answer to the question posed by Job's innocent suffering, so in Habakkuk, God's answer is not the one that Habakkuk had wanted to hear: that Babylon's assault would be measured and that Judah would be preserved (cf. 1:12). Habakkuk 2:4-5a sounds like a vindication of the LORD's harsh judgment in response to the prophet's earlier complaint (cf. Ezek 9:9). God's answer to the prophet's implicit prayer for preservation ("We shall not die," 1:12) is that Judah's end *will* come, and soon.

This dark vision has not been permitted to stand, however. Habakkuk's editors have revised this work, so that both Habakkuk's vision and the woes that follow relate instead to Babylon. In the final form of Habakkuk, the prophet hails *Babylon's* end. Little wonder that in the history of the interpretation of this book, so many have viewed Habakkuk's vision as one of hope rather than destruction. This shift is already under way in the shaping of this book for its place among the Twelve Prophets, which Jesus ben Sirach says "comforted the people of Jacob and delivered them with confident hope" (Sir 49:10). Floyd summarizes the message of Habakkuk in its final form succinctly:

> Yahweh can be seen as responsible for Babylon's rise, as the oracle in 1:5-11 asserts, but not for the injustice that has accompanied the imposition of their rule. If one recognizes that Babylon is now destined to fall and trusts that Yahweh will eventually bring about this destiny, faith in him as Lord of history can become compatible with a commitment to justice. (Floyd 2000, 83)

Yet one can still discern Habakkuk's original message in this text, and it deserves a hearing. Indeed, if we are to understand this text in its final form, we must be attentive to the process that has produced it.

The transition from Habakkuk's vision of the end to the woes that follow comes in 2:4-5, which contrasts the puffed-up pride of the wealthy and arrogant with the faithful perseverance of the righteous. The term *'uphlah* (NRSV "the proud") in 2:4 requires some consideration. The LXX has "If he falls back [Greek *huposteiletai*]," reading perhaps *'alaph*, "he becomes faint," instead of *'uphlah*. However, 1QpHab supports the MT here. *Targum Nebi'im* reads "the wicked ones" (Aramaic *rashi'aya'*), influenced perhaps by 1:4 and 13, where "the wicked" and "the righteous" are set in parallel (cf. Gowan 1976, 41). Most likely, *'uphlah* is a form of the verb *'aphal*, also found in Numbers 14:44: "But they *presumed* to go up to the heights" (emphasis mine). The NRSV "Look at the proud!" reads *'uphlah* as a participle or a noun related to this root. It then takes the next clause independently: "Their spirit [altered for reasons of inclusivity; the Hebrew has *naphsho*: 'his life, spirit'] is not right in them [Heb., 'him']." The LXX reads, "my spirit [i.e., God's] has no pleasure in him" (quoted, with some rearrangement, in Heb 10:38: "My soul takes no pleasure in anyone who shrinks back"). It is best, however, to read 2:4a with the NJPS, "Lo, his spirit within him is puffed up, not upright," which takes "his spirit within him" (that is, "his life"; cf. 2 Sam 1:9; Ps 107:5) as the subject of both the verb *'uphlah* ("is puffed up") and of the phrase *lo'-yasherah* ("not upright"; both verbs are feminine in form, as is the noun *nephesh*, "spirit, life"; cf. also the KJV). The implied subject, as *Tg. Neb.* recognizes, is the "wicked," who in 1:4 stand in contrast to "the righteous." Those who are "not upright" are "puffed up"—arrogant and proud (cf. 1:7, 11, 16). By contrast, "the righteous live by their faith" (2:4b).

As one of the pivotal texts Paul cites for the doctrine of justification by grace through faith (cf. Rom 1:17 and Gal 3:11), Habakkuk 2:4b stands as both "the keystone of Paul's theology" and "a rallying cry of both Lutheran and Reformed theology" (Gowan 1976, 11). In Jewish tradition as well, this half-verse assumes significance far out of proportion to its meaning in context. The Talmud records the teaching of Rabbi Simlai that the 613 commandments in Torah are condensed into eleven by David (Ps 15), into six by Isaiah (Isa 33:15-16), into three by Micah (Mic 6:8); into two by Isaiah (56:1), and into one by Amos ("For thus says the LORD to the house of Israel: Seek me and live," Amos 5:4) and by Habakkuk (Hab 2:4b; cf. *b. Mak.* 23b-24a). The interpreter of Habakkuk therefore faces the double danger of either paying too much attention to this passage in isolation from its setting, or else of ignoring its resonances in history and tradition, and correspondingly paying it too little attention. We will try to split the difference by considering the meaning of this passage in context and then weighing its use in the New Testament and the Talmud against that meaning.

The Hebrew *'emunah* (rendered "faith" in the NRSV) typically has to do with steadfastness, trustworthiness, and reliability. *Targum Nebi'im* assumes that it is the truth (Aramaic *qushtekhun*, "their truthfulness") of "all of these"—presumably, Habakkuk's words, regarded as nothing by the wicked—that the righteous rely upon (*yithqayyemun*). Similarly, Robert Haak translates 2:4b as "the righteous one because of its fidelity will live" (Haak 1992, 55; cf. also Seifrid 2007, 610). While "the antecedent is understood as the vision" (cf. 2:2-3), Haak deems the ambiguity in this expression to be intentional: "the reliability of the vision," of its content (which Haak understands to be the coming of the Chaldeans), and of the LORD are "interdependent" (Haak 1992, 59). This interpretation, however, misses the contrast in 2:4 between the righteous one (Heb., *tsaddiq*) and the one who is "not upright." The latter, we hear, is arrogant: "puffed up." The righteous instead "live by their [changed in the NRSV for reasons of inclusivity; MT reads "his"] faith" (Heb., *be'emunato yikhyeh*). If "his" refers, as seems simplest, to the righteous one, then "his faith" refers to the steadfastness, trustworthiness, and reliability of the righteous: in a word, to their commitment. Unlike the wicked, who are concerned only for themselves, the righteous live lives of commitment and devotion to God and to God's *torah* (so Jewett 2007, 145). So, the *pesher* on 2:4b in 1QpHab 8:1-3 reads that this passage "concerns all in the house of Judah who observe the *torah*, who God has removed from the house of judgment on account of their hard labor and their faithfulness to the Teacher of Righteousness." The LXX, which has first- rather than third-person pronouns at significant points in this verse (Codex Sinaiticus and the Freer Codex of the Twelve read both "my [i.e., God's] spirit" and "my [God's] faith," rather than, with the MT, "his spirit" and "his faith"), may reflect a common scribal error (the third-person and first-person pronominal endings are often confused). Nevertheless, it is also possible that the LXX translators are interpreting the text here (so Seifrid 2007, 609; note that the Greek text of the Twelve from Nahal Khever, 8KhevXIIgr 17.30, follows the MT). At any rate, although refocusing the verse on God's faithfulness, the LXX captures its point: in contrast to the self-righteous, who are self-centered and proud, the *truly* righteous are characterized by their devotion to God (cf. the NJPS, "the righteous man is rewarded with life for his fidelity"). Habakkuk 2:5 and the woes that follow in 2:6-20 serve by contrast to describe the selfish, arrogant lifestyle of the wicked, and so to legitimate God's judgment upon them.

Paul cites Habakkuk 2:4 twice. In Galatians 3, Paul calls on this community not to trust in ritual observances to deliver them, but rather to return to the gospel that he had proclaimed. Paul advances a series of scriptural arguments elucidating his fundamental point: that God's original promise to Abraham is not restricted to Abraham's physical descendants but rather applies to all, Jew and Gentile alike, who like Abraham believe God's word (Gal 3:6-14). In that connection, Paul asserts, "Now it is evident that no one is justified before God by the law; for 'The one who is righteous will live by faith'" (Gal 3:11). Similarly, Paul cites our passage from Habakkuk in Romans 1:17 as part of his larger argument for the commonality of Jew and Gentile before God: first in condemnation, and then in salvation through Christ (cf. Rom 2:9-29; 3:21-26). Paul says that the gospel of God's son Jesus "is the power of God for salvation to everyone who has faith, to the Jew first and also to the Greek" (Rom 1:16). To demonstrate this truth, Paul cites Habakkuk 2:4b: "For in it [i.e., the gospel] the righteousness of God is revealed through faith for faith; as it is written, 'The one who is righteous will live by faith'" (Rom 1:17). Paul's point, in both Galatians and Romans, is the inclusion of the Gentiles, not the exclusion of the Jews (cf. Rom 9–11, especially 11:13-24, 26) or the rejection of the Torah (cf. Gal 3:19-29).

Notably, Paul's citations of 2:4b follow neither the MT ("his faith") nor the LXX ("my faith"). Since Paul customarily quotes from the LXX, this shift is certainly significant, making it unlikely (as some claim, e.g., Seifrid 2007, 610) that Paul simply intended, with the LXX, to refer to God's faithfulness here (cf. Hays 2002, 140). James Dunn sees Paul as charting a middle course between the MT and LXX, embracing both (Dunn 1988, 45). He therefore argues that "Paul's citation is *deliberately* ambiguous" (Dunn 1988, 48; emphasis his). Referring back to the previous clause in Romans 1:17, where God's righteousness is revealed "from faith to faith," Dunn sees the Habakkuk citation as referring to faith in both senses:

> He who is maintained within or has been brought into the relationship with God which brings about salvation, by the outreach of God's faithfulness to his own faith, shall experience the fullness of life which God intended for humankind as he lives in the dependence of faith on the continuing faithfulness of God. (Dunn 1988, 48)

Robert Jewett recognizes another ambiguity in Paul's usage, depending on whether, as in "the classic Lutheran interpretation of Romans," "by faith" is attached to "the righteous," hence describing "the means by which justification is achieved," or whether, as in "Catholic or pietist" interpretations, one attaches faith to the following verb, indicating that the righteous one is to live faithfully (Jewett 2007, 146). Arguing that it is best to resolve this question grammatically, rather than by appeal to theological presuppositions, Jewett notes that elsewhere, when Paul intends to refer to "the process by which righteousness is gained," he uses the verb *logizein* ("to judge, reckon;" used 19 times in Rom, especially in Rom 4 regarding Abraham as "justified" by faith). He therefore concludes that this is not Paul's intent in citing

Habakkuk 2:4b; as in the MT, Paul affirms that the righteous live lives characterized by faithfulness (Jewett 2007, 146).

Like Dunn, Richard Hays proposes that Paul's citation is purposefully ambiguous, but in a different sense. As Paul uses it in Galatians 3:11, the phrase from Habakkuk 2:4 means:

> (a) The Messiah [i.e., the Righteous One] will live by (his own) faith(fullness).
> (b) The righteous person will live as a result of the Messiah's faith(fullness).
> (c) The righteous person will live by (his own) faith in the Messiah. (Hays 2002, 140)]

The second option is of greatest interest for Hayes, who argues that "for Paul the obedience and faithfulness of Jesus Christ are of central soteriological significance. . . . Jesus' faith is not merely exemplary, as in nineteenth-century liberal theology, but vicariously efficacious" (Hays 2002, 210). In any case, Paul's citation of Habakkuk intends all three: "Paul's thought is rendered wholly intelligible only if all three of these interpretations are held together and affirmed as correct" (Hays 2002, 140).

In the deepest sense, then, what Paul affirms in his use of Habakkuk 2:4b is not unlike what the Talmud affirms in the claim that all of the commandments in Torah find their heart in this passage and in Amos 5:4. Rabbi Simlai and Paul alike affirm that a dynamic, committed relationship with the Divine must come first and remain foremost in our lives. Of course, Rabbi Simlai would affirm that the one who seeks God and is faithful will also strive to observe all 613 of the commandments in God's Torah! Paul denies that such observance is necessary for those who find relationship with God through Christ (cf. Gal 4:10; 5:6). Yet Paul also insists that faith has definite consequences for the life of the believer. Throughout his ministry, Paul struggled against a serious misinterpretation of his gospel: the claim that, since our justification is God's free gift offered through Jesus Christ, we can live as we please (e.g., Rom 6:1). Paul everywhere denies that this is the case. The believer, he affirms, has died to sin and to the world (Rom 6:1-4), and has been born into a new life, lived under the direction of God's Spirit (Rom 8:1-17). Deeds of love, justice, and mercy will of course follow from such a life (e.g., Gal 5:22-25), but they alone cannot produce it. The point of Paul's vehemence regarding the inefficacy of works, particularly in Galatians, is that nothing can be added to the free, gracious gift of God in Christ. We cannot earn our salvation, but can only respond to God's gracious gift (see especially

Rom 5)—a truth that the Hebrew Bible also affirms (e.g., Deut 7:6-8; Ezek 20:4).

The citation of Habakkuk 2:4b from the LXX in Hebrews 10:38 shifts the order of the clauses, and reads *mou* not with *pisteos* but with *dikaios*: hence, rather than "the righteous will live by my faith," this passage has "my righteous one will live by faith." The difference may result from the author using a different text of the LXX (Codex Alexandrinus and Codex Ephraemi Syri Rescriptus have "my righteous one"; but cf. Hays 2002, 139, who proposes instead that these two texts "result from assimilation to the text of Hebrews"); however, it may also be that the differences are owed to the author citing the passage from memory (cf. Heb 2:6). Still, it is intriguing that, as in Paul's letters, the citation of this passage in Hebrews does not follow the LXX reading "my faith." Perhaps Paul influenced the writer of Hebrews in this decision. In any case, the citation of Habakkuk 2:4b in Hebrews 10:38 introduces the rehearsal of great heroes of faith from the biblical story in Hebrews 11. The climax of that rehearsal in turn is the call, following the example of "Jesus the pioneer and perfecter of our faith" (Heb 12:2), to "lay aside every weight, and the sin that clings so closely, and . . . run with perseverance the race that is set before us" (Heb 12:1). The broader context of this citation in Hebrews, then, upholds the theme of persistence and commitment found in Habakkuk.

Habakkuk 2:5 continues to describe the wicked in contrast to the righteous:

> Moreover, wealth is treacherous;
> the arrogant do not endure.
> They open their throats wide as Sheol;
> like Death they never have enough.

The MT has instead *hayyayin boged* ("wine is treacherous," cf. KJV; NIV), which is also assumed by LXX and *Tg. Neb.*, but the following verse says nothing about wine or drunkenness. 1QpHab 8.3 reads not *hayyayin boged* but *hwn ybgwd* ("wealth [Heb., *hon*] will betray"), which fits the context much better than "wine." The NRSV accordingly has "wealth is treacherous" (the NJPS, which relates *hwn* instead to the verb *hawan*, "make light" [cf. Deut 1:41] reads, "How much less then shall the defiant go unpunished").

Sheol is an ancient name for the underworld, or the place of the dead. It is mentioned sixty-six times in Scripture (e.g., Gen 37:35; Isa 38:18-19; Pss 6:6 [5]; 139:8) but only five times in the Twelve (Hos 13:14 [twice]; Amos 9:2; Jonah 2:3; Hab 2:5). Fully half of the references to Sheol come from the

Psalms (16 times) and from wisdom literature (9 times in Proverbs, 8 times in Job, 1 time in Ecclesiastes), so the use of the term by the central intermediary Habakkuk is not surprising. The depiction of the underworld and death as insatiable and eager to devour recalls the portrayal of the god *Mot* ("Death") in the poetry of old Canaan (cf. Roberts 1991, 117), but the comparison of the wealthy and arrogant to a ravenous Sheol once more calls to mind wisdom parallels. In Proverbs 1:12, sinners plan to ambush the innocent: "like Sheol let us swallow them alive, / and whole, like those who go down to the pit." The statement "like death they never have enough" (Hab 2:5) recalls Proverbs 30:15-16, which lists Sheol together with the barren womb, the dry earth in a time of drought, and fire as four things that are "never satisfied" and "never say, 'Enough.'" There as here, the point of the comparison is that the greedy and self-centered, who take rather than give, threaten the community—like fire, drought, barrenness, and death itself.

Up to this point, the reader assumes that the target of this verse is *Judah's* proud: those accused in 1:1-4 of perverting justice, whom 1:5 calls *bogedim* ("traitors"; cf. the discussion of 1:5 above, and 2:5 for wealth as *boged*, "treacherous"), who have brought down God's judgment upon their own people. The final line of the verse shifts the focus, however: "They gather all nations for themselves, and collect all peoples as their own" (2:5). Clearly, this line alludes to the fisherman allegory in 1:15-17, where Babylon scoops up nations in its net. Like the allegory, which presupposes the exile, this line is the work of Habakkuk's editors. Inspired perhaps by Habakkuk 1:13, where the prophet, evidently referring to the Babylonian invaders, asks why God is "silent when the wicked swallow those more righteous than they," the editors have transferred Habakkuk's prophecy of judgment, indeed of the end, from Jerusalem to Babylon.

Habakkuk 2:6a leads explicitly into the five woe oracles that follow (2:6b-8, 9-11, 12-14, 15-17, 19; significantly, each begins with *hoi*, "woe," rendered "Alas" in the NRSV), calling on everyone to join in pronouncing those woes on the wealthy and proud, against whom God's judgment is directed. The terms used in this summons, *mashal* (NRSV "taunt"), *melitsah*, and *khidot* (the NRSV reads these two terms together as "mocking riddles"), appear together elsewhere only in Proverbs 1:6. This verse, part of the prologue to the entire book of Proverbs (Prov 1:1-7), says that to gain wisdom, the young sage must learn "to understand a proverb [*mashal*] and a figure [*melitsah*], the words of the wise and their riddles [*khidot*]." In Proverbs, each of these terms refers to a saying requiring an interpretation: what we might call a riddle, a parable, or a proverb. *Mashal* sometimes designates a proverb or epigram (e.g., 1 Sam 10:12); indeed, the Hebrew title of the book of Proverbs is *meshalim*, the plural of *mashal*. On the other hand, a *mashal* can also be a parable or allegory (e.g., Ezek 17:2); indeed, the LXX commonly translates *mashal* as *parabole*, the word used in the NT for Jesus' parables. Further, the expression "raise a *mashal*" (*mashal* with the verb *nasa'* ["lift up"]), translated "taunt" in the NRSV of Habakkuk 2:6, introduces Balaam's attempted curses against Israel (Num 23:7, 18; 24:3, 15, 20, 21, 23), prophetic taunt songs against Babylon (Isa 14:4) and Jerusalem (Mic 2:4), and Job's final speeches (Job 27:1; 29:1). In short, it is difficult to generalize about either the form or the content of a *mashal*. Similarly, *khidah*, commonly rendered "riddle," describes Samson's riddle of the beehive (Judg 14) and Ezekiel's allegory of the eagle and the vine (Ezek 17:2; also called a *mashal*, note), as well as the riddles used by the Queen of Sheba to test Solomon's wisdom (1 Kgs 10:1//2 Chr 9:1). Furthermore, Numbers 12:8 also uses it for the veiled sayings of the prophets, as contrasted with the clear, face-to-face communication between God and Moses. The term *melitsah* appears only in Habakkuk 2:6 and Proverbs 1:6. The Aramaic *Targumim* on these two passages render the word differently: *Targum Nebi'im* renders the word in Habakkuk as *sho'i* ("derisive talk, sneer, byword;" cf. Jastrow 1926, 1538), while the *Targum Kethubim* (*Tg. Ket.*) reads *pl'h*, "puzzle, allegory." Similarly, the LXX of Habakkuk renders the term as *problema* ("riddle, problem"), while in Proverbs it is rendered as *skoteion logon* ("a dark word"). James Crenshaw proposes that these are "sayings that carry a sting hidden within their clever formulation, and may by extension refer to admonitions and warnings" (Crenshaw 1998, 23).

One may draw two conclusions from this brief consideration of the terminology in 2:6a. First, it is evident that these terms are at home in the wisdom tradition; Habakkuk's use of them shows us, once more, his familiarity with the language of the sages, and underlines the likelihood that as a professional prophet he has studied in the upper-class academies. Second, the nearly unanimous conclusion of the translators (e.g., NRSV, NJPS, NIV, and KJV) that these terms imply derision does not seem necessarily to follow from their usage elsewhere. Reading Habakkuk 2:6-20 as a taunt song seems to depend particularly on comparison with Nahum 3. Habakkuk's editors have recast the judgment in 2:5 and the woes in 2:6-20 to relate to Babylon rather than Jerusalem; this further supports the parallel with the mock dirge for Nineveh in Nahum 3, as well as with Isaiah 14, where Babylon is again the target. In its final form as a part of the Book of the Twelve, paired with Nahum, Habakkuk 2:6-20 does seem to function as a taunt song. Still, one wonders if perhaps Habakkuk's original intent in these oracles was not mockery but mourning (cf. the discussion of *hoi* in Nah 3:1, above).

The first woe (2:6b-8) deals with theft ("Alas for you who heap up what is not your own!" 2:6b; the Hebrew more literally reads, "the one who heaps up what is not his own"), although the theft described does not seem to be straightforward robbery or burglary. Habakkuk says that these thieves heap upon themselves *'abtit* (NRSV "goods taken in pledge"), a word that occurs only here; the LXX translators, uncertain what to do with it, render it as *kloion* (evidently a yoke or slave collar; the KJV, following the Vulgate, has "thick clay"). It is likely, however, that this word is related to the noun *'abot* used for a pledge given on a loan (Deut 24:10-13), and the verb *'abat* used for borrowing against a pledge (Deut 15:6), for taking an item given in pledge (Deut 24:10), and for lending after taking a pledge (Deut 15:6, 8; notably, *Tg. Neb.* of Hab 2:6 has *tequph khobin*, "strong debt"[?]). These passages take care to ensure that the dignity of the borrower is preserved and that the lender shows compassion in taking a pledge. In particular, Deuteronomy 24:12-13 states that, should a poor person's cloak be taken in pledge, it cannot be kept overnight: "You shall give the pledge back by sunset, so that your neighbor may sleep in the cloak and bless you; and it will be to your credit before the LORD your God" (Deut 24:13). The principle is expressed elsewhere, although with different vocabulary (cf. Exod 22:26–27; Ezek 18:7-8, 16; Amos 2:8). Most likely, then, Habakkuk too deals with abusive lending practices. In his opening complaint concerning social injustice, inequity, and violence in the land, Habakkuk cried out to the LORD, "How long?" (1:2; Heb., *'ad-'anah*; cf. Jer 47:6; Ps 13:2-3 [1-2]). Here, that question is raised again (2:6; Heb., *'ad-matay*; cf., e.g., Isa 6:11; Jer 4:14; Ps 82:2; Prov 1:22), and once more, the offenders are the wealthy and arrogant, the religious and secular leaders of Judah. Now, however, Habakkuk says, the worm is about to turn: "Will not your own creditors suddenly rise, / and those who make you tremble wake up? / Then you will be booty for them" (2:7).

The theme of the poor exalted and the rich brought low features prominently in Scripture (e.g., the song of Hannah in 1 Sam 2:1-10). Our passage particularly recalls the plundering of the Egyptians by the Hebrews in the Exodus story (cf. Exod 3:22; 12:33-36). Christian readers will think of Mary's Magnificat (Luke 1:46-55), and the dramatic and unexpected reversals of fortune in the parables of Jesus (e.g., Matt 20:1-16; Mark 9:33-37; Luke 13:20-30). The mention of booty has apparently prompted an editorial expansion in 2:8. While 2:6-7 are concerned with wealth taken through abusive lending practices (Nogalski 1993b, 130), 2:8 describes conquest, and the vengeance of the vanquished:

> Because you have plundered many nations,
> all that survive of the peoples shall plunder you—
> because of human bloodshed, and violence to the earth,
> to cities and all who live in them.

This addition effectively redirects the woe from the leaders of Judah to the armies of Babylon.

The second woe (2:9-11) similarly deals with dishonest gain. The expression *botsea' betsa'* elsewhere refers to greedy, unjust gain (Prov 1:19; 15:27), and particularly to the wealthy and powerful preying on the poor and powerless (Jer 6:13; 8:10; Ezek 22:27); however, Habakkuk intensifies this depiction by adding the adjective *ra'* ("wicked, evil"): "Alas for you who get *evil* gain for your houses" (2:9, emphasis mine). Often in Hebrew, "house" refers to one's family, but the following verses show that here the term is used literally to refer to the solid, secure mansions of the rich (cf. Amos 5:11; Isa 5:9). Habakkuk accuses the rich of using their unjust gains for "setting your nest on high / to be safe from the reach of harm!" (2:9). The use of "nest" as a snug metaphor for "home," familiar in English usage, is also found in Hebrew (Job 29:18; Prov 27:8). The reference to a nest set "on high" calls to mind the eagle's nest (Job 39:27) used as a metaphor for security. Indeed, the Song of Moses (Deut 32:1-43) compares God's providential care and protection of Israel in the wilderness to the eagle nurturing its young in their nest (Deut 32:11). Elsewhere, however, this metaphor depicts a vain quest for safety; those who seek, like the eagle, to set their nest high in the rocks will be brought down (Num 24:21; Jer 49:16; Obad 3-4). Thus, robbing the poor to set up strong and secure houses will bring the wealthy no security. Instead of gaining security, by the pursuit of dishonest gain, "[y]ou have devised shame for your house"—now used for the family rather than for the physical structure—and indeed, "you have forfeited your life" (2:10). Just as in 2:7, the wronged creditors rise up to plunder their fraudulent lenders, so in 2:11, "The very stones will cry out from the wall, / and the plaster [Heb., *kaphis*; better "beam" or "rafter," with KJV, NJPS, NIV] will respond from the woodwork."

This passage is cited in Luke's account of the triumphal entry into Jerusalem, where in response to the Pharisees' demand that Jesus silence his disciples, Jesus says, "I tell you, if these were silent, the stones would shout out" (Luke 19:40). Given that Habakkuk too opposes the religious and secular leadership of Judah for refusing to hear the outcry of the poor, Luke's citation seems particularly apt. Once more, however, the final form of Habakkuk shifts the focus outward, to the Babylonian invaders: Habakkuk

2:10 accuses those this woe targets of "cutting off many peoples." The reference cannot be to Judah's leadership but must rather be to an imperial power asserting authority over multiple nations. The allusion, once more, is to the fisherman allegory in 1:14-17, which depicts Babylon "destroying nations without mercy" (1:17). Once more, this expansion may relate to language in the oracle concerning plunder, a possible meaning of the noun *betsa'* ("[unjust] gain"; but cf. Judg 5:19, and perhaps Prov 28:16). Although it is difficult to see what it might mean for imperial Babylon to set its nest "on high to be safe from the reach of harm," the final form of the text nonetheless targets the invader rather than Judah itself.

Habakkuk's third woe (2:12-14) once more accuses its target of injustice and oppression, although this time with direct reference to the military threat posed by Babylon. Those who rob the poor through dishonest practices and fraudulent loans (2:6b-8) in order to build for themselves fine, strong, and secure houses (2:9-11) in truth "labor only to feed the flames" (2:13): the day of their doom and destruction is coming. In context, the natural referent for these words would seem to be Jerusalem's imminent assault and ultimate destruction by Babylon. On the other hand, reading this passage in relation to Nahum yields a different understanding. In Nahum, *Nineveh* is the bloody city (Nah 3:12; cf. Hab 2:12) whose citizens labor in vain building defenses destined for the flames (Nah 3:13-14). Indeed, just as the LORD of hosts (Heb., *Yhwh tseba'oth*) brought on Nineveh's devastation (cf. Nah 3:5), so the LORD of hosts will bring about the judgment Habakkuk describes (2:13). Habakkuk's editors, then, would have had no difficulty viewing this woe as addressed toward the foreign aggressor Babylon. There is no need to attribute these words to the editors, however. Read as applying to Jerusalem, they provide a fitting climax to the first three oracles. Indeed, even if the parallels with Nahum reflect the deliberate use of that text, there is no reason to think that Habakkuk himself could not have known of Nahum's oracles: particularly if, as many have proposed, both were central intermediaries connected to the palace and the temple. Habakkuk pronounces woe upon those "who build a town by bloodshed, / and found a city on iniquity!" (2:12). In its immediate context in the Book of the Twelve, this accusation resonates strongly with Nahum 3:1, but the closest parallel to this passage is Micah 3:10, where the message of Zion's destruction is proclaimed to those "who build Zion with blood and Jerusalem with wrong [*'awlah*, rendered "iniquity" in the NRSV of Hab 2:12]!" So too, Ezekiel speaks of Jerusalem as a bloody city (Ezek 7:23; 9:9; 22:2, 3; 24:6, 9). In the time after the Babylonian exile, Trito-Isaiah warns his community of God's renewed judgment, "For your hands are defiled with blood and your fingers with iniquity"

(Isa 59:3). Quite likely, then, Habakkuk too was directing his words against corrupt Judah's leadership, although in the book's final form, Babylon seems the target.

The first three interrelated woes build to a climax: "But the earth will be filled / with the knowledge of the glory of the LORD, / as the waters cover the sea" (2:14). Elsewhere, one finds the affirmation that the glory of the LORD fills the earth (cf. Num 14:21, Isa 6:3; Ps 72:19), but Habakkuk avows that one day all will know and experience this truth: "the *knowledge* of the glory of the LORD" will fill the earth. As a noun, the Hebrew *da'at* ("knowledge") occurs ninety times in the Hebrew Bible, forty times in Proverbs. Here, however, *da'at* appears in a verbal form that intensifies the experiential, relational sense of the word: Habakkuk speaks not of the intellectual grasp of static data about God but of *knowing* God. With this affirmation, the prophet brings us back to the contrast between the arrogance of the wicked and the faithfulness of the righteous (2:4). Ultimately, Habakkuk declares, the faithfulness of the righteous will prevail, when all presumption and pretense are swallowed up in the oceanic experience of God's glory.

After this climactic declaration, the fourth and fifth woes seem like an afterthought. Indeed, as these woes in particular target Babylon, one might wonder whether the Twelve's editors have tacked the last two woes onto Habakkuk's original, neat sequence of three. Yet we can well imagine that Habakkuk would have been deeply concerned about Babylon's ultimate fate. Further, 2:18, which as we will see is clearly a late insertion, presupposes 2:19-20. Perhaps Habakkuk originally presented three woes against Judah's leaders, a fourth woe against Babylon, and a fifth woe directed at both. In the final form, the editors have simplified and clarified this sequence, so that all five woes address the Babylonian invaders.

Both the target of the fourth woe (2:15-17) and the offense that this oracle describes are unclear at first. Habakkuk 2:15 seems to condemn a strange act of personal immorality: getting one's neighbor drunk in order to "gaze on their nakedness" (2:15; cf. Gen 9:20-27). Some have proposed emending the Hebrew *mesape'akh* ("pouring out") to *missaph* ("from the cup"; e.g., Roberts 1991, 115; cf. KJV, NIV), but the MT is supported by the versions and by 1QpHab 11.2. However, it is not wine that the accused pours out, but "his wrath" (2:15). The Hebrew *khemah* ("wrath") can describe the heat or glow felt from drinking wine (Hos 7:5), which would support the idea that this is after all ordinary wine used in an act aimed at personal humiliation. Nevertheless, the use of the plural ("*their* nakedness") reveals that this is not an isolated act of mischief; indeed, 1QpHab 11.2 has *r'yhw*, "his neighbors," rather than the MT *re'ehu*, "his neighbor." This is an act against the community, not against individuals. Further, 2:17 describes violence and devastation done "to the earth": here including the natural world (the forests of Lebanon and the wild animals) as well as "cities and all who live in them." The communal, indeed global, character of the offense makes it plain that imperial Babylon is the target.

Once the target is clarified, the offense also becomes clear. As we have seen, drunkenness can function as a metaphor for the shame of military defeat (cf. the discussion of Nah 1:10 and 3:11). The woe condemns the victors for bringing shame upon the vanquished. What might it mean, then, that Babylon makes its neighbors drink "in order to gaze on their nakedness" (2:15)? A clear parallel to this passage is Lamentations 4:21, where Edom, which had rejoiced at Jerusalem's shame, is grimly assured, "to you also the cup shall pass; / you shall become drunk and strip yourself bare." Similarly, Ezekiel 23 employs both drunkenness and stripping to depict God's judgment upon Samaria and Jerusalem. The reference is likely to the practice, common in the ancient Near East, of sexually humiliating prisoners of war by stripping them naked (Smith-Christopher 2005, 154; cf. the discussion of Nah 3:4-7).

God has used Babylon to punish Judah (cf. 1:12), but this does not mean that Babylon will escape punishment for its crimes. Habakkuk pronounces a woe upon the invader and declares,

> You will be sated with contempt instead of glory.
> Drink, you yourself, and stagger!
> The cup in the LORD's right hand
> will come around to you,
> and shame will come upon your glory! (2:16).

Instead of "stagger," the MT of 2:16 has "be circumcised [?]" (Heb., *wehe'arel*); *Tg. Neb.* renders this as "be naked" (cf. KJV, NIV). The NRSV reading "stagger" follows the LXX, which has *diasaleutheti kai seistheti* ("stumble and stagger"), evidently reading *wehera'el* ("stagger") instead of *wehe'arel* (cf. Aquila, the Syriac, and the Vulgate). As this is indeed the reading that 1QpHab 11.9 has (*whr'l*), we do best to emend the text accordingly. Babylon as well will drink from "[t]he cup in the LORD's right hand," and become shamefully, staggeringly drunk.

God's cup is a biblical image of judgment and suffering. Psalm 75:8 describes God's judgment as "a cup with foaming wine, well mixed" from which the wicked must drink (cf. Ps 11:6, where judgment is instead poured out upon the wicked). Ezekiel 23:31-34 describes Babylon's assault on

Jerusalem as "a cup of horror and desolation" (Ezek 23:33) that the LORD has given Jerusalem to drink—the same cup, indeed, from which Samaria had drunk. Similarly, Jeremiah 25:15-29 refers to "this cup of the wine of wrath" (Jer 25:15) in God's hand from which the nations must drink (cf. Jer 49:12, where Ammon drinks the cup); indeed, Babylon itself is called "a gold cup in the LORD's hand, making all the earth drunken" (Jer 51:7). Isaiah 51:17-23 assures Jerusalem, who has "drunk at the hand of the LORD the cup of his wrath" (51:17), that the time of punishment is now ended: "See, I have taken from your hand the cup of staggering; / you shall drink no more from the bowl of my wrath" (Isa 51:22).

The bowls of wrath in Revelation 16:1-21 and the gold cup in the hand of Babylon the Great in Revelation 17:1-6 are apocalyptic transformations of this image. Jesus' prayer in Gethsemane also reflects the cup of suffering poured out from God's hand: "My Father, if it is possible, let this cup be taken from me; yet not what I want but what you want" (Matt 26:39; cf. Mark 14:36 and Luke 22:42; as well as Mark 10:38//Matt 20:22). In broad terms, then, the cup of wrath and judgment is in God's hand. Although Babylon's assault represented God's judgment on Judah, Babylon too was subject to God's judgment.

The work of Habakkuk's editors is evident in 2:17. The specific mention of Lebanon recalls the editorial expansion regarding Lebanon in Nahum 1:4 (cf. the discussion of that passage, above), and the reference to Babylon's devastation across the earth reflects knowledge of imperial Babylon's later victories. It is certainly possible, however, that the remainder of this woe could have come from Habakkuk.

Habakkuk 2:18 clearly relates not to the verses preceding it but to the following woe regarding idolatry (2:19-20). Therefore, this verse breaks the pattern of this section, in which each new unit begins with *hoi* ("woe"; "Alas!" in the NRSV). The scribal paragraphing also sets this verse apart, with breaks both before and after it, indicating that the scribes realized its distinctiveness. All of this suggests that 2:18 has been secondarily inserted into its context. The clear allusions to Isaiah 44:9-10 in the verse confirm this impression: the verb *ya'al* ("profit"), the participle *yotsar* ("maker"), and the noun *pesel* ("idol") all appear in both contexts, as does the idea of casting an image (the noun *massekah*, "cast image," in Hab 2:18 derives from the verb *nasak*, "pour out," used in Isa 44:10 for casting an idol). Plainly, then, Habakkuk 2:18 is an addition in the language of Deutero-Isaiah, intended to connect the woe against idolatry in 2:19 to the Babylonian practices described and condemned in Isaiah 44:9-20. In this way, the insertion directs the final woe in the chapter from Judah to Babylon.

Unlike the first four woes, which condemn social injustice, the fifth woe (2:19-20) condemns false worship. This shift, however, need not indicate that the fifth woe is not from Habakkuk. Even when focusing particular attention on one or the other, the prophets never separate right living and right worship (e.g., Amos 2:6-8; Ezek 8:17; cf. also Ps 24). Indeed, the expansion evident in 2:18 presupposes 2:19, making it likely that this woe was already part of the text when the editors reshaped it as part of the Book of the Twelve.

The fifth woe reads:

> Alas for you who say to the wood, "Wake up!"
> to silent stone, "Rouse yourself!"
> Can it teach?
> See, it is gold and silver plated,
> and there is no breath in it at all (2:19).

This verse could be addressed against Babylonian practice (cf. Isa 40:18-20 and 44:9-20, especially 44:9-10, to which the insert at Hab 2:18 certainly alludes). In particular, the reference to attempts to rouse the image to respond and the mocking question "Can it teach?" call to mind Babylonian texts describing the *mis pi* ritual for "opening the mouth" of an idol so that it could serve as a means of communion with the god (Hurowitz 2003, 147–50). Indeed, as Victor Hurowitz observes, these Mesopotamian ritual texts assume that the god-image was "born biologically and not fabricated mechanically" (Hurowitz 2003, 150). The assumption refuted in 2:19—that the idol is a living thing, birthed by the gods rather than made by human hands—may reflect contact with Babylonian practice. There is reason to think that Israel would have encountered this idea long before the exile, however. For example, in the story of the golden calf, Aaron claims that the image formed itself: "I threw it [i.e., the gold jewelry the people had given him] into the fire, and out came this calf!" (Exod 32:24). Intriguingly, a variety of Jewish legends hold that Aaron was telling the truth: that the image, whether deliberately or accidentally, formed itself by magical means, and even that the calf had come forth alive from the flames (cited by Hurowitz 2003, 154–55). The golden calf incident in Exodus clearly condemns idolatry and rejects Aaron's account of the "birth" of the image. Still, Aaron's claim reflects the similar claims made by the artificers of divine images in Mesopotamia. The presence of this idea in Habakkuk need not argue for a late date, then; nor need it require that this final woe be directed against foreign practice. Indeed, the parallel of wood and stone in 2:19 recalls a formula designating idolatrous worship in Deuteronomy: to "serve other gods . . . of wood and stone"

(Deut 4:28; 28:38, 64; cf. also 29:17, and Ezek 20:32). In these contexts, worshiping "wood and stone" is a practice by which Israel becomes "like the nations." In contrast, the woe condemning idolatry addresses the practice, not a particular group; it rejects Judean and Babylonian idolatry alike as dangerous foolishness.

The living God experienced in Israel's worship stands in sharp contrast to dead idols in which "there is no breath" (2:19). Habakkuk 2:20, which affirms God's presence in the Jerusalem temple and its liturgy, also returns us once more to the contrast between the faithful persistence of the righteous, who will find vindication, and the woeful arrogance of the wicked, who will be overthrown. The opening clause ("The LORD is in his holy temple") quotes Psalm 11:4, which depicts God's judgment of "the wicked and the righteous" (Ps 11:5); intriguingly, in this psalm the wicked receive "fire and sulfur" and "scorching wind" as "the portion of their cup" (Ps 11:6; cf. Hab 2:15-17), while the "the upright shall behold his face" (Ps 11:7). The second clause of this verse, "let all the earth keep silence before him!" (2:20), assumes a setting before God's throne of judgment. Thus, Zephaniah 1:7 reads, "Be silent before the Lord GOD! For the day of the LORD is at hand" (cf. Amos 8:3; Zech 2:13). This verse therefore serves both as a fitting close to the five woes and as a hymnic transition to Habakkuk's closing psalm.

Framing Psalm (3:1-19)

While Nahum opens with a psalm (Nah 1:2-11), Habakkuk concludes with a psalm (Hab 3:1-19). The title in 3:1, the liturgical note at the psalm's conclusion (3:19), and the appearance of *selah* in 3:3, 9, 13 (the only use of this enigmatic expression outside the book of Psalms) suggest to many interpreters that this poem had a life apart from this book in the temple liturgy (with, e.g., Rudolph 1975, 239–40). The ascription of the psalm to "Habakkuk the prophet" in 3:1 may be secondary, reflecting the book's scribal superscription (cf. Hab 1:1). Indeed, the LXX ascribes Psalms 145–148 (Ps 146–148 in the MT; Ps 147 divides into two poems [MT 147:1-11 and 12-20] in the LXX) to Haggai and Zechariah (Hiebert 1986, 130). Further, it is intriguing that the psalm is missing from 1QpHab. Could it be that the Qumran community knew of a text of Habakkuk *without* the psalm, or that they sensed that the psalm stood apart from the book proper?

On the other hand, 3:1-19 is undeniably present in other ancient witnesses to the text of Habakkuk. The first century CE versions of the Twelve found at Nahal Khever (8KhevXIIgr) and Wadi Murabba'at (MurXII) include the psalm, as do, of course, the LXX and *Tg. Neb.* Further, as we will see, the psalm in Habakkuk 3 appears to have been reworked, so that an ancient theophanic hymn (3:3-15) has become a prayer for help. Perhaps, as in Nahum, the inclusion and adaptation of this poem reflect the work of Habakkuk's editors (Hiebert 1986, 137–39; 1996, 652–55; Nogalski 1993b, 134). Certainly, in the final form of the text, these two psalms function as a frame around Nahum and Habakkuk (cf. the discussions in the Introduction, and in "Habakkuk and Nahum," above). But Habakkuk 3 seems at odds with the editorial expansions in Habakkuk 1–2. These expansions confirm God's judgment upon Babylon, so that, like Nahum's declaration of judgment upon Nineveh, the word of Babylon's demise in Habakkuk prefigures the coming Day of the LORD (e.g., Hab 1:6). In contrast, Habakkuk 3 expresses concern about God's seeming absence, although defiantly declaring God's faithfulness in the face of tragedy:

> Though the fig tree does not blossom,
> and no fruit is on the vines;
> though the produce of the olive fails
> and the fields yield no food;
> though the flock is cut off from the fold
> and there is no herd in the stalls,
> yet I will rejoice in the LORD;
> I will exult in the God of my salvation (Hab 3:18).

This message, while in tension with the position of Habakkuk's editors, is perfectly consistent with the message here proposed for the original prophecy. Evidence for assigning the adaptation of this ancient psalm to Habakkuk rather than to his editors may be found in 3:17, where the prophet resolves to praise God "though the flock is cut off [Heb., *gazar*] from the fold." The verb *gazar* is not common, appearing only twelve times in the Hebrew Bible. The oldest meaning of the word seems to be "cut in two" (1 Kgs 3:25-26; Ps 136:13; notably *gezarim*, a noun used in Gen 15:17 for the severed halves of the animals in Abraham's ritual and in Ps 136:13 for the divided parts of the Red Sea, is related to this root) or "cut down" (2 Kgs 6:4). Ezekiel 37:11, Lamentations 3:54, and Isaiah 53:8, which all come from the exilic period, use *gazar* in an abstract sense for the separation of death (cf. also Ps 88:5). Late texts use *gazar* in contexts where earlier texts would use *karat* ("cut"). Thus, 2 Chronicles 26:21 records that King Uzziah was "excluded [*nigzar*, that is, "cut off"] from the house of the LORD" due to his leprosy; priestly law (e.g., Lev. 7:20-21; 17:10-11; 18:29; 19:8; 20:5-6) uses *karat* ("cut off") for expulsion from the worshiping congregation. Esther 2:1 and Job 22:28 both use *gazar* for issuing a decree, again reminiscent of *karat*, often used for making a covenant (e.g., Deut 29:11; 1 Kgs 8:9; Hag 2:5). Habakkuk's use of *gazar* for sheep missing from the fold—presumably lost, stolen, or dead—is closest to the exilic usage cited above; indeed, those passages presuppose the sense of *gazar* found in Habakkuk, rather than the original sense of the term. We will propose that the prophet himself reworked this psalm and included it as the conclusion of his prophecy.

The psalm in Habakkuk 3 is titled "A prayer (Heb., *tephillah*) of the prophet Habakkuk according to Shigionoth" (Hab 3:1). This pattern (*'al* ["according to"] followed by what seems to be a song title) occurs sixteen times in the titles of Psalms to indicate musical accompaniment for the psalm or a tune to which the poem may be sung (cf. Pss 6, 8, 9, 12, 22, 45, 46, 53, 56, 60, 62, 69, 77, 81, 84, 88). These notations do not appear in the last two books of the Hebrew Psalter; indeed, all but four are found in Books One and Two (sometimes referred to as the Davidic psalter; cf. Ps 72:20), suggesting that such titles may reflect an older tradition in the composition of the Psalter. The word *tephillah* ("prayer") likewise appears predominantly in the Psalter (32 of its 77 occurrences are in this book); in the prophets, it appears only in Isaiah (1:15; 37:4//2 Kgs 19:4; 38:5//2 Kgs 20:5; 56:7), Jeremiah (7:16; 11:14), Jonah 2:7, and here in Habakkuk 3:1. The use of this word in Jonah is particularly intriguing, as Jonah 2:3-10, like Habakkuk 3, is often regarded as an originally independent psalm secondarily incorporated into its context (e.g., Nogalski 1993b, 265; Trible 1996, 464–65; Jack Sasson, while reading the poem in continuity with the prose of Jonah, nonetheless recognizes its distinctiveness and does not claim that it was composed for its place in the book [Sasson 1990, 165]).

Following the KJV, the NRSV simply transliterates the Hebrew *shigyonot*, proposing no translation for this obscure term (cf. NJPS, NIV). Two poems in Scripture are designated as *shigyonot*: Habakkuk 3 and Psalm 7, called in the NRSV "A Shiggaion of David." The LXX renders the term as "psalm" (*psalmos* in Ps 7; cf. the Vulgate *psalmus*) or "song" (*odes* in Hab 3:1); similarly Koehler-Baumgartner, declaring arguments from derivation and context alike to be inconclusive, says only that *shiggayon* is "a technical term for a specific type of cultic song" (*HALOT* 2000, 1414).

Many scholars, however, have attempted to identify the etymology and meaning of this term. Some propose that *shiggayon* is related to Hebrew *shagah* ("stray, stagger, do wrong") and translate the term as "an enthusiastic, rambling, or ecstatic song" (e.g., Sellin 1930, 406, who emphasizes the ecstatic, visionary character of the poem in its context in Habakkuk, and Dahood 1965, 41, who renders *shiggayon* as "dithyramb": a wild, ecstatic song [the term originally related to the worship of Dionysus]). Evidently assuming the same root but a different meaning, the Vulgate reads *shigyonot* in Habakkuk 3:1 as *ignorantionibus* ("errors," or perhaps "ignorances"; cf. *Tg. Neb.* and the Greek translations of Aquila, Symmachus, and Theodotion); significantly, in Jerome's Psalter translated from the Hebrew rather than the Greek, a similar reading is found in the title of Psalm 7.

The most probable derivation for *shiggayon* is from the Akkadian *shigu*, a term for penitential prayer (with Seux 1981, 438). This interpretation may be strengthened by its pairing in 3:1 with *tephillah*, a term often used in prayers for help found in the Psalter (e.g., Ps 4:2 [1]; 17:1; 54:4 [2]; 55:2 [1]; 61:2 [1]). The reading "penitential prayer" fits well with Psalm 7, which is indeed a prayer for help (cf. Ps 7:4-6 [3-5]). Unfortunately, it does not seem, at least initially, to describe Habakkuk 3. Like its parallel in Nahum 1, this poem is a hymnic depiction of the LORD as the divine warrior manifest in the storm. The opening verse of the psalm seems atypical, however. Rather than calling upon the community to join in praise, this verse contrasts the action of God in the following psalm with the poet's present circumstance: "In our own time revive it; / in our own time make it known; / in wrath may you remember mercy" (3:2).

There is also a clear shift in Habakkuk 3:16, not only grammatically (from second-person descriptions of God's activity in 3:8-15 to a first-person account of the poet's experience in 3:16-19) but also thematically. The poet confesses that the power of the LORD described in this psalm elicits not confidence but confusion and bewildered disappointment. Why would such a God fail to act against Babylon? While in Psalm 7 the LORD wields the LORD's weaponry against the enemy in response to the psalmist's prayer (Ps 7:12-16), Habakkuk sees no evidence of God's activity but must instead sigh and wait "for the day of calamity to come upon the people who attack us" (Hab 3:16). These additions transform the poem into a prayer for help. A comparable transformation of an older hymn for a new situation is Psalm 89, which reads like a royal song praising God for God's faithfulness manifest in the eternal preservation of David's line, until v. 38, when the tone abruptly shifts:

> But now you have spurned and rejected him;
> you are full of wrath against your anointed.
> You have renounced the covenant with your servant;
> you have defiled his crown in the dust (Ps 89:38-39).

Just as the fall of Jerusalem and the end of kingship prompted the psalmist to respond to the confidence of Psalm 89:1-7 with an anguished protest, so the threat not merely of punishment but of annihilation by Babylon prompts Habakkuk to revise the ancient theophanic hymn in 3:3-15. If this reading is correct, then Habakkuk himself may be responsible for designating this poem a *shiggayon.*

The book of Habakkuk concludes with a dedication and a musical instruction pertaining to this psalm: "To the choirmaster: with stringed instruments" (3:19b). Apart from the end of Habakkuk, the dedication *lamnatseakh* (rendered "To the choirmaster" in the NRSV of Hab 3:19 and "To the leader" in the Psalms) appears only in the Psalter (55 times; the term *menatsekhim,* "overseers," occurs in 2 Chr 2:1, 17; 34:13). The word *binginotay* ("with stringed instruments") also appears only here and in the Psalms, always following *lamnatseakh* (five times; cf. Pss 4; 6; 55; 67; 76); indeed, in every instance apart from Habakkuk, these expressions appear in the title of a psalm. Based on the colophons in Akkadian literature, which are placed at the end of a work rather than the beginning, Haim Gevaryahu has argued that biblical colophons also were originally found at the end of texts (as in Hab 3:19), and have been moved to the beginning by editors (Gevaryahu 1975). Bruce Waltke, though unpersuaded by Gevaryahu's alleged Akkadian parallels, also regards Habakkuk 3 as "the parade example" for the original pattern, which he finds both in the cognate literature and in Scripture apart from the Psalms (cf. Isa 38:9-10), of "compositional elements, genre classification, and author in the superscriptions, and matters pertaining to performance, preservation, and collections in the postscripts" (Waltke 1991, 595; Waltke proposes that the original *lamnatseach* postscripts were shifted to the following psalms by scribal error [Waltke 1991, 594]). In either case, the presence of this postscript in Habakkuk 3:19 provides further evidence for the antiquity of the original psalm (so Hiebert 1986, 141–42).

In the MT, the scribes divide the poem in Habakkuk 3 into three parts: 3:1-7, God's march from the south; vv. 8-13, God's manifestation in the storm; and vv. 14-19, God's ancient victory and the poet's situation in contrast. We should note, however, another system of division evident in the text itself, based on the expression *selah.* Apart from Habakkuk, this expression appears only in Psalms, where it occurs seventy times. In Habakkuk 3, *selah* appears at the middle of v. 3, the middle of v. 9, and the end of v. 13. Both the meaning and the derivation of this term are obscure: *selah* may indicate a change of pitch, a pause, an instrumental interlude, or a coda. Still, it functions in the Psalms to mark a transition from one section to another. Habakkuk 3:3-15, where *selah* appears, is also the section in which "[t]he archaic features of the poetry are concentrated" (Roberts 1991, 148, though like Albright [1950, 8–9] he regards the poem as composed by Habakkuk based on older texts); thematically, these are the verses that describe God as the divine warrior victorious over unruly water. In short, it seems likely that the term *selah* reflects the structure of the original psalm prior to its incorporation into this book: the title/call to praise in 3:3a, the depiction of God's warlike advance in 3:3b-9a, the storm theophany in 3:9b-13, and the announcement of God's victory in 3:14-15.

Habakkuk 3:1-7 takes the reader from the psalm title in v. 1 through the description of the divine warrior's march from the south, to which the poet is a witness (3:7). At first, the poem seems to begin, like the typical hymn, with praise: "O LORD, I have heard of your renown, and I stand in awe, O LORD, of your work" (3:2). Yet a contrast is swiftly apparent between the speaker in this opening verse, who has only *heard* of the LORD's renown, and the poet in the ancient hymn, who says, "I *saw* the tents of Cushan under affliction; the tent-curtains of the land of Midian trembled" (3:7, emphasis mine). In Job's response to the LORD's appearance in the whirlwind, he says, "I had heard of you by the hearing of the ear, but now my eye sees you" (Job 42:5). In contrast, the speaker in 3:2 has *only* heard, and has not seen, as the remainder of this verse makes clear: he prays for God to manifest Godself here and now, and prays, "in your wrath remember mercy" (3:2; cf. the plea for moderation in judgment in 1:12-13). Similarly, Isaiah 64:1-3 reflects the dissonance between the traditional stories of God's saving acts and God's apparent absence from the contemporary world: "O that you would tear open the heavens and come down" (Isa 64:1). The reference to hearing in Habakkuk 3:2 parallels the statement in 3:16, "I hear, and I tremble within" (so Roberts 1991, 149), bracketing the original poem in 3:3-15 and also expressing neatly the theme of the poem in its final form: I have heard of God's mighty acts of salvation, but where is God now? No answer is given; Habakkuk's solution is paradoxically to affirm God's presence in a world from which God appears to be absent (3:17-19). A Christian reader may think of Jesus' words to Thomas in John 20:29: "Blessed are those who have not seen and yet have come to believe."

The expression rendered "in our own time" in the NRSV (used two times in 3:2) reads literally "in the midst of years" (Heb., *beqereb shanim*), and is found nowhere else. The LXX, as well as a late first-second century CE Greek translation of Habakkuk 3 from Alexandria called the "Barberini version" (Good 1959, 28–30; Bucur and Mueller 2011, 91–92; though Good holds that Barberini and the LXX are conflated in 3:1-2 [Good 1959, 12]), render this phrase in its first occurrence (NRSV "in our own time revive it") as "between the two living creatures," reading *shanim* ("years") as *shtayim* ("two") and the verb *khayyehu* ("revive") as the noun *khayyot* ("living creatures"). While it may be that the LXX translators, as Origen proposed (cf. the discussion in Bucur and Mueller 2011, 92–94), were thinking here of the mercy seat with its two cherubim, between which the LORD appeared to Moses and Aaron (e.g., Exod 25:18-22; so Origen, *Comm. Rom.* 3.8.2-8), or of the seraphim in Isaiah 6 (so Origen, *Princ.* 1.3.4), it is more likely that they have in mind the living creatures accompanying the Glory in Ezekiel's visions (significantly, the same Greek word, *zoon*, is used in the LXX of Hab 3:2 and to translate the Hebrew *khayyah* ["living creature"] in Ezek 1:5, 13, 14, 19-20, 22; 3:13; 10:15, 20; cf. Bucur and Mueller 2011, 96–99). At any rate, Christian interpreters from Tertullian to the Venerable Bede found reference here to Jesus' Transfiguration appearance with Moses and Elijah (Bucur and Mueller 2011, 94–95). Theodoret of Cyrus finds reference rather "to lives, the present and the future, between which the just Judge appears" (Hill 2006, 200). While the interpreter of Habakkuk should be attentive to the rich interpretive history of the LXX, it is better to stay with the Hebrew, which, while difficult, is meaningful: *beqereb shanim*, rendered in the NJPS as "in these years," could be aptly paraphrased "right now." The prophet longs for God to manifest God's power clearly and unmistakably against oppression in his own day, as God did in times past.

Habakkuk 3:3-7 is rich in ancient themes and vocabulary. The psalmist declares, "God came from Teman, the Holy One from Mount Paran" (3:3); he is manifest among "the tents of Cushan" and in "the land of Midian" (3:7). The location of Teman is uncertain, though the name is consistently used in reference to Edom, a nation to the southeast of Judah (cf. Gen 36:11,15, 35, 42[//1 Chr 1:36, 45, 53]; Jer 49:7, 20; Ezek 25:13; Amos 1:12; Obad 9; Job 2:11; 4:1; 15:1; 22:1; 42:7, 9). Paran refers to a site in the Sinai wilderness; Mount Paran likely is a poetic reference to Mount Sinai, the mountain of God (cf. Deut 33:2, which also says that the LORD "dawned from Seir [i.e., Edom]"). The LXX renders this as "the dark, shady mountain" (though Barberini has *Pharan*; cf. Good 1959, 12–13). Theodoret (Hill 2006, 200) and Irenaeus (*Haer.* 4.33.11) interpret this as predicting Jesus' birth in Bethlehem, to the south of the "shady mountain," that is, Zion. Cushan is mentioned only here; the LXX has "Ethiopia," evidently reading "Cush" (e.g., Jer 46:9; Ezek 29:10), while *Tg. Neb.* assumes the reference is to Cushan-rishathaim ("Cushan the Doubly Wicked"), an enemy of Israel in Judges 3:7-11 (*Tg. Neb.* reads "Cushan the Sinner" in both places). Nevertheless, given the reference to tents, and the parallel with the "land of Midian" (the Midianites were a coalition of Arab tribes associated particularly with the Sinai; e.g., Gen 37:28, 36; Exod 2:15-16), Cushan was probably an otherwise unknown Arab tribe. As in most ancient songs of the divine warrior, then, God marches into battle out of the south (cf. Deut 33:2-3; Judg 5:4-5).

The NRSV and NIV of 3:4 imagine the light accompanying God's appearing as a sunrise: however, the word "sun" does not appear in this verse. Indeed, as the following verses show, this psalm depicts God not as the sun but as the approaching storm. Gregory of Nazianzus, who sees Habakkuk 3 as a vision of the risen Christ, writes of this theophany: "behold a man riding on the clouds and he is very high, and his countenance is like the countenance of an angel, and his vesture is like the brightness of piercing lightning" (*Orat.* 45:1, cited by Bucur and Mueller 2011, 99). The reference to the "rays" (Heb., *qarnayim,* literally "two horns") coming from God's hand makes the image clear: God manifest in the storm wields a forked lightning bolt as a weapon (so Roberts 1991, 128). The "brilliant light" (NJPS; Heb., *wenogah ka'or*) of God's manifestation is the lightning flash (with Roberts 1991, 134; cf. Job 36:30, 32; 37:11, 15).

Continuing the image of God's warlike advance is the depiction of God's retinue. While the NRSV and NJPS alike read "pestilence" and "plague" in 3:5 as though describing ordinary diseases, it is better to capitalize these as Pestilence and Plague personified, or to leave them untranslated, as divine names: *Deber* and *Resheph* (cf. Hiebert 1986, 4, 92–94; del Olmo Lete 1999, 232; Xella 1999, 703). Similarly, in the Babylonian creation epic *Enuma 'elish,* when Marduk goes into battle against the sea monster Tiamat, he is flanked by fearsome warrior demons: "On his right he posted *Smiter,* fearsome in battle, / On the left the Combat, which repels all the zealous" (Speiser 1969, 660; cf. del Olmo Lete 1999, 232). That a retinue of divine beings accompanies the warrior God may be surprising to us, but while later traditions in the Old Testament are uncompromisingly monotheistic, worshiping a unique and singular God (e.g., Isa 45:5-7), earlier traditions rather stress Israel's exclusive devotion to the LORD above all gods. For example, the Ten Commandments reject the worship of other gods, not because there *are* no other gods but because "I the LORD your God am a jealous God" (Exod 20:5//Deut 5:9; cf. the discussion of Nah 1:2, above). Even the Shema, Israel's ancient confession of faith, is more about Israel's absolute allegiance to the LORD than it is about how many gods there are: "Hear, O Israel: The LORD is our God, the LORD alone" (Deut 6:4 in NRSV and NJPS; compare the traditional rendering in the KJV, "Hear, O Israel: The LORD our God, the LORD is one"). The other heavenly beings are not worshiped but are assigned a role in the cosmos. According to the ancient Song of Moses (Deut 32:1-43), "When the Most High apportioned the nations, when he divided humankind, he fixed the boundaries of the peoples according to the number of the gods" (Deut 32:8). The NRSV here reads *bene 'elohim*, "sons of the gods," with 4QDeutj, our oldest witness to the text of Deuteronomy from Qumran; the LXX "angels of God" also assumes this reading. The meaning of this passage is clear: God set Israel apart as God's own special, particular possession (Deut 32:9) and apportioned the other nations among the *bene 'elohim*—a notion so offensive to later monotheistic scribes that they altered the text to read "according to the number of the sons of *Israel*" (the MT reads "*bene Yisra'el*"; cf. the KJV and NIV). In Job 2:1, the expression *bene 'elohim* is used for "the heavenly beings"—including *hassatan*, the Accuser—who "present themselves before the LORD." Likewise, in Habakkuk 3:5, *Deber* and *Resheph*, or Pestilence and Plague, are terrible heavenly beings, marching alongside their lord as God goes into battle.

The description in 3:6 of the earth shaken, nations trembling, and mountains shattered at God's advance recalls Nahum 1:5-6; here as there, it is typical of the storm theophany (cf. Judg 5:4-5; Ps 18:7-15; Theodoret of Cyrus understands this with reference to the earthquake associated with Jesus' crucifixion in Matt 27:51 [Hill 2006, 201]). The emphasis on antiquity in this verse ("eternal mountains," "ancient pathways," "everlasting hills") recalls the divine warrior's defeat of chaos and establishment of order at the dawn of time (cf. 3:8-11). God also acts before the psalmist's eyes, however: "I saw the tents of Cushan under affliction; / the tent-curtains of the land of Midian trembled" (3:7). The phrase rendered "under affliction" in the NRSV (Heb., *takhat 'awen*) appears nowhere else; it is oddly placed at the beginning of the verse, and is omitted by Barberini (Good 1959, 14). Some interpreters propose that it belongs to the former verse and suggest that the MT is a corruption of *tekhate'nah*, from a conjectured root *khata'* ("crushed"?) otherwise unknown in Hebrew, but found in Ugaritic, Akkadian, and Arabic (so Heibert 1986, 21–22; Albright, 1950, 11, 14–15; *HALOT* 2000, 363). The LXX, however, seems to be trying to make sense of the text as we have it. The Hebrew is meaningful, if unusual; the point is that God's advance in the storm threatens the tents of Cushan (cf. NRSV; NIV; NJPS).

Habakkuk 3:8-13 opens with a question: "Was your wrath against the rivers, O LORD?" This seems an odd question to a modern reader: why would God be angry with a body of water? In the ancient Near East, however, the creation of the world was often imagined as the imposition of order upon chaos, brought about by the victory of the creator god over the personifications of unruly water. Thus, in the Babylonian myth Marduk defeated Tiamat ("Salt Water"), while in old Canaan Ba'al defeated *Yamm/Nahar*, or "Prince Sea, Judge River." Indeed, the form *neharim* ("rivers") is unusual;

the plural of *nahar* is usually *naharot*. This suggests that the Hebrew originally read *naharayim*: that is, "two rivers," used in Canaanite myth for the dwelling of the high god 'El "at the source of the twin rivers, by the pools of the double-deep" (Tuell 2000, 180; cf. Roberts 1991, 137–38; Hiebert 1986, 23). As in 3:5, then, it is best either to capitalize "Rivers" and "Sea" (cf. footnotes in NRSV) or leave them untranslated (cf. NJPS). The fact, however, that this verse takes the form of a question raises the possibility that God's opponent is not after all the mythic monsters of River and Sea. The resolution of that riddle is left for 3:13. In the meantime, the poet describes the divine warrior's power manifest in the storm. God rides into battle, leading the heavenly chariotry (3:8; cf. 2 Kgs 2:11-12; 6:17; 7:6; 13:14; 23:11; Zech 6:1-8; Ps 68:18 [17]; cf. also the depictions of the LORD riding on the storm, e.g. Ps 18:9-12 [10-13], and the depiction of the wheeled throne of the LORD in Ezek 1 and Dan 7) and wielding a bow against the enemy (3:9; for God's bow and arrows, see also e.g., Gen 9:12-17; Ps 18:14, and compare *Enuma 'elish* Tablet 4.100-104; Speiser 1969, 67).

The MT of 3:9a is difficult, as the awkward rendering of the NJPS, "Sworn are the rods of your word (?)," demonstrates. In Hebrew, this clause concludes with three nouns in a row, *shebu'ot mattot 'omer*: mechanistically, "oaths staves speech." The word *matteh* ("staff") can also refer to a tribe, so *Tg. Neb.* and the Vulgate understand this phrase to refer to the power of God's sworn oath to the tribes (cf. KJV); however, nothing is said before or after this of God's oath or of the tribes. Staying with the imagery of God's warlike advance, in parallel with the bow and in keeping with the Syriac and the Barberini version (*bolis*, "missile"; Good 1959, 15), it is best to read *mattot* as referring to arrow shafts (with NRSV and NIV). Similarly, *shebu'ot* seems likely to be a corruption of *sibba'ta*, from *saba'*, "be satiated," so that the LORD sates his arrows with the lives of the slain (with Barberini, *echortasas* ["filled, satisfied;" Good 1959, 15]; so, e.g., Hiebert 1986, 26–27; Roberts 1991, 139; NRSV). All the versions presuppose the last word in this phrase, *'omer*, though it is difficult to determine what it might mean in context. The LXX adds the divine name and reads it as a verb: "says the LORD" (cf. NIV, which also reads this word as a verb: "you called for many arrows"). Syriac and *Tg. Neb.* stay with the noun but add "your" (so NRSV, NJPS). Barberini has "his quiver" (Good 1959, 15). Other interpreters despair of making any sense of this word and either understand it as a gloss based on the mistaken reading "oaths" or as a corruption of *yeter* or *metar* ("bowstring"; cf. Hiebert 1986, 140; Roberts 1991, 139–40). The NRSV "sated were the arrows at your command" is as close as we are likely to come to deciphering this obscure poetic line.

The earth, the mountains, Sun, and Moon (again, best regarded as personified heavenly powers; cf. footnotes in NRSV) witness God's victory. The opponent God comes to vanquish is now made clear, however. It is not after all against cosmic, mythic enemies that God marches to battle, but against earthly, historical ones:

> In fury you trod the earth,
> in anger you trampled nations.
> You came forth to save your people,
> to save your anointed (3:12-13).

Instead of coming to crush the head of the chaos monster (cf. Ps 74:13-14), God comes to crush "the head of the wicked house" (3:13). The juxtaposition of God's power as creator and God's deliverance from historical oppressors is a very old idea. The Song of the Sea, perhaps the oldest text in Scripture (Exod 15:1-18), relates God's victory over the Sea directly to God's defeat of earthly oppressors—specifically, Pharaoh (Exod 15:4). Similarly, in the ancient Song of Deborah (Judg 5:2-31), God marches out of the south and manifests Godself in the storm to defeat the forces of Sisera. Indeed, Nahum 1:4, too, juxtaposes the exodus out of Egypt and God's creative power to express God's triumph over Assyria (cf. also Isa 51:9-11). The divine warrior who comes in the storm comes to deliver!

The ancient poem reaches its climax with the dual assertion of God's power over the earthly oppressor, who falls pierced by his own arrows (3:14), and over cosmic chaos: "You trampled the sea with your horses, / churning the mighty waters" (3:15). In the poem as it now stands, however, reflection on God's sovereign power leads not to praise but to confusion. Habakkuk's response to this paean to divine power (3:16) is sometimes understood positively: the prophet is overwhelmed by God's glory (e.g., Achtemeier 1986, 53–54; Roberts 1991, 157). Yet the language of the verse does not support such an optimistic take on the passage. Elsewhere, the verb used for "trembling" (Heb., *ragaz*) refers to panic at the approach of a foe (Deut 2:25; 2 Sam 18:33), to overwhelming grief (2 Sam 18:33), to shame (Prov 29:9), or to divine judgment (Isa 5:25; Jer 33:9; 50:34; Ezek 16:43); it is not used anywhere else for a faithful person's response to a theophany. Rottenness of the bones, similarly, refers elsewhere to overwhelming shame (Prov 12:4; 14:3). In short, the prophet's response to this poem is not exaltation and awe, but shame and terror. Indeed, Habakkuk's description of his own reaction—shaky, weak, lips numb and trembling—sounds as though the prophet is in shock!

The reason for this reaction takes us back to the theodicy dialogue in 1:1-17 and to God's message of destruction in 2:1-3. The Babylonian assault does not resolve Habakkuk's original complaint against the violence he sees in Judah, abetted by its corrupt or incompetent leaders. Indeed, Babylon brings more violence and oppression! God's response to the prophet's complaint, when it comes, offers no hope: this is indeed the end for Judah. Therefore, Habakkuk lives in a disconnect between the traditional language of his faith, which affirms God as victorious over all oppression, and his own experience. Although he longs for vengeance, he will never see it: Babylon of course would fall, but that day was a lifetime off. Meanwhile, Habakkuk says, "I wait quietly for the day of calamity to come upon the people who attack us" (3:17).

The honesty of the prophet's language before God may be startling to us, although it is typical of the prophets and of the psalmists (e.g., Ps 3:8 [7]; Jer 11:20). Significantly, Habakkuk does not stay with that anger. He resolves to worship God, despite his circumstances. In the face of famine, hardship, and loss, Habakkuk declares, "yet I will rejoice in the LORD; I will exult in the God of my salvation" (3:18). Similarly, the apostle Paul wrote to the church at Rome, "For I am convinced that neither death, nor life, nor angels, nor rulers, nor things present, nor things to come, nor powers, nor height, nor depth, nor anything else in all creation, will be able to separate us from the love of God in Christ Jesus our Lord" (Rom 8:38-39). In an uncertain world, where sometimes the worst thing that could happen does indeed happen, God's love is the only security we can have. Yet generations of believers affirm that that is the only security we truly need.

Engaging in honest prayer and determined praise proves effective: Habakkuk does experience God's presence in the midst of his trouble. He affirms "GOD, the Lord, is my strength; / he makes my feet like the feet of a deer, / and makes me tread upon the heights" (Hab 3:19). In keeping with the Wisdom tradition (e.g., 1 Kgs 4:33; Prov 30:24-28), meditation on the natural world has brought the prophet to a profound spiritual insight, yielding a powerful poetic image securely lodged in Jewish and Christian devotional practice. A deer can make its way through seemingly impassible terrain. Although the prophet can see no way through the obstacles that lie before him, or over the precipices that rise to cover him, he trusts that God has given him feet like a deer, to carry him through his times. This is surely a worthy closing prayer: that God will give us as well the courage to meet whatever obstacles lie ahead and the resolve to make our way through, confident that, seen or unseen, God is with us.

In the Vulgate, Habakkuk's psalm is titled *oratio Abacuc prophetae pro ignorationibus*: "a speech of the prophet Habakkuk on behalf of his errors," or perhaps, "his ignorances." Although this translation of the Hebrew *shiggayon* is unlikely, the Latin title is nonetheless evocative. To be sure, this poem *does* address our ignorance: what do we do when God's will and way are unclear, when indeed God seems absent from our world? The Book of the Twelve as a whole holds fast to the promise that the Day of the Lord will come one day, and with it a clear resolution to our present conflicts, but Habakkuk is concerned with what we are to do meanwhile: how are we to live today, in the midst of the struggle? The answer Habakkuk offers is therefore existential, not theological (Gowan 1976, 10–11). Although God's justice will prevail, we ourselves may not see it. Therefore, in the meantime, we must reject the counsel of despair, and with Habakkuk, resolve to praise God despite our circumstances. Don Gowan's last word on this passage captures its power: "We cannot explain why we must endure it all. But we know that we do not endure it alone, for God comes, as Habakkuk learned, and he suffers it with us, as the Cross reveals" (Gowan 1976, 91).

Zephaniah

Reading Zephaniah

The central theme of the book of Zephaniah is the day of the Lord, depicted as "a day of wrath" (1:15; cf. 1:18; 2:2-3; O'Brien 2004, 86). Some Christians, contrasting an alleged Old Testament "God of wrath" with the New Testament "God of love," complain that wrath is the theme of the *entire* Hebrew Bible. Of course, this canard holds some truth: the oldest images of God in Scripture, as we have seen, are of God as a warrior, pouring out wrath on God's enemies (cf. Exod 15:1-18; Judg 5:1-31). Yet God's love and grace also feature prominently in the Hebrew Bible (e.g., Zeph 3:14-15), while divine wrath is found in the New Testament as well (e.g., Rev 16:1-11, which features wrath by the bowlful!). We cannot avoid the "God of wrath" unless we manage our Bible reading very carefully.

Still, we must approach this topic with care and caution. Otherwise, it is far too easy for us to read God's wrath simplistically and naively onto the tragedies and vicissitudes of life: God saved us because we are good; God injured them because they are bad. Too often, those who preach the wrath of God are all too certain that they know the *mind* of God and can identify the targets of God's wrath. The message of God's wrath then becomes a message of self-vindication that legitimates contempt, even violence, toward others. But the wrath of God is not a weapon for us to wield, as though God were our tool. Rather, God's wrath reminds us that God is *God* and does as God chooses.

Zephaniah uses the concept of God's wrath in ways that may surprise us. Zephaniah 2:1-3 opens a collection of oracles directed against foreign nations, including Assyria, so we might at first think that God directs God's wrath toward outsiders. But the prophet's audience is not the nations; it is his own people in Judah. These oracles expressly address "you humble of the land, who do his commands" (2:3). Thus, the "shameless nation" in 2:1

is not a foreign power but Judah. At the end of this chapter, the prophet moves without transition from an oracle against Nineveh, Assyria's capital (2:13-15), to an oracle concerning the "soiled, defiled, oppressing city" (3:1) of *Jerusalem* (3:1-8)! Further, in Zephaniah, God's wrath calls the community to come together "before there comes upon you the day of the LORD's wrath" (2:2): to seek the LORD in righteousness and humility, so that "perhaps you may be hidden on the day of the LORD's wrath" (2:3). Wrath language, then, serves more as a warning for the faithful than as a condemnation of the faithless.

Similarly, Jesus delivered his message of judgment not to the Romans or to the nations but to fellow Jews: to "insiders." As pastor and author Rob Bell writes, "Jesus did not use hell to try and compel 'heathens' and 'pagans' to believe in God, so they wouldn't burn when they die. He talked about hell to very religious people to warn them about the consequences of straying from their God-given calling and identity to show the world God's love" (Bell 2011, 82).

If the biblical message of wrath intends to effect change within the community, then wrath is God's response to our unresponsiveness. This circumstance is evident in the prophets' understanding of the great disasters of Israel's history—from the fall of the northern kingdom to the fall of Jerusalem and the exile—as God's judgment upon Israel for failing to heed God's word. While we may bridle at an oppressed population interpreting its suffering as divine wrath, such self-blame can be a potent strategy for survival. By taking responsibility for its circumstances, a community embraces action rather than despair, hope rather than fatalistic surrender. As Daniel Smith-Christopher observes, in this way oppressed peoples "creatively reinterpret their defeat, and 'dis-empower' their conquerors" (Smith-Christopher 2005, 157).

In personal terms, our suffering may drive us to realize our own inadequacy and vulnerability, and therefore lead us to confession, new life, and deepened faith. As C. S. Lewis wrote, "God whispers to us in our pleasures, speaks to us in our conscience, but shouts in our pains: It is His megaphone to rouse a deaf world" (Lewis 1976, 93). Of course, we can only have this revelatory experience with regard to our *own* pain; we cannot foist it off onto others, declaring that *their* pain is due to God's wrath. Our only legitimate response to the suffering of others is compassion, prompting us to alleviate that suffering as best we can.

Is God indeed a God of wrath? If, as Julia O'Brien succinctly states, "A moral God cares about what happens to the world" (O'Brien 2004, 95), then the answer must be a resounding yes! Rob Bell writes,

> When we hear people saying that they can't believe in a God who gets angry—yes, they can. How should God react to a child being forced into prostitution? How should God feel about a country starving while warlords hoard the food supply? What kind of God wouldn't get angry at a financial scheme that robs thousands of people of their life savings? (Bell 2011, 38)

God's wrath is not opposed to God's love; rather, God is a God of wrath *because* God is a God of love. God's wrath is directed against injustice because God loves justice. God's wrath is directed against oppression because God loves the oppressed. That is what the day of the Lord means—and that, in brief, is Zephaniah's theme.

Authorship, Date, and Setting

The name "Zephaniah" (Heb., *Tsephanyah* and the related form *Tsephanyahu*) is, like many Hebrew names, theophoric: that is, it contains a form of a divine name (in this case, the Name *Yhwh*, commonly rendered by English translations as "the Lord"; cf. the discussion of the Name in Nah 3:5). The derivation of "Zephaniah" is uncertain. It may be related to the verb *tsaphan* ("hide, store"), and mean something like "the Lord has preserved." The LXX renders the name as *Sophonias,* however, suggesting a link to Zaphon, the divinized mountain dwelling of Ba'al in Canaanite myth (Niehr 1999, 928) that Psalm 48:3 (2) associates with Zion (cf. Isa 14:13; Job 26:7; 37:22). In that case, "Zephaniah" would mean "the Lord is Zaphon" (so Sabottka 1972, 1–3). Roberts finds this derivation unlikely, as "personal names that equate Yahweh with another divinity or even with a sacred mountain are hardly well attested" (Roberts 1991, 165). Yet both Joel and Elijah mean "the Lord is 'El," and Psalm 48:15 (14) certainly does equate God with Zion. Further, an association of "Zephaniah" with Zion/Zaphon may account for the use of this name in priestly circles.

Scripture apart from this book mentions at least three different people named "Zephaniah." The first was an ancestor of Heman, a Levitical musician from the clan of Kohath installed in the Jerusalem shrine by David (1 Chr 6:21 [36]). The second was a priest living in the time of Zedekiah, last king in Jerusalem (597–587/6 BCE), called "Zephaniah son of Maaseiah" (Jer 21:1, 29:25, 29; 52:24; cf. 37:3, where the spelling is *Tsephanyahu*); likely, he was the same person as "the second priest [better, "priest of the second order"] Zephaniah" (Heb., *Tsephanyahu*), deported and executed by the king of Babylon (2 Kgs 25:18). As the priests of the second order evidently performed non-sacrificial duties (i.e., "the priests who have charge of the temple" in Ezek 40:45; cf. Tuell 1992, 129–32; 2001, 60–63), this Zephaniah may have been descended from the first. The third Zephaniah, however, was certainly a sacrificial priest, and so a Zadokite, as he was the father of Joshua (Zech 6:10, 14), high priest in Jerusalem in the early years following the exile (c. 520 BCE). We will return to the topic of priestly descent, and the issues pertaining to priesthood in the Judean Restoration, when we turn our attention to Haggai, Zechariah, and Malachi. For now, these links could lead us to expect that the prophet Zephaniah, like Jeremiah (Jer 1:1) and Ezekiel (Ezek 1:3), was of priestly ancestry. Yet the superscription to Zephaniah claims that the prophet belongs to a different lineage: he is a great-great-grandson of King Hezekiah (727–697 BCE). While this genealogy comes from Zephaniah's editors rather than from the prophet himself, it is difficult to see why they would have invented such a connection. The prophet Zephaniah, it seems, was a member of Jerusalem's nobility.

The superscription also places Zephaniah chronologically: this is "The word of the LORD that came to Zephaniah . . . in the days of King Josiah son of Amon of Judah" (Zeph 1:1), who reigned from 640–609 BCE. We can probably specify Zephaniah's setting more closely, however. Zephaniah's harsh judgment against Jerusalem's ruling class (e.g., 3:1-4) makes no mention of Josiah's reforms, begun in his eighteenth year (approximately 622 BCE), which addressed both religious corruption and social injustice (cf. 2 Kgs 22:1–23:25). Indeed, according to Chronicles, "Josiah began to seek the God of his ancestor David" at age sixteen (2 Chr 34:3), and began his reforms in his twelfth year—that is, as soon as he turned twenty, the age of majority (cf. 1 Chr 23:24, 27; 27:23; and 2 Chr 31:17), and assumed full authority as king (2 Chr 34:3). It seems probable, then, that Zephaniah dates from before Josiah's reforms, in the years of his minority.

In support of this dating, the oracles against the nations in Zephaniah 2:1-15 do not mention Babylon. Instead, the great international powers mentioned are Ethiopia (2:12) and Assyria (2:13-15), both of whom "lost their power in the 7th century" (Nogalski 1993a, 175). As Edom is often condemned in exilic and postexilic texts for its participation in the sacking of Jerusalem (e.g., Ps. 137:7; Lam 4:21-22; Obad; cf. Nogalski 1993a, 172), its absence from Zephaniah's oracles may also indicate a pre-exilic setting. Ehud ben Zvi, although agreeing that this list depicts a seventh-century setting, argues that that setting is fictional: these nations are viewed retrospectively, from the standpoint of the period after the exile (cf. ben Zvi 1991, 298–306). Still, as Sweeney notes, Zephaniah's oracles do "list nations that are of direct concern to Josiah's Judah" (Sweeney 2003, 17). Likely, the oracles against the nations in Zephaniah confirm the superscription's seventh century dating.

Of course, this does not mean that the entire book dates to Josiah's reign. Rudolph agrees that the oracles against the nations in Zephaniah 2 likely precede the exile (Rudolph 1975, 279). However, he regards 3:1-15 as exilic, and 3:16-20 as postexilic (further expanded at 1:8; 2:7, 9b, 10; 3:8; cf. Rudolph, 1975, 256). The final form of Zephaniah certainly reflects later editing for its incorporation into the Twelve, evident particularly in 3:14-20 (as we will see), but the content of the book substantially reflects the seventh century date of its superscription (with Robertson 1990, 300).

Structure

According to Nogalski (1993a, 171), Zephaniah follows "the typical tripartite eschatological prophetic pattern: judgment (1:2–2:3), oracles against the nations (2:4–3:8), and salvation (3:9-14)" (cf. Roberts 1991, 162–63, whose division is 1:2–2:3, 2:4-15; 3:1-20)—the same pattern that Walther Zimmerli (1979, 481–96) found in Isaiah, Ezekiel, and the LXX text of Jeremiah (cf. also Rex Mason: "Zephaniah encapsulates in miniature almost the whole range of Old Testament prophecy" [1994, 17]). This broad pattern masks a greater complexity, however (with O'Brien 2004, 90–91). After all, 1:1–2:3 concerns judgment, not only against Judah and Jerusalem but also against the entire earth (1:2-3; 17-18; cf. Rudolph 1975, 256, 264–65), while the oracles against the nations in 2:4-15 emerge out of judgment against Judah in 2:1-3, and segue seamlessly back into the oracle against Jerusalem in 3:1-7.

Further, the MT structure does not reflect this threefold thematic division. The scribal tradition preserved in Codex Leningradensis and followed in BHS (the standard critical edition of the Hebrew Bible) breaks the book into six paragraphs that blur the distinctions between two of the three alleged divisions:

1. 1:1-9, breaking at *ne'um Yhwh* ("says the LORD") in 1:10, which explicitly resumes the divine speech begun in 1:2-3 (the Aleppo Codex, a somewhat older witness to the Ben Asher scribal tradition, breaks after v. 11; cf. Berlin 1994, 18).
2. 1:10-18, breaking at the end of chapter 1 (rather than at 2:3).
3. 2:1-4, joining the judgment against Judah in 2:1-3 to the oracles against the nations in 2:4-15.
4. 2:5-15, observing the shift of address in 3:1.
5. 3:1-13, observing the shift from the promise of deliverance in 3:8-13 to the summons to rejoice in 3:14.
6. 3:14-20, a unit also recognized in the common lectionary (3:14-20 is appointed for the third Sunday of Advent, Year C, and every year in the

Easter Vigil; note that the Aleppo Codex breaks this into two units, 3:14-15 and 16-20; cf. Berlin 1994, 18).

Influenced by these subdivisions, this study will propose a modified three-part outline. With O'Brien (2004, 90–91) and Floyd (2000, 170), we will treat the first chapter, after the superscription (1:1), as a single unit concerning the day of the LORD, bracketed by accounts of wholesale destruction (1:2-3, 18). The second major unit (2:1–3:13) consists of oracles of judgment, with judgment upon the nations (2:4-15) bracketed at beginning and end by judgment upon Judah (2:1-3) and Jerusalem (3:1-13). The third major unit, 3:14-20, relates Jerusalem's promised restoration.

Zephaniah and the Book of the Four

Although Habakkuk follows Nahum both canonically and chronologically, Zephaniah, set in the reign of Josiah, certainly precedes Habakkuk and likely precedes Nahum as well. The best explanation is that Nahum–Habakkuk as an edited unit was inserted into another, preexisting collection: a "book of the Four" consisting of Hosea, Amos, Micah, and Zephaniah (Albertz 2003; cf. Nogalski 1993a, 278–80 and Schart 1998). A canonical approach to Zephaniah, then, must consider this book as shaped first for incorporation into the Four and then for incorporation into the Twelve.

Among the Twelve, Zephaniah shares with Hosea, Amos, Micah, Haggai, and Zechariah an explicit statement of its historical setting given in the superscription. While the superscriptions (and the dates within) Haggai and Zechariah set these books in the time after the Babylonian exile, however, Hosea, Amos, Micah, and Zephaniah all date before the exile: indeed, the first three date to the eighth century. The last king mentioned in these books, Hezekiah (Hos 1:1; Mic 1:1), is Zephaniah's great-great-grandfather (according to the genealogy in Zeph 1:1), so that the prophet himself bridges the gap between the mid-eighth century and the late seventh century.

Other parallels between Zephaniah and these other pre-exilic prophetic books are easily drawn. Zephaniah opens with the divine word formula, "The word of the LORD that came to Zephaniah" (Zeph 1:1). This expression, in a variety of formulations, is fairly common, particularly among the prophets (e.g., Isa 38:4; Jer 14:1; Ezek 1:3; Jonah 3:1). But the specific pattern found in Zephaniah 1:1 (*dabar Yhwh 'asher hayah 'el* plus a proper name) appears only in the superscriptions of Hosea, Joel, Micah, and Zephaniah. Among these four, the superscription of Joel lacks any date formula, suggesting that Joel's opening has been patterned after the others. This shared pattern strengthens the connections among Zephaniah, Hosea, and Micah, and supports the likelihood of an earlier collection, including these three books plus Amos (which, like them, features explicit dating).

Although Amos has its own unique superscription, there are other links connecting this book and Zephaniah. In particular, the oracles against the nations in Amos 1:1–2:5 and in Zephaniah 2:5-15 reflect a shared pattern and purpose. Though the specific nations addressed differ (Aram, Philistia, Tyre, Edom, Ammon, Moab, and Judah in Amos; Philistia, Moab, Ammon, Ethiopia and Assyria in Zeph), both lists climax in an oracle against the prophet's audience (Israel in Amos 2:6-15; Jerusalem in Zeph 3:1-13). Further, in each case, the shift emphasizes continuity between the audience and the "heathen" nations: in Amos, by a continuation of the pattern of the judgments against the nations ("For three transgressions of X, and for four, I will not withhold the punishment"); in Zephaniah, by a direct shift without transition from the oracle against Assyria in 2:13-15 to the oracle against Jerusalem in 3:1-7, so that initially it appears that *Nineveh* is the target!

In a variety of ways, Zephaniah functions as a transitional text, serving to sew the Four into the Twelve. As we have seen, by inserting Nahum and Habakkuk out of sequence, prior to Zephaniah, our editors have deliberately woven the Four into the temporal structure of the Twelve through overlapping dates (cf. Zech 1:1, which predates Hag 2:10 and 20). Further, the statement of God's love for Israel in Hosea, at the beginning of the Twelve (Hos 3:1; cf. also 11:1 and 14:5 [4]), and in Malachi, at its close (Mal 1:2; 2:11; cf. Watts 2000b, 212), finds expression in Zephaniah 3:17-18, which declares that the LORD

> will rejoice over you with gladness,
> he will renew you in his love;
> he will exult over you with loud singing
> as on a day of festival.

Although the Twelve mentions God's love for Israel nowhere else, its appearance at these key junctures reorients the message of the whole: all that God does, in blessing or in judgment, is seen in light of God's love. As ben Sirach observes, the Twelve Prophets "comforted the people of Jacob and delivered them with confident hope" (Sir 49:10).

Commentary

Superscription (1:1)

Prophetic superscriptions often introduce the prophet to us as "the son of" his father (Isa 1:1; Jer 1:1; Ezek 1:3; Hos 1:1; Joel 1:1; Jonah 1:1; Zeph 1:1;

Zech 1:1). Only three instances give more than this bare minimum lineage. Jeremiah's father Hilkiah, we learn, was "of the priests who were in Anathoth in the land of Benjamin" (Jer 1:1). For Zechariah, the lineage goes back to his grandfather: he is the "son of Berechiah son of Iddo" (Zech 1:1; see the discussion of this passage below in context). Only for Zephaniah, however, are we given what amounts to a genealogy, tracing the prophet's ancestry back four generations, to Hezekiah. Given the lengths gone to demonstrate the connection, this is almost certainly the Hezekiah who ruled as king at the height of the Assyrian Empire's power (727–697 BCE) and whose failed rebellion against Assyria set the stage for the entirely complicit reigns of Manasseh and Amon. Although Zephaniah's genealogy reveals that he came from the upper classes, indeed from the royal family, he pulls no punches in his condemnation of Jerusalem's priesthood (cf. 1:4-7; 3:4) and aristocracy (cf. 1:8; 3:3), calling to mind comparisons with Hosea, Amos, and Micah—as well as Habakkuk (cf. Hab 1:2-4; 2:4-14).

This book is set in the reign of Josiah (Zeph 1:1), who was also a great-great-grandson of Hezekiah. Zephaniah makes no mention of Josiah's reforms, however: hence, as we have seen, it most likely dates from early in Josiah's reign. Among the Twelve, this explicit setting in time, tied to an Israelite or Judean king, parallels the superscriptions of Hosea, Amos, and Micah, the other members of the "Book of the Four," and stands in curious tension with Haggai and Zechariah, which are dated by the regnal years of the foreign ruler Darius (cf. Hag 1:1; Zech 1:1).

The Day of the LORD (1:2-18)

The book of Zephaniah begins by depicting universal destruction: "I will utterly sweep away everything from the face of the earth, says the LORD" (Zeph 1:2). Noting parallels with the flood account in Genesis, Sabottka proposes that Zephaniah's new word from God abrogates the divine promise made after Noah's sacrifice: "I will never again curse the ground because of humankind . . . nor will I ever again destroy every living creature as I have done" (Gen 8:21; cf. Sabottka 1972, 11–12). Yet, while possible links to the flood story are intriguing (note in particular the use of *'asap*, "sweep away, destroy" in both contexts), a more persuasive parallel is evident between Zephaniah 1:2-3 and Genesis 1:20-31. Zephaniah 1:3 lists the living creatures created by God on the fifth and sixth days of creation. However, as Michael De Roche has observed, they are listed in reverse order, moving backwards from humanity (De Roche 1980, 106–107): "I will sweep away humans and animals; / I will sweep away the birds of the air / and the fish of the sea." The LORD's impending judgment is *un-creation*: the inversion of God's gracious acts in calling the world into being.

De Roche takes this allusion to Genesis 1 as evidence for the early dating of Genesis 1–11 due to the seventh century setting of Zephaniah (De Roche 1980, 108). Nogalski, on the contrary, finds the post-exilic dating of Genesis 1 a good reason to assign Zephaniah 1:2-3 to the post-exilic editing of this book (cf. Nogalski 1993a, 188). Ehud ben Zvi claims that there is no allusion to Genesis here at all: the mention of these creatures of air, water, and land emphasizes the totality of destruction in the LORD's judgment but has no significance beyond that (ben Zvi 1991, 55–58; cf. Sweeney 2003, 62–64). Still, the reference to these creatures, in this particular order, must surely be significant. Further, there is a middle ground. While, as a broad consensus of scholarship holds, there are good reasons for thinking that the final editing of the Pentateuch belongs in the time after the exile, there are also reasons for thinking that the priestly traditions included in the Pentateuch have a long prehistory, extending back into the time of the monarchy (e.g., Polzin 1976, 159; Hurvitz 1982, 150–51; Tuell 1992, 145–46; Schniedewind 2004). Zephaniah could, therefore, allude to a priestly tradition of the order of creation without presupposing the written text of Genesis 1 in its final form. Jeremiah 4:23, the only place outside of Genesis 1:2 where the expression *tohu wabohu* ("formless void") appears, supports a pre-exilic priestly creation tradition. In short, Zephaniah 1:2-3 may both allude to the priestly creation tradition underlying Genesis 1 and also derive from the seventh-century prophet. That said, the psalms bracketing Nahum–Habakkuk (Nah 1:2-11; Hab 3) also evoke creation themes, suggesting another reason the editors of the Twelve placed that unit prior to Zephaniah. The divine warrior who defeated chaos and brought an ordered world into being (Nah 1:3-4; Hab 3:8) can also undo that order and return the world to the chaos from which it came. Indeed, Habakkuk 3:8, 13 makes this claim, interpreting cosmic creation and destruction in terms of divine judgment against a human foe—a move also underway in Zephaniah.

"I will make the wicked stumble" (1:3 in the NRSV) is a reconstruction from the Hebrew *hammakshelot eth-haresha'im*, which *Tg. Neb.* reads as "stumbling-blocks for the wicked." The MT, however, is intelligible as it stands, meaning "the ruins with the wicked." This phrase does not appear in the LXX and likely represents an insertion; however, it forecasts the movement underway in this chapter from the day of the LORD as universal judgment on all creation (1:2-3) to the day of the LORD as particular judgment within history upon particular human communities (specifically against Judah and Jerusalem) for particular human sins (1:4-17)—and then back again (1:18).

A variety of schemes for tracing the composition history of this chapter separate these ideas into different layers from different times (e.g., Schart 1998, 206–207, who dates 1:2-3 and the final form of 1:18 to the final editing of Zeph). The final form of the text, however, effectively communicates the interconnection of these two themes. The certitude of divine judgment at the end of time, and the assurance that God's justice will prevail, gives us courage to stand for God's justice in our own time and place, despite the apparent might of forces arrayed on the side of injustice and oppression. The words of abolitionist Theodore Parker, which echo in the speeches of Martin Luther King, Jr. and Desmond Tutu, express this confidence:

> I do not pretend to understand the moral universe; the arc is a long one, my eye reaches but little ways; I cannot calculate the curve and complete the figure by the experience of sight; I can divine it by conscience. And from what I see I am sure it bends towards justice. (Parker 1867, 48)

Conversely, events in history can give credence to this confidence in God's ultimate triumph, and ground hope in realistic expectation. As for Parker, history's oft-told tale of despotism overthrown—particularly, in the American Revolution—raised the hope that the injustice of slavery would end to a certainty, so for the editors of the Twelve, the fall of Assyria and Babylon grounded hope in God's ultimate triumph.

The word of universal judgment and destruction in 1:2-3 applies immediately to the impending judgment on Judah and Jerusalem. Much as the judgment on all the earth then focuses more tightly on Jerusalem, however, so the judgment on "all the inhabitants of Jerusalem" (1:4) tightens further to the condemnation of idolatrous worship and the religious leaders responsible. The LXX ignores the unusual term *kemarim* ("idolatrous priests") in 1:4, while the MT provides an interpretive gloss (*'im-hakkohanim*, "with the priests;" cf. LXX, the Vulgate, and the KJV). Likely, the Hebrew *komer* comes from the Ugaritic *kumru* and refers to a priest serving foreign gods; certainly, the Aramaic equivalent refers to idolatrous priests in later literature. This term appears elsewhere in the MT only in 2 Kings 23:5 and Hosea 10:5, though some conjecture that *komer* should also be read in Deuteronomy 18:8 and Hosea 4:4 (cf. *HALOT* 482). Its use in Zephaniah 1:4, then, supports the dating found in Zephaniah's superscription: *kemarim* is a term we might expect a seventh-century prophet to use for officials of the Baal cult.

In addition to the cult of Baal, Zephaniah condemns "those who bow down on the roofs to the host of heaven" (1:5). While the host of heaven may refer to heavenly beings subordinate to God (1 Kgs 22:19, and the divine title "LORD of hosts"; cf. Nah 2:14; 3:5), it also may refer to the worship of the sun, moon, and stars as deities in their own right (Niehr 1999, 428–29). Nowhere else does the Twelve mention the "host of heaven," and the only prophetic books apart from Zephaniah to use this expression are Isaiah and Jeremiah. Isaiah 34:4 and Jeremiah 33:22 use the expression poetically for the stars (cf. also Dan 8:10; Neh 9:6). Jeremiah 9:2 and 19:13, however, have the worship of astral deities in view; indeed, 19:13 parallels both the practice described in Zephaniah 1:5 (worship on rooftops) and the social group condemned in this chapter (for a parallel to the condemnation of the royal house in Jer 19:13, cf. Zeph 1:8). Elsewhere, as the Jeremiah reference leads us to expect, the cult of the host of heaven is condemned, especially in Deuteronomy (4:19; 17:3) and in the Deuteronomistic History (2 Kgs 17:16; 21:3, 5 [//2 Chr 33:3, 5]; 23:4-5). The condemnation of the astral cult in particular, then, also fits the seventh century date that Zephaniah 1:1 claims.

Zephaniah further condemns those "who swear by Milcom" (1:5). The NRSV reading "Milcom," the national god of Ammon (1 Kgs 11:5, 33; 2 Kgs 23:13), follows the Greek recension of Lucian, the Syriac, and the Vulgate (cf. KJV "Malcham" and NJPS "Malcam"; the NIV "Molek" is unlikely, as Molech and Milkom were separate deities [cf. Puech 1999, 576]); similarly, *Tg. Neb.* has "swear by the name of his idol." The MT and the LXX read rather "the ones who swear by (or, are sworn to) their king" (Heb., *bemalkam*), suggesting political identity rather than religious faithlessness (so Sweeney 2003, 55). The Hebrew word for "their king" in 1:5 (*malkam*) and the divine name *Milkom* are identical, however, in ancient Hebrew, written without vowel markings. These terms are evidently confused elsewhere. For example, the MT of 2 Samuel 12:30//1 Chronicles 20:2 says that, after occupying Rammah, David took the crown of "their king" (*malkam*) and placed it on his own head (cf. KJV, NIV)—a reasonable enough action on the part of a conqueror. Yet our texts say that the crown "weighed a talent of gold" (2 Sam 12:30//1 Chr 20:2), or over seventy-five pounds: far too heavy for any human king to wear! A more likely reading, suggested by the Latin, Arabic, and some Greek versions and followed by the NRSV (cf. the NIV footnote on this verse), is that David took Milcom's crown, completing the subjugation of Ammon by defacing the image of Ammon's god and claiming his crown for himself (cf. Amos 1:15; Jer 49:1, 3). Most likely, Milcom should be read in Zephaniah 1:5 as well, as further evidence of Jerusalem's idolatry.

Zephaniah 1:4-9 describes more than the survival of idolatrous practices in Judah, however. The prophet claims that Jerusalem's religious practices *combine* the worship of the LORD with the recognition of foreign gods: "those who bow down and swear to the LORD, but also swear by Milcom" (1:5). Religion scholars refer to such merging of religious ideas and practices as *syncretism.* Clearly, Zephaniah regards syncretism as the rejection of Israel's traditional faith. Those who follow these practices, he declares, may think that they "bow down and swear to the LORD," but in fact they "have turned back from following the LORD" and "have not sought the LORD or inquired of him" (1:6). Josiah's reforms also firmly rejected syncretism; he removed from the temple "all the vessels made for Baal, for Asherah, and for all the host of heaven; he burned them outside Jerusalem in the fields of the Kidron, and carried their ashes to Bethel" (2 Kgs 23:4). Once more, then, Zephaniah seems to depict Jerusalem *before* those reforms, early in the boy king's reign.

Zephaniah goes further than condemning religious syncretism. Stepping over the threshold (1:9) was likely a superstitious custom, reflecting old ideas concerning doorways as numinous spaces (e.g., 1 Sam 5:5; Ps 24:7-10; cf. Roberts 1991, 179)—much like our modern superstition about stepping over cracks in pavement. It scarcely seems to rise to the level of idolatry. Yet the LORD declares, "On that day I will punish all who leap over the threshold," and equates this practice with "violence and fraud" (1:9). So too, Zephaniah condemns the royal household (his own kin, recall; cf. 1:1) for wearing foreign clothing (1:8). To this zealous prophet *any* cultural compromise is dangerous, no matter how innocuous it may seem, and reflects Judah's slide into corruption.

To arrest that slide, Zephaniah declares, God is about to act: "Be silent before the Lord GOD! For the day of the LORD is at hand" (1:7; cf. Amos 8:3; Hab 2:20; Zech 2:13). The day of the LORD's judgment is described liturgically: "the LORD has prepared a sacrifice, / he has consecrated his guests" (1:7). Indeed, the day that the LORD "will punish the officials and the king's sons" is called "the day of the LORD's sacrifice" (1:8). Ominously, this implies that the nobles and religious leaders themselves *are* the sacrifice, that they have been consecrated, not to join in the sacred feast but for the slaughter. While startling, this use of sacrificial imagery for judgment is not unique. Isaiah 29:1-8 calls Zion "Ariel," the term designating the altar hearth (cf. Ezek 43:15-16 and the Moabite Stone inscription), to indicate that Jerusalem will become a place of burning and slaughter. Similarly, Ezekiel 39:17-24 describes the slain of Gog as a sacrifice (39:17, 19), consumed by birds and wild animals in a grim mockery of the sacred meal. Zephaniah declares that, because of their religious corruption, cultural impurity, and social injustice, Judah's nobility will be sacrificed on the day of the LORD.

Zephaniah 1:10-18, the next unit identified by the scribes, opens "On that day, says the LORD" (1:10). The Hebrew expression *ne'um Yhwh* ("says the LORD") commonly marks the conclusion of a prophetic oracle; here, however, it explicitly continues the divine speech begun in 1:2. "That day," of course, is "the day of the LORD" (1:7): the theme of Zephaniah and a major theme of the Book of the Twelve (see Introduction, and cf. Nah 1:8). In this chapter, Zephaniah refers to the day of the LORD in many ways: the "day of the LORD's sacrifice" (1:8), "that day" (1:9, 10, 15), "at that time" (1:12), "the great day of the LORD" (1:14), and "the day of the LORD's wrath" (1:18). By any name, the day of the LORD is the day of reckoning, when God's just rule will be confirmed—when, in the words of the Lord's Prayer, God's will at last will "be done, on earth as it is in heaven" (Matt 6:10). In the first half of this chapter, the description of judgment moved from the universal to the particular: God's universal judgment (1:2-3) focused down to Jerusalem and, more tightly still, to its corrupt religious leaders. The direction shifts in the verses that follow. God's judgment on specific persons and neighborhoods in Jerusalem (1:10-13) expands to incorporate broader regions ("against the fortified cities and against the lofty battlements," 1:16), until finally "the whole earth shall be consumed" (1:18).

In 1:10-11, the Fish Gate (2 Chr 33:14; for the rebuilding of the gate, cf. Neh 3:3; 12:39), the Second Quarter (in Hebrew, the *Mishneh*; cf. 2 Kgs 22:14//2 Chr 34:22), and the Mortar (or the Hollow: perhaps the Tyropoean Valley, west of the Temple Mount) all refer to the newer, northwest part of Jerusalem, expanded under Hezekiah (Negev et al. 1986, 198) and Manasseh (2 Chr 33:14), where the wealthier citizens likely lived. The "loud crash from the hills" (1:10) could refer to the sound of advancing armies (so Sweeney 2003, 89–90). Yet, since *gib'ah*, the word used for hill here, often refers to places of idolatrous worship (Deut 12:2; 1 Kgs 14:23; 2 Kgs 16:4//2 Chr 28:4; 17:10; Isa 65:7; Jer 2:20; 3:23; 13:27; 17:2; Ezek 6:13; 20:28; Hos 4:13), Zephaniah may have particularly in mind the collapse of the shrines of Baal and the other gods condemned in 1:4-9.

The cause of this consternation and collapse is that "all the traders have perished; all who weigh out silver are cut off" (1:11). The MT has *kol-'am kena'an* here: literally, "all the people of Canaan," a reading reflected in *Tg. Neb.*, the LXX, and the Vulgate. To make sense of the Canaanites' presence in a passage condemning Jerusalem, *Tg. Neb.* and LXX read the verb here not as *damah*, "destroy," but as its homophone, meaning "be like," so that those cut off by the LORD are all who are *like* the Canaanites—picking up, presumably, on the condemnation of syncretism and cultural compromise in the first half of the chapter (so Sweeney 2003, 91–92). The Vulgate says that the Canaanites are *conticiut* ("silenced"), assuming the root to be *damam*, "be silent." With most English translations (KJV, NRSV, JPSV, and

NIV), it is best to understand "people of Canaan" here as a roundabout way of saying "merchants" (so Rudolph 1975, 263)—a figure of speech found elsewhere in Scripture (cf. Hos 12:8; Zech 14:21; Prov 31:24; Job 41:6; and note the unique word *kin'an*, evidently meaning "tradesman," in Isa 23:8), particularly given the parallel with "all who weigh out silver" (1:11). Financial ruin has brought distress to the people in the high-rent district and caused the collapse of the hill shrines. The day of the LORD hits the idle rich and the idolaters of Jerusalem where it hurts!

God's action is neither random nor hasty, however. "At that time," the LORD says, "I will search Jerusalem with lamps" (1:12). Similarly, in Jeremiah 5:1, God commands the prophet,

> Run to and fro through the streets of Jerusalem,
> look around and take note!
> Search its squares and see
> if you can find one person
> who acts justly
> and seeks truth—
> so that I may pardon Jerusalem.

In Zephaniah, however, the LORD searches not for the innocent but for the guilty, "who rest complacently on their dregs" (1:12). The word rendered "who rest complacently" in the NRSV is *haqqophe'im*: "those who stiffen, congeal" (*Tg. Neb.* renders this as *deshalen shelewa'*, "who are peacefully at ease"). The rare verb *qapa'* occurs elsewhere only in Exodus 15:8 (for the deeps foaming or congealing at the crossing of the Red Sea), Zechariah 14:6 (for ice freezing; cf. also Sir 43:20), and Job 10:10 (where Job declares that God had fashioned him in the womb: "Did you not pour me out like milk, and curdle me like cheese?"). The versions show some confusion over *shimrehem*, interpreting it as derived from *shamar*, "keep watch," rather than *shemer*, for the sediments of wine (commonly called the lees, or the dregs, of the wine). Hence, LXX declares that God will punish those who despise the ones for whom they are responsible (*phulagmata auton*), and *Tg. Neb.* condemns those who rest over their possessions—that is, who fail to keep watch. Still, the MT is meaningful, and the point of the image seems clear in the context: the uncaring nobles of Jerusalem are content to drink themselves into a stupor, heedless of the religious corruption and injustice all around them. This accusation is reminiscent of Amos's condemnation of those "who are at ease in Zion" (Amos 6:1).

These sluggards believe God to be as apathetic as they are: "The LORD will not do good, nor will he do harm" (1:12; cf. Mal 2:17; 3:14-15). Yet their declaration of the irrelevance of faith is about to be revealed for the lie that it is. As in 1:11, the day of the LORD hits them right in the pocketbook: "Their wealth shall be plundered, and their houses laid waste" (1:13). The statement of the financial ruin to be experienced by Jerusalem's elite ("Though they build houses, they shall not inhabit them; though they plant vineyards, they shall not drink wine from them") may be reflected in Ezekiel 28:26, which neatly inverts this judgment into a promise of future restoration: "They shall live in safety in it, and shall build houses and plant vineyards" (cf. Isa 65:21, and compare Jer 29:5, 28).

The language Zephaniah uses for the day of the LORD is typical of the Twelve and of the prophets generally. First, "The day of the LORD is near, near and hastening fast" (1:14; e.g., Isa 13:6; Ezek 7:10-12; Zeph 1:7; Mal 3:1-2). As we have seen, the description of Babylon in Habakkuk 1:6 recalls this verse. Zephaniah describes the day of the LORD as *maher* ("hastening fast"); NRSV renders *wehannimhar*, another form of the same verb "impetuous" in Habakkuk 1:6. Zephaniah declares, "the sound of the day of the LORD is bitter [Heb., *mar*]; the warrior cries aloud there" (1:14). The same word, rendered "fierce," describes Babylon in Habakkuk 1:6. Zephaniah's "soon," in the early seventh century, thus becomes Habakkuk's "soon," late in the seventh century. Just so, Mark summed up the proclamation of Jesus quite simply: "The time is fulfilled, and the kingdom of God has come near; repent, and believe in the good news" (Mark 1:15). The reign of God is never a message for *someday*, in the indefinite future: it speaks with imminence and urgency, and calls us to action here and now. Perhaps for this reason, Zephaniah 1:7, 12-18 is the alternate Old Testament reading for Proper 28, Year A in the Revised Common Lectionary, read together with 1 Thessalonians 5:1-11 (regarding "the day of the Lord" coming "as a thief in the night") and Matthew 25:14-30 (the parable of the talents, which portrays God's final judgment).

Zephaniah further describes the day of the LORD as "a day of darkness and gloom, a day of clouds and thick darkness" (1:15; e.g., Ezek 34:12; Joel 2:2; Amos 5:18-20). Typically, as is the case through most of this chapter, the "distress and anguish," "ruin and devastation" (1:15) of this day are pronounced on Israel and its leaders (e.g., Joel 2:1-2; Amos 8:1-10; Lam 2:2). However, the day of the LORD can also be a day of judgment on the nations (e.g., Isa 13:6, 9; Ezek 30:3; Jer 46:10). This, one recalls, is the point of 1:2-3, which announces judgment on all creation; the message then shifts in 1:4 from universal judgment to God's particular judgment on Jerusalem.

A shift back may already be underway in 1:16, which speaks not of judgment on Jerusalem alone but rather of "a day of trumpet blast and battle cry / against the fortified cities / and against the lofty battlements." While the cities and fortifications of Judah alone may be intended, this is not stated. Similarly, the terrible punishments depicted in 1:17 are meted out against people who "have sinned against the LORD," which certainly need not refer to Judah alone. Zephaniah 1:18 alludes to the idle rich of 1:8-12: "Neither their silver nor their gold / will be able to save them / on the day of the LORD's wrath." Ezekiel 7:19 quotes this verse with reference to the nobility in Jerusalem's final days before the Babylonian conquest. Yet nothing in Zephaniah requires one to read this statement of the impotence of wealth to save with reference to Jerusalem alone. Christian readers may recall Jesus saying, "It is easier for a camel to go through the eye of a needle than for someone who is rich to enter the kingdom of God" (Mark 10:25; cf. Matt 19:24; Luke 18:25).

Certainly, the final lines of Zephaniah 1:18 present the day of the LORD as universal judgment, and total devastation:

> in the fire of his passion
> the whole earth shall be consumed;
> for a full, a terrible end
> he will make of all the inhabitants of the earth (1:18; cf. Nah 1:8-9; Hab 2:3).

We might expect that the broadening of the day of the LORD to encompass the entire earth (1:18) would lead naturally into Zephaniah's oracles against the nations (2:4-15). But the structure of this book is not so simple. Instead, judgments against Judah (2:1-3) introduce the oracles against the nations.

Oracles of Judgment (2:1–3:13)

One could make an argument for reading 2:1-3 in relation to the first chapter (so Roberts 1991, 162–63; Nogalski 1993a, 171). After all, this passage does speak of the day of the LORD, calling it "the day of the LORD's wrath" (2:2-3; cf. 1:15, 18). The scribal paragraphing, however, breaks at the end of chapter 1 and marks the next subunit as 2:1-4, including the first verse of the oracle against the Philistines into the judgment against Judah—a reading that links 2:1-3 to the oracles against the nations that follow. Once again, Zephaniah presents God's judgment upon Israel and the nations as inextricably interwoven.

An Oracle against Judah (2:1-3)

The referent of the judgment in 2:1-3 is not immediately apparent. The passage begins ambiguously: "Gather together, gather, O shameless nation" (2:1). Indeed, only in 2:3 ("Seek the LORD, all you humble of the land, who do his commands") does it become clear that this passage addresses God's own people, making the "shameless nation" of 2:1-3 the nation of Judah.

The translation of 2:1-2 poses numerous problems, beginning with the expression *haggoy lo' niksaph* (2:1). While the NRSV, JPSV, and NIV all render this as "shameless nation" (influenced by the parallels in Akkadian and Aramaic; cf. O'Brien 2004, 113), the root is used elsewhere in the Hebrew Bible to mean "desire" (Gen 31:30; Pss 17:12; 84:3[2]; Job 14:15): hence the Vulgate *gens non amabilis* ("unlovable nation") and the KJV "O nation not desired" (so Roberts 1991, 185–87; Berlin 1994, 96; Sweeney 2003, 110). The image of Jerusalem or Israel as an unwanted or unloved child, though painful and disturbing, occurs in Scripture (e.g., Ezek 16:4-5; Hos 1:6). But this verb in the form found here is used elsewhere actively, not passively: hence, not "undesired nation," but "nation that does not desire. . . ." This is reflected in *Tg. Neb.*, which interprets the phrase as meaning "the people of the generation that does not desire to return to the Torah," and perhaps by the LXX, which has *to ethnos to apaideuton* ("ignorant nation," that is, the nation that does not desire to be taught). On the other hand, the absence of an object for the verb may be deliberate (e.g., Ps 23:1, "I shall not want [anything]"; or Ps 139:1, "O LORD, you have searched me and you know [everything]"). The apathetic, wine-sotted community (cf. 1:11-12) condemned by Zephaniah for its compromises and lack of commitment (cf. 1:4-9) is in view here as well: Judah is a nation without zeal, without passion—a nation that does not desire *anything*, let alone the LORD.

Yet this community is called to choose, and to decide, right now. The MT of 2:2a is difficult and likely corrupt, as the awkward but faithful rendering in the JPSV makes clear: "Before the day of the decree is born—The day flies by like chaff" (cf. KJV). The word "day" seems out of place here, and it is difficult to make any sense in context out of the Hebrew *khoq*, "decree." The emendation proposed by Roberts (1991, 187–88) and followed by the NRSV seems to yield the best sense: "before you are driven away like the drifting chaff." In any case, however, this verse presents a concatenation of "befores" (Heb., *beterem*), underscoring once more the immediacy of God's judgment. Apathetic Judah must rouse itself and act quickly,

> before there comes upon you
> the fierce anger of the LORD,

before there comes upon you
the day of the LORD's wrath (2:2).

In contrast to the leadership condemned in 2:1-2, Zephaniah turns in v. 3 to "the humble of the land" (Heb., *'anwe ha'arets*), an expression that elsewhere refers to the oppressed poor (Isa 11:4; Amos 8:4; Ps 76:10[9]). It is immediately apparent, however, that the prophet refers not so much to the economically humbled as to those "who do [God's] commands" (2:3): who humble themselves before the LORD (cf. Num 12:3, of Moses; and compare Matt 5:3; Jas 2:5-7). These righteous persons, it seems, are intended to form the nucleus of a community that gathers itself together to "seek righteousness, seek humility" (2:3) before the day of the LORD comes. For those who sought to join the Methodist societies, John Wesley had "only one condition previously required . . . a desire to flee the wrath to come" (Outler 1964, 178). Just so, it seems, Zephaniah sought to gather an assembly of the faithful in Judah before it was too late.

Nonetheless, the prophet offers no guarantees that gathering to seek the LORD will save even the righteous in Judah. He will say only, "perhaps you may be hidden on the day of the LORD's wrath" (2:3; cf. Jonah 3:9). Similarly, in Ezekiel 9, while it initially appears that "those who sigh and groan over the abominations that are committed" in Jerusalem (9:4) are marked for preservation, the description of those cut down in the judgment is all inclusive: "old men, young men and young women, little children and women" (9:6). For Ezekiel as for Zephaniah, the judgment called down upon Judah cannot be neatly restricted to the guilty; rather, the righteous may well suffer along with the wicked (cf. Tuell 2011, 200–202).

Oracles against the Nations (2:4-15)

Oracles against foreign nations were an important part of the prophetic repertoire: so much so that collections of such oracles often appear in prophetic books (Isa 13–23; Jer 46–51; Ezek 25–32; Amos 1–2; Zech 9:1-8; and arguably, the entire short book of Obadiah). Although they target foreign nations, it is unlikely that any foreigner ever actually heard these oracles. Their intended audience was the people of Israel—just as, in our own day, politicians often make pronouncements about international affairs intended for domestic consumption (see the discussion above of Amos 1:3–2:16). Clearly, this was true of Zephaniah, whose oracles against the nations (2:4-15) begin with an oracle against Judah (2:1-3) and lead seamlessly into an oracle against Jerusalem (3:1-13).

Why does Zephaniah condemn these nations in particular? The five city-states of Philistia (2:4-7) were long-time rivals of Judah, and prophetic collections of oracles against the nations often condemn them, whether collectively or singly. Although the term "Cherethites" (Zeph 2:5) appears elsewhere in the prophets only in Ezek 25:16, these people are condemned as "Philistines" (Zeph 2:5) in Isa 11:14; Jer 47:1, 4; Ezek 25:15-16; Amos 1:8; Obad 19 (outside of the oracle collections, cf. Jer 25:20; Ezek 16:27, 57; Amos 6:2). The Philistine city-states are also condemned separately in oracles against the nations: Gaza (Zeph 2:4) in Jer 47:1, 5; Amos 1:6-7; Zech 9:5 (outside the collections, Jer 25:20); Ashkelon (Zeph 2:4, 7) in Jer 47:5, 7; Amos 1:8; Zech 9:5 (outside the collections, Jer 25:20); Ashdod (Zeph 2:4) in Amos 1:8 and Zech 9:6 (outside the collections, Isa 20:1; Jer 25:20; Amos 3:9); and Ekron (Zeph 2:4) in Amos 1:8 and Zech 9:5, 7 (outside the collections, Jer 25:20). Intriguingly Gath, which is not mentioned in Zeph 2, is absent from the other collections of oracles against the nations as well (but cf. Amos 6:2; Mic 1:10). The minor kingdoms of Moab and Ammon (2:8-11) were close neighbors of Judah and are commonly mentioned in these collections: for Moab, cf. Isaiah 11:14; 15:1–16:14; Ezekiel 25:8-11; Amos 2:1-3; for Ammon, cf. Isaiah 11:14; Ezekiel 25:1-7; Amos 1:13-15. Likewise, we expect the oracle against Assyria (2:13-15), given Zephaniah's seventh century setting.

In contrast, the oracle against the people of Cush (the NRSV reads "Ethiopians"; cf. 2:12) is a surprise. While Cush does appear in other collections of oracles against the nations, it is either used as a place name indicating Egypt's border (Isa 18:1, where the land "beyond the rivers of Ethiopia [i.e., Cush]" is Egypt [cf. Zeph 3:10]; Ezek 29:10) or mentioned as an ally of Egypt (Isa 20:3-5 [cf. 43:3; 45:14]; Jer 46:9; Ezek 30:4, 5, 9). Only Zephaniah's oracles against the nations address an oracle against the Cushites *as* Cushites (but cf. Amos 9:7). Robert Bennet, noting that the genealogy in 1:1 identifies Zephaniah as *ben-Kushi* ("son of a Cushite/Ethiopian"[?]), proposes that the prophet had "an African heritage," which explains his attention to Cush in 2:12 and 3:10 (Bennett 1996, 659, 661, 690–91, 699). "Cushi" (Jer 36:14), "Cush" (Ps 7:1; although *Tg. Ket.* reads "Saul son of Kish" here), and "Cushan" (Judg 3:8, 10) are used as personal names, however, and since the point of the genealogy is to emphasize Zephaniah's links to Judean nobility, it is doubtful that an Ethiopian connection is intended.

Adele Berlin proposes that Cush in 2:12 refers to the Assyrians, since the table of nations in Genesis 10 lists Cush as Assyria's ancestor; indeed, only Zephaniah 2 and Genesis 10 mention Cush and Assyria together (Gen 10:8-10; Berlin 1994, 112–13; cf. O'Dell 2000, 673). Berlin finds many other links between Zephaniah's oracles against the nations and Genesis 10 (Berlin 1994, 13–14, 111–13, 120–24; cf. Nogalski 2012, 704–706). The phrase "islands of the nations" (Heb., *'iyye haggoyim*) appears only in Zephaniah 2:11 and Genesis 10:5 (Berlin 1994, 111). Zephaniah describes Philistia as "Canaan, the land of the Philistines" (2:5) and declares, "Moab shall become like Sodom and the Ammonites like Gomorrah" (2:9)—intriguing, since Genesis 10:19 places the descendants of Canaan "as far as Gaza, and in the direction of Sodom, Gomorrah, Admah, and Zeboiim" (Berlin 1994, 121). Berlin concludes that, just as Zephaniah 1:3 alludes to Genesis 1, so Zephaniah's oracles against the nations place their condemnation of Assyria and its cronies in the mythic context of Genesis 10, with the descendants of Japheth (the "islands of the nations") and particularly Ham (Canaan [Philistia, Ammon, Moab] and Cush [Assyria]) set against Israel, the descendant of Shem (Gen 10:22; cf. 11:10-26; Berlin 1994, 120, 124). This context, for Berlin, explains why Edom is not mentioned after Ammon and Moab, as we would expect, since Edom/Esau, like his brother Jacob/Israel, descends from Shem (Berlin 1994, 121–22).

While intriguing, Berlin's proposal pushes the evidence too far. As any audience familiar with the table of nations would know, not only Edom but also Ammon and Moab were Shemites (cf. Gen 10:30); it is too far-fetched to conclude from the Sodom and Gomorrah comparison that Zephaniah regards Ammon and Moab as "eastern Canaanites" (Berlin 1994, 121). Further, while the use of the phrase *'iyye haggoyim* ("the islands of the nations") in both contexts is interesting, it seems most likely that Zephaniah and the Genesis table of nations have different referents in view. While Genesis 10:5 clearly intends the descendants of Japheth, the context of the phrase in Zephaniah 2:11 suggests that it refers back to the Philistines, who were, after all, Sea Peoples from the Aegean settled on the coast of Palestine (as the NRSV paraphrase "all the coasts and islands of the nations" infers).

Why, then, does Zephaniah refer to Cush? First, it does seem most likely that the term here intends Ethiopia: the LXX and the Vulgate alike render *Kushim* in 2:12 as "Ethiopians," supporting the NRSV, "You also, O Ethiopians, shall be killed by my sword." The high-water mark of Ethiopian power was Egypt's 25th Dynasty, Ethiopian in origin, which ruled both Ethiopia and Egypt from 770 to 664 BCE. The last pharaoh in this dynasty, Taharqa (690–664 BCE; called "Tirhakah" in 2 Kgs 19:9//Isa 37:9) was defeated by the Assyrian Assurbanipal (669–627 BCE). This happened years before Josiah came to the throne, however. What relevance would Ethiopia have to Zephaniah's context? Here, the translation in the NRSV ("*shall be* killed by my sword") misleads. The Hebrew is phrased as a description, not as a prediction: the Ethiopians are "ones who were/are slain by my sword" (so too the LXX, although the Vulgate and *Tg. Neb.* render this as future). Likely, the prophet recalls Cush here, at the beginning of his oracle against Assyria and Nineveh (2:13-15), for the same reason that Nahum recalls the fall of Thebes in his oracles against Nineveh (Nah 3:8-10; cf. Bennett 1996, 690–91): what Assyria had done to Cush would now be done to Assyria. Although God had once used the sword of Assyria to punish the nations (including Israel and Judah; cf. Nah 1:12-13; Isa 10:5; and compare Ezek 21, where *Babylon* is God's sword), now Assyria itself is judged and condemned.

Although Zephaniah's oracles against the nations declare that their targets will be destroyed, they give no specific reasons for this judgment. The statement that God will give Philistine lands to "the remnant of the house of Judah" in order to "restore their fortunes" (2:7) may respond to land seizure by the Philistines, in retaliation for Hezekiah's annexation of Philistine territory (2 Kgs 18:8), but that is certainly not stated here. Comparing Moab to Sodom and Ammon to Gomorrah (2:9) may imply that, like those famously wicked cities, Moab and Ammon were guilty of idolatry and injustice to the poor (cf. Ezek 16:49-50), but it is far more likely that Sodom and Gomorrah are used, as is typically the case, as bywords for total destruction wrought by God's judgment (e.g., Gen 13:10, 13; Deut 29:23; Isa 1:9-15; Jer 23:14; Amos 4:11; Matt 10:15//Luke 10:12; 2 Pet 2:6). Moab and Ammon are condemned broadly for ridiculing Judah ("they have taunted my people and made boasts against their territory," 2:8; cf. Ezek 25:3, 8), not for any particular instance of idolatry or injustice. The references throughout these oracles to "the remnant" (2:7, 9) could be a reference to Judean exiles and therefore reflect a postexilic setting, either for the composition or editing of these oracles, but that too is not necessarily the case. The reference may simply be to whoever survives the sweeping judgments depicted in chapter 1.

Particularly interesting in light of the condemnations of idolatry in 1:4-13 is 2:11: "he will shrivel the gods of the earth." The verb *razah* ("shrivel" in the NRSV and JPS; "famish" in KJV; "destroys" in NIV) occurs only here and in Isaiah 17:4. Sabottka proposed deriving *razah* in Zephaniah 2:11 from *razon* ("dignitary"), so that the LORD *rules* over the gods (Sabottka 1972, 90–91), but that seems unlikely in light of Zephaniah's utter rejection of anything remotely associated with idolatry. In Isaiah 17:4, the passive meaning of this verb is "grow lean"; likely, the point here is that God will cause these false deities to wither away. "Shrivel" is a good rendering. The expression "the gods of the earth" brings to mind Assyrian ruler Sennacherib's bold claim to Hezekiah, "Who among all the gods of the countries have delivered their countries out of my hand, that the LORD should deliver Jerusalem out of my hand?" (2 Kgs 18:35//Isa 36:20). Just as then God had delivered Jerusalem from Assyria, so now, in the reign of Hezekiah's great-great-grandson, God is about to destroy Assyria, its allies, and their gods.

Indeed, the oracle against Assyria and Nineveh (2:13-15) is also vague. No specific charges are laid—but then, none are needed. Assyria's evil was certainly well known. The statement that the LORD "will stretch out his hand against the north" (2:13) recalls Isaiah 14:31, which describes Assyria as a fire "out of the north." Although Assyria was to the east of Israel, geography forced its armies to march north around the desert wastes, then south along the coastal plain, approaching Palestine from the north. The other great Mesopotamian power, Babylon, will also be called the enemy from the north (18 times in Jeremiah: e.g., Jer 1:13-16; 3:12,18; 6:1, 22-25; cf. Ezek 9:2; 23:24; Zech 2:6-7; 6:8). Indeed, the "enemy from the north" becomes a trope for all threats against Israel (Joel 2:20; Ezek 38–39; Dan 11:40-45).

Like Moab and Ammon, Nineveh is cursed: the city will become a wasteland, the haunt of wild creatures and birds. Curiously, while *Tg. Neb.* and the LXX alike read "wild animals" in 2:14 (assuming the Hebrew *khayat-ha'arets*, "beast of the earth," or *khayat-hassadeh*, "beast of the field," both typical idioms for "wild animal" in Hebrew), the MT has *kol-khayto-goy*: "every beast of a nation." It is difficult to account for this as a textual error (though Rudolph 1975, 278, suggests that *goy* is an error for *naweh*, "meadow," which is visually similar in Hebrew; cf. also Roberts 1991, 193): rather, the versions seem to be interpreting the Hebrew original we have before us. As Sweeney observes, the purpose of this unique Hebrew expression may be to connect with "the concerns of the oracles against the nations" (Sweeney 2003, 153).

Nineveh expresses its arrogance in a marvelously contemptuous dismissal of all rivals (cf. Roberts 1991, 204): "I am, and there is no one else" (2:15). Deutero-Isaiah will use this same expression to describe the arrogance of Babylon in its last days (Isa 47:8-11; cf. Sweeney 2003, 155). The same arrogance of empire, selfish and careless of consequences, rings in the declaration commonly attributed to Louis XV, "*Apres moi, le deluge*"—that is, "After me, let the flood come." I alone matter. In our own Western context, this sounds like our culture's cult of the individual, ignoring the common good in favor of so-called "enlightened self-interest." Yet it may also describe the attitudes of those in ministry who insist that they alone are competent, or capable, or caring enough to meet their peoples' needs. Scripture condemns such self-idolatry in all its forms (cf. Exod 18:13-27; 1 Kgs 19:9-18). Proud Nineveh will become "a desolation . . . a lair for wild animals" (2:15). Instead of the fear and awe that it had held to be its due, the ruined city will be regarded with contempt (for hissing as a sign of contempt, see Jer 19:8; Lam 2:15-16; Ezek 27:36).

An Oracle against Jerusalem (3:1-13)

The chapter begins "Ah, soiled, defiled, oppressing city!" (3:1). Since the vilified city is unnamed, the reader assumes that Zephaniah is still talking about Nineveh (2:13-15). Yet, then 3:2 says of this city, "It has not trusted in the LORD; it has not drawn near to its God"—surely a strange accusation to raise against foreign Nineveh. It is only with the statement "The LORD within it is righteous" (3:5), however, that the identification of the "soiled, defiled, oppressing city" becomes unmistakable: this must be *Jerusalem.* Just as Amos uses the same forms of speech to critique Israel that he had used to critique its neighbors (Amos 1–2), and just as an oracle against Judah in 2:1-3 introduces the oracles against the nations in Zephaniah 2:4-15, so the prophet here invites his audience to see Jerusalem as no different than Nineveh!

Now we see why the oracles against the nations are so vague and nonspecific—especially as compared to Zephaniah's very specific and particular accusations against Judah. Zephaniah is not greatly concerned about the wickedness of foreigners. His real concern is with his own people who, judging by their actions, seem to have forgotten who they are: they have lost their distinctiveness (cf. 1:8-9) and become just like the nations.

Beginning in 3:3, Zephaniah extends his critique to specific officials in Jerusalem (cf. Ezek 22:25-29, which is based on Zeph 3:3-4; so Duguid 1994, 72–75; Tuell 2009, 146–48). First, its secular ("officials" and "judges"; 3:3) then its religious leadership ("prophets" and "priests"; 3:4) stand condemned. The term *sar* (rendered "officials" in the NRSV of 3:3) "is a very general term for an officer" (Roberts 2005, 147). Such officials could be, like Zephaniah himself (1:1), members of the nobility (cf. 1:8, where *hassarim* ["the officials"] are condemned alongside "the king's sons," and Ezek 22:25), but this need not be the case. As Roberts (2005, 147; cf. Sweeney 2003, 162–63) notes, *sar* "was used for officials of cabinet rank (1 Kgs 4:1-6), including the commander-in-chief of the army (1 Sam 14:50; 2 Sam 24:2), but it was also used for leaders of much smaller units, units of a thousand, a hundred, fifty, and even down to a unit of ten (Exod 18:25)." According to some traditions, judges were to be Levites (1 Chr 23:4; 26:29-32; 2 Chr 19:4-10), indeed priests (Exod 21:6; 22:7-8; Deut 21:1-5; Ezek 44:24); since the priests are separately and specifically critiqued in 3:4, however, it is more likely that secular officials are intended here (cf. Exod 18:21-23). The officials and judges of Jerusalem are described as beasts: lions and wolves preying on the people they were charged to protect (cf. Hab 1:8, where the Babylonians are described in bestial terms; the expression *ze'ebe 'ereb* ["wolves of the evening"] appears only in these two contexts).

While Zephaniah condemns Jerusalem's secular leaders for their rapacity, he condemns its religious leaders for their carelessness. The prophets are "reckless, faithless persons" (3:4), insolent and unreliable. The priests, responsible for teaching Torah and for preserving the distinction between sacred and profane things (e.g., Lev 10:10-11; Deut 33:8-10; 2 Kgs 17:27-28; Ezek 44:23-24; 2 Chr 15:3), have instead "profaned what is sacred," so that "they have done violence to the law" (cf. Hab 1:4). Through their inattentiveness and lack of zeal, these religious leaders have betrayed both their responsibilities and their people.

A similar rebuke to the leadership of Jerusalem appears in Micah 3:9-12, where the city's rulers (Heb., *ro'sheha*, "its chiefs"), priests, and judges alike are condemned for taking bribes. Micah condemns these leaders for saying, despite their corruption, "Surely the LORD is with us! No harm shall come upon us" (Mic 3:11; cf. Jer 7:4). Unlike Micah, however, who dismissively declares Zion's destruction (Mic 3:12), Zephaniah remains confident that the LORD is indeed present in Jerusalem:

> The LORD within it is righteous;
> he does no wrong.
> Every morning he renders his judgment,
> each dawn without fail (Zeph 3:5).

God's faithfulness, then, stands in sharp contrast to the faithlessness of Jerusalem's leaders.

Zephaniah 3:6-8 recapitulates chapter 1, once more setting God's judgment upon Jerusalem in the context of universal judgment. The condemnation of the nations described in 2:4-15 is lifted up in 3:6 as an example to Jerusalem. Surely, having seen God's judgment on its neighbors, the city will respond to God and repent. The NRSV of 3:7 ("Surely the city will fear me") blurs the personal nature of God's appeal; the Hebrew could better be rendered, "I said, 'Surely *you* [that is, "you, Lady Jerusalem"] will fear me, *you* will accept correction'" (the verbs are feminine singular; both *Tg. Neb.* and LXX have plurals, assuming that the people rather than the personified city are addressed). The NRSV "it will not lose sight" follows the Syriac and LXX, which evidently read "from her eye" rather than the MT "her dwelling" (so also Roberts 1991, 209). The MT *welo' yikkaret me'ona* ("her dwelling will not be cut off"; cf. KJV) is meaningful, though, and reflected in both

Tg. Neb. and the Vulgate (with Sweeney 2003, 167). God hopes that the devastation worked in the cities of the nations (3:6) will not need to be visited on Jerusalem.

Nonetheless, sadly, Jerusalem has learned nothing from God's judgment on the nations. Zephaniah 3:8 is strongly reminiscent of 1:2-3, where God's wrath is poured out on the entire earth. The expression "in the fire of my passion all the earth shall be consumed" (3:8) recalls 1:18, where virtually the same phrase occurs. This recapitulation of the beginning and ending of the first chapter suggests that 3:8 was the original ending of Zephaniah's prophecy: because Jerusalem had become in all points like the nations, it would share their fate on the day of the LORD's wrath (cf. Nogalski 1993a, 177).

This is not the end of the *book*, however! In its final form, Zephaniah concludes not with judgment but with hope. Zephaniah 3:9-13 deals with the restoration of Judah after the exile, and so likely dates in large measure to the time of the exile (so Rudolph, 1975, 256) or later. This promise of restoration, however, begins not with the exiles of Judah but with the nations. The Hebrew *ki-'az 'ekhpok 'el-'amim saphah berurtah* ("then I will change to the peoples a pure speech") in 3:9 clearly assumes that *something* unspecified will be changed, but the versions, which seem to be working with the same ambiguous text that we have, are no help. The NRSV "At that time I will change *the speech of* the peoples to a pure speech" seems the best rendering of this clause. The passage alludes to Babel (Gen 11:1-9; ben Zvi [1991, 24–25] notes that Zeph 3:9-17, 20 was read together with Gen 11:1 in the old triennial cycle of readings once used in the synagogue), where God confused the speech (again, *saphah*; cf. Gen 11:7) of the nations, so that humanity, which had been united by "one language and the same words" (Gen 11:1), became scattered (cf. Berlin 1994,14; Sweeney 2003, 183; Nogalski 2011, 705–706, 743–45). Zephaniah envisions the undoing of Babel's curse, to the end "that all of them may call on the name of the LORD / and serve him with one accord" (3:9).

This promise that the nations will be reunited in the worship and service of the LORD calls to mind the Zion song in Isaiah 2:1-4 (contrast Mic 4:1-5, where this same song is used instead to contrast faithful Israel with the faithless nations), and the role of the nations in the Servant Songs (cf. especially Isa 42:1, 4, 6; 49:1, 6-7; 52:15). Christian readers will think of the allusion to the Babel story in Acts 2:1-13, where the Holy Spirit conveys the gift of tongues to those praying in the upper room, prompting Pentecost pilgrims from across the Roman world to declare, "in our own languages we hear them speaking about God's word of power" (Acts 2:11). In Zephaniah, reversing the curse of Babel in turn reverses the curse of exile (Zeph 3:10). Just as, through the confusion (Heb., *balal*; Gen 11:7) of their speech the nations had been scattered (Heb., *puts*; Gen 11:8), so through the purification (Heb., *barar*; Zeph 3:9) of the nations' speech God returns the exiles—those God calls "my scattered ones" (Heb., *bath-putsay*; Zeph 3:10)—"From beyond the rivers of Ethiopia" (3:10), that is, from Egypt (cf. Isa 18:1; Ezek 29:10). This may be literal, referring to the Egyptian Diaspora (cf. Jer 43:8–44:30), or it may be figurative, using Egypt as a symbol for captivity (cf. Hos 11:5). In either case, the returnees come back to Jerusalem to offer sacrifices on Zion (Zeph 3:10-11). The description of Zion as "my holy mountain" (3:11) appears elsewhere in the Twelve only in the late books Joel (2:1; 4:17 [3:17]) and Obadiah (16). This expression appears primarily in the Psalms (six times) and in Isaiah (also six times), particularly in Trito-Isaiah (cf. 56:7; 57:13; 65:11, 25; 66:20; the other occurrences of this phrase are Isa 11:9; Ezek 20:40 and Dan 9:16). Particularly intriguing are the parallels with Isaiah 56:7, where the context also deals with a rebuke to the haughtiness of Judah, and 66:20, which also deals with the end of the exile. Likely, this passage too comes from after the exile, although the editors have related this expansion clearly to Zephaniah 3:5, which affirms God's presence in the midst of Jerusalem.

Just as God has purified the speech of the nations, reuniting them in order to deliver God's people from exile, so also God purifies the people Israel. The restored nation will no longer be haughty, but "humble and lowly" (3:12; Heb., *'oni wadal*), like those righteous ones to whom Zephaniah had appealed in 2:3: "all you humble [Heb., *'onwe*, closely related to *'oni*] in the land, who do his commands." This "remnant of Israel"

> shall do no wrong
> and utter no lies,
> nor shall a deceitful tongue
> be found in their mouths (3:13).

Thus, Israel's speech will be purified, just like the speech of the nations! The description of restored Israel as the flock of the LORD, which will "pasture and lie down, and no one shall make them afraid" (3:13), calls to mind Ezekiel's description of the LORD as the good shepherd (Ezek 34:11-16; cf. John 10), as well as Psalm 23 (cf. 23:2, 4), and contrasts sharply with the image of Assyria's kings as failed shepherds in Nahum 3:17-18.

Jerusalem Renewed (3:14-20)

The concluding section of Zephaniah is recognized as a unit, not only by the Masoretic scribes but also in the Revised Common Lectionary, which designates 3:14-20 for reading on the third Sunday of Advent, Year C, and every year in the Easter Vigil. Both of these settings in the Christian liturgical year reflect the message of salvation and deliverance in this passage. Thus, Theodoret of Cyrus, while acknowledging that these verses relate to the return of the exiles and the restoration of Jerusalem, nonetheless affirms, "But you can find a more exact outcome after the Incarnation of our savior: then it was that he healed the oppressed in heart in the washing of regeneration, then it was that he renewed human nature, loving us so much as to give his life for us" (Hill 2006, 218).

The passage begins with a call to praise:

> Sing aloud, O daughter Zion;
> shout, O Israel!
> Rejoice and exult with all your heart,
> O daughter Jerusalem! (3:14).

While Jerusalem was implicitly personified in 3:1-2 and 7, this verse makes the depiction of Jerusalem as a woman explicit. While that depiction is frequently negative in Scripture (cf. the discussion of Nah 3:4-7), here it is unrelievedly positive. As in Isaiah 40:1-2, daughter Zion is assured of God's forgiveness and deliverance (3:15). Since this message of salvation is at odds with Zephaniah's earlier message of universal destruction and devastation, 3:14-20 most likely belongs to the final editing of Zephaniah for inclusion in the Book of the Twelve. This is particularly evident in Zephaniah 3:17: "he will rejoice over you with gladness, / he will renew you in his love." The NRSV here follows the LXX and Syriac; the MT has *yakharish be'ahabato* ("he will be silent in his love" [?]). As the verse goes on to describe God's joyous ululation (Heb., *rinnah*) over Jerusalem, however, it is likely that the MT is an error for *yekhadesh* ("he will renew"). Therefore, God joins in Zion's song (very different from Amos 5:23, where God rejects the songs of Israel), restoring even the weak and lame (3:19)—a reminder that it is not our strength that makes the difference in the end, but God's! Edith Humphrey recalls that in C. S. Lewis's novel *The Magician's Nephew*, the lion Aslan, Lewis's Christ figure, sings the world of Narnia into being. Although there are few biblical references to God singing, she observes, "[A]ll songs are inspired by that One. . . . Nor are all the songs of God laments: for he promised by the prophet Zephaniah (3:17) to utter his *rinnah*, his ulululation or great cry of triumph, when we his people are renewed" (Humphrey 2011, 197). Thus, too, Gregory of Nazianzus prayed, "All things breathe you a prayer, / A silent hymn of your own composing" (trans. W. Mitchell; cited by Humphrey 2011, 197). All creation is caught up in God's exultant song of joy.

Apart from Hosea 3:1 (cf. also 11:1 and 14:5 [4]) and Malachi 1:2; 2:11, Zephaniah 3:17 is the only mention of God's love in the Twelve (though here, the noun *'ahabah* is used, not the verb *'ahab* found in Hosea and Malachi). This verse, then, reflects the final form of the Twelve, in which love begins, ends, and in effect centers the entire collection. It is appropriate then that Zephaniah, which began in wrath, should end in joy and renewal:

> I will make you renowned and praised
> among all the peoples of the earth,
> when I restore your fortunes
> before your eyes, says the Lord (3:20).

Haggai

Reading Haggai

Haggai was an establishment prophet. Unlike Amos or Zephaniah, who staunchly opposed the powers that be, Haggai was closely tied to the central institutions of government and religion. His oracles are dated by the regnal years of Darius, the Persian overlord, and are directed to Zerubbabel, the governor of Judah under Persian auspices, and to Joshua the high priest (Hag 1:1). Perhaps this is one reason his book is so rarely studied: we are far more attracted to the rebel, standing alone against the system, than to a loyal company man like Haggai. As Goldingay wryly observes, "We are more comfortable with Amos than with Haggai, even if in the end we take no notice of Amos" (Goldingay 2009, 147). Indeed, Hans Walter Wolff describes Haggai as "one of the most minor of the minor prophets, indeed one of the most despised" (Wolff 1988, 11). Yet Haggai, no less than Amos or Zephaniah, claims to speak the LORD's word, and Haggai's book is included in the Scriptures. His rebuilding program may not be as exciting as Zephaniah's exuberant vision of rebirth and restoration (cf. Zeph 3:14-20), but even so Haggai has an important word for us. Indeed, Haggai's message of preservation and rebuilding may be more important now than ever before.

In his book *A Generation of Seekers: The Spiritual Journeys of the Baby Boom Generation,* Wade Clark Roof concludes that, while Americans born between 1946 and 1964 are very interested in spiritual questions, they are disenchanted with traditional, organized religion. In fact, of the people in this age group that Roof surveyed, 66 percent of conservatives, 79 percent of moderates, and 94 percent of all others agreed with the statement, "a person can be a good Christian or Jew if he or she doesn't attend church or synagogue" (Roof 1993, 110–11). Such attitudes have, if anything, increased in succeeding years (cf. Lugo et al. 2012; Cooperman et al. 2015). The Pew Research Institute has determined that 22.8 percent of Americans identify themselves as unaffiliated with any particular religion. Further, while only 11 percent of those born 1928–1945 are unaffiliated with any church or religious group, 17 percent of those born 1946–1964, 23 percent of those born 1965–1980, 34 percent of those born 1981–1989, and 36 percent of those born 1990–1996 identify themselves as unaffiliated—indeed, "none" is the fastest-growing religious group among young adults (Cooperman et al. 2015). In another disturbing statistic, a 2013 Gallup poll reveals that 77 percent of Americans believe "religion is losing its influence on American life"—the highest negative number polled on this question since 1970, when 75 percent of Americans thought that this was true (Newport 2013).

These statistics mark the death of an illusion to which the church has clung since the days of Constantine (272–337 CE), when Christianity not only became legal but also took on the trappings of official power. We had come to think that we Christians belong with the popular and powerful rather than the shunned and the powerless. We had come to believe that we ought to be able to dictate our values to the world rather than demonstrating our values through lives of engagement and service. We forgot that we serve a crucified Lord whose only crown was a crown of thorns. Perhaps now that "Christendom" lies dead or dying, we can be the church again and seek the kingdom of God.

Looking at these same statistics, Diana Butler Bass sees not decline but transformation. She proposes that we are in the second stage of a fourth Great Awakening, which began in the 1960s, was slowed by a "powerful nativist backlash" from 1975 to 1995, and is now once more gaining steam (Bass 2012, 241). Bass describes the story of this Fourth Great Awakening as "deceptively simple":

> Conventional religion is failing and a new form of faith, which some call "spirituality" . . . is in the process of reshaping most religions by emphasizing relationships, practices, and experience that connects people to deeper awareness of self, to their neighbors in global community, and to God. (Bass 2012, 259)

Frustration with the church in our day is palpable and easily understood: like all institutions, the church has been slow to change when change is needed. Still, the institutional organization of the church remains the means by which ministry gets done. God's presence is still experienced, and God's will made known, in and through religious institutions—despite their many troubles and conflicts. We need to learn new ways to be the church in a rapidly changing culture, without losing our identity in the face of change.

Like Haggai, we need to devote ourselves to rebuilding: to finding in our day new ways to tell the old story.

Authorship, Date, and Setting

The name "Haggai" means "festal," and so may have been a name given to children born on a feast day. In the Hebrew Bible, a son of Gad (Gen 46:16; Num 26:15) and a Levite, the son of Shimea (1 Chr 6:15), are also called Haggai; Haggith, a feminine form of the name, was one of David's wives, the mother of Adonijah (2 Sam 3:4; 1 Kgs 1:5; 1:11; 2:13; 1 Chr 3:2). The name "Haggai" occurs nine times in the book of Haggai (1:1, 3, 12, 13; 2:1, 10, 13, 14, 20), as well as in Ezra 5:1 and 6:14, where Haggai and Zechariah appear together as the prophetic cheerleaders of the Judean restoration, advocating for the rebuilding of the temple that the Babylonians had destroyed. While Haggai 1:13 identifies Haggai as "the messenger of the LORD [*mal'ak Yhwh*]," and Haggai 2:13, 14, and 20 provide the name alone, the other seven passages all identify Haggai as "*the* prophet" (Heb., *hannabi'* in Haggai; Aramaic *nabia'* in Ezra). As in the case of Habakkuk (cf. the discussion of Hab 1:1, above), this suggests that Haggai was a central intermediary (only Habakkuk, Haggai, and Zechariah are identified *as* prophets in the opening verses of their books). The identity of Haggai's audience confirms this impression. Although he sometimes also addresses "the people" (1:13), "the remnant of the people" (2:2), or "you people of the land" (2:4), Haggai speaks primarily to religious and secular leaders: to "Zerubbabel son of Shealtiel, governor of Judah, and to Joshua son of Jehozadak, the high priest" (1:1; 2:2), to the priests (2:10), and to Zerubbabel alone (2:21).

According to the royal genealogy in 1 Chronicles 3:17-19, the first governors of Judah under Persian auspices were descendants of David through King Jeconiah (also called Jehoiachin [2 Kgs 24:6-17; 2 Chr 36:8-9] and Coniah [Jer 22:24]), who was taken to Babylon as an exile in 597 BCE. Second Kings 25:27-30 states that Jehoiachin was released from prison by Evil-merodach (likely Amel-marduk, who ruled in Babylon from 562–560 BCE), given a living allowance, and honored among the other exiled kings in Babylon, so it certainly is possible that he could have fathered children in Babylon. The Chronicler's genealogy records seven sons born to Jeconiah in exile. The fourth son, Shenazzar, was apparently the first Persian-period governor of Judah, called Sheshbazzar in Ezra 1:8-11 (both names are forms of the Akkadian *Sin-ab-utsur*). Zerubbabel, Jeconiah's grandchild through his third son Pedaiah, is likely the second governor, under whose authority the second temple was completed (Ezra 3:8; 5:2; Neh 12:1; Hag 1:1; 2:1-4, 21-32; Zech 4:6-10). Haggai, Ezra, and Nehemiah call Zerubbabel the son of Shealtiel, Jeconiah's eldest son, rather than the son of Pedaiah, which may reflect the practice of levirate marriage. By this custom, if a man died childless, his brother was obligated to marry the widow; the first son born from their union was considered for purposes of inheritance the child of the deceased man (cf. Gen 38:8-11; Deut 25:5-10). Hence, Zerubbabel could have been the biological son of Pedaiah, as Chronicles states, and still legally the son of his uncle Shealtiel. In any case, it seems probable that Zerubbabel was descended from David.

Jehozadak, father of Joshua the high priest (Hag 1:1, 12, 14; 2:2, 4; Zech 3:1, 3, 6, 8; 6:11) appears in the high priestly genealogy in 1 Chronicles 6:4-15, which traces the lineage of the high priests from Eleazar the son of Aaron to Jehozadak, who "went into exile when the LORD sent Judah and Jerusalem into exile by the hand of Nebuchadnezzar" (1 Chr 6:15). Nehemiah 12:10-11 picks up where this list leaves off, with Joshua (there called Jeshua, but cf. Ezra 3:8; 4:3; Neh 12:1), who would have been born in exile. Joshua and Zerubbabel, then, were the religious and secular leaders, respectively, of the Judean community during the reign of the Persian emperor Darius. Moving from Zephaniah, set in the reign of Josiah in the mid-sixth century, to Haggai, set in the late fifth century (August to December of 520 BCE, to be precise) involves a leap of more than a century.

A series of nine quite precise date formulae link Haggai to Zechariah (Hag 1:1, 15; 2:1, 10, 18, 20; Zech 1:1, 7; 7:1). All but four of these specify the year, the month, and the day (Hag 2:1 gives the month and the day, but see the discussion on 1:15–2:1 in "Structure" below; 2:18 gives the day and month, and 2:20 gives only the day, but both refer explicitly back to the date in 2:10; Zech 1:1 gives only the year and month). This precision in dating calls to mind the book of Ezekiel, the only other biblical text that features dating precise to the day (cf. Tuell 2003, 283). In Ezekiel, the dating formulae typically follow the order year-day-month (cf. 1:1; 8:1; 20:1; 24:1; 29:1; 29:17; 30:20; 31:1; 32:1; 33:21; 40:1; in 1:2; 26:1; and 32:17 only the year and day are given). But in Haggai and Zechariah, the formula is not fixed: the order is year-month-day in Haggai 1:1; month-day in Haggai 2:1 (possibly year-month-day, if the year in 1:15b is presumed); day-month-year in Haggai 1:15; 2:10 (for this same date, 2:18 has day-month, and 2:20 has only the day); and Zechariah 1:7; month-year in Zechariah 1:1; and year-day-month in Zechariah 7:1.

Usually, as in Ezekiel, each date formula introduces a unit (but cf. 1:15). Also as in Ezekiel, the dates are in the main sequential (in Ezekiel, only the dates in the Egypt oracles [29–32] are out of sequence; cf. Tuell 2009, 168). The exception is Zechariah 1:1, which predates Haggai 2:10, 18, 20. Seth

Sykes proposes that these overlapping dates "reinforce a thematic connection between the two prophetic texts"; in this way, the overlap contributes to the unity of Haggai–Zechariah 1–8 as a "unified, whole utterance" (Sykes 2002, 27; see the discussion of "Haggai and Zechariah 1–8," below). The most remarkable feature of these dates, however, is that they are calculated by the regnal years of a foreign king, the Persian emperor Darius I (522–486 BCE)—a move without precedent in the prophetic corpus (Meyers and Meyers 1987, 5).

The Early Persian Period

In 539 BCE, Cyrus the Great (558–530 BCE) conquered Babylon, and the Neo-Babylonian Empire ended. The Cyrus Cylinder, an inscription on a clay barrel dating to this time, describes Cyrus's policy toward at least some of the peoples exiled by the Babylonians:

> (As to the region) from . . . as far as Ashur and Susa, Agade, Eshunna, the towns of Zamban, Me-Turnu, Der as well as the region of the Gutians, I returned to (these) sacred cities on the other side of the Tigris, the sanctuaries of which have been in ruins for a long time, the images which (used) to live therein and established for them permanent sanctuaries. I (also) gathered all their (former) inhabitants and returned (to them) their habitations. (Oppenheimer 1969, 316)

Ezra records two versions of an edict from Cyrus regarding the exiles from Judah, one in Hebrew (Ezra 1:2-4) and one in Aramaic (6:3-5), permitting them as well to return home and rebuild their temple, assisted by contributions from their neighbors. Cyrus further directed that the gold and silver vessels stolen from the Jerusalem temple were to be handed over to Sheshbazzar, the "prince of Judah" and leader of the returnees (Ezra 1:5-11), who would then return these sacred objects to the rebuilt temple.

The temple was not rebuilt, however. Cyrus had not provided explicitly for the funding of this project. Also, laborers were few—after a generation lived in exile, few were willing to leave Babylon, the only home they had ever known, for an uncertain life in Judah. That both Sheshbazzar and Zerubbabel had Akkadian rather than Hebrew names testifies to how thoroughly acclimated to Babylon the exiles had become. Further, the returnees refused to accept help that was offered by the people in the land who had not been taken off into exile, rejecting their claim that "we worship your God as you do" (Ezra 4:1-3). Whatever their reasons, then, the returnees gave up on their plans for rebuilding the temple, deciding to do the best that they could for themselves and their own families (cf. Hag 1:2, 4).

Meanwhile, Cambyses (530–522 BCE), son of Cyrus, took the Persian throne after his father's death. Preoccupied with the conquest of Egypt, Cambyses apparently paid no attention to Jerusalem and its ruined shrine; he is not mentioned in Scripture. Still, his conduct of affairs in Egypt confirms that he followed the pattern set by his father Cyrus, of selective, deliberate intervention into the religious lives of subject peoples (so Tuell 1992, 84–87). Thus, while Cambyses destroyed or defunded some Egyptian temples, he supported the temple of Neith and the House of Life at Sais (cf. the Udjahoresne inscription, trans. Lichtheim 1980, 38–39), as well as the temple of the Hebrew community at Elephantine (cf. the Elephantine Papyri, AP 30, in Cowley 1923). This pattern, which extends through other Persian rulers as well, lends credence to the biblical witness regarding the support of Cyrus and Darius in particular for the rebuilding of the Jerusalem shrine.

With the death of Cambyses far from home in Egypt, the succession was thrown into question. First Bardiya, the brother of Cambyses, claimed the throne. Then Darius, a popular general in the field, ousted him in a military coup, justifying this action with the assertion that the real Bardiya was dead, and that the man who had claimed Persia's throne was an impostor. Darius expressed his apology for this usurpation in the grandest and most public manner possible, writing it on a massive inscription carved into a cliff face at Behistun (cf. Weissbach 1911, 17). Whether his claim to the throne was legitimate or not, Darius became after Cyrus the greatest of Persia's kings: indeed, one could say that it was Darius who unified the empire and made it work.

According to Ezra 5–6, Darius was in no small measure responsible for ensuring that the Jerusalem temple was finally rebuilt. In response to inquiries from the regional governors of the province of Abar-Nahara, of which Yehud (Persian-period Judah) was a part (Ezra 5:6-17), Darius initiated a search of the archives, to determine whether Cyrus had indeed empowered the Judeans to build their shrine. When a copy of Cyrus's decree was uncovered (Ezra 6:3-5), Darius added his own decree, giving teeth to the edict (6:6-12). Darius directed that the temple be rebuilt with money from the royal treasury, and its cult supported with money from the tribute paid by the province: that is, the temple would be a state-supported enterprise. If anyone opposed this edict, he declared, "a beam shall be pulled out of the house of the perpetrator, who then shall be impaled on it. The house shall be made a dunghill" (Ezra 6:11)! From what we can learn from Darius's own royal inscriptions and other sources concerning his policies elsewhere, this concern for ensuring that the edict of Cyrus was indeed carried out is entirely consistent with Darius's character and policies. For example, Darius's "Restoration of Order" inscription reads,

> Says Darius the king: Much evil that had been done, that I made (into) good. Provinces, seething, which smote one another, I made that they not smite: (that) these, as they were previously, so they should be, as many as were provinces.
>
> Says Darius the king: that I did by the will of Ahuramazda, that one man the other not smite: I in his place each one put; the law which was mine, of that they had respect; so that the strong the weak neither smite nor harm. (trans. Kent 1934, 44)

For Darius, it was the task of the king to preserve on earth the order established from heaven by the creator Ahuramazda.

Despite his eventual success at bringing order to the realm, Darius's coup initially threw the empire into disarray. The Egyptians and Babylonians, taking advantage of the confusion, rebelled against the Persians. It was two years before Darius finally managed to subdue all the rebel provinces and consolidate his own claim to the throne. It is against this backdrop of confusion, conflict, and disillusionment (cf. Hag 2:20-22) that the prophecies of Haggai, which are all dated in Darius's second year, must be read.

Structure

The structure of Haggai in its final form must certainly relate to the recurring date formulae in Haggai–Zechariah 1–8. That said, however, there is some controversy as to how those dates structure this work. Haggai 1:1-11; 2:1-9, 10-19 (note that this passage involves a conversation between Haggai and the priests as well as a word of the LORD from the prophet), and 20-23 seem to fit the expected pattern from Ezekiel of a date formula introducing an oracle. But 1:12-15, a narrative depicting the response to the prophet's first oracle, instead *concludes* with a date (1:15). The MT paragraphing treats 1:1-2 as an introduction to the entire book; it then divides Haggai into seven parts: 1:3-6, 7-11 (each introduced by the messenger formula "Thus says the LORD of hosts"; cf. 1:2, 7), 12-14; 1:15(? odd, as this paragraph thus begins with two different dates)–2:5, 2:6-9 (again breaking at the messenger formula; cf. 2:6), 10-19 and 20-23. Once more, 1:15 presents a problem, particularly the phrase "in the second year of King Darius" in 1:15b. As the text now stands, it is unclear whether this year belongs with the preceding date in 1:15a or the following date in 2:1, which is missing a year.

Hans Walter Wolff argued that 1:15a is a free-floating fragment (Wolff 1951, 20–21; 1988, 59–60). This date originally belonged with the oracle now found in 2:15-19. But the "Haggai-chronicler," as Wolff called the final redactor of this text, moved 2:15-19 from its original position following 1:15a, so that the blessing promised in 2:19 would be associated not with rebuilding but with the rejection of the unclean from participation. Meyers and Meyers note that 1:15, which presents the date as day-month-year, forms a neat envelope with 1:1, which has year-month-day. They therefore propose that the date in 1:15 was intended to conclude the first chapter. Meyers and Meyers also suggest that Haggai 2:1 originally began, "In the second year of Darius," but this phrase was lost when the scribe's eye skipped to the second, identical date and missed the repetition—a common scribal error known as *haplography* (Meyers and Meyers 1987, 36–37; cf. Beuken 1967, 31–33). They accordingly divide Haggai into two parts, 1:1-15 and 2:1-23 (Meyers and Meyers 1987, xlviii, 36–37). But as the date formulae in Haggai-Zechariah 1–8 do not follow any set pattern (see the discussion of the date formulae in Haggai and Zechariah in "Authorship, Date, and Setting," above), it is probably not a good idea to build an argument on their arrangement. David Petersen proposes that Haggai 1:1-15a be divided into two units, one beginning with a date formula (1:1-11; Petersen 1984, 41–54), the other ending with one (1:12-15a; Petersen 1984, 55–60); further, he carries the year designation in 1:15b over to the month and day in 2:1 (Petersen 1984, 62; note that the NRSV and the JPSV also follow this arrangement).

The solution to this puzzle, however, makes little difference as to the structure of the book. Petersen divides Haggai into six dated units: 1:1-11, 12-15; 2:1-9; 10-14, 15-19, 20-23 (Petersen 1984, 5). Meyers and Meyers (1987, xlviii) recognize these as subunits within their two-part structure, although they count 2:10-19 as a single unit (cf. Nogalski 2011, 769). This structure coincides rather neatly with the scribal units, apart from the scribes' tendency to break at indications of divine speech, subdividing the first and third units at the messenger formula. We will therefore consider this book in six parts: 1:1-2 (proposing, with the MT, that 1:1-2 functions as an introduction to the book), 3-11, 12-15; 1:15b–2:9, 10-19, and 20-23.

Haggai and Zechariah 1–8

In his *Geschichte des Volkes Israel bis zur Restauration unter Esra und Nehemia*, August Klostermann proposed that Haggai–Zechariah 1–8 was originally a single narrative, secondarily divided into two books (Klostermann 1896, 213). While the distinctiveness of Haggai and Zechariah makes this proposal highly unlikely, that it could be made at all testifies to the continuity evident between Haggai and Zechariah 1–8. A broad scholarly consensus holds that Haggai and Zechariah 1–8 were edited together as a unit, although differing markedly on complexity and the dating of that process (e.g., Ackroyd 1952, 155–56; Beuken 1967, 331; Meyers and Meyers 1987, xliv–xlix; Redditt 1995, 37; 42–43; Sykes 2002, 25–46; Nogalski 1993a, 235; 2011, 763; Hallaschka 2010, 13–14). Although David Petersen insists on the distinct composition and redaction of Haggai and Zechariah, he too recognizes a connection between the books (Petersen 1984, 124).

As we have already seen, date formulae precise to the day sew Haggai and Zechariah together, and so clearly belong to the editing of Haggai-Zechariah 1–8. Some scholars (e.g., Beuken 1967, Wolff 1988, Nogalski 1993) assign this activity to an editor from the same time and setting as Chronicles. We have no reason to doubt the accuracy of these dates, however, any more than we have to doubt the accuracy of the likewise precise dates in Ezekiel (*contra* Petersen 1984, 32–36, who proposes that Haggai is rather a prophetic novella: a "brief apologetic historical narrative" [Petersen 1984, 35] comparable to Jer 26; 36; 37–41, or perhaps to Jonah or Ruth), suggesting an editor not far removed in historical and social setting from Haggai.

The use of this dating system strongly suggests the influence of Ezekiel on the editor of Haggai and Zechariah, although the formulae are used differently in these two works. In Ezekiel's case, the slow passage of the exile is in view as he marks off the days, one by one. In Haggai–Zechariah 1–8, as Carol and Eric Meyers propose, the dates are a "countdown" to the end of the disruption brought by exile, thanks to the rebuilding of the LORD's temple (Meyers and Meyers 1987, 6). The date formulae in Ezekiel appear to be original to the prophet, but less significant for the structure of that book; the dates in Haggai and Zechariah, however, are both a major redactional link between these books and also a key structural feature in their shape. Three of Haggai's dates (Hag 2:10, 18, 20) refer to the same day: "On the twenty-fourth day of the ninth month, in the second year of Darius" (Hag 2:10). Meyers and Meyers propose that this may have been the date for the re-foundation ceremony of the temple (Meyers and Meyers 1987, xlvii). Redactionally speaking, this date stands at the center of Haggai–Zechariah 1–8, with three dates before it and three after (so Sykes 2002, 28–29).

That Haggai and Zechariah mark time by the reign of the Persian Darius would appear to indicate at least an acknowledgment of Persian domination, and perhaps even a pro-Persian bias (Hanson 1979, 244–45; Petersen 1984, 42–43; Meyers and Meyers 1987, 5–6). However, Sykes proposes rather that the "chronistic" structure of Haggai–Zechariah 1–8 involves a transformation of an old Babylonian chronicle genre (Sykes 2002; following Grayson

1975, who identifies twenty-four Mesopotamian texts as chronicles, fourteen of which precede Haggai and Zechariah). The Babylonian chronicles maintained royal support of the temple and cult at Esagila by selectively chronicling the reigns of "good" and "bad" kings. The ideal king, as presented in the Babylonian chronicles, preserves Babylon and its temples and so is blessed by the gods. By dating in accordance with the reign of Darius, Haggai and Zechariah appear to be following in that same vein, implicitly eliciting the support of Darius for their temple project by promising God's blessing on his reign.

The focus of the work is not on the rule of the Persian monarch, however. One of the most distinctive features of Haggai and Zechariah is the use of the divine title "LORD of hosts" (Heb., *Yhwh tseba'oth*; cf. the discussion of this title in Nah 3:5, above). In texts expressive of the old Zion theology, this title depicts the LORD enthroned above the cherubim in the Most Holy Place; it appears fourteen times in Haggai; and fifty-three times in Zechariah (though only nine times in Zech 9–14). As Meyers and Meyers demonstrate, while Haggai constitutes only 0.2 percent of the Hebrew Bible, 5 percent of the references to *Yhwh tseba'oth* in Scripture occur in this book. Similarly, Zechariah 1–8, at 0.6 percent of the Hebrew Bible, accounts for 14 percent of its references to this divine title (Meyers and Meyers 1987, 18). To say the least, it is clear that *Yhwh tseba'oth* is a characteristic expression of Haggai-Zechariah 1–8. The focus of this text, then, is not the rule of Darius but the rule of the LORD! As Sykes observes, Haggai–Zechariah 1–8 "subverts the historical reality of Persian imperial rule by depicting the universal and eternal rule of Yahweh" (Sykes 2002, 149–50).

Another characteristic feature of Haggai–Zechariah 1–8 is the use of the messenger formula *koh 'amar Yhwh* ("thus says the LORD"; cf. the discussion of this formula in Nah 1:12). In the six books with which we are concerned, this key feature of prophetic literature appears once each in Nahum (1:12) and Malachi (Mal 1:4), and not at all in Habakkuk or Zephaniah. However, the messenger formula occurs five times in Haggai (Hag 1:2, 5, 7; 2:6, 11), and twenty times in Zechariah—though only once (Zech 11:4) in Zechariah 9–14. Given the frequent use of the messenger formula by contemporaries Ezekiel (125 times) and Jeremiah (153 times), it appears that the formula became particularly important shortly before the exile; certainly Ezekiel understood this expression to be normative for prophetic speech: "I am sending you to them, and you shall say to them, 'Thus says the Lord GOD'" (Ezek 2:4; cf. 13:6-7). The frequency of the messenger formula in Haggai–Zechariah 1–8, particularly when compared to its scarcity in or absence from the likely postexilic compositions Joel, Obadiah, Jonah, and Malachi, again reflects the formal dependence of this work on Ezekiel.

Once we observe the literary distinctiveness of Haggai–Zechariah 1–8, other features become apparent. Haggai–Zechariah 1–8 (and for that matter, Malachi) is written in prose, in contrast to Nahum, Habakkuk, and Zephaniah, which like most prophetic books are mostly if not entirely poetry (cf. Goldingay 2009, 136). As Meyers and Meyers observe (Meyers and Meyers 1987, xliv–lxiii), numerous thematic and verbal links tie Haggai to Zechariah 1–8, and particularly, to Zechariah 7–8 (Meyers and Meyers 1987, xlix). For example, Haggai 1:1-11 opens with a date formula (1:1), as does Zechariah 7:1; describes the land as devastated (1:6), as does Zechariah 7:14; relates temple building to fertility (1:6-11), as does Zechariah 8:12; and parallels the produce of the land to the dew of heaven (1:10), as does Zechariah 8:12.

In sum, there are good reasons for thinking, in keeping with a large consensus of scholarship, that Haggai–Zechariah 1–8 was edited into a unit. Further, as we will see, there are good reasons for proposing that Zechariah and his disciples assembled this unit (with Klostermann 1896, 213; Meyers and Meyers 1987, 268). In the final form of Zechariah, of course, chapters 9–14 have been woven into the text, requiring us to consider the ways in which these chapters function in their final location. That is a question for later, however, as we consider the final shaping of Zechariah in the Book of the Twelve.

Commentary

Introduction (1:1-2)

Properly speaking, Haggai lacks a superscription, beginning instead with the date of its opening oracle (so Andersen and Freedman 1988, 143; Watts 2000a, 112)—another likely indication of the influence of Ezekiel on this composition (cf. Ezek 1:1). Nonetheless, the paragraphing of the Masoretic scribes observes a distinction between the opening statement of Haggai's prophecy (1:2) and his first oracle (1:3-6, 7-11). The repetition of the prophet's name coupled with the divine word formula at 1:1 and 3 (*wayehi debar-Yhwh beyad Khaggay hannabi'*, "Then the word of the LORD came by [literally, "by the hand of"] the prophet Haggai"), further suggests that, in the final form of the book, 1:1-2 has been set apart to serve as an introduction to what follows. Similarly, Amos opens with an introductory statement of the prophet's message: "The LORD roars from Zion . . ." (Amos 1:2; Sweeney calls this a "motto" [cf. Sweeney 2003, 184–85]), and Hosea's message commences after the superscription (Hos 1:1) with a repetition of the prophet's name, coupled with "the word of the LORD" (Hos 1:2). Likely, then, this reworking reflects the incorporation of Haggai–Zechariah 1–8 into the Book of the Twelve.

Among the Twelve, only Haggai 1:1, 3; 2:1; and Malachi 1:1 state that the word of the LORD comes "by the hand of" the prophet. In other prophetic books, this expression for the prophet as the bearer of God's word (*dabar Yhwh* with *beyad* followed by the prophet's name) only occurs at Isaiah 20:2 and in Jeremiah 37:2; 50:1. Torah uses this expression for Moses' role (Exod 9:35; Lev 10:11; Num 16:40; 27:23; cf. 2 Chr 35:6). But the Deuteronomistic History often describes prophetic activity in this way: especially in 1 and 2 Kings, where *dabar Yhwh* with *beyad* is used twelve times for the message of a specific prophet (Ahijah the Shilonite in 1 Kgs 12:15; 14:18; 15:29; Jehu son of Hanani in 1 Kgs 16:7, 10; Joshua in 1 Kgs 16:34; Elijah in 1 Kgs 17:16; 2 Kgs 9:36; 10:10; Jonah in 2 Kgs 14:25) or for the collective message of "his servants the prophets" (2 Kgs 21:10; 22:4). Perhaps this formula marks the inclusion of both Haggai–Zechariah 1–8 and Malachi into the Book of the Twelve, although in that case it is odd that this expression does not appear in Joel or Jonah. At any rate, it emphasizes the role of the prophet as intermediary (cf. Petersen 1984, 45).

The brief statement of Haggai's message in 1:2 neatly expresses the circumstance that this prophet confronted: "These people say the time has not yet come to rebuild the LORD's house" (Hag 1:2). It is perhaps little wonder that the people had come to this decision. With Jerusalem in ruins, and resources scarce, we can easily understand how the returnees could have decided to do their best for themselves and their families first, and to think about God later. Haggai, however, challenges this apparently reasonable course, and calls for the community to build the temple and put worship first.

Consider How You Have Fared (1:3-11)

The principal theme of Haggai's prophecy, the rebuilding of the temple (Ackroyd 1985, 367; Redditt 1995, 13), comes immediately into play in the opening section of the book. Haggai 1:3-11 echoes the dual themes of fertility and material prosperity, linked to the divine presence enshrined and celebrated in the right temple with the right cult, themes that are also found in Ezekiel 47:1-12 (Tuell 1992, 68–71; 2000, 171–89, esp. 181–86)—although in a negative rather than a positive sense. While in Ezekiel's vision, the river of paradise flows out of the glorified temple, bringing natural (Ezek 47:9, 12) and economic (Ezek 47:10-11) abundance, in Haggai the *failure* of the postexilic community to rebuild the temple has meant disaster not only for the human community but also for the land itself. Just as the presence of God, honored and celebrated in the temple, brings life and blessing to the land, the absence of God's temple has brought death, infertility, and drought (Hag 1:10-11).

Haggai challenges his community, "Consider how you have fared" (1:5). In a series of vivid images, he describes their circumstances: "You have sown much, and harvested little; you eat, but you never have enough; you drink, but you never have your fill; you clothe yourselves, but no one is warm; and you that earn wages earn wages to put them into a bag with holes" (1:6). By any standard, the community was not doing well. No one had enough, and no one seemed able to do anything more than just get by. The people were dissatisfied and unfulfilled. Stephen Cook (2010) relates this depiction of the postexilic community to "futility curses" for covenant breaking found in the Holiness Code (Lev 17–26; cf. 26:14-33), specifically Leviticus 26:20 ("Your strength shall be spent to no purpose: your land shall not yield its produce, and the trees of the land shall not yield their fruit") and 26 ("though you eat, you shall not be satisfied"). As Ezekiel too relates powerfully to the Holiness Code (e.g., compare Ezek 18:6, 19; 22:11; 33:26 with Lev 18:19; cf. Tuell 2009, 3; Lyons 2009, 157–61), Cook proposes that Haggai may have been a follower of Ezekiel in the exile (2010; cf. Hanson 1975, 174). Such a close relationship is not required, however, to explain Haggai's use of broad themes relating to Israel's temple ideology. Much of Ezekiel's characteristic vocabulary is either absent from or used differently in Haggai. For example, the term *hekal* is used in Ezekiel for the long central chamber of the temple (41:1, 4, 15, 21, 23, 25; 42:8), but in Haggai (Hag 2:15, 18; cf. Zech 6:12-15; 8:9), as elsewhere in postexilic literature (e.g., Isa 44:28; 66:6; Mal 3:1; Ezra 3:6, 10; 4:1; Neh 6:10, 11), it is used for the entire temple. Ezekiel's favorite term for the presence of the Lord, the priestly expression *kabod* ("glory"), is used in Haggai 2:3, 7, and 9 to mean "splendor" but does not explicitly indicate divine presence (*contra* Meyers and Meyers 1987, 54), while the expression *Yhwh tseba'oth*, typical of Haggai, never appears in Ezekiel. The strongest parallel between Ezekiel and Haggai, the dating formulae, relates to the book's shaping, together with Zechariah 1–8, rather than to Haggai's oracles or themes. While both Haggai and Ezekiel reflect priestly concerns, and more specifically relate to the concerns of the Holiness Code, Haggai's dreams are distinct from Ezekiel's (cf. Tuell 2003, 280).

Not only the people but also the land itself suffered from the temple's absence. Haggai declares, "Therefore the heavens above you have withheld the dew, and the earth has withheld its produce" (1:10). As Cook observes, Haggai makes a clear connection between the temple lying "in ruins" (Heb., *khareb*) and the "drought [Heb., *khoreb*] on the land" (1:11; cf. Cook 2010). For Haggai, since God's presence in the temple was the source of life and fertility in all the land, the refusal of the people to rebuild the temple resulted in God's absence, and so in infertility and drought. Jubilees 8:19, which also reflects this assumption, places Zion "in the midst of the navel of the earth." Scholar of religion Mircea Eliade described the myth of the center, or "navel," of the earth as a common theme in the history of religions (Eliade 1974). Since the cosmic center, identified with the temple, was the source of life and meaning for all creation, the presence of the Divine in the temple meant both fertility and material prosperity.

This belief regarding the temple occurs elsewhere throughout the ancient Near East. The Gudea Cylinders, an ancient Mesopotamian text dealing with the building of a temple to Ningirsu at Lagash, describe the preparation of a royal bedchamber in the temple for the god and his consort, resulting in fertility as well as material prosperity (Cylinder B, 14.19-24). Similarly, in old Canaanite mythology, temple building results in both natural and economic abundance. When El decrees that a house is to be built for Baal, Lady Asherah jubilantly responds,

> Now, indeed, his rainy season
> Baal will appoint; the season of ships upon the waves.
> Now he will give his voice in the clouds;
> He will loose lightnings upon the earth.
> The house of cedar, he may build it;
> Even the house of brick, he may raise it! (CTA 4.5.68-73, my translation)

The temple of Baal was a blessing to merchant as well as farmer, bringing material prosperity as well as natural abundance. Although the sexual imagery of the Gudea Cylinders is absent from the Hebrew Bible, the themes of abundance linked to temple building are clearly found there as well (cf. Ezek 47:1-12; Hag 1:2-11). The building of the temples at Lagash and Ugarit called for precious woods, stones, and metals (cf. the list of materials in Gudea Cylinder A, and in CTA 4.5.74-81; 91-97 [98-102]). The descriptions of the tabernacle in Exodus 25–27, and of Solomon's temple in 1 Kings 6–7, also emphasize gold, cedar, and other precious materials. Haggai 1:2-11, then, echoes a common theme of prosperity linked to the divine presence, enshrined and celebrated in the right temple with the right cult.

A modern reader may see connections between Haggai's temple theology and the "prosperity gospel," which promises health, wealth, and success to those who believe the right things and pray in the right way (Gifford

2007). But this so-called "gospel" is actually an egregious misappropriation of Haggai's theology. In contrast, Haggai does not tell his community what they must do in order to prosper. Indeed, he lays the blame for their currently unfulfilled lives on the pursuit of their own prosperity. Haggai 1:4 asks, "Is it a time for you yourselves to live in your paneled houses, while this house lies in ruins?" The reference to paneling (Heb., *saphun*) calls to mind the opulence of the first temple (1 Kgs 6:9) and of the royal palaces of Solomon (1 Kgs 7:3, 7) and Jehoiakim (Jer 22:13-15). Haggai's community, with their "paneled houses," had aspired to that former wealth and prosperity, and in so doing had placed themselves first and God last. But this way of living had not brought them the satisfaction and fulfillment they sought. Only by obeying God's command through the prophet to rebuild the temple, and so place God first, could Haggai's community find the fulfillment that had eluded them. For Christian readers, this paradox calls to mind the words of Jesus, "[T]hose who want to save their life will lose it, and those who lose their life for my sake, and for the sake of the gospel, will save it" (Mark 8:35).

The People Respond (1:12-15a)

David Petersen describes Haggai as a "brief apologetic historical narrative" comparable to Jeremiah 26; 36; 37–41 (Petersen 1984, 32–36). Both Jeremiah and Haggai demonstrate a "skillful interweaving of prophetic word with narrative context," but Petersen observes an intriguing contrast between these two prophets: "Whereas Jeremiah's words received a fundamentally negative response, e.g., Jer. 36, Haggai's words by contrast elicit a positive response" (Petersen 1984, 34; cf. Wolff 1988, 11). Haggai's success is the subject of the brief narrative unit in 1:12-15. In these few verses, the description of the response of the people and their leadership (described in nearly identical terms in 1:12 and 14) brackets a word of assurance from the prophet: "Then Haggai, the messenger of the LORD [*mal'ak Yhwh*], spoke to the people with the LORD's message, saying, I am with you, says the LORD" (Hag 1:13). The word "message" (Heb., *mal'akut*) appears only here in the Hebrew Bible. The expression *mal'ak Yhwh*, commonly used for the angel of God's presence (cf. Zech 1:11-12; 3:1, 5, 6; 12:8), refers to a human messenger only here and in Malachi 2:7 (which refers to God's ideal priest as "the messenger of the LORD of hosts"). This dual emphasis on the unique role of Haggai suggests that, again like Jeremiah, he is being cast in this narrative as the prophet, like Moses (cf. Deut 18:15; McBride 2009, 181). This connection is made more likely by the word of the LORD Haggai proclaims, a promise also given to Moses: "I am with you" (Hag 1:13; cf. Exod 3:12). Just as Moses was given a vision of the tabernacle his people were to build (Exod 25:9), so Haggai calls his community in his day to build a shrine for the LORD. The promise of divine presence will remind Christian readers of Jesus' words at the conclusion of Matthew's Gospel: "And remember, I am with you always, to the end of the age" (Matt 28:20).

Inspired by Haggai's challenge, the leadership and the community set about rebuilding the Jerusalem temple. The book of Haggai describes that community as "all the remnant of the people" (Heb., *kol she'erith ha'am*; Hag 1:12, 14; cf. Hag 2:2). In the Book of the Twelve, the term "remnant" (Heb., *she'ar*) occurs seventeen times: three in Amos (1:8, of the Philistines; 5:15, of Joseph; 9:12, of Edom), five in Micah (2:12; 4:7; 5:7-8; 7:18; all of Israel), and three each in Zephaniah (2:7, 9; 3:13), Haggai (1:12, 14; 2:2), and Zechariah (8:6, 11, 12). As we saw in Zephaniah 2:7, 9, *she'ar* may refer to the survivors of any catastrophe. Most commonly, however, the word refers to the remnant who survived the destruction of Jerusalem (note that the *she'ar* appears most often, 24 times, in Jeremiah), and hence to the restored community after the exile (as in Zeph 3:13 and in Haggai–Zechariah 1–8).

Take Courage! (1:15b–2:9)

As successful as Haggai's initial proclamation may have been, it was less than a month (assuming that the year in 1:15b and 2:1 is the same; see the discussion in "Authorship, Date, and Setting," above) before discouragement set in. Of course, reality always falls short of our dreams and ideals. As C. S. Lewis's Screwtape trenchantly observes, God

> allows this disappointment to occur on the threshold of every human endeavour. It occurs when the boy who has been enchanted in the nursery by *Stories from the Odyssey* buckles down to really learning Greek. It occurs when lovers have got married and begin the real task of learning to live together. In every department of life it marks the transition from dreaming aspiration to laborious doing. (Lewis 1960, 17)

But for the already disillusioned community of returnees from the exile, disappointment was a particular problem. They had surely heard grand stories of the wonders of Solomon's temple, and in its surviving foundation lines and ruined walls they could doubtless sense at first hand something of its majesty. Now, as their own far more modest structure began to take shape, the contrast between what was now and what once had been became, for some, overwhelming.

Haggai responds to this disillusionment with straightforward honesty: "Who is left among you that saw this house in its former glory? How does it look to you now? Is it not in your sight as nothing?" (Hag 2:3). Haggai does not deny either the glories of the past or the apparent insignificance of the present. He refuses, however, to succumb to despair. To the leaders of the community and to the people themselves, Haggai issues a renewed call to "take courage" and "work, for I am with you, says the LORD of hosts" (Hag 2:4). Much like Deutero-Isaiah, who had described Judah's coming restoration as a new exodus (e.g., Isa 40:3-4; 43:16-17, 19-20; 53:13), Haggai relates God's promise to be with his community to "the promise that I made you when you came out of Egypt" (2:5). As we have seen, this promise of divine presence recalls God's words to Moses, faced with the seemingly impossible task of delivering the people out of the hand of Pharaoh: "I will be with you" (Exod 3:12). So too Joshua, Moses' successor, was commanded, "Be strong and courageous; do not be frightened or dismayed, for the LORD your God is with you wherever you go" (Josh 1:9; cf. 1:6-7, 18). God's promise in those days of Israel's beginnings had proven true. Now, God assures the returnees that the promise remains sure. God will be with them, and they will become a great people once more.

But the renewal of Israel, Haggai declares, will require a cosmic upheaval: "For thus says the LORD of hosts: Once again, in a little while, I will shake the heavens and the earth and the sea and the dry land" (2:6; cf. 2:21). The language is reminiscent of ancient storm theophanies (e.g., Judg 5:4; 2 Sam 22:8; Nah 1:5; Pss 18:8[7]; 68:9[8]) as well as depictions of the day of the LORD (e.g., Joel 2:10; 3:16). In Zephaniah, cosmic upheaval relates to God's judgment on Judah (cf. Zeph 1:1-3, 18), but for Haggai, the nations are shaken so that their riches might flow into Jerusalem (Hag 2:7-8), to the end that "The latter splendor of this house shall be greater than the former" (2:9).

Reading this passage, many may hear in the back of their heads the Christmas section of George Handel's magnificent oratorio *Messiah*. Charles Jennens's libretto for this section understands Haggai 2:6-7 as a prediction of the coming Messiah (and also reads this passage, as we will see, in continuity with Mal 3:1-3). This messianic reading of Haggai depends in large measure on the translation of 2:7. While the NRSV reads "the treasure of all nations shall come," the KJV, following the Latin Vulgate, has "the *desire* of all nations shall come."

Jennens was far from the first Christian reader to make this move. Augustine (*City of God* 18.35) understood Haggai 2:6 to relate to Jesus' first coming (the shaking of the heavens relating to the angelic host [Luke 2:8-14] and the star [Matt 2:1-10], the shaking of earth and sea to the spread of the gospel), and 2:7 to his second coming: Jesus, of course, being the "desire of all nations." Similarly, in the Latin "O Antiphons" of Advent, dating certainly from the eleventh century and possibly from as early as the time of Charlemagne, the church sings "*O Rex gentium et desideratus*" ("O King and desire of the nations"). "O Come, O Come Emmanuel," the familiar carol based on these antiphons, hails Jesus as the "Desire of Nations." Intriguingly, the Revised Common Lectionary assigns Haggai 1:15b–2:9 for reading on Proper 27 in Year C, paired with 2 Thessalonians 2:1-5, 13-17, on Christ's second coming.

At issue in the translation and interpretation of Haggai 2:7 is the word *khemdath*, which means something precious or desirable (cf. the NIV, which reads "what is desired by all nations"). The LXX, however, reads *eklekta*: "the *elect* of all nations," apparently understanding the one desired by the nations to be God's elect ruler. The "O Antiphon" likely conflates this reading with the Vulgate *et veniet desideratus cunctis gentibus* ("and the desired of all nations shall come"). In context, *khemdath* seems rather to refer to the silver and gold in 2:8, brought into Jerusalem from the nations to glorify the rebuilt temple. *Targum Nebi'im* clarifies this by construing the word as plural ("the desired *things*" rather than the MT "desired thing or one"; cf. the JPSV translation "the precious things"). Ezekiel's favorite term for divine presence, *kabod* ("glory"), appears in Haggai 2:3, 7, and 9, but it is used differently than in Ezekiel: not for the LORD's glory but for the splendor of the temple, assured by God's decision to bring the wealth of the nations into Jerusalem. God can do this because the wealth the nations prize does not in truth belong to them: "The silver is mine, and the gold is mine, says the LORD of hosts" (2:8).

As O'Brien (2004, 149) notes, 2:6-9 is often called "eschatological" by commentators, and assigned to the later expansion of the book (e.g., Hallashka 2011, 62). These words, however, fit neatly into the time frame to which the date in 1:15b–2:1 assigns them. In the chaos surrounding Darius's reestablishment of order in the empire following his usurpation (see "The Early Persian Period" above in "Author, Date, and Setting"), Haggai hoped that God would act to restore Judah's prosperity and independence under Zerubbabel (cf. 2:20-23).

A Priestly Torah, and Its Implications (2:10-19)

This passage reports a conversation between Haggai and the priests, initiated at God's direction. Two date formulae (Hag 2:10, 18; cf. 2:20) refer to the same day, "the twenty-fourth day of the ninth month, in the second year of Darius" (Hag 2:10). This date stands at the center of Haggai–Zechariah 1–8, with three dates before it and three after (so Sykes 2002, 28–29), showing its importance in the book. Likely, as Meyers and Meyers propose, this was the day of the temple re-foundation ceremony (Meyers and Meyers 1987, xlvii;

cf. Ezra 3:8-13). On this day, the LORD commands Haggai to ask the priests for a *torah*—that is, an authoritative ruling (cf. Lev 10:10-11; Jer 18:18)—regarding holiness and defilement (2:11-13).

In the priest's worldview, the holy, the common, the clean, and the unclean marked the borders of life lived in relationship to God and to one another. The holy is God's peculiar sphere, while the common is the sphere of ordinary life: what we in the modern world might call the sacred and the secular. The story of Uzzah, who touched the holy ark of the covenant and immediately died (2 Sam 6:7//1 Chr 13:10), provides a grim reminder that the holy and the common must remain separate! Haggai asks the priests what would happen if they carried "consecrated meat" out of the temple precincts into unconsecrated space and touched ordinary, common food with it (2:12). This thought experiment would have horrified them. Priestly teaching consistently holds that consecrated meat is to be consumed within the bounds of sacred space, in the immediate environs of the temple's inner court. Leftovers must be burned, and anything that comes into contact with the consecrated meat must either be thoroughly cleaned within the temple walls, so that not even the smallest trace of the sacrificial offering is carried out of sacred space, or be destroyed (cf. Exod 29:34; Lev 6:19-23 [26-30]). Certainly, then, food and drink touched by such meat would not themselves become holy.

The clean and unclean relate to the spheres of the permissible and impermissible, not in moral but in ritual terms: what the people Israel can and cannot eat, drink, plant, use, wear, or even touch. Contact with unclean things—in Haggai's example (2:13), with a corpse (cf. Num 19:1-21)—makes a person and anything she or he touches unclean, unless the defilement is purged by right ritual and sacrifice. The priests therefore rightly rule that a person contaminated by corpse contagion would make any food he touched unclean.

Since a major responsibility of the priesthood was to know how to distinguish among the holy, the common, the clean, and the unclean, and to teach these distinctions to the people by word and example (Lev 10:10-11; cf. Ezek 7:26; 22:26), Haggai's question is not controversial (O'Brien 2004, 152), and the ruling of the priests is perfectly in line with the teaching in Torah. The question is why the prophet asks for this ruling and how he develops its implications. In view of the date of this oracle, Cook (2010) proposes that Haggai is "speaking at a re-foundation ceremony for the new temple" (cf. O'Brien 2004, 150–51; Meyers and Meyers 1987, 76–82), in order to call the whole community to spiritual discipline. In that case, however, it is difficult to understand the point of the analogy: in what way is his audience "like" someone with corpse contagion, and what is the point of the question about consecrated meat? Petersen (1984, 85; cf. O'Brien 2004, 151) proposes that Haggai's analogy is about sacrifice, specifically the need to purify the altar: "Haggai is arguing that when Judahites appear at the temple to present sacrifices, what they offer becomes unclean because it comes in contact with an altar and a temple that have not yet been purified." Yet Haggai has said nothing before this about the need for rituals of consecration or purification. If, as seems likely, the date of the oracle is the date of the temple's refoundation ceremony in Darius's second year, and if the priests are indeed (as they appear to be from their *torah*) cognizant of the importance of observing the holy, common, clean, and unclean, surely those rites were performed as a part of that ceremony (Ezra 3:10 states that everything was done "according to the directions of King David of Israel," the founder of the temple's liturgy; cf. 1 Chr 28:11-19; Tuell 2001, 92–93; 108–109).

One way into this analogy may be rethinking the audience of the oracle. Although 2:14 does talk about "this people" and "this nation," it does so in third person: "and so with every work of *their* hands; and what *they* offer there is unclean" (emphasis mine). Surely, if this narrative were reporting on a speech of Haggai to the people, he would address them in second person. It is instead most likely that the audience of the oracle is the priests, whom Haggai had asked for a *torah*. If we ask what about the *priests* might result in unacceptable and unclean sacrifices, the legitimacy of the priesthood itself comes to mind.

Biblical texts dating to the early Persian Period, not only Haggai, Zechariah, and Malachi but also Ezra-Nehemiah, Isaiah 56–66 (Trito-Isaiah), and Ezekiel 40–48 (the Law of the Temple), indicate that the years after the Babylonian exile were a time of intense conflict between those returning from the exile and those people in the land who had never left (Tuell 2005, 183–87; McBride 2000, 35; Hanson 1979, 209–11). A major issue in this conflict was right priesthood and right worship. The religious leaders of the people of the land were Levites left behind when the Zadokite priests of the Jerusalem temple were taken away into exile, while the returnees were led by Zadokites such as Joshua, the high priest. Both sides in this conflict are represented in Scripture. On the one hand, Zechariah 3:6-10 affirms that priestly access to the LORD is given to Joshua and the other priests who had returned from exile, while Ezekiel 44:1-14 restricts priesthood to this group, the Zadokites, alone. On the other hand, Trito-Isaiah (e.g., Isa 65:5; 66:3) sharply critiques the priesthood of the restored temple, while Malachi 2:1-9 advocates for God's covenant with the *whole* tribe of Levi (cf. see also Deut 18:1; Jer 33:19-22), not just the single Levitical family of Zadok.

The strong connection between the central intermediary Haggai and the two leaders of his community, the governor Zerubbabel and the high priest Joshua, make plain where Haggai stood in this conflict. Now that the right temple was coming into place (according to Ezra 6:15, the temple would be completed four years later), Haggai subtly reminds the priests that right worship requires not only the right shrine and the right ritual but also the right priesthood. Contact with holy things would not sanctify illegitimate priests. Instead, unclean cult personnel would defile the offerings of the people (cf. Ezek 44:9-14).

To underline this message, Haggai recapitulates his earlier oracle linking the temple to fertility in the land and fulfillment in the human community (2:15-19). Repeated calls in these verses to "consider" (Heb., *simu-nah lebabkem*; "put your heart [to]"; 2:15, 18; cf. 1:5, 7) "this day" (2:15, 18, 19) emphasize the significance of the beginning that has been made. The founding of the temple will prove a turning point, Haggai declares: "From this day on I will bless you" (Hag 2:19).

The LORD's Signet Ring (2:20-23)

Just as the narrative in 2:10-19 addresses the religious leadership of Judah, so in this final oracle Haggai addresses the political leader, the governor Zerubbabel. Once more, the language of cosmic cataclysm ("I am about to shake the heavens and the earth," 2:21; cf. 2:6) prompts some to refer to this passage as eschatological (Meyers and Meyers 1987, 82), and some correspondingly to regard it as a late addition to the book (Hallaschka 2011, 321). The exalted view of Zerubbabel in this passage, however, is difficult to square with later contexts, which largely ignore this figure (contrast the significant space given to Zerubbabel in Haggai–Zechariah 1–8, or in 1 Esdras 3–4, with his virtual absence in Ezra-Nehemiah; cf. Cross 1975, 194–98; Tuell 2001, 11–12). Indeed, even Haggai's contemporary Zechariah had to defend Zerubbabel against his detractors (cf. Zech 4:6, 10). In contrast, Haggai compares Zerubbabel to the LORD's "signet ring" (Heb., *khotam*) and declares, "I have chosen you, says the LORD of hosts" (2:23).

The word *khotam* ("seal") is not common, appearing elsewhere primarily in the description of the priestly vestments (Exod 28:11, 21, 36; 39:6, 14, 30; cf. Ezek 28:12) or in poetic contexts (Job 38:14; 41:7[15]; Song 8:6). Still, the use of the term in Genesis 38:18 and 1 Kings 21:8, together with archaeological evidence (numerous clay document seals and jar handles bearing seal impressions have survived), suffice to demonstrate the importance and use of the signet: its impression indicated that the document or item so sealed came from, belonged to, or bore the authority of the seal's owner. Particularly significant for understanding Haggai 2:23 is Jeremiah 22:24: "As I live, says the LORD, even if King Coniah son of Jehoiakim of Judah were the signet ring on my right hand, even from there I would tear you off." Haggai, like Jeremiah, is using royal imagery: to be the king is to act on divine authority; to be, as it were, God's signet. For Jeremiah, the image demonstrates both God's authority and Jehoiachin's irrelevance: even if Jehoiachin *had been* God's signet ring, God had removed him, just as one takes a ring from one's finger. Haggai's choice of this image, however, is tremendously significant and potentially dangerous. Jehoiachin had at least been a king for a little while. Zerubbabel may have been a descendant of David (1 Chr 3:19; see "Authorship, Date, and Setting," above), but he is explicitly called *pekhah*: governor, not king. For him openly to claim the title "king" would be to join the leaders of Babylon and Egypt in their rebellion against Darius.

Haggai does not propose a rebellion. Instead, he is confident that God is at work in the tumultuous political events of his day to bring about Zerubbabel's rise. Just as Deutero-Isaiah had confidently proclaimed that Cyrus of Persia would be used by God to break the power of Babylon (Isa 45:1-19), so Haggai is convinced that the rebellions against Darius will lead to the fall of Persia and to independence for Judah. God is about "to overthrow the throne of kingdoms" (Heb., *kisse' mamlakot*, 2:22). The LXX has "*thrones* of kingdoms," which Wolff regards as original (Wolff 1988, 98, 103). Both *Tg. Neb.* and the Vulgate, however, also have the singular, and while it is easy to see why a Greek translator would have thought that the two terms should agree in number, it is difficult to see how the opposite move could occur. Elsewhere, the expression "the throne of (his/your) kingdom" (with "kingdom" in the singular) is used of David's throne, over Israel (Deut 17:18; 2 Sam 7:13; 1 Kgs 9:5). But here, the singular throne over multiple kingdoms must surely refer to imperial power: in context, to Persia (cf. Meyers and Meyers 1987, 67; Sweeney 2000, 553–54; *contra* Petersen 1984, 96, 98–100).

Of course, Haggai was wrong. Darius did not fall—thankfully, since according to Ezra it was largely through his intervention that the temple was at last built. Zerubbabel did not rise to kingship; instead, he faded into obscurity. This is but one of many examples from across Scripture of prophecies that did not come to pass: to name but a few, Huldah's promise that Josiah would die in peace (2 Chr 34:28//2 Kgs 22:20; cf. 2 Kgs 23:29-30; 2 Chr 35:20-27), Ezekiel's prediction that Tyre would fall to Nebuchadrezzar (26:1-14; cf. Ezek 29:17-21), Jonah's declaration of Nineveh's fall (Jonah 3:4; cf. 3:10), and the many New Testament predictions of the imminent end of the world (e.g., Mark 13:30; 1 Cor 7:29-31; Rev 22:12, 20). This is a problem if we believe the prophets to be fortune-tellers; after all, Deuteronomy 18:22

does claim that accurate prediction is a test of prophetic authenticity. The prophets themselves, however, seem untroubled by this standard. Instead, the Bible presents the prophets as God's messengers, communicating what God has revealed as best they can. God remains free to act as God chooses, in response to God's people (cf. Jonah 4:1-2, 11). We need not, then, root Haggai from the canon because he misread his times. We may, however, find in his last oracle a cautionary tale about the dangers of identifying our faith too closely with any political figure or movement.

Zechariah

Reading Zechariah

The primary message of Zechariah is communicated through eight visions (1:7-17; 2:1-4 [1:18-21]; 2:5-9 [1-5]; 3:1-10; 4:1-5, 10b-14; 5:1-4, 5-11; 6:1-8), ranging from heavenly horsemen (1:7-17) to the high priest Joshua dressed in filthy rags on trial in the heavenly court (3:1-10), to women with wings like storks, bearing a basket in which another woman, called "Wickedness," is imprisoned (5:5-11). Zechariah's guide and interpreter in these visions is an angel whom the prophet calls "the angel who talked with me" (Zech 1:9, 19; 2:3-5; 4:10-14; 5:3, 6-8, 10-11; 6:5-6). The prophet says that his interpreting angel "wakened me, as one is wakened from sleep" (Zech 4:1), suggesting to some that his visions should be understood as dreams (cf. Zech 1:8; Dan 7:1-2). That is not what Zechariah says, however. He compares his visions not to dreaming but to being "*wakened* from sleep"—entering the vision state was not like falling asleep but like waking up (Meyers and Meyers 1987, 229)! Like his predecessor Ezekiel (cf. Ezek 1:3; 3:14, 3:22; 8:1-4; 37:1; 40:1), Zechariah speaks out of a prophetic ecstasy in which he is taken up into another reality. For Zechariah, that reality—the world of God's revelation—is not less real but *more* real than the waking world.

By twenty-first-century Western standards, one could think that Zechariah was insane. Indeed, Jack Miles calls Zechariah's fellow visionary Ezekiel "the psychotic articulation of the prophetic message" (Miles 1995, 197). Alternatively, one could propose that Zechariah's alleged "visions" are actually literary conceits: fictions no more real than the poet Dante's "visions" of heaven, hell, and purgatory.

But before we dismiss Zechariah too quickly as either a psychotic or an author of fiction, we must consider four issues pertaining to visions generally. First, seeing things or hearing things that others do not is not necessarily a symptom of mental illness. In his book *Hallucinations* (2012), neurologist

Oliver Sacks relates the experiences of numerous persons, clearly sane, who nonetheless have reported hearing voices or sounds, or seeing people and objects, that were not physically present. Yet, in a 1973 study conducted by psychologist David Rosenhan, when perfectly normal researchers presented themselves at hospitals across the country, reporting no symptom at all other than "hearing voices" (all of them reported that the voices were indistinct but that they could make out the words "empty," "hollow," and "thud"), all of them were hospitalized, for up to two months, and prescribed antipsychotic drugs (Sacks 2012, 53–54). Sacks reports that such pat diagnoses are a fairly modern phenomenon: indeed, an 1894 study of 17,000 people (none of whom had any "obvious medical or psychological problems") found that 10 percent reported visual or auditory hallucinations, with a third of those saying that they had heard voices (Sacks 2012, 57).

Second, it is not at all clear why such experiences, even if rationally explained, could not be means of divine revelation. Christian mystic Hildegard of Bingen's visions involved auras, jagged shapes, and streaks of light, and were accompanied by debilitating physical illness—prompting some modern interpreters to propose that she suffered from migraines (Sacks 1970, 112–15). This diagnosis, however, in no way lessens the spiritual depth of Hildegard's insights; nor can her poems and songs be reduced to manifestations of neurological symptoms. As Oliver Sacks observes, Hildegard's visions "provide a unique example of the manner in which a physiological event, banal, hateful, or meaningless to the vast majority of people, can become, in a privileged consciousness, the substrate of a supreme ecstatic inspiration" (Sacks 1970, 115). Similarly, in Augustine's account of his conversion, he reports hearing a child's voice chanting, "Take up and read. Take up and read" (*Confessiones* 8.12). In response to this prompt, Augustine opened his Bible and read the first thing he saw: Romans 13:13-14. Convicted by these words of Scripture, he became a Christian. The reality of Augustine's experience cannot be questioned, whether the voice he heard was a child playing next door, a random neurological incident, or (as Augustine himself believed) the voice of God. Rational explanations for the experiences of Hildegard, or Augustine, or countless other believers, do not explain these experiences *away*.

Third, we must ask if our society's standards of mental illness apply to Zechariah or to his fellow prophets. As Robert Wilson observes, cultures in which ecstatic behavior is part of the expected range of religious experience do not confuse insanity with spiritual experience; in fact, in such cultures, an intermediary accused of insanity may be removed from office (Wilson 1980, 44–45). Certainly, Ezekiel and Zechariah were not the only prophets who behaved oddly (e.g., Isa 20:2-6; Jer 23:9). Indeed, Hosea records, "Israel cries, / 'The prophet is a fool, / the man of the spirit is mad!'" (Hos 9:7). Christian readers may recall that Jesus' own family said of him, "He has gone out of his mind" (Mark 3:21). Seen in the context of prophetic activity in the ancient world, then, Zechariah's behavior is not extreme.

Finally, to say that Zechariah's visions must be either hallucinations or fictions is a false dilemma, based on the presumption that reality consists only of what we can measure and analyze. Surely any person of faith will want to affirm the reality of the world of the spirit, and therefore the possibility that a person who claims, as Zechariah did, to have accessed that realm may be telling the truth. Of course, not everyone who claims such an experience must be heeded: many are certainly deceivers, or self-deceived. But we should not dismiss visions, or visionaries, out of hand. First John 4:1 advises, "Beloved, do not believe every spirit, but try the spirits to see whether they are from God." Of course, in the case of Zechariah, the community of faith has already undertaken that task of discernment: weird though they may be, Zechariah's visions are part of the canon of Jewish and Christian Scripture. The only question is what we are to do with them.

Authorship, Date, and Setting

"Zechariah" is a theophoric name (see the discussion of "Zephaniah," above) meaning "the LORD remembers," and a relatively common name in the Bible. Over thirty different people in Scripture are called "Zechariah" (Shuler 1996, 1238), among them a king of Israel, the son of Jeroboam II (2 Kgs 14:29; 15:11; possibly also King Hezekiah's maternal grandfather; cf. 2 Kgs 18:2), and various priestly or Levitical figures (e.g., 1 Chr 15:18; 26:2; Ezra 8:16; Neh 8:4), including most prominently a prophet stoned to death in the time of Joash (2 Chr 24:20-23; cf. Matt 23:35; Luke 11:51) and the father of John the Baptist (Luke 1:5).

Our prophet is named four times in this book (Zech 1:1, 7; 7:1, 8), as well as in Ezra 5:1 and 6:14, which credit Zechariah and Haggai for inspiring the people of Judah first to start and then to finish rebuilding the temple. Curiously, neither Zechariah nor Haggai mentions the other in his book; but then, contemporaries Jeremiah and Ezekiel do not mention one another either, despite signs of mutual influence (e.g., Jer 31:29-30 and Ezek 18:2). Zechariah's two central visions, in chapters 3 and 4, deal with the two central figures of restoration society, the high priest Joshua (3:1-10) and the governor Zerubbabel (4:6-10), suggesting that, like Haggai, he was a central intermediary.

A brief genealogy at the opening of the book identifies Zechariah as "son of Berechiah son of Iddo" (1:1; cf. 1:7). Both the narrative in Ezra (5:1; 6:14) and the priestly genealogy in Nehemiah 12:16 identify Zechariah as the son rather than the grandson of Iddo; however, Berechiah is also a name with Levitical connections (e.g., 1 Chr 6:39; Neh 3:4, 30). The name "Iddo" is likely related to an Aramaic word found in an eighth-century inscription from King Zakir of Hamat and Lu'ath. The king records his prayer for deliverance from Hazael of Aram and his allies, and says that the answer to his prayer came from Baal Shamayin ("the lord of the heavens") by *khzyn* ("seers"; compare Heb., *khozeh*, "seer"; e.g., Amos 7:12, and *khozen*, "vision," e.g., Nah 1:1) and *'ddyn* ("prophets" or "intermediaries;" cf. Wilson 1980, 130–32). Likely, then, "Iddo" means "prophet" (cf. 2 Chr 12:15; 13:22), confirming Zechariah's prophetic heritage. Indeed, it is unclear in the Hebrew whether the title *hannabi'* ("the prophet") in Zechariah 1:1 properly belongs to Zechariah (cf. NRSV, JPSV) or to his grandfather (KJV).

The three dates in Zechariah (Zech 1:1, 7; 7:1) fall within a two-year span, from the second to the fourth years of Darius's reign (see "The Early Persian Period" in the introduction to Haggai, above). Like the other dates in Haggai–Zechariah 1–8, these three are far more precise than is usually the case (compare Zeph 1:1), and seem to be influenced by the date formulae in Ezekiel. The only date in this collection that is not sequential is Zechariah 1:1, "In the eighth month, in the second year of Darius," which precedes the dates in Haggai 2:10, 18, 20. This overlap tends to strengthen the link between Haggai and Zechariah 1–8. The other two dates in Zechariah use names as well as numbers for the months: Shebat for the eleventh month (1:7), Chislev for the ninth (7:1). These Babylonian names would later become a standard feature of the Jewish calendar (cf. Jerusalem Talmud, *Rosh Hashannah* 1.56d; Vanderkam 2006, 523–24), but are used for the first time here.

No dates at all appear in Zechariah 9–14, which is commonly regarded as a later expansion to this book. Indeed, the disparate character of this material makes it likely that multiple hands composed these chapters at various times. Still, a clue to the dating of the latter chapters may be found in 9:13: "I will arouse your sons, O Zion, against your sons, O Greece [Heb., *Yawan*, or Iona]." The mention of Greece here, together with evidence of conflict and unrest in these chapters, suggests to many that this material dates to the wars between Persia and Greece in the fifth century, when the Persians experienced defeat at Marathon (490 BCE) and Salamis (480 BCE; so Meyers and Meyers 1993; Petersen 1995, 3–5; Cook 2011).

Structure

Broadly speaking, Zechariah falls into two parts, 1–8 and 9–14; indeed, some commentators treat these sections separately, as though they were two different books (e.g., Meyers and Meyers 1993; Petersen 1995; O'Brien 2004). The justification for regarding Zechariah 9–14 as a later addition to the book will be discussed below. Attempting to reflect the canonical unity of the book of Zechariah, some scholars describe the structure differently: Sweeney divides the book into an introduction (1:1-6) and the "Narrative Presentation of YHWH's words to Zechariah" (1:7–14:21; cf. Sweeney 2000, 567, 573), while Nogalski identifies nine parts: 1:1-6; 1:7–6:15; 7:1–8:23; 9:1-17; 10:1–11:3; 11:4-17; 12:1-14; 13:1-9; and 14:1-21 (Nogalski 2011, 821–22). Still, Zechariah 1–8 is bracketed by references to "the former prophets" (Heb., *hannebi'im harishonim*) at 1:4 and 7:7, 12, and set apart in other ways as well (see "Zechariah 1–8 and 9–14," below); we do best to recognize its unity.

This first part of the book may in turn be divided into three sections: eight vision reports with interspersed oracles (1:1–6:8), a sign-act (6:9-15), and a priestly *torah* and its application (7–8). Although the introduction in 1:1-6 is likely the work of the editors responsible for joining Haggai-Zechariah 1–8 to the Twelve, in the present form of the book it is an integral part of the whole, paralleled by the corresponding editorial conclusion in the final form of 7–8. Likewise, the formal distinction between the vision reports that dominate Zechariah 1:1–6:8 and the sign-act in 6:9-15 legitimates distinguishing 6:9-15 as a separate unit.

The second part of this book is divided into two collections, 9–11 and 12–14, each titled "An Oracle" (Heb., *massa'*; 9:1; 12:1). Following Nogalski (2011, 822), each collection may be further divided into three parts: the first at 9:1-17; 10:1–11:3; and 11:4-17; the second at 12:1–13:1 (departing from Nogalski, who reads 13:1-9 as a unit); 13:2-9; and 14:1-21.

Zechariah 1–8 and 9–14

While the prophet Zechariah is mentioned by name four times in Zechariah 1–8 (1:1, 7; 7:1, 8), this name does not appear at all in the last six chapters of the book. The messenger formula, found nineteen times in Zechariah 1–8, occurs only once (11:4) in 9–14. Of the two most characteristic features of Haggai–Zechariah 1–8, the date formulae and the divine title *Yhwh tseba'ot* ("the LORD of hosts"; see "Haggai and Zechariah 1–8," above), the date formula does not appear at all in Zechariah 9–14, while "the LORD of hosts" appears nearly five times as often in Zechariah 1–8 as in 9–14.

Haggai–Zechariah 1–8 (and for that matter, Malachi) are written in prose, while Zechariah 9–14 is roughly half poetry (9:1-11:3; 11:12; 13:7-9). All of this suggests that Zechariah 9–14 was not originally a part of the book but has been added later—most likely, after Haggai–Zechariah 1–8 was incorporated into the Twelve (Nogalski 1993a, 278; 1993b, 274–79).

The content of Zechariah 9–14 confirms this impression. As has long been recognized (e.g., Hanson 1979, 282–83), Zechariah 9–14 emphasizes *apocalyptic* themes. The words "apocalypse" and "apocalyptic" come from the Greek *apocalupsis* (cf. Rev 1:1), meaning literally "unveiling," or pulling back a curtain. Apocalypses are concerned with the revelation of hidden truth. Most scholars would agree that the essential features of an apocalypse are the revelation of another world to a human seer by means of a heavenly being or angel (Hanson 1976a, 29). This other world may be the future world, or it may be the heavenly world—or it may be both. We might think that this definition fits prophecy as well—after all, prophets do speak the word of the LORD, which may involve (as in Zechariah) visions of the divine world or predictions of future events. Prophetic visions and predictions, however, are aimed at affecting actions in the present, within human history. By contrast, apocalypses assume a great gulf between the world of the revelation and the human world—that is why an angel is needed as a go-between. The world of God is infinitely removed from the world we live in. Further, the future envisioned in apocalypses is infinitely removed from anything our own efforts can accomplish. For example, Zechariah 14:1-21 depicts the day of the LORD as a time of cosmic transformation, ranging from the Mount of Olives splitting in two (14:4) to continuous day without cold or frost (14:6-7) to the leveling of Judean hill country around Jerusalem into a great plain (14:10). From the apocalyptic viewpoint, only God can bring in the future world. Human efforts cannot bring about God's future; but neither can any human power prevent God's future from coming into being.

Stephen Cook, while agreeing that Zechariah 9–14 represents a later expansion to the book, sees this material as a continuation of apocalyptic themes already present in Zechariah 1–8 (Cook 1995, 133; 2003, 104). Certainly, the opening chapters of this book were mined by later apocalyptists (e.g., the four horsemen in Zech 1:7-17; cf. Rev 6:1-8; the four horns in 2:1-4 [1:18-21]; cf. Dan 7:24; Rev 17:9-11). But nonetheless, Zechariah 1–8 remains tied to the historical circumstances of the sixth-century prophet. In contrast, Zechariah 9–14 moves away from this world and toward a future only God can bring, approaching the thoroughly apocalyptic perception of God and the world in Daniel and Revelation.

The intent of this commentary, however, is to take seriously the final canonical shape of the text by considering the integration of these two parts in the book's final form (cf. Sweeney 2000, 566). As Julia O'Brien notes, both parts of this book share "the primary concern with the restoration of Jerusalem, the belief that the nations that oppose Jerusalem must be punished, and hints of tension between Jerusalem and the rest of Yehud [Judah in the Persian period]" (O'Brien 2004, 232). Despite the disparate character of the material in Zechariah 9–14 and the likelihood that these chapters are not an original part of Haggai–Zechariah 1–8, this continuity of theme suggests that the inclusion of these chapters in this place is not accidental. The authors of these oracles likely understood themselves to be carrying on Zechariah's legacy, much as Deutero-Isaiah and Trito-Isaiah continued Isaiah's legacy, or the editors of the Law of the Temple (Ezek 40–48) continued Ezekiel's.

While this commentary has argued that Haggai and Zechariah 1–8 were carefully and deliberately intertwined, it is unlikely that they were *composed* as a unit; the two remain in many ways distinct. For example, vision reports play no role at all in Haggai, while Zechariah's prophecy is characterized by visions (1:7-17; 2:1-4 [1:18-21]; 2:5-9 [1-5]; 3:1-10; 4:1-5, 10b-14; 5:1-4, 5-11; and 6:1-8). The angel who serves as Zechariah's guide and interpreter in these visions (Zech 1:9, 2:2 [1:19]; 2:7-9 [3-5]; 4:10-14; 5:3, 6-8, 10-11; 6:5-6) has no role at all in Haggai: indeed, in Haggai 1:13, it is the prophet, not an angel, who is the *mal'ak Yhwh* ("the messenger of the LORD"; cf. Zech 1:11-12; 3:1, 5, 6; 12:8). Both of these features of Zechariah reflect the influence of the book of Ezekiel, likewise a visionary (cf. Ezek 1-3; 8-11; 37:1-14; 40–48) who in his last great vision is guided by an angel (Ezek 40:3-4). Another distinctive feature of Zechariah 1–8, and one that it also shares with Ezekiel, is the use of the first person: indeed, in the entire canon of the Hebrew Bible, only these two books are written entirely in the first person (cf. Tuell 2003, 287).

Why then were Haggai and Zechariah 1–8 combined? Haggai–Zechariah 1–8, Ezekiel 40–48 in its final form (cf. Tuell 1992, 20–22; Konkel 2001, 24), and quite possibly the beginnings of both Chronicles (cf. Freedman 1961, 439–40; Schneidewind 1995, 249; Tuell 2001, 10–12; Hahn 2012, 1) and the Pentateuch (cf. Blenkinsopp 1987, 413–14; Tuell 1992, 145–46) all date to the early Persian Period. This tremendous burst of literary activity may have been sparked by a decree that Darius I issued in c. 520 BCE, described in a papyrus manuscript sometimes called the Demotic Chronicle:

> As for Darius, it heeded him . . . the land (of Egypt) in its entirety because of the excellence of his character. He issued a decree concerning Egypt to

> his satrap in (his) third regnal year, as follows: "Let be brought unto me the learned men . . . from among the (military) officers, the priests, (and) the scribes of Egypt so that, being assembled together, they may in concert write the law of Egypt which had been (observed) formerly through the forty-fourth regnal year of Pharaoh Amasis, (that is) the fifth pharaonic law, (concerning) the temples (and) the people." (Spiegelberg 1914, 30–31; translated here from the Demotic by S. Dean McBride, Jr.)

While the decree mentioned in the Demotic Chronicle concerns Egyptian civil and religious law, it likely reflects broader policy during Darius's reign. Even if such an order was not given directly to the religious and political leadership of Judah, however, the Persian demand for a written, official document containing the "law . . . (concerning) the temples (and) the people" in Egypt would surely have galvanized Jewish communities, both in Babylon and in Palestine, to write down their own authoritative collections. Eric Meyers suggests that this "Persian encouragement to codify laws in the provinces could well have been the impetus to combine Zechariah 1–8 with Haggai into a single composite piece that was probably intended for presentation at the rededication ceremony of the Second Temple" (Meyers 1987, 513; cf. Meyers and Meyers 1987, 380).

Meyers's proposal is intriguing, but Haggai–Zechariah 1–8 really cannot be described as a "law . . . (concerning) the temples (and) the people." Ezekiel 40–48, however, can (cf. Greenberg 1984, 189–90; Tuell 1992, 20-22; Block 1998, 498; Konkel 2001, 24). Indeed, in striking parallel to the language of the Demotic Chronicle, Ezekiel 43:12 twice declares, "This is the law of the temple," suggesting that Ezekiel 40–48 responds to Darius's command. The collection of Haggai–Zechariah 1–8 into a book, then, responds at best *indirectly* to this Persian edict; it relates directly, though, to Ezekiel.

In its final form, Ezekiel's work has the consistency of style and theme we expect to find in an intentionally written work, rather than a loose assembly of oral speeches secondarily collected in writing. That is, Ezekiel and his earliest interpreters have written a *book* (cf. Gunkel 1906, 82; Davis 1989, 65–66; Wilson 2000, 588). So also, in Haggai–Zechariah 1–8 *Zechariah* has written a book, modeled stylistically after Ezekiel.

Meyers and Meyers observe in the later prophets "an increasingly greater awareness of and dependence on sacred literature"; indeed, they suggest that "the availability of written, sacred tradition as revelation from God must have been one critical factor" in prophecy's decline (Meyers and Meyers 1987, 201; cf. Sommer 1996, 46–47). This emerging notion of text—that is, of *Bible*—as the word of God extends from Ezekiel through Haggai–Zechariah

1–8 (cf. "the former prophets" in Zech 1:4; 7:7, 12) and into Chronicles, where "the word of the LORD" often refers to the words of Scripture, especially the Torah of Moses (1 Chr 15:15; 2 Chr 30:12; 34:21; 35:6), and where prophets write books (cf. Samuel, Nathan and Gad in 1 Chr 29:29; Nathan, Ahijah, and Iddo in 2 Chr 9:29; Shemaiah and Iddo in 2 Chr 12:15; Iddo in 2 Chr 13:22; Jehu ben Hanani in 2 Chr 20:34; Isaiah in 2 Chr 26:22 and 32:32). The trajectory continues into Ezra-Nehemiah where, with the exception of Haggai and Zechariah, prophets and prophecy no longer function as the means of God's revelation. Thus, Ezra is not a prophet but a scribe: "an inspired text interpreter" (Schniedewind 1995, 250). The great Temple Scroll from Qumran marks a far point on this arc, as this book claims to be the very plan (Heb., *tabnith*) revealed to Moses (Exod 25:9, 40), then handed on to Solomon by David (1 Chr 28:19; cf. Yadin 1983, 177 and 182).

Along that trajectory falls the Book of the Twelve, assembled through the manipulation, expansion, and combination of preexisting blocks of text. The Book of the Four (Hosea-Amos-Micah-Zephaniah) plus Haggai–Zechariah 1–8 plus Malachi provided the frame into which the editors inserted Nahum-Habakkuk, Obadiah, and Joel. The later addition of Jonah and Zechariah 9–14 made the collection complete. Zechariah, however, was likely the impetus for the entire collection: "the lens through which the other prophets were read—and perhaps the template by which they were written and edited" (cf. O'Brien 2007, 172).

Commentary

Zechariah 1-8

Vision Reports and Oracles (1:1–6:8)

On the one hand, Zechariah's visions seem in character very like Ezekiel's. Like Ezekiel's visions, Zechariah's abound in fantastic imagery (e.g., the wheels with eyes in Ezek 1:16-18; 10:2, 6, 13; the seven "eyes of the Lord" in Zech 4:10) and supernatural beings (the four-faced creatures in Ezek 1:5-10; 10:20; *hassatan* in Zech 3:1-2). Ezekiel's climactic vision features an angelic interpreter (40:3-4 and again throughout chs. 40–42; 47), as do nearly all of Zechariah's visions (Zech 1:9, 19; 2:3-5; 4:10-14; 5:3, 6-8, 10-11; 6:5-6). On the other hand, Ezekiel's characteristic visionary vocabulary is absent from Zechariah, as his characteristic temple vocabulary was absent from Haggai. While Ezekiel's signature visions are given the title *mar'ot 'elohim* ("visions of God"; 1:1; 8:3; 40:2) and dated, precise to the day (1:1; 8:1; 40:1), Zechariah's visions are neither titled nor individually dated. Ezekiel's expression for entering the vision state, "the hand of the LORD [*yad Yhwh*] was upon me/him" (1:3; 3:14, 3:22; 8:1-4; 37:1; 40:1), does not appear in Zechariah 1–8. Finally, the content of Zechariah's visions is, generally speaking, entirely distinctive. For example, Zechariah 5:1-4 involves a scroll, like Ezekiel 2:8–3:3 (as well as measurement, like Ezek 40–42, or 48:1-35). Yet these two visions unfold in quite different ways: Ezekiel eats his (presumably normal sized) scroll, while Zechariah's giant, thirty-foot-long scroll flies through the air! Ezekiel has certainly influenced Zechariah, in the prominence both books give to visions and in the role played by the interpreting angel. In content, however, Zechariah's visions stand apart.

First oracle: introduction (1:1-6). Much like Haggai (see the discussion of Hag 1:1), Zechariah's book begins not with a superscription but with the date of his first oracle, "In the eighth month, in the second year of Darius" (Zech 1:1). As we have seen, this is the only date in Haggai–Zechariah 1–8 that is not in chronological sequence, as it precedes the dates in Haggai 2:10, 18, 20. Seth Sykes proposes that these overlapping dates "reinforce a thematic connection between the two prophetic texts"; in this way, the overlap contributes to the unity of Haggai–Zechariah as a "unified, whole utterance" (Sykes 2002, 27). While there is no set form for the dates in Haggai–Zechariah 1–8, every date in the unit but this one mentions the day. These distinctive features of the date in Zechariah 1:1 suggest that this opening oracle of the book may be a part of its final editing.

The expression *hannebi'im harishonim* ("former prophets") in 1:4 supports this conclusion. This expression appears in Scripture only in the book of Zechariah, in this opening oracle of the book (1:4) and in the final unit of Haggai–Zechariah 1–8 (7:7, 12). Likely both the introduction and the conclusion reflect the work of Zechariah's editors, incorporating Haggai–Zechariah 1–8 into the Twelve.

By the Middle Ages, the "Former Prophets" had come to refer to the books of Joshua, Judges, Samuel, and Kings (Brettler 2004, 451). But Julia O'Brien proposes that our passage has a more immediate referent in mind: "Hosea through Zephaniah were consciously edited as a preface to Zechariah, providing a portrayal of the 'former prophets' useful to the writer of Zechariah" (O'Brien 2007, 180). If the previous books of the Twelve are the "former prophets" to which 1:1-6 alludes, then the sum total of their message is understood by these editors as leading up to Zechariah's call to repentance.

Those former prophets, Zechariah declares, had said to the ancestors, again and again, "Thus says the LORD of hosts, 'Return from your evil ways and from your evil deeds'" (1:4). This summons was vital, for the nation was in danger: "The LORD was very angry with your ancestors" (Zech 1:2). The effect of God's righteous anger is clear, looking back: Israel did not listen to Hosea or Amos, and now it is gone. Judah did not listen to Micah, to Zephaniah, or to Habakkuk, and now it is gone. As the text poignantly asks, "Your ancestors, where are they?" (1:5). One might, of course, cynically ask if the same is not true of the prophets who had called the ancestors to repentance: "do they live forever?" (1:5). Have they not, as well, been swallowed up in the dust and flotsam of rising and falling empires? But the answer, clearly, is "No!" This book, the Book of the Twelve, preserves their words, and so they still speak. Zechariah joins their chorus: "Return to me, says the LORD of hosts, and I will return to you, says the LORD of hosts" (Zech 1:3).

The story of the former prophets is not only a tragic account of Israel's past but also a road map for its future. When overtaken by God's judgment, at least some of the ancestors had turned back to the LORD in repentance (1:6), with the result that the enemies who had afflicted them were overturned (cf. 1:15, 21; 2:10-17 [6-13]). Thus, Nahum depicts the fall of Assyria, and the final form of Habakkuk depicts judgment on Babylon. The point for Zechariah's community is clear. If we do not repent, then we too will vanish from history, but if we *do* repent, then we have hope!

Zechariah's predecessors are identified not only as the "former prophets" but also as "my servants the prophets" (1:6). While this expression does appear, once, in Ezekiel (38:17), that reference belongs to one of the latest-dated portions of the book (Tuell 2012, 266–67) and is unlikely to have influenced Zechariah or his editors. The title "my/your/his servant(s) the prophet(s)" is found twenty times in the Old Testament, most often in material influenced by Deuteronomy: eight times in the Deuteronomistic History (1 Kgs 14:18; 18:36; 2 Kgs 9:7; 14:25; 17:13, 23; 21:10; 24:2) and six times in Jeremiah (7:25; 25:4; 26:5; 29:19; 35:15; 44:4). In the Book of the Twelve apart from Zechariah, it is found only in Amos 3:7. In Zechariah 1:6, the editors likely have the use of this expression in Deuteronomic contexts in mind. Second Kings 17:12, 23 attributes the fall of the northern kingdom to their failure to heed "my servants the prophets"; 2 Kings 21:10, which lays the blame for Judah's fall on Manasseh, bases this assessment on the word of the LORD to "his servants the prophets." To the editors of the Twelve, hope for the future depended on not following their ancestors' example, and heeding the ancient prophetic word, reverberating now in the words of Zechariah (compare the use of this phrase in Ezra 9:11 and Dan 9:6, 10).

Zechariah 1:2-4 became in turn the source and model for 2 Chronicles 30:6-9, a letter from King Hezekiah inviting "all Israel and Judah" to his Passover (so Williamson 1982, 367–68). Each passage repudiates the sins of previous generations (cf. 2 Chr 30:8 and Zech 1:4), so that the wrath of the

Lord, once directed against the ancestors, might not fall on their descendants as well (2 Chr 30:8; Zech 1:2). Both the author of Chronicles and the editors of the Twelve call the postexilic community to respond to God's faithfulness with faithfulness, by seeking God in the temple.

First vision: the four horsemen (1:7-17). Zechariah sees "a man riding a red horse" (1:8). As his vision unfolds, he realizes that the figure is not alone; in a grove of myrtle trees behind him are other horses, "red, sorrel, and white" (1:8; curiously, the LXX has *four* colors, red, grey, piebald, and white, likely reflecting Zech 6:1-2). Riders for the other horses are not mentioned but can be inferred, as the rider on the red horse tells the prophet, "They are those who the Lord has sent to patrol the earth" (1:10). Christian readers will think immediately of the four horsemen in Revelation 6:1-8, also distinguished by the color of their mounts (there, white, red, black, and pale green—influenced, perhaps, by the LXX list). While the horsemen in John's vision represent images of war, however (conquest in 6:1-2; slaughter in 6:3-4; scarcity and war profiteering in 6:5-7; famine and plague in 6:7-8), Zechariah's horsemen report a world at peace (1:10-11)—presumably pacified by Persian might. Curiously, Darius's second year was not a peaceful time: indeed, Darius's first four years were occupied with reestablishing order in the provinces, putting down revolts in Egypt and Babylon. Still, the point of the vision is the contrast between the apparent peace and prosperity enjoyed by the rest of the world and the continued suffering of the people of Judah.

The horsemen report to "the angel of the Lord" (Heb., *mal'ak Yhwh*), a figure who appears in the prophets only in Isaiah 37:36 (//2 Kgs 19:35) and in Zechariah (1:11-12; 3:1, 5, 6; 12:8; note that Hag 1:13 and Mal 2:7 refer to human messengers). Usually, the angel of the Lord is an extension of the Lord's own person—a *hypostasis* (that is, the personification of a divine attribute; cf. Prov 8:1-36, where divine Wisdom is personified) of God's very presence (e.g., Gen 22:11; Exod 3:20; Num 22:22-27). In Zechariah 1:12, however, *mal'ak Yhwh* challenges the Lord: "O Lord of hosts, how long will you withhold mercy from Jerusalem and the cities of Judah, with which you have been angry these seventy years?" (Zech 1:12; cf. *Talmud b. Sanh.* 38b; 94a; 97b; 103a; *b. Shabb.* 55a, where God is taken to task by divine Justice personified). The prophet Jeremiah had declared that the exile would last seventy years (Jer 25:11-12; 29:10), doubtless intended to indicate the span of a human life: no one going into exile should expect to return (cf. Jer 29:4-14). As it happened, the exile actually lasted closer to fifty years, from the fall of Jerusalem in 587 to the conquest of Babylon and Cyrus's edict in c. 539 BCE (see "The Early Persian Period," above). Yet despite the return of the exiles to their homeland, the full restoration of Judah lagged (cf. Hag 1:5-11). In time, Jeremiah's seventy years took on harsher colors, as a symbolic representation of God's continued judgment on Israel (cf. 2 Chr 36:21; Dan 9:2).

God responds not to the *mal'ak Yhwh* but to Zechariah's personal angelic interpreter, "the angel who talked with me" (1:13). Earlier, this angel had interceded on Zechariah's behalf, to learn the identity of the four horsemen (1:9); now, the angel communicates God's "gracious and comforting words" to Zechariah (1:13). Earlier prophets had spoken with God directly (e.g., Isa 6:8-13; Jer 1:4-10; Ezek 2:1-7), but Zechariah's message comes through his angel, who conveys God's word and interprets Zechariah's visions. This new model of angelic intermediation rather than direct communication between God and the prophet becomes a standard feature of apocalypses (e.g., Dan 7:15-16; 8:15-17; Rev 1:1-2).

First, the LORD declares, "I am very jealous for Jerusalem and for Zion" (1:14). The verb used here, *qana'*, might better be rendered "zealous" or "passionate." God is intensely committed to God's people, and calls for a correspondingly zealous devotion from them (cf. Exod 20:5-6). Then, the nations that have humbled Judah are condemned: "for while I was only a little angry, they made the disaster worse" (1:14). This is similar to 2 Chronicles 28:9, where the prophet Oded intercedes with the people of Samaria on behalf of 200,000 Judean prisoners taken in the Syro-Ephraimite War: "Because the LORD, the God of your ancestors, was angry with Judah, he gave them into your hand, but you have killed them in a rage that has reached up to heaven." In keeping with the prophets generally, Zechariah (like Oded) regards Judah's victorious enemies as tools used by God to punish a rebellious people. But that does not excuse these nations for their cruelty (cf. Hab 1:11; Isa 10:12-15; Ezek 21:35-37 [30-32]): indeed, they are condemned for taking matters further than God had intended! Finally, God declares God's intention to restore both the city and the temple: "I have returned to Jerusalem with compassion; my house shall be built in it, says the LORD of hosts, and the measuring line shall be stretched out over Jerusalem" (1:16; cf. 2:5-9 [1-5]; 4:6-10a). Like his contemporary Haggai (cf. Hag 2:6-9), Zechariah declares that with that rebuilding, prosperity will return to Jerusalem (1:16-17).

Second vision: the four horns and the smiths (2:1-4 [1:18-21]). In the Hebrew text, this vision opens a new chapter. The scribes divided this passage into two units: the horns (2:1-2 [1:18-19]) and the smiths (2:3-4 [1:20-21]), suggesting that the Masoretes considered these two separate visions. Since they are given a single, unified interpretation in 2:4 (1:21), however, we will regard this as a single vision.

In the Old Testament, horns represent power—in particular, power in battle. Often, horns represent the power of a leader to deliver a people from their enemies (e.g., Num 23:22; Deut 33:17; 2 Sam 22:3). Here, however, the four horns represent the powers "that have scattered Judah, Israel, and Jerusalem" (2:2 [1:19]): perhaps Egypt, Assyria, Babylon, and Persia. Elsewhere in Scripture, a horn can refer to a king: so, in Psalm 132:17 the horn is a descendant of David, while in Daniel 7:24 and Revelation 17:9-11, horns represent, as in Zechariah, the kings of nations opposed to God's people. Further, in Daniel 2:31-45 and 7:1-8, as in Zechariah, four is the number of Israel's oppressors—though, of course, a *different* four. This ongoing reinterpretation of images is common within apocalypses; for example, Daniel's fourth beast (7:7-8), likely Greece in its context, becomes Rome in 4 Ezra 12:10-12 and Revelation 17:9.

It may seem strange that the figures who oppose these powers are not warriors but "blacksmiths" (2:3 [1:20]; so also NJPS). The term *kharashim*, rendered "blacksmiths" in the NRSV, refers more broadly to artisans (cf. Sweeney 2000, 583; KJV has "carpenters," and NIV reads "craftsmen")—such as engravers or carvers in horn. The Hebrew word for "horn" (*qeren*) is also used for a variety of containers made from horn, used to store oil (1 Sam 16:1, 13; 1 Kgs 1:39), ink (Ezek 9:2-11), and cosmetics (Job 42:14); also, of course, horns could be crafted into musical instruments (Josh 6:5). Zechariah's vision anthropomorphizes the horns (that is, it treats them as though they were people with feelings), so that the approaching craftsmen "terrify them" (Heb., *lekharid 'otham*). Still, the vision is not as bizarre as it may seem; indeed, it likely presents an everyday scene given a supernatural interpretation (cf. Amos 8:1-3). Just as craftsmen cut off animal horns for use in a variety of crafts, so the LORD will cut off the powers oppressing Israel.

Third vision: the measuring line (2:5-9 [1-5]). This study argues that the visions of Zechariah, while formally influenced by Ezekiel, are distinctive in content. The exception that proves this rule is Zechariah 2:5-9 (1-5). Here, Zechariah sees "a man with a measuring line (*khebel midah*) in his hand" (2:5[1]). This is certainly an allusion to Ezekiel 40:3, where the prophet first encounters his own angelic guide: "a man . . . whose appearance shone like bronze, with a linen cord [*petil-pishtim*] and a measuring reed in his hand." Although different terms are used for the cord, the correspondence is striking. Since the linen cord is not mentioned again in Ezekiel (but cf. 47:3, where the man uses a cord [here *qaw* in Heb.; cf. Zech 1:16] to measure the river flowing from Ezekiel's visionary temple), Zechariah's vision provides an explanation for it. In Ezekiel's vision, the man measures the visionary temple complex (40–42) and the fabulous river that flows out of it (47:1-12). In

Zechariah's vision, when the prophet asks the man with the measuring line where he is going, he replies, "To measure Jerusalem, to see what is its width and what its length" (2:6[2]; cf. Ezek 48:30-35, though the dimensions of the city are not reported by Ezekiel's guide). Little wonder that Meyers and Meyers (1987, 151) see a virtual correspondence between these two visions.

In fact, however, Zechariah's vision is not a parallel to Ezekiel's but a parody of it. In Ezekiel's vision, the man measures the temple but *not* the city. This is no oversight. The "very high mountain" (Ezek 40:2) to which the hand of the LORD carries Ezekiel at the beginning of his final vision report (40–48), atop which his visionary temple is located, is of course Zion. In Ezekiel, however, the mountain is never *called* Zion. Further, in Ezekiel's vision Jerusalem is not on the mountain, so the temple is not in the city. The focus on Jerusalem in Zechariah is therefore at odds with Ezekiel's vision. Second, detailed, careful measurement is the point of Ezekiel 40–42: the perfect dimensions of the sanctuary demonstrate its holiness. But in Zechariah's vision, the man with the measuring line never actually measures anything. Zechariah clearly alludes to Ezekiel here, but his own vision moves in an entirely different direction (cf. Petersen 1984, 169).

As David Petersen observes, before the man in Zechariah's vision can carry out his task of measuring the borders of Jerusalem, "[a]n angelic interpreter interrupts these proceedings and proclaims that the new Jerusalem will exist without boundaries" (Petersen 2000, 678). This reference to a Jerusalem without walls has a dual significance. First, the city cannot be restricted by boundaries "because of the multitude of people and animals in it" (2:8[4]; cf. 1:16-17); its growth will explode any such restrictions. Second, defensive walls of stone will be unnecessary, "For I will be a wall of fire all around it, says the LORD, and I will be the glory within it" (2:9[5]). This promise stands in intriguing conflict with the later building project of Nehemiah, who restores Jerusalem's walls.

Second oracle: the day of the LORD (2:10-17 [6-13]). While to this point, the scribal paragraphing has largely coincided with our determination of natural units, the MT divides this second oracle into three paragraphs: 2:10-11 (6-7), 12-13 (8-9), and 14-17 (10-13). The first break coincides with the messenger formula "For thus said the LORD of hosts" in 2:12 (8), and the second with the invitation to Zion to "sing and rejoice" (2:14[10]). Still there is a clear thematic unity to these three paragraphs: the LORD is about to strike down Israel's oppressors and bring all God's people home. While the actual expression does not appear, this clearly describes the day of the LORD (cf. Zeph 1:7; and the discussion of this term at Nah 1:8). The certainty of God's judgment and Israel's full restoration is the seal of the oracle's authenticity (2:13 [9], 15 [11]).

The oracle opens with the LORD's call for the exiles, whom the LORD had "spread abroad . . . like the four winds of heaven" (2:10 [6]; for God's responsibility for the exile cf. Hab 1:2-17) to "Flee from the land of the north"—that is, Babylon (2:11 [7]; cf. the discussion of Zeph 2:13)—to Zion (2:11 [7], following the LXX). The NRSV renders the Hebrew *hoi* as an exclamation: "Up! Up!" (2:10-11 [6-7]). While defensible, this translation misses the connections with other passages in the Twelve, particularly Nahum 3:1; Habakkuk 2:6, 9, 12, 15, 19 (cf. Boda 2008, 186–87); and Zephaniah 2:5; 3:1, where woe is pronounced upon Israel's enemies.

This reference to the exiles and to the punishment of Babylon seems odd in light of the dates in 1:1, 7 and 7:1, which set this material between the second and fourth years of Darius I of Persia, well after Cyrus conquered Babylon and liberated the exiles (see "The Early Persian Period" in the introduction to Haggai, above). Paul Redditt proposes that Zechariah's visions and oracles originally addressed the exiles in Babylon, and that they have been secondarily accommodated to a postexilic setting by the insertion of material concerning Joshua and Zerubbabel (1992, 258–59). Still, all the exiles clearly did *not* return by Darius's second year, or even by his fourth: in fact, Babylon remained a major center of Jewish life and learning down into the Middle Ages. Further, while Cyrus had indeed effectively suppressed Babylon in 539 BCE, Babylonian resentment against the Persians continued to simmer and erupted into revolt twice in the early years of Darius's reign: first in 522 BCE under Nidintu-bel, who called himself Nebuchadrezzar III; then again under Arakha, styled Nebuchadrezzar IV, in 521 BCE (Roux 1980, 376–77). We need not predate Zechariah's oracle to understand his concern for the exiles in Babylon.

Once all of God's people have escaped to Zion, God will carry out God's vengeance on Israel's oppressors (2:12-13 [8-9]). Zechariah 2:12 (8) is obscure, but both the versions and the best evidence for the Hebrew of this verse confirm the wording of the MT. The problem, then, is how to make sense of the verse. The NRSV takes the opening words of the oracle after the messenger formula to be a parenthetical statement: "For thus said the LORD of hosts (after his glory sent me) regarding the nations that plundered you" (2:12 [8]). While plausible, this reading is effectively meaningless (one can scarcely go *before* one is sent), and requires the reader to go against the plain sense of *'el-haggoyim*: not, as the NRSV has, "concerning the nations," but rather "*to* the nations." Further, in the Hebrew the word *kabod* ("glory") lacks any suffix meaning "his." The Glory is a way of designating divine presence in priestly material (e.g., Exod 24:16-17; Num 14:21-22; cf. 1 Kgs 8:11; Isa 6:3), and particularly in Ezekiel (e.g., Ezek 1:28; 10:4; 43:4; cf. Mettinger 1982; Tuell 2009, 7, 11–12). Most likely, then, "Glory" appears here as a further designation for "the LORD of hosts" (cf. Meyer and Meyers 1987, 165; Tuell 2003, 280). Indeed, Sweeney proposes that *'akhar* ("after" or "behind") *kabod* alludes to Exodus 33:12–34:9, where Moses sees the "back" of the LORD; so that this entire expression becomes "a cryptic reference to YHWH" (Sweeney 2000, 588–89).

The LORD has "sent me" to "the nations that plundered you" (Zech 2:12 [8]) with a message of judgment: "See now, I am going to raise my hand against them, and they shall become plunder for their own slaves" (2:13 [9]). The speaker could be the prophet: prophets do elsewhere pronounce oracles against foreign nations (e.g., Zeph 2), and can even be described as acting metaphorically in God's stead (e.g., Ezek 21:19 [14]). But it is more likely that the prophet's angelic interpreter, who spoke in 2:8-9 (4-5), continues speaking here (cf. Sweeney 2000, 587–92).

God's retribution will be poured out on those nations because "one who touches you touches the apple of my eye" (2:12 [8]). Our expression "the apple of my eye," indicating someone of whom we are particularly fond, is traditionally used here and elsewhere in English translations of Scripture (cf. the KJV of Deut 32:10 and Prov 7:2, where the Hebrew back of the English word "apple" is *'ishon* ["little man"?]; Lam 2:18, which has *bat* ["daughter"]; and Ps 17:8, which combines the two), but is not particularly helpful for understanding the intent of this passage. The Hebrew *babah*, rendered "apple" in the NRSV of Zechariah 2:12 (8), appears only here but is likely related to Aramaic and Arabic terms referring to the pupil of the eye (*HALOT*, 107). The *Tg. Neb.* reading *galgal* ("wheel") and the Vulgate *pupilla* ("pupil") also suggest that this word refers to the round opening of the eye itself. Curiously, the LXX reading *kore* ("little girl"?), found not only in Zechariah 2:12 (8) but also in Deuteronomy 32:10; Psalm 17:8; and Proverbs 7:2 supports this reading, since the Hebrew *'ishon* and *bat* as well as the Latin *pupilla* also literally mean a small person: perhaps the image reflected in the pupil? The best translation, then, is "the pupil of the eye" (cf. CEB).

But to whose eye does the passage refer? The MT and the versions all have "his eye," which could refer to the eye of the one plundering Israel, so that one who touches them might as well be poking himself in the eye! The NRSV "my [i.e., God's] eye" responds to an ancient Jewish tradition (*Mekhilta Shir* 6.10) identifying this passage as one of the *Tiqqune Sopherim*: places in Scripture where the scribes may have altered a reference to the Divine out of respect (cf. the discussion of Hab 1:12, above). In this instance, however, as the speaker is the LORD's messenger (whether the prophet or his angel) rather than the LORD directly, "his eye" could also refer to the Divine. The point of this passage, then, is not that God is fond of Israel (as the traditional translation "apple of my eye" suggests) but rather that anyone who harms Israel assaults God.

With 2:14-17 (10-13), the theme of the oracle shifts from judgment on the oppressors to the restoration of God's people. Just as the word of judgment began with a command to flee, this word of promise opens with a summons to worship and praise: "Sing and rejoice, O daughter Zion!" (2:14 [10]; cf. Zeph 3:14). God declares, "I will come and dwell in your midst" (2:14 [10]), a promise that certainly relates to the rebuilding of God's house, the temple (cf. Hag 1:3-11). After God's judgment on Israel's oppressors has established God's rule over the whole world, the rebuilding of the temple will lead to the reorientation of the world around Zion as its center: "Many nations shall join themselves to the LORD on that day, and shall be my people" (2:15 [11]; cf. Isa 2:3-4). Still, alluding to the Song of Moses in Deuteronomy 32:1-43, Zechariah describes Judah as the LORD's special inheritance and portion among the nations (2:16 [12]; cf. Deut 32:8-9), and Jerusalem as, once more, God's chosen place of dwelling. A final imperative concludes this oracle: "Be silent, all people, before the LORD; for he has roused himself from his holy dwelling" (2:17 [13]). As in Amos 8:3, Habakkuk 2:20, and Zephaniah 1:7, this command underlines God's determination to act, in judgment and in restoration, on the day of the LORD. The visions and oracles that follow will further describe God's acts of restoration, specifically with regard to the Jerusalem temple and God's judgment.

Fourth vision: Joshua on trial (3:1-10). The Masoretic paragraphing throughout this section emphasizes connections across units. Thus, the scribes mark 3:1–4:7 as a single paragraph, reading the vision of Joshua's trial (3:1-10) in continuity with the vision of the lampstand (4:1-5, 10b-14) and the third oracle (4:6-10a). This makes sense since these two visions and this oracle share the important issue of the sanctity and role of the priesthood.

Priesthood figures prominently in Haggai–Zechariah 1–8. Two of Haggai's four oracles are addressed to Joshua the high priest, as well as to Zerubbabel the governor (Hag 1:1; 2:2, 4; Joshua also figures prominently in the narrative depicting the temple rebuilding in Hag 1:12-15), while another oracle explores the implications of a priestly *torah* that Haggai requests (Hag 2:10-19). In Zechariah 1–8, the high priest Joshua is the central figure in 3:1-10; 6:9-15 and appears to be one of the two olive trees/"anointed ones" in 4:1-14. Zechariah 7–8, where a priestly *torah* (7:1-3; 8:18-19) again provides the occasion for a prophetic oracle (cf. Hag 2:10-19), also underlines the importance of right priesthood for this prophet.

In Zechariah 3:1, the prophet sees the high priest Joshua "standing before the angel of the LORD [cf. 1:11-12], and Satan standing at his right hand to accuse him." The NRSV rendering of this verse suggests that Joshua's accuser is the personal devil of the New Testament, where "Satan" (Greek *Satanas*) occurs thirty-five times, always as a personal name used for the Enemy. The NRSV is mistaken, however. The Hebrew has not the proper name "Satan" but a title: *hassatan* means "the *satan*," that is, "the adversary" or perhaps "the accuser."

Satan designates a heavenly being in four passages (elsewhere, the term *satan* appears in the Hebrew Bible with reference to a human adversary; cf. 1 Sam 29:4; 2 Sam 19:22; 1 Kgs 5:4; 11:14, 23, 25; Ps 109:6). First, in Numbers 22:22, 32, the angel of the LORD is a *satan* (the NRSV reads "adversary") to the prophet Balaam. Second, in our passage (Zech 3:1-2), the *satan* stands in God's presence, ready to accuse the high priest Joshua, until the LORD's rebuke. Evidently, *hassatan* is an official in the LORD's court, a kind of celestial prosecuting attorney. The third passage is Job 1–2, where *satan* appears (as in Zech 3:1-2) with the article, as a title: "the *satan*." Here too, *hassatan* is a member of God's court, one of the "heavenly beings" (Heb., *bene 'elohim*, literally "sons of the gods" or "sons of God") who "present themselves before the LORD" (Job 1:6; 2:1). Also as in Zechariah, *hassatan* is the accuser of the faithful, accusing the righteous Job of serving the LORD out of self-interest, because God has always blessed him (Job 1:9-11). In the fourth passage, 1 Chronicles 21:1, David's disastrous decision to carry out a census is attributed to the enticement of "Satan," who "stood up against Israel, and incited David to count the people of Israel." This passage uses *satan* without the article, making it likely that here Satan *is* a proper name—the first such occurrence in Scripture, the only one in the Hebrew Bible, and the first step in the development that leads to the personification of evil in the New Testament as Satan (so Tuell 2001, 85–88; *contra* Japhet 1993, 374–75 and Knoppers 2004, 751, who see David's *satan* as a human advisor). But that later development should not be read back onto Zechariah 3:1-2, which presents *hassatan* not as God's enemy but merely as Joshua's accuser in the heavenly court.

As observed in the commentary on Haggai 2:10-19, priesthood was a contentious issue in the early postexilic period. Paul Hanson observes that Zechariah's vision may have arisen "in response to charges from a rival group that the Zadokite Joshua was unsuited for the high-priestly office" (Hanson 1996, 1239). Alternatively, while the Law of the Temple in Ezekiel 40–48 affirms an exclusively Zadokite priesthood, it makes no mention of a high priest; perhaps the office itself was in contention (cf. Tuell 1992, 146–51).

No case against Joshua is ever presented, however; he is vindicated by divine *fiat*. The LORD rebukes *hassatan* and declares, "Is not this man a brand plucked from the fire?" (3:2). Likely this is an allusion to Amos 4:11, the only other place in Scripture to describe someone as snatched (in each context, *mutsal*) from the fire (*misserephah* in Amos 4:11; *me'esh* in Zech 3:2). In Amos, this refers to Israel's past deliverance from judgment (in contrast to Sodom and Gomorrah, which were destroyed). Here, Joshua is depicted as one saved from exile, representative of a priesthood spared against all expectation from the destruction of Jerusalem and its temple. John Wesley, who as a child had been saved from a fire at his father's rectory, described himself as "a brand plucked from the burning" (Wallace 1997, 64). Zechariah and Wesley alike, it seems, intend this image to convey that *this* person has been spared for some divine purpose.

In Zechariah's vision, Joshua is wearing "filthy clothes" (although the word *tso'* is found only here, it is evidently related to *tse'ah*, meaning "excrement"; cf. Ezek 4:12). But at the angel of the LORD's command, those vile garments are taken away, and the high priest is dressed up for a festival, in fine clothes and a turban. In the MT, the prophet himself calls for the turban: "And I said, 'Let them put a clean turban on his head'" (3:5). This seems odd: nowhere else does the prophet intervene in his visions; further, the LXX lacks this intervention. Likely, then, we should treat this as a scribal error for "And *he* said." Given Joshua's priestly status, it is tempting to think that the angels are clothing him in priestly vestments. The words used for both the garments and the turban, however, are never used elsewhere for priestly dress; indeed, the only other place that these words appear together is Isaiah 3:22-23, describing the rich garments of the wealthy women of Jerusalem (for the turban, cf. Isa 62:3; Job 29:14). Likely, all that the vision report conveys is the sharp contrast between Joshua's former low status and the high status that the angel of the LORD now grants him.

As the interpretation of the vision unfolds, however, Joshua's elevation explicitly involves priestly privilege: "Thus says the LORD of hosts: If you will walk in my ways and keep my requirements, then you shall rule my house and have charge of my courts, and I will give you the right of access among those who are standing here" (Zech 3:7). While "those standing here" could be the angels, implying Joshua's access as priest to heavenly places, it is more likely, in light of 3:8, that the reference is to Joshua's fellow Zadokites, extending to them, as to Joshua, access to sacred space (cf. Ezek 40:44-46, where the expression "have charge" [Heb., *mishmeret*] also appears). What is more, Joshua and his fellow priests will become "an omen [Heb., *mophet*, or "sign"] of things to come" (3:8; for people as signs, cf. Isa 8:18; Ezek 12:6, 11; 24:24, 27; Ps 71:7). Specifically, the elevation of Joshua and the other priests is a sign of the coming of "my servant the Branch" (3:8). The word "Branch" (Heb., *tsemakh*) is used in the sign-act of the crowns (6:9-15) to refer to the one who "shall build the temple of the LORD; he shall bear royal honor, and he shall sit and rule on his throne" (6:13). Jeremiah 23:5; 33:15 and Ezekiel 17:9-10 use this image for a descendant of David (cf. Isa 11:1, where a different word meaning "branch" is used). Likely, then, the Branch in Zechariah 3:8 is Zerubbabel the governor, a descendant of David who, while *not* a king, is charged with the kingly task of rebuilding the ruined temple (cf. Hag 2:20-23; Zech 4:6b-10a).

To Joshua, meanwhile, is given "a single stone with seven facets" (3:9; literally, "seven *eyes*;" cf. 4:10), bearing an inscription from God's own hand. The inscribed stone given to the high priest recalls the golden seal on Aaron's turban (Exod 28:36-38), on which was engraved "like the engraving of a signet [Heb., *khotam*; cf. Hag 2:23], 'Holy to the LORD'" (Exod 28:36)—although, as the parallel with the seven "eyes of the LORD" in 4:10 reveals, it is doubtful that this priestly association exhausts the meaning of the mysterious stone (cf. Rev 2:17). Indeed, rather than charging the newly established priests with the task of making atonement for the land and its people (e.g., Lev 4–6; 16:1-34), the LORD declares, "I will remove the guilt of this land in a single day" (3:9; for the LORD making atonement, rather than human agents, cf. Deut 32:43; Ezek 16:63; 2 Chr 30:18-19), after which God's people will once more live securely and prosper in the land (3:10; cf. Hag 2:18-19). Zechariah does not even use the ritual language of the temple liturgy: rather than *kipper* ("atone") or the like, he uses the secular term *mush* ("remove") for God's activity. While right priests and priesthood matter, the coming cleansing is God's work and God's alone—just as the building of the temple, although involving Zerubbabel, will be accomplished "Not by might, nor by power, but by my spirit, says the LORD of hosts" (Zech 4:6).

Fifth vision (the lampstand; 4:1-5, 10b-14) and third oracle (4:6-10a). In the Masoretic paragraphing, this complex unit is combined both with the vision of Joshua's trial (3:1-10) that precedes it (the Masoretic paragraphing reads 3:1–4:7 as a unit, breaking at the divine word formula in 4:8) and with the two visions that follow it (the next paragraph, 4:8–5:8, reads the interpretation of the lampstand vision in continuity with the visions of the scroll [5:1-4] and the woman in the basket [5:5-8], although keeping the related vision of the winged women [5:9-11] separate). As a result, the lampstand vision occupies a central place in this book, as the linchpin between the first four and the last three visions of the prophet.

An angel, whom the prophet says "wakened me, as one is wakened from sleep" (Zech 4:1), takes Zechariah into the visionary state. This could mean that the vision of the lampstand that follows came to the prophet in a dream while he was sleeping (cf. Zech 1:8; compare Dan 7:1-2). The language of the verse (*ke'ish 'asher-ye'or*, that is, "*like* one wakened"; so RSV) suggests, however, that the prophet intends rather to *compare* being summoned by the angel to being "wakened from sleep." For Zechariah, the world of God's revelation is more real than the waking world; entry into that world was like waking up (Meyers and Meyers 1987, 229)!

In his vision, Zechariah sees a lampstand (4:1-5). The word translated "lampstand" in 4:2 is *menorah*: the same word used today for the seven-branched candlestick that is a symbol of the modern state of Israel. Ordinarily, lampstands in the ancient world were made of clay, but Zechariah's is made of gold, like the golden lampstands of the tabernacle and the temple of Solomon. The single golden *menorah* of the ancient tabernacle had three branches on each side like the modern menorah, providing space for seven lamps (Exod 25:31-40). Solomon's temple contained ten golden lampstands (1 Kgs 7:49). Nothing is said of any of them having branches like the one in the tabernacle—although the *menorah* in the depiction of the sack of Jerusalem on the Arch of Titus in Rome shows that the lampstands in Herod's temple did. The single, branchless lampstand of Zechariah's vision with its seven lamps represents a compromise between these two old memories of service in God's presence.

The Hebrew text describing Zechariah's lampstand is in places very difficult, suggesting that later scribes, unfamiliar with the kind of lampstand and lamps that appear in Zechariah's vision, were also confused by this description. To picture the object in Zechariah's vision, the reader must first remember that the *menorah* is not a lamp but a lamp *holder*. Lamps were placed on top of a lampstand so that their light could spread through a room, as in Jesus' parable of the lamp and the lampstand (Matt 5:15). The lampstand of Zechariah's vision has at its top a structure like a bowl (Heb., *gullah*; 4:2; so Eccl 12:6; cf. also Josh 15:19; Judg 1:15, for the pool of a spring, and 1 Kgs 7:27-28//2 Chr 4:12-13, for the bowl-shaped structures atop the freestanding pillars at the entrance to Solomon's temple). Seven lamps are placed around its rim, like cups hung on the rim of a punch bowl. Archaeologists have found lampstands rather like the one Zechariah describes, datable to the Persian period (Meyers and Meyers 1987, 235–38; 290, fig. 13).

The versions reveal some confusion around the number seven in this vision report. The MT reads that on the *menorah* were seven lamps, with *sheb'a wesheb'a mutsaqot*: that is, "seven and seven lips/spouts." The NRSV follows the LXX, which reads simply *hepta eparustrides* ("seven spouts;" cf. NJPS). The doubled sevens are also found in *Tg. Neb.*, however, and do make sense once the reader has the entire description of the lamps and the lampstand in mind.

Until the Greeks introduced closed lamps into the Middle East, lamps were open saucers of oil, with a cloth wick draped over the side. The lip of the saucer would be pinched together into a spout to hold the wick in place; the end of the wick, extending from this spout, would support the flame. Such lamps usually had space only for a single wick; however, a lamp from Tell Dothan, dated to around 1000 BCE, has seven spouts, like the lamps in Zechariah's vision (Meyers and Meyers 1987, 290, fig. 12). The prophet saw seven of these seven-spouted lamps arranged atop the golden *menorah*, so that seven *times* seven, or forty-nine, flames would have been blazing from the lampstand!

Flanking the *menorah* are two olive trees—the source of the oil used for lamps. Later in the chapter, we learn that these trees are directly linked to the lampstand and its seven lamps by golden pipes (4:12). This image makes no literal sense, but in the dreamlike context of Zechariah's vision, it conveys the idea that the lamps are continually refilled and perpetually burning. Still today, synagogues have a *Ner Tamid*: an Eternal Light that is always burning, placed above the Ark that holds the Torah scrolls. Tending the sanctuary lamps was an important responsibility of the priesthood (Num 8:1-4; 2 Chr 13:11), which strongly suggests that the lampstands in both temple and tabernacle were not mere light fixtures, but had symbolic significance.

Light was the first creation of God (Gen 1:3) and is often used in Scripture as a symbol of God's presence and guidance, particularly in the Psalms (e.g., Pss 27:1; 43:3; 119:105). Christian readers will remember that Jesus said, "I am the light of the world" (John 8:12; 9:5). Just as we light candles in our places of worship to signify God's presence, the lampstands in the temple represented God's presence in the worship of ancient Israel (cf. the seven lampstands representing the seven churches in Rev 1:12-20).

The treelike arrangement of seven branches on the tabernacle *menorah* suggests another symbolic interpretation: the lampstand as a sign of God's presence in the fruitfulness of the earth (Meyers and Meyers 1987, 233–34). The lampstands from Solomon's temple may not have had branches, but carvings of trees and flowers covered the temple's walls (1 Kgs 6:29). The temple was a microcosm, reflecting in small the fertility of the whole world

(Levenson 1984). In Zechariah's vision, two olive trees flank the golden lampstand (Zech 4:3), so that here as well, the notion of life-giving fertility is joined to God's presence (cf. Hag 1:7-11). The subject of God's revelation to the prophet, as these images make clear, is the promise of God's presence, bringing light and life to the world—a presence encountered, in Israel's experience, in temple worship. These ideas and images should have been familiar to Zechariah. Perhaps this explains the angel's puzzled response when the prophet asks for an explanation: "Do you not know what these are?" (4:5).

At this point, an oracle concerning Zerubbabel (4:6b-10a) interrupts the prophet's vision report, coming squarely between the vision (4:1-5) and its interpretation (4:10b-14). Indeed, 4:10b presupposes the opening words of 4:6 in Hebrew; with the insertion removed, the text flows seamlessly. Although many scholars (e.g., Hanson 1976b, 982; Petersen 1984, 244; Redditt 1995, 39) hold that later editors made this insertion, Meyers and Meyers (1987, 242) argue that the oracle and the vision were likely arranged together by Zechariah himself. This is particularly likely since the oracle serves to confirm the connection between the vision and the rebuilt temple.

The LORD's first words to Zerubbabel are, "Not by might, nor by power, but by my spirit, says the LORD of hosts" (Zech 4:6). "Might" (*khayil*) and "power" (*koakh*) refer to military strength, usually understood to be at the command of the king (Ps 33:16; Dan 11:25; 2 Chr 26:13). These are *not* given to Zerubbabel—as is appropriate, for while Zerubbabel was a descendant of David (1 Chr 3:17-19; cf. Hag 2:20-23), he was not a king. Apparently, Zerubbabel's ambiguous position was troubling to many in the Restoration community. The very fact that Zerubbabel, son of David, was merely a governor under Persian authority must have been humiliating to many. Zechariah 4:10 speaks of those who "despised the day of small things"—referring, evidently, to the diminished power and significance of David's house. Contemporary American churches, faced with declining membership, worship attendance, and cultural influence, may find these words painfully apt. As the gaps in our pews grow wider (and the heads in those pews grow whiter), we too are learning what it is to live in a time of dreams deferred, of reduced expectations—a "day of small things."

Zerubbabel's reduced status was more than a matter of wounded pride. In the ancient world, temple-building was a project carried out by kings—just as Solomon had built the Jerusalem temple (cf. Redditt 2008b, 61). How could the returnees build a temple without a king? Yet God's words to Zerubbabel express confidence and offer a promise: the temple *would* be built—not by the power or authority of Zerubbabel or of any human king but "by my spirit, says the LORD of hosts" (4:6).

The specific provisions of the Zerubbabel oracle relate to the rituals of temple rebuilding usually performed by the king. Before Zerubbabel, the LORD declares, the top of the temple mount shall become a smooth, level place, prepared for rebuilding (Meyers and Meyers 1987, 244–45). Into this construction site Zerubbabel will carry *ha'eben haro'shah* ("the top stone"), to the peoples' acclamation (Zech 4:7). The "top stone," or perhaps better the "first" or "premier stone," could be the equivalent of the first brick in Babylonian temples, ceremonially placed by the king. Alternatively, Zerubbabel's "top stone" could be a stone from the first temple, ceremonially preserved from the ruins for inclusion in the new temple. Both customs were attested in Babylon (Meyers and Meyers 1987, 246–48; Petersen 1984, 240–41).

Also said to be in Zerubbabel's hand is *ha'eben habbedil* (literally, "the tin stone"; Zech 4:10). Traditionally, this phrase has been understood to refer to a plumb bob and has been translated as "plummet" (so KJV, NIV, NRSV; the JPSV emends the text to read "stone of distinction"). If this is accurate, then our passage once more shows Zerubbabel's involvement in rebuilding the temple, by checking that the temple walls are laid true. It seems odd, however, to refer to a plummet, which would more likely have been made of stone or lead, as "the *tin* stone." Deposits of precious materials, and of symbolic metal objects such as nails, were often placed in temple foundations. Perhaps *ha'eben habbedil* is such a foundation deposit (with Meyers and Meyers 1987, 253–54; and Petersen 1984, 243–44). Whatever the meaning of this obscure phrase, the implication of seeing this object in the hands of Zerubbabel is clear. Onlookers, even the skeptics who "despised the day of small things" (4:10), will find this convincing proof that the spirit of the LORD is at work in Zerubbabel. Having restored the foundations of the temple, he will also complete its rebuilding (4:9; cf. Hag 2:18).

Just as twenty-first-century Christians may find our present circumstances mirrored in a sense by those of Zerubbabel, we may also find in the prophet's oracle hope and challenge for our day. The way forward is not the way back—we cannot reclaim past glories, and indeed we should not try to do so. But we may learn to be attentive to the movement of God's spirit in our own context, and trust that spirit to enliven and empower us for ministry in our own age, "Not by might, nor by power, but by my spirit, says the LORD of hosts" (4:6).

Abruptly, in the middle of 4:10, the vision report resumes with the angel's answer to Zechariah's question in 4:6a. The seven lamps on the golden lampstand "are the eyes of the LORD, which range through the whole earth" (4:10b; cf. 3:9). This verse is quoted in 2 Chronicles 16:9, which understands it to mean that God is attentive to the needs of God's people everywhere, "to strengthen those whose heart is true to him." Similarly, in Revelation 5:6, the Lamb of John's vision has "seven eyes, which are the seven spirits of God sent out into all the earth" (conflating Zech 4:10 with traditions regarding the seven archangels; cf. Rev 1:4; Tob 12:15; 1 Enoch 20:1-7). In Zechariah 4:10 as well, the seven "eyes of the LORD" are a symbol not only of divine omniscience but also of divine presence and involvement. God is with God's people, providing power and help by means of God's spirit.

In Zechariah 4:11-12, the prophet expands his original question, revealing in the process a detail not found in the initial description of the *menorah* and the two olive trees. A branch of each tree stretches toward the *menorah*, and through golden pipes extending from these branches golden-hued olive oil is flowing, to fill the seven lamps. The two olive trees, then, provide oil continually to keep the lamps burning. But what (or whom) do the trees represent? In the NRSV, the angel says, "These are the two anointed ones who stand by the LORD of the whole earth" (Zech 4:14). The Hebrew word *meshiakh* ("anointed one"), from which our word "Messiah" comes, is not used here, however. Instead, the phrase translated "anointed ones" is *bene-hayyitshar*: that is, "sons of oil." The term *yitshar* refers to fresh olive oil (e.g., 2 Kgs 18:32; Hos 2:10, 24[8, 22]; Hag 1:11) and is never used elsewhere for anointing oil. The point of this vision is not that Joshua the high priest and Zerubbabel the governor are "Messiahs"—although the Essenes of Qumran did expect both a priestly and a kingly Messiah (e.g., 1QS 9:11; 1QSa 2:11-21; cf. Vermes 1995, 60; 2000, 165–66), likely because of Zechariah 4:10 and 6:9-15. Rather, just as the two olive trees in Zechariah's vision provide oil for the lamps, so the high priest and the governor together are expected both to rebuild and to provide for the temple, where God's presence would be experienced and celebrated (cf. 2:14-17 [10-13]).

Sixth vision: the flying scroll (5:1-4). In the Masoretic division of this book, 4:8–5:8 forms a single paragraph, inviting us to read the third oracle (4:6b-10a), the interpretation of the lampstand vision (4:10b-14), and the sixth and seventh visions (the flying scroll [5:1-4] and the woman in the basket [5:5-8]) in continuity. The reason for the break at 4:7 seems clear, as there is an explicit marker of divine speech in 4:8. There is no corresponding marker at 5:9, however; nor is it apparent what these units have in common. Perhaps, as is observed above, all that can be said is that, by joining the vision and oracle in Zechariah 4 both to the units preceding it and to those following it, the scribes emphasize the centrality of that chapter to the message of the book.

The word *megillah* ("scroll") appears in the Hebrew Bible twenty-one times, but in only four books—indeed, in only four passages within those books: fourteen times in Jeremiah 36 (the story of the scroll of Jeremiah's prophecy, prepared by Baruch at the prophet's dictation, destroyed by King Jehoiakim, then restored by Jeremiah and Baruch), four times in Ezekiel 2:8–3:3 (the prophet's vision of the scroll filled with "words of lamentation and mourning and woe" [2:10] which he was commanded to eat), twice in Zechariah 5:1-2, and once in Psalm 40:8 (7).The relative rarity of this word may account in part for the LXX *drepanon* ("sickle"), misreading *megillah* as the even rarer *maggal* ("sickle"; cf. Jer 50:16; Joel 4:13) and accounting for early Christian interpretations of this passage (e.g., Hill 2006, 245; Augustine's letter to Bishop Alypius [*Ep.* 125]; John Chrysostom, *Hom on Matt*, 3.7.4) as depicting a weapon of God's wrath.

While Zechariah may have been aware of any of these biblical passages, he would certainly have been aware of the Ezekiel text; still, his vision has its own logic. Like Ezekiel's vision, Zechariah's represents a message of condemnation and judgment: indeed, the prophet's angel describes the flying scroll as a curse (5:3). In Ezekiel's vision, the scroll is filled with writing, front and back, to express the sheer quantity of "lamentation and mourning and woe" it contains; in Zechariah's, the magnitude of the curse is shown by the size of the scroll: thirty feet long and fifteen feet across. The curse, however, does not need to be ingested by Zechariah or even pronounced by him: "I have sent it out, says the LORD of hosts" (5:4). The scroll flies independently "over the face of the whole land" (5:3) and does its work against all thieves and against "anyone who swears falsely by my name" (5:4), consuming their houses, "both timber and stones" (5:4).

To this point, Zechariah's visions have all expressed blessing upon Judah, and God's power and grace given for the land's restoration. The oracles have expressed judgment, but on foreign nations or on past generations rather than on the prophet's own audience. This sixth vision, however, proclaims judgment against Zechariah's own community, since the commands not to steal (Exod 20:15; Deut 5:19) and particularly not to misuse God's name (Exod 20:7; Deut 5:11) come from the Decalogue: the foundational statement of Israel's covenant with God. The effect of the curse, the devastation of the wrongdoers' house, may suggest why these two commands in particular have been singled out. Haggai accused this community of putting its own prosperity ahead of worship: "Is it time for you yourselves to live in your paneled houses while this house lies in ruins?" (Hag 1:4). Indeed, Malachi will say that those who withhold their tithe are robbing God, to the end that they will be "cursed with a curse" (Mal 3:8-9). Perhaps these are the thieves Zechariah has in mind: not burglars or pickpockets but those who did not support the rebuilding of the temple, as well as those who pledged to do so in the LORD's name but did not fulfill their pledge. Such persons would not benefit from their treachery; their own houses would be lost to God's curse (cf. Hab 2:9-11).

Seventh vision: the woman in the basket (5:5-11). This vision has two interrelated parts, the woman in the basket (5:5-8) and the winged women who carry the basket away (5:9-11); each part is interpreted to Zechariah by "the angel who talked with me" (5:5, 10). The word rendered "basket" is in Hebrew *'ephah*, a measure of volume equal to about two-thirds of a bushel. Into this relatively small measure is crammed Judah's sins: "their iniquity in all the land" (5:6). The MT has *'aynam* ("their eye"?), but both the context of this passage and the agreement of the versions (LXX and Syriac; note that *Tg. Neb.* has "lie") make plain that *'aynam* is a scribal error for *'awonam* ("their iniquity").

A leaden cover over the basket is lifted to reveal imprisoned there a woman called Wickedness (Heb., *rishah*). This vision likely personifies wickedness as a woman because in Hebrew, where (as in some modern languages, such as French and Spanish) nouns have gender, the word *rishah* is feminine (cf. the feminine *khokmah* [Wisdom], also personified as a woman in Prov 8:1-36). Some might use 5:5-11 to condemn women as inherently wicked or as responsible for the iniquity of Judah (cf. the discussion of Nah 3:4, above). This does not appear to be the way that early Christian interpreters read this passage, however. Instead, they focused on the weightiness of the lead cover as symbolizing the burden of sin (see citations in Ferreiro 2003, 246–47). In any case, since in this vision it is also women, "with wings like the wings of a stork" (5:9), who remove the evil from the land, no hostility toward women is apparent.

Like Zechariah's other visions, 5:5-11 is a *vision*, not an allegory: we ought not press too hard for what the women "represent" or what it *means* to say that they have wings "like the wings of a stork." While there are allegorical elements in some of these visions (such as the two olive trees in Zech 4), in no case is there a clear point-for-point equation of elements in the vision with people, places, or events in the world. The visions retain a core of irreducible mystery. The white stork is a large bird whose wingspan can approach seven feet; its spring migration takes it through Palestine. A friend who has witnessed this migration describes the birds spiraling up and up into the heavens on thermals, then soaring off on their way from that great height. Likely, the stork's size and its soaring flight bring this association to the prophet's mind.

The winged women, evidently heavenly beings, carry the basket containing Judah's wickedness off to Shinar. In the Old Testament, this term usually refers to all of Mesopotamia (so *HALOT*, 1608; cf. Gen 10:10; 11:2; 14:1, 9; Josh 7:21; Isa 11:11), but in Daniel 1:2, Shinar is Babylon: a usage likely derived from this passage. According to Ezekiel, those left in the land during the Babylonian crisis claimed that God had sent the corrupt and impure away into exile, leaving behind a righteous remnant (Ezek 11:3, 15). That claim had of course been false. But now, Zechariah promises, God will remove all wickedness from the land (cf. 3:9), sending it off to be destroyed along with the wicked oppressors of Shinar (cf. 2:10-17 [6-13]).

Eighth vision: four chariots (6:1-8). Zechariah's visions conclude as they had begun, with a vision of horses (cf. 1:7-17)—although this time he sees four *teams* of horses, each team drawing a chariot. As in the first vision, the horses are distinguished by color: the first team is red, the second white, the third black, and the fourth dappled (6:1-2). In 1:8, the horses are red, sorrel, and white, though the Hebrew word for "sorrel" (*sheruqim*) sounds very like the word for "black" (*shekhorim*) in 6:2, so that either could perhaps have been misheard as the other. The LXX lists are more similar, although not identical: the word used for "black" in 1:8 is *psaroi*, while 6:23 has *melanes*. In short, while this last vision of Zechariah has apparently influenced the LXX version of his first vision (note that the LXX has four colors in each context), neither the visionary nor the scribes engaged in the later transmission of the book have made any great attempt to accommodate the language of either vision to the other.

The chariots come "from between two mountains—mountains of bronze" (6:1). The "mountains of bronze" could prompt one to think of the altar of burnt offering, which was sheathed in bronze (cf. 2 Chr 4:1; Ezek 9:2; compare Exod 35:30-33; 38:1-2) and whose bronze hearth is called *har 'el*, "the mountain of God," in Ezekiel 43:15. But the MT and the versions of Zechariah 6:1 agree on *two* mountains, and there was always only one altar of burnt offering. Cook (2010) proposes that the two bronze mountains correspond to the two bronze pillars, called Jachin and Boaz, that had stood at the entrance to the Jerusalem temple (1 Kgs 7:17–22//2 Chr 3:15–17; Ezek 40:49), and that the chariots in this vision correspond to the horses and chariots of the sun once placed in that temple. These items were removed from the temple in Josiah's reforms (2 Kgs 23:11), but solar associations with the LORD and the temple are both old and long-standing (e.g., Ezek 8:16; Ps 84:12; cf. Smith 1990, 15–16), extending to depictions of the solar chariot in mosaics from early synagogues at Beth Alpha (Goodenough 1953–68, 1:248; 3: fig. 640), Naaran (Goodenough 1953–68, 1:255; 3: fig. 644), and Hamath Tiberius (Goodenough 1953–68, 12:45); portions of such mosaics were also found at Yafa (Goodenough 1953–68, 1:217) and

Isfiya (Goodenough 1953–68, 1:258; 3: fig. 658). But it is difficult to square this identification either with the number of the chariots (why four?) or with the interpretation of the vision given by Zechariah's angel. Ezekiel's visions describe heavenly beings as gleaming like bronze (Ezek 1:7; 40:3). Perhaps the most we can say, then, is that the chariots come from a valley between two heavenly mountains, located beyond this world.

Zechariah's angel tells him, "These are the four winds of heaven going out, after presenting themselves before the LORD of all the earth" (6:5). In 2:10 (6), this was the image used for the exile of Israel: "I have spread you abroad like the four winds of heaven, says the LORD." Now, it seems, God sends the winds forth not to scatter but to bring word concerning those who had *been* scattered, particularly to the north—that is, to Babylon (cf. 2:11 [7]). The news is good: "Then he cried out to me, 'Lo, those who go toward the north country have set my spirit at rest in the north country'" (6:8). The summons in 2:10-11 (6-7) has been heeded; the exiles have returned, so that God's judgment can be meted out on the oppressors—particularly Babylon, to which the LORD has shipped the wickedness of Judah (cf. 5:11).

The Sign-Act of the Crowns (6:9-15)

Zechariah 6:9-15 describes a prophetic sign-act (6:10-11) interpreted by an oracle (6:12-15). Such signs were part of the standard repertoire of Israel's prophets. Some sign-acts are miracles, such as the signs that the LORD gave to Moses, to prove that the LORD has sent him (Exod 4:1-8). But most are symbolic performances that enact the meaning of a prophetic message. Thus, Hosea's tormented marriage to Gomer embodied the strained relations between the LORD and Israel (Hos 1:2), while Jeremiah's ox yoke effectively expressed submission to Babylon (Jer 27:1-22). These vivid demonstrations would have commanded the attention of the prophet's audience and made his or her message more persuasive (cf. Friebel 1999, 40). But sign-acts were more than object lessons. When, for example, Ezekiel is told to lie on his left side for 390 days (Ezek 4:4-8), this act represents the 390 years of the temple as the years of Israel's sin. But the LORD also says, "you shall bear their punishment [better, "their iniquity"] for the number of the days that you lie there" (Ezek 4:4; cf. Tuell 2012, 25–26). Ezekiel's sign-act is more than an illustration; it *accomplishes* something. By performing a sign-act, the prophet embodies and participates in God's activity; she or he becomes an agent of the LORD, for judgment or deliverance.

Reports of sign-acts usually present both the command to the prophet to perform the sign-act and a description of the performance itself (e.g.,

Hos 1:2-3; Ezek 24:15-24). But while Zechariah 6:9-15 presents the LORD's command to "Collect silver and gold from the exiles . . . make a crown [MT has "crowns"; see the discussion below], and set it on the head of the high priest Joshua" (6:10-11), it describes neither the actual performance nor the reaction of Zechariah's audience—let alone the reaction of Persian officialdom! The reason, likely, is that this is a *literary* sign-act rather than one actually performed by the prophet. Similarly, Ezekiel 4:4-8 describes no performance, and in this instance, Ezekiel could not have performed the sign literally as described. Quite apart from the terrible physical toll it would have taken on the prophet to lie in one position for over a year, or the fact that Ezekiel was supposedly performing other sign-acts as well at this time (cf. Ezek 4:9–5:17), the next dated oracle in the book finds the prophet sitting in his house surrounded by the elders (8:1) when, according to a strictly literal reading of the text, he should still have been lying immobile.

Almost certainly, Zechariah could not have performed his sign, either. The prophet is told to approach certain people in the community to obtain silver and gold for the crowns he is to fashion (6:10). These potential donors all bear names found elsewhere in priestly and levitical lists and genealogies (for Heldai, cf. 1 Chr 27:15; for Tobiah, cf. Ezra 2:60 [perhaps the father of the Tobiah who was Nehemiah's opponent in Neh 6:10-14, 17-19; 13:4-6; cf. Mazar 1957; Meyers and Meyers 1987, 351–43]; for Jedaiah, cf. Ezra 2:36; Neh 7:39; 11:10; 12:6, 19, 21; 1 Chr 9:10; 24:27). These same three benefactors (Syriac has Heldai instead of Helem in 6:14), plus "Hen the son of Zephaniah" (following the Hebrew, with the KJV; NRSV follows the Syriac, reading "Josiah" instead of "Hen"; the LXX has only the name of Zephaniah, and translates the Hebrew "*khen*" as "grace") are charged with keeping and caring for the crowns "as a memorial in the temple of the LORD" (6:14). This suggests that they may have been priests themselves: Joshua's peers and presumed allies. Whether priests or not, however, they are identified as *haggolah*: that is, as returnees from the Babylonian exile (cf. the discussion of this term in Nah 3:5, 10). Ezra 4:1-3 similarly depicts the postexilic community as divided between the *golah* Jews, who had come back to the land from exile in Babylon, and the people in the land, who had never left it. This tension will be particularly evident as we move from Haggai-Zechariah 1–8 to the book of Malachi. Both Haggai (1:1-11; 2:2) and Zechariah (1:12; 4:10) stress the limited resources of the *golah* community, making it doubtful that they had any surplus silver and gold lying around. But even assuming that Zechariah could have gathered sufficient silver and gold from these donors to fashion crowns (not just one but likely two; see the discussion below), and assuming that he had the necessary tools and skill to craft crowns from these materials, both making such crowns and using them in the coronation of Jewish officials would have been acts of rebellion against Persia. Neither Haggai nor Zechariah called for such a rebellion, however.

For the purposes of the prophetic book, it does not matter whether Zechariah actually *performed* this sign or not. In a written text, the description of the act is enough for the reader to understand the sign-act's meaning. But before the meaning of the act can be deciphered, we must first deal with the number of crowns imagined in Zechariah 6:9-15. Although only one crown is actually *used* in the final form of the text, the plural *'atarot* ("crowns") in the MT of 6:11 and 14 raises intriguing questions. Perhaps *'atarot,* although plural in form, is singular in meaning: in the MT of 6:14, this plural noun takes a singular verb (Gelston 2010, 139–40*; Gelston also cites Job 31:36 as another instance, although that passage is itself obscure). In that case, there would be only one crown, and the sign-act would serve, like the vision of Joshua's trial (3:1-10), to exalt the high priest.

Still, 6:12-13 reads, "[S]ay to him, 'Thus says the LORD of hosts: Here is a man whose name is Branch [Heb., *tsemakh*]: for he shall branch out in his place, and he shall build the temple of the LORD. It is he that shall build the temple of the LORD; he shall bear royal honor, and shall sit and rule on his throne.'" This enthroned figure cannot be Joshua, as he is the one being addressed ("say to *him*," 6:12). Indeed, in 3:8, Joshua and his fellow priests are a sign that the royal Branch (cf. Jer 23:5; 33:15; Ezek 17:9-10) is coming. Further, in Zechariah's third oracle (4:6-10a), Zerubbabel (not Joshua) is charged with building the temple. Finally, 6:13 concludes, "There shall be a priest by his throne, with peaceful understanding between the two of them." As the "priest by his throne" is certainly Joshua, this clinches the distinction: *two* crowned figures are identified here, a priest and a king (cf. Redditt 2008b, 62). The plural "crowns" remains in the final form of this passage as a reminder that the original sign-act envisioned crowns for both Joshua and the Branch, likely Zerubbabel (so Hanson 1979, 256 and 1976, 983). Apparently the editors have removed the explicit reference to Zerubbabel as the messianic Branch in the final form of this book, since Zerubbabel ultimately proved a disappointment (see the discussion of Hag 2:10-19, above). As a result, the Branch becomes a promise opening into the future hope connected to the day of the LORD in the Book of the Twelve.

This sign-act gives the dual leadership of the postexilic community divine sanction. This view is consistent with the remainder of this book (cf. especially Zech 4:14), as well as with the book of Haggai, which is addressed to both Zerubbabel and Joshua. This dual leadership model has also influenced later ideas of kingship. The Hasmonean monarchs, who ruled in Jerusalem from the Maccabean revolt to the rise of the Roman Empire, claimed the title of high priest as well as king. As we have seen, the Essenes at Qumran expected two messiahs, one a priest and one a king (e.g., 1QS 9:11; 1QSa 2:11-21; cf. Vermes 1995, 60; 2000, 165–66). Christian readers may think particularly of Hebrews, where the image of the priest-king Melchizedek (Gen 14:18-20; Ps 109:4) enables this author to describe Jesus as at once high priest and king (Heb 5:6, 10; 6:20; 7:1-28).

For Zechariah, as for Haggai, the practical point of this partnership is the completion of the temple (6:15). Zechariah calls for the community to rally around these leaders and "obey the voice of the LORD your God," but he also stakes his prophetic reputation on the accomplishment of their purpose: it is when, under Joshua and Zerubbabel's leadership, "[t]hose who are far off . . . come and help to build the temple of the LORD" that "you shall know that the LORD of hosts has sent me to you" (6:15).

A Priestly/Prophetic Torah and Its Application (7–8)

In the Masoretic text, these chapters are divided into multiple subunits, usually at indications of divine speech (particularly the messenger formula): 7:1-3, 4-7, 8-14; 8:1-3, 4-5, 6, 7-8, 9-13, 14-17, 18-19, 20-22, 23. This complexity may indicate the scribes' awareness that the editors of the Twelve have extensively reworked these chapters. For example, the recollection of the "former prophets" in 7:8-14 refers back to the editorial introduction at 1:1-6, while the wording of Zechariah 7:2; 8:21-22 links Haggai–Zechariah 1–8 to Malachi 1:9. Still, as Nogalski notes, this "overabundance of beginnings" and "the resulting staccato character of these chapters masks the pivotal role as thematic summary that these chapters perform within the book" (Nogalski 2011, 885–86). This summary is held together by a priestly and prophetic *torah* (7:1-3; 8:18-19), and consists of prophetic interpretations of and responses to that *torah*.

The reader will recall that in Haggai 2:10-19, the priests are approached for an authoritative ruling, which provides the occasion for a prophetic oracle. So too, in Zechariah 7:1-3, a request for a ruling about fasting comes to "the priests of the house of the LORD of hosts and the prophets" from the people of Bethel: "Should I mourn and practice abstinence in the fifth month, as I have done for so many years?"(7:3). Since it was in the fifth month that Nebuchadnezzar "burned the house of the LORD, the king's house, and all the houses of Jerusalem" (2 Kgs 25:9//Jer 52:13), this fast was certainly initiated as a remembrance for the destruction of the first temple. Later tradition established the Ninth of Ab as the day to mourn both the first and second temple, both of which are said to have fallen on the same day. Both this question and the fact that it is addressed to temple staff strongly suggest that by this time—two years after the date in 1:7—the temple, although certainly not completed, was near enough to completion to function liturgically. Given the existence of a new temple, then, is it still necessary to mourn the loss of the old one?

The answer to this query is given in 8:18-19. Not only the former fast of the fifth month but also fasts in the fourth month (perhaps commemorating the breaching of Jerusalem's walls and the end of kingship; cf. 2 Kgs 25:2-7), the seventh month (likely commemorating the assassination of Gedaliah, ill-fated governor of Judah under the Babylonians; cf. 2 Kgs 25:25; Jer 41:1-3; Zech 7:6), and the tenth month (perhaps recalling the beginning of Nebuchadnezzar's siege; cf. 2 Kgs 25:1//Jer 52:4; Ezek 24:1) are to become "seasons of joy and gladness, and cheerful festivals for the house of Judah" (8:19). This celebration is not devoid of ethical content, as though the standards of former times could be laid aside. God commands the community to "love truth and peace" (8:19), to devote itself to standards of right and wholeness (cf. 5:1-4, where liars and thieves, who violate truth and community, are placed under a curse). But God also gives them permission to stop mourning for the past and to celebrate the new thing that God is doing in a new day.

Within (and without; cf. 8:20-23) these brackets, Zechariah 7–8 uses this *torah* as a key to the meaning not only of this book but also of the Book of the Twelve as a whole. Zechariah 7:4-7 presents the following two chapters as a unit, responding to the question posed by the people of Bethel. The divine word formula in 7:4 recapitulates the formula in 7:1, expressly continuing the idea that, in all that follows, Zechariah is speaking the word of the LORD.

God asks, "When you fasted and lamented in the fifth month and in the seventh, for these seventy years, was it for me that you fasted?" (7:5). Here, as in 8:19, an observance in the seventh month is added to the fast in the fifth month, although the other two fasts addressed in the response to the request at 8:18-19 are not mentioned. This may be because, at the time this passage was composed, only these two fasts were still being observed. Then again, as the fast in the seventh month mourned the assassination of Gedaliah, it may be that the names of the emissaries from Bethel, Sharezer and Regel-melech (7:2), called to mind Sharezer and Adrammelech, who assassinated Sennacherib (2 Kgs 19:37//Isa 37:38; cf. Roux 1980, 298). The "seventy years" during which the people have observed these fasts are Jeremiah's seventy years of exile (Jer 25:11-12; 29:10; cf. Nogalski 2011, 888), mentioned at the beginning of this book (cf. 1:12).

The expected answer to God's question in 7:5—"was it for me that you fasted?"—is clearly "No." Whether in their fasting, mourning their own loss and tragedy, or eating and drinking (7:6), this community has been concerned only with itself, not with discerning and following the will of its God (cf. Hag 1:3-11). In this, sadly, they have followed the example of their forebears, and so Zechariah's message is in continuity with the message of "the former prophets, when Jerusalem was inhabited and in prosperity, along with the towns around it, and when the Negeb and the Shephelah were inhabited" (7:7). Just as the mention of Jeremiah's seventy years recalls the interpretation of Zechariah's first vision (1:7-17), so this reference to the former prophets recalls his first oracle (cf. 1:1-6). It also points forward, however, to the summary of their message—and purportedly, Zechariah's own—in 7:8-14.

The summative message in 7:8-14 opens with the divine word formula in the third person, "The word of the LORD came to Zechariah" (7:8), just as in 1:1, 7, and 7:1—in contrast to 7:4, where the formula is in the first person. The ethical content of this message, while perhaps presumed in the earlier units, has not been expressed in these terms to this point in the book—although 1:1-6 speaks of "my words and my statutes, which I commanded my servants the prophets" (1:6). The themes, however, are familiar ones. The expression *mishpat 'emet* ("true judgments") in 7:9 is found elsewhere only in Ezekiel 18:8, in that prophet's depiction of the righteous person (18:5-9). The wording of the command "do not oppress the widow, the orphan, the alien, or the poor" is unique to 7:10, but the concept, of course, is widespread in Scripture. The first three terms in this list regularly occur together in Deuteronomy (e.g., Deut 10:18; 24:17), and the command to treat these persons justly is also found in Jeremiah 7:6; 22:3; Ezekiel 22:7; and Malachi 3:5.

As 1:1-6 also records, the commandments and warnings of the former prophets were not heeded: "They made their hearts adamant in order not to hear the law and the words that the LORD of hosts had sent by his spirit through the former prophets" (7:12). The NRSV "adamant" follows the Vulgate *adamas*; the Hebrew *shamir* likely means "diamond." Although *shamir* is used three times in the Hebrew Bible, always expressing stubborn resistance to God's will (Jer 17:1; Ezek 3:9; Zech 7:12), each usage is distinctive: in Jeremiah, the sin of the people is ineradicable, engraved "with a diamond point" on their hearts and altar; in Ezekiel, it is their foreheads that are "[l]ike the hardest stone [Heb., *shamir*], harder than flint." But the image of the hardened heart does occur elsewhere: for example, in Ezekiel's "heart of stone" texts (11:19; 36:26) and, most famously, in the plagues stories in Exodus, where Pharaoh's heart is, more precisely, "strengthened" (*hazaq*) or "made heavy" (*kabed*). The point is clear. Because the people did not respond to the former prophets, they suffered the consequences of their disobedience: "I scattered them with a whirlwind among all the nations that they had not known. Thus the land they left was desolate, so that no one went to and fro, and a pleasant land was made desolate" (7:14).

Zechariah used the image of exiled Israel scattered by the winds earlier in this book (2:10 [6]; 6:5), although again, the expression here is different (Heb., *we'esa'arem*: "I blew them away"; cf. Hab 3:14, which uses the same verb). The theme of the desolated (Heb., *shamam*) land has not appeared before this in Zechariah (but cf. Hag 1:3-11). It is an important theme in Ezekiel, however (25 times; e.g., 36:3-4, 34-36), drawing on ancient covenant curses (e.g., Lev 26:14-45; Deut 28:25-37; cf. Rom-Shiloni 2005, 11), and occurs elsewhere in the Twelve in Hosea 2:14 (12); Joel 1:17; Amos 7:9; 9:14; Micah 6:14; and Zephaniah 3:6. Ideology to one side, however, the land was not in fact emptied by the Babylonian exile; although the people left in the land were regarded as illegitimate by the population returning from exile, they were indeed present (cf. O'Brien 2004, 216–17). This myth of the "empty land" was also back of European colonization of the Americas, with devastating consequences for the Native American populations who were, in fact, there. Chaim Weizmann, the first president of the state of Israel, famously said in 1914, "there is a country which happens to be called Palestine, a country without a people, and, on the other hand, there exists the Jewish people, and it has no country. What else is necessary, then, than to fit the gem into the ring, to unite this people with this country?" (cited in Masalha 2009, 47). Thus the rightly celebrated establishment of the state of Israel in 1948 as a homeland for the Jewish people also became, tragically, the *Nakba* ("Catastrophe") for Palestinian Arabs, many of whose villages were destroyed and depopulated. Nur Masalha writes, "the indigenous people earmarked for dispossession are usually invisible. They are simultaneously divested of their human and national reality and classed as a marginal non-entity" (Masalha 2009, 46). While we can understand the perspective of the returning exiles presented in Haggai–Zechariah 1–8 and related texts, we must be careful not to accept that perspective uncritically.

The opposite of the desolated land is the land restored, populated, and fertile. This is a major theme of the Twelve (cf. Nogalski 2007, 128–30) that finds expression in Zechariah 8. Now that God's judgment is past, the prophet announces a new day for Jerusalem and its people. The first eight verses of Zechariah 8 are a rollicking chorus of celebration at God's deliverance and Jerusalem's rejuvenation. The frequent "beginnings" (to use Nogalski's [2011, 885] expression: cf. the divine word formula in 8:1; the messenger formulae in 8:2, 3, 4, 6, and 7) create a "call and response" feeling, as excitement builds from line to line. Echoing the beginning of the book (cf. 1:14-15), 8:1-3 speaks of God's wrath against Israel's oppressors, and God's jealousy—better, God's zealous passion—for Israel. For these reasons, the LORD declares, "I will return to Zion, and will dwell in the midst of Jerusalem; Jerusalem shall be called the faithful city, and the mountain of the LORD of hosts shall be called the holy mountain" (8:3; cf. 2:14 [10]). Not only shall the LORD return to Jerusalem; its people shall return as well. In 8:4-5, old and young alike fill the city's streets (cf. Joel 3:1-2 [2:28-29], where God's spirit is poured out on everyone, old and young alike).

In the MT, the scribal paragraphing sets 8:6 apart from the verses that precede and follow it, emphasizing the importance of this declaration: "Thus says the LORD of hosts: Even though it seems impossible to the remnant of this people in these days, should it also seem impossible to me, says the LORD of hosts?" Christian readers will think of the saying of Jesus that likely alluded to this passage, "For mortals it is impossible, but not for God; for God all things are possible" (Mark 10:27; cf. the parallels in Matt 19:26 and Luke 18:27; also Luke 1:37); indeed, the NRSV follows the LXX, which like the Gospels has *adunatesei* ("be impossible") here; similarly, *Tg. Neb.* has *tiyqar* ("be difficult"). The Hebrew, however, has *yippale'*, the same term used in God's gently chiding question to Abraham and Sarah: "Is anything too wonderful for the LORD?"(Gen 18:14; cf. Jer 32:17, 27). Jerusalem's rebirth will be a wonder, as miraculous as Israel's own beginnings had been!

God's deliverance will extend to wherever God's people have been scattered: "I will save my people from the east country and the west country" (8:7). The Hebrew reads more literally, "from the land of the rising and from the land of the setting of the sun"—that is, from one end of the world to the other (so O'Brien 2004, 218). Earlier, Zechariah's promises of deliverance focused on Babylon, the *north* country (2:10-11 [6-7]; 6:8). Now, however, all the dispersed are to be gathered home, from wherever they might have been scattered. Of this restored population, God declares, "They shall be my people, and I will be their God, in faithfulness and in righteousness" (8:8). This exact phrase ("They shall be my people, and I will be their God") appears elsewhere only in Ezekiel 11:20; 14:11; 37:2; and Jeremiah 32:38. Although in the days of the exodus, God had promised, "I will walk among you, and will be your God, and you shall be my people" (Lev 26:12; cf. Exod 6:7; Jer 7:23; 11:4), that relationship was broken through Israel's idolatry and injustice, prompting Hosea to declare, "you are not my people and I am not your God" (Hos 1:9). For Ezekiel, only after idolatry has been purged from the hearts of God's people will the LORD again say, "[Y]ou shall be my people, and I will be your God" (Ezek 36:28; compare Jer 30:22). The final form of Zechariah assumes, then, that Israel is not only restored to the land but also restored to its original faithful relationship with God.

Zechariah 8:9-13 calls the community to act on the opportunity this restored relationship with God represents. These verses both begin and end with the exhortation, "Let your hands be strong" (8:9, 13). David used those same words in a message to the people of Jabesh-gilead, both reassuring them that they need not fear retribution for their support of Saul and also calling upon them now to support his own rule (2 Sam 2:7). Readers may also recall Joshua 1, which repeatedly urges Moses' successor, "Be strong and courageous" (Josh 1:6, 7, 9). Similarly Haggai compared his time of rebuilding to "when you came out of Egypt" (Hag 2:5). Indeed, the editor of Zechariah here refers to "the prophets who were present when the foundation was laid for the rebuilding of the temple" (Zech 8:9)—clearly, Haggai and Zechariah. Like all of these, this oracle speaks into a time of transition. Like Haggai (cf. Hag 2:18-19), the prophet contrasts the time that is coming, when "the vine shall yield its fruit, the ground shall give its produce, and the skies shall give their dew" (8:12), with the time past, when "there were no wages for people or for animals, nor was there any safety from the foe for those who went out or came in, and I set them against one another" (8:10).

Indeed, this oracle speaks even more starkly of the contrast between then and now: "Just as you have been a cursing [literally, "a curse"] among the nations, O house of Judah and house of Israel, so I will save you and you shall be a blessing. Do not be afraid, but let your hands be strong" (8:13). This view of exiled Israel not as accursed but *as themselves* a curse (Heb., *qelalah*) reflects the perspective, if not the language, of Ezekiel 36:16-23a. For Ezekiel, the exile was necessary to spare the land from the defilement of Israel's injustice and idolatry and to give the land the opportunity to heal (36:18-19; cf. Lev 26:27-45). The exile also posed a problem, however: "But when they came to the nations, wherever they came, they profaned my holy name, in that it was said of them, 'These are the people of the LORD, and yet they had to go out of his land'" (36:20). The exiles profane the LORD's name, not by anything that they do but because of who they are: their exile implies that the LORD had been unable to save them, calling God's honor into question. For Ezekiel, it is for this reason alone—to vindicate the LORD's honor—that the LORD will rescue the exiles: "It is not for your sake, O house of Israel, that I am about to act, but for the sake of my holy name, which you have profaned among the nations to which you came" (36:22). In Zechariah, on the other hand, God's deliverance changes Israel from a curse to a blessing among the nations, calling to mind God's promise to Abraham, "in you all the families of the earth shall be blessed" (Gen 12:3). Once more, Jerusalem's physical restoration also involves its spiritual restoration.

As with Zechariah 1:2-4, the Chronicler used 8:9-13 in composing a speech for his own history: in this case, for Azariah son of Oded, addressed to Asa king of Judah following his stunning victory over the hosts of Zerah the Ethiopian (2 Chr 15:1-7; cf. Japhet 1993, 721; Tuell 2001, 169–70). Azariah describes the lawless period before kingship much as Zechariah describes the time before the rebuilding of the temple (compare Zech 8:10 and 2 Chr 15:5-6). Just as the LORD assures Zechariah's community that, now that the temple has been built, "there shall be a sowing of peace . . . and I will cause the remnant of this people to possess all these things" (Zech 8:12), so Azariah assures Asa, "But you, take courage! Do not let your hands be weak, for your work shall be rewarded" (2 Chr 15:7). In the Chronicler's story, Asa responds to this speech with building and reform projects of his own (cf. 2 Chr 15:8-9); but by using this text from Zechariah, the Chronicler implicitly urges his own community to continued faithfulness.

In 8:14-17, the editors issue a renewed call for righteousness, grounded in God's faithfulness: God has kept God's promises, for good (8:15) and for ill (8:14). The word used for God's intention (translated "purposed" in 8:14 and 15) is the relatively rare term *zamam*, found only fourteen times in Scripture. Yet in Zechariah this word appears three times, in 1:6 and in 8:14-15—further evidence that 1:1-6 and the expanded material in chapters 7–8 reflects the editors' introduction and conclusion to this book. The standards of righteousness set forth in 8:16-17 recall the summary of the message of the former prophets in 7:8-14. Once more, truth and justice are the hallmarks of a life lived in right relationship to God. This depiction of the life of the righteous person, in combination with the stress on temple worship, brings to mind entrance liturgies such as Psalms 15 and 24, which also emphasize truthfulness (compare Zech 8:16 with Pss 15:2 and 24:4), good intentions toward others (compare Zech 8:17 with Ps 15:3), and not swearing false oaths (compare Zech 8:17 with Pss 15:3-4 and 24:4). Little wonder that the writer of Ephesians quotes Zechariah 8:16 in his own list of practical instructions for the life of faith (cf. Eph 4:25).

After Zechariah's answer to the request for an oracle (8:18-19; cf. 7:1-3) comes the conclusion of Haggai–Zechariah 1–8. In 8:20-23, what God has done in Jerusalem has universal consequences, as the nations are drawn to Jerusalem (cf. 2:15 [11]). The sentiment is not unlike that expressed in the

Zion song at Isaiah 2:2-4//Micah 4:1-3, but is here presented in a far more personal and winsome fashion: "Peoples shall yet come, the inhabitants of many cities; the inhabitants of one city shall go to another, saying, 'Come, let us go to entreat the favor of the LORD, and to seek the LORD of hosts; I myself am going'" (8:20-21). There is also an unparalleled intensity to the desire of the nations to encounter Israel's God: "Thus says the LORD of hosts: In those days ten men from nations of every language shall take hold of a Jew, grasping his garment and saying, 'Let us go with you, for we have heard that God is with you'" (8:23). Similarly, in Isaiah 66:18-21, the nations come to Jerusalem, bringing with them the exiles of Israel, and find not merely acceptance but also affirmation and inclusion. The statement about the inclusion of the nations at the close of Zechariah 1–8 echoes the statement of the earth's nations at peace in 1:11. There, the comparative well-being of the rest of the world is the spur to an anguished question: why, then, are God's own people still not made whole? In contrast, 8:20-23 views the nations positively. The reader will likely be struck as well by the contrast with Nahum, or with the oracle against the nations in Zephaniah 2. The final form of the Twelve, however, emphasizes the inclusion of the nations. Indeed, Nogalski proposes that Jonah found a home among the Twelve for this very reason: "The narrative was selected as a contrast to the views of Nahum, whose bitter denunciation of Nineveh (within the context of cosmic judgment) leaves no room for YHWH's salvific action among the nations" (Nogalski 1993b, 270–71).

Zechariah 9–14

The last six chapters of this book are the ones most familiar to Christian readers—although they may not know it (cf. LaCocque 1998, 401). Here we find several passages quoted or alluded to by the Gospel writers in their accounts of Jesus' passion: the triumphal entry into Jerusalem (Matt 21:5; John 12:15; cf. Zech 9:9), Judas's thirty pieces of silver (Matt 26:15; 27:9-10; cf. Zech 11:12-13), Jesus' prediction of the disciples' betrayal ("I will strike the shepherd, and the sheep of the flock will be scattered"; Matt 26:31//Mark 14:27; cf. Zech 13:7), and the piercing of Jesus' side (John 19:37; Rev 1:7; cf. Zech 12:10) all draw on these chapters of Zechariah (cf. Matt 9:36//Mark 6:34, which may allude to Zech 10:2). The heavy dependence of the Gospel writers on the latter part of this book, particularly in their understanding of Jesus' suffering and death, likely relates to the intensity of messianic expectation in Zechariah 9–14. This expectation builds on the royalist ideas present in Haggai–Zechariah 1–8 (Hag 2:20-23; Zech 3:8; 4:6-10a; 6:9-15) but makes them explicit. Zechariah 9:1-10 speaks not metaphorically of a signet ring (Hag 2:23) or a branch (cf. Zech 3:8; 6:12-13), but quite explicitly of a coming king (9:9-10). A prevalent image in these chapters is the shepherd, an image commonly used in the ancient Near East for the king (10:3-5; 11:4-17; 13:7-9; cf. the discussion of Nah 3:18). Further, as Paul Redditt observes, Zechariah 12:7, 8, 10, 12 and 13:1 all explicitly name the "house of David" (Redditt 2008b, 78).

That said, it is also plain that this messianic expectation is qualified and reassessed in the final form of Zechariah 9–14 (Redditt 2008b, 79). As Redditt also observes, "the author apparently had struggled to understand why the glorious future the prophets had predicted had not come to fruition and had concluded that the fault lay with the leadership in Jerusalem, not with God and not even primarily with the populace as a whole" (Redditt 2008b, 79). Although the perspective of Zechariah 9–14 in its final form is "not incompatible" with messianic hopes, "it does, however, manifest a level of disenchantment" (Redditt 2008b, 80). Yet that very ambiguity may have been part of the appeal of these chapters, making them a natural source for early Christians struggling to come to terms with the scandal of a crucified Messiah.

This second part of Zechariah is divided into two collections, 9–11 and 12–14, each called an oracle (Heb., *massa'*; 9:1; 12:1). Each oracle is in turn divided into three parts, coinciding generally with the chapter divisions (Nogalski 2011, 822): the first at 9:1-17; 10:1–11:3; and 11:4-17; the second at 12:1–13:1 (departing from Nogalski's divisions here; see the discussion in context below); 13:2-9; and 14:1-21. As this commentary observed regarding Nahum 1:1, in most places where *massa'* refers to a prophetic pronouncement, it designates a judgment oracle (cf. Achtemeier 1986, 7). In the apocalyptic framework of Zechariah 9–14, that judgment is pronounced on all reality (e.g., 9:1-8; 14:1-15; cf. Zeph 1:2-3, 18).

First Oracle (9–11)

"Lo, your king comes to you" (9:1-17). Zechariah 9:1 designates the first major section of Zechariah 9–14 as a *massa'*. It also opens the first part of that first oracle with an intriguing shift on the divine word formula. Usually, we would expect something like "The word of the LORD came to Zechariah" (cf. 7:1, 8). But here, the formula does not mention the recipient of the word, only its target (the nations and cities in 9:1-8). The MT divides this unit into two parts, the oracles against the nations of Syria-Palestine in 9:1-8 (breaking at the invitation to Zion to rejoice in 9:9; cf. 2:14 [10]) and 9:9–10:2 (at the shift from third person speech about God to first person speech from God:

"*My* anger is hot"). Although there is no clear indication of the end of the unit (such as "says the LORD" in 10:12), 10:1-2 is sharply negative in tone, contrasting with the oracle of salvation in 9:1-17. We do best, then, to treat Zechariah 9 as a unit in its final form. Paul Redditt proposes that 9:1-10, culminating in the triumphal entrance of Jerusalem's king, constitutes the first expansion to Haggai–Zechariah 1–8, likely from a time soon after this unit was combined with the Book of the Four (Redditt 2008b, 78).

Zechariah 9:1-8 reads like a collection of oracles against foreign nations (see the discussion of Zeph 2:4-15). The specific nations targeted, however, are all in Syria-Palestine. Their conquest clears the way for Israel to expand to its proper borders, according to ancient tradition (cf. Num 34:1-12; Josh 15:1-4; Ezek 47:13–48:35). The list begins in the north, with sites in Syria: Hadrach (mentioned in the Hebrew Bible only in Zech 9:1, but identified in ancient inscriptions as a Syrian district; cf. Negev 1986, 164; Meyers and Meyers 1993, 91–92); Syria's former capital, Damascus (9:1; cf. Amos 1:3); and Hamath, often cited as marking Israel's northernmost border (9:2; e.g., Num 34:8; Josh 13:5; 1 Kgs 8:65; 2 Kgs 14:25). The NRSV reading "to the LORD belongs the capital of Aram" (9:1) emends the Hebrew *'en* ("eye") to *'ir* ("city") and *'adam* ("human") to Aram (another name for Syria)—which makes good sense in context but has no textual support. The versions all assume, and struggle to make sense of, the MT *la Yhwh 'en 'adam* (mechanistically, "to the LORD the eye of humanity"[?]): for example, LXX has "the Lord watches over humans [*ephora anthropous*]," and *Tg. Neb.* has "the LORD reveals the deeds of humans [*gelan 'ubadebene 'anasha*]." The JPSV reads, "all men's eyes will turn to the LORD," interpreting this positively, perhaps with a view back to 8:20-23. David Petersen proposes, "Yahweh truly has a view of all humanity" (Petersen 1995, 39–40; cf. LXX and *Tg. Neb.*), which fits well in the context. God acts with an eye to all the nations but with decided preference for "all the tribes of Israel" (9:1).

From Syria, the text moves south and to the coast, addressing the Phoenician cities Tyre and Sidon (9:2b-4). The mention of Tyre is notable, since by the Persian period Tyre was no longer a city of extraordinary wealth, with "silver like dust, and gold like the dirt of the streets" (9:3). Carthage, the great north African port founded by Tyre in 814 BCE, and Tyre's sister city Sidon had taken Tyre's place as mercantile powers long before Tyre fell to Alexander the Great in 332 BCE. This passage deals less with the actual city of Tyre than with its literary depiction in Ezekiel 26:1–28:19 (which also emphasizes the association of Tyre with wisdom; cf. Ezek 28:2-4). Largely because of Ezekiel, "Tyre and Sidon" became a formulaic pair in Scripture, continuing to connote the Phoenician coast long after Tyre itself had faded from historical significance (e.g., Jer 47:4; Joel 3:4; 1 Macc 5:15; Matt 11:21-22; Mark 3:8; Luke 6:17; Acts 12:20). Indeed, with the sole exception of Judith 2:28, Tyre is always mentioned *first.* In Zechariah, Tyre's total destruction clears the way for Jerusalem's rejuvenation (cf. Ezek 26:2-6): "But now, the LORD will strip it of its possessions / and hurl its wealth into the sea, / and it shall be devoured by fire" (9:4).

Finally, the passage traces the coastline south to Philistia (9:5-7): the Philistine city states Ashkelon, Gaza, Ekron, and Ashdod (cf. Zeph 2:4-7; curiously, Gath is again absent) are displaced, so that "the pride of Philistia" (9:6) "shall be a remnant for our God; / it shall be like a clan in Judah, / and Ekron shall be like the Jebusites" (9:7). The Philistines are described (9:7) as defiled and polluted, eating blood and unclean food (Heb., *shiqquts*; NRSV "abominations"). But the LORD will take this corruption away, the prophet states. This could mean that the Philistines are conquered and their lands taken (as David had taken Jerusalem from the Jebusites, cf. 2 Sam 5:1-10//1 Chr 11:1-9; so O'Brien 2004, 234–36). But it may mean that they are converted and absorbed into the people Israel (so Hanson 1979, 319–20; Petersen 1995, 51–53). In any case, God establishes God's people in their own land, and declares that they will never again be driven from their place:

> I will encamp at my house as a guard,
> so that no one shall march to and fro;
> no oppressor shall again overrun them,
> for now I have seen with my own eyes (9:8).

Likely, the declaration "I have seen with my own eyes" is meant to parallel the statement regarding the LORD's eye on humanity in 9:1 (cf. the references to God's "eye[s]" in 2:12 [8]; 4:10; and perhaps 3:9). God watches over God's own.

The only reading from Zechariah in the Revised Common Lectionary is 9:9-12, which is the alternate Old Testament lection for Year A, Proper 9 (the Gospel for that day is Matt 11:16-19, 25-30). Curiously, this is not one of the readings appointed for Palm Sunday, although Matthew and John both quote Zechariah 9:9 in their accounts of Jesus' triumphal entry into Jerusalem (Matt 21:5 and John 12:15; cf. Mark 11:1-11 and Luke 19:28-40, which both use the word *polon*, "colt," found in the LXX of Zech 9:9):

> Rejoice greatly, O daughter Zion!
> Shout aloud, O daughter Jerusalem!
> Lo, your king comes to you;

triumphant and victorious is he,
humble and riding on a donkey,
on a colt, the foal of a donkey (9:9).

Applying to this passage a wooden literalism, Matthew describes Jesus entering Jerusalem mounted on both an ass and her colt (Matt 21:6-7)! This bizarre image was doubtless intended to ram the point home, making absolutely certain that the reader could not miss the connection. Similarly, Theodoret of Cyrus records, "This acquires a clear interpretation in actual events: the king who is prophesied has come" (Hill 2006, 256).

The NRSV translation "triumphant and victorious" (9:9) is difficult to understand (but cf. JPSV). The Hebrew reads *tsaddiq wenosha'*. The first term means "righteous," perhaps defending "the royal legitimacy of the king" (Meyers and Meyers 1993, 127), although it may also refer to his morality (*Tg. Neb.* has *zaqay*: "innocent"). The second is a passive participle meaning literally "one who is saved" (reflected also in the Aramaic of *Tg. Neb.*). The LXX renders this as *sozon*, an active participle ("saving"). Petersen, who translates these two words as "Righteous and victorious," says that the LXX reading "seems to be the required sense" (Petersen 1995, 55; cf. CEB). Carol and Eric Meyers, however, stay with the plain sense of the Hebrew: "Yahweh is victorious over the enemies, with the result that the king is 'saved,' thereby enabled to assume power" (Meyers and Meyers 1993, 127). In short, this is already a transformed notion of kingship, grounded not in dynastic and regal pomp but in God's own action (cf. Zech 4:6).

As this passage unfolds, it continues to draw distinctions between *this* king and other, previous kings. Although the humble mount in 9:9 derives from a long tradition of kingly processions involving the king riding an ass (Meyers and Meyers 1993, 129), this passage surely catches the point of that tradition: by riding an ass rather than a war horse or chariot, the king shows humility and declares that he comes in peace. Yet this time, the prophet declares, this is no pretense: this king truly *is* humble, and not only comes in peace but also comes to *bring* peace:

He will cut off the chariot from Ephraim
and the war horse from Jerusalem;
and the battle bow shall be cut off,
and he shall command peace to the nations;
his dominion shall be from sea to sea,
and from the River to the ends of the earth (9:10).

In the Persian period, the satrapy to which Yehud (or Judah) belonged was Abar-Nahara: that is, the lands "Beyond the River," across the Euphrates and west toward the Mediterranean Sea (cf. Tuell 1991). This verse seems to envision Jerusalem's sway extended throughout this region (Petersen 1995, 53), an idea also found in the Law of the Temple (cf. Ezek 47:13–48:35; so Tuell 1992, 170–74). Further, the mention of Ephraim (the largest of the northern tribes, often used to represent the entire northern kingdom of Israel, e.g., Isa 7:2; Jer 7:15; Ezek 37:19; Hos 5:3) shows that this renewed kingdom will include those formerly excluded, the "lost tribes" from the northern kingdom destroyed and dispersed by the Assyrians long before (cf. 9:13; 10:6-7; Ezek 37:15-28; contrast, however, Zech 11:14).

It is little wonder that this passage so captured the imagination of the Gospel writers. While the first Christians confessed Jesus as *christos*, the term used in the LXX for Hebrew *meshiakh* ("Messiah"), it is clear that their understanding (and Jesus' own understanding) of what being "Messiah" means transformed this image. Mark 1:1 identifies Jesus not only as *Christos*, or Messiah, but also as "the Son of God." While related to the idea of the king as God's adopted son (Pss 2; 45:6), this confession goes much further than any Jewish conception of Messiah: Jesus the Messiah *is* God! This confession creates new problems, raising the need for the church to affirm that "Christ has come in the flesh" (1 John 4:2; cf. John 1:14). But while on the one hand Christian confessions about Jesus exalt the role of Messiah far beyond traditional Jewish expectations, on the other hand these ideas subvert the idea of Messiah as king. In debate with the Pharisees, who believed in a literal future Messiah, Jesus asks, "'What do you think of the Messiah? Whose son is he?' They said to him, 'The son of David'" (Matt 22:42). In response, Jesus quotes Psalm 110:1: "The LORD says to my lord, / 'Sit at my right hand / until I make your enemies your footstool.'" Assuming the speaker to be David (in both MT and LXX, the title of this psalm identifies it as a psalm of David), Jesus asks, "If David thus calls him [that is, the Messiah] Lord, how can he be his son?" (Matt 22:45). Although Matthew's genealogy takes pains to demonstrate Jesus' descent from David (Matt 1:6, 17), Christ is more than David's son.

Particularly subversive of traditional Messianic expectation is the Christian view that the Christ must be understood in terms of suffering. Thus, in Mark, Peter's confession at Caesarea Philippi that Jesus is *Christos* is inadequate: faced with Jesus' determination to suffer and die, Peter rebukes him and is in turn himself rebuked by Jesus (Mark 8:29-33). Indeed, in Mark, the first human to make a *full* confession about Jesus is his executioner, who declares when Jesus dies, "Truly this man was God's son" (Mark 15:39). It may well be that Jesus understood his own role in terms of the Suffering Servant in Deutero-Isaiah (42:1-4; 49:1-6; 50:4-11; 52:13–53:12). Certainly, early Christians did (1 Cor 15:3; Acts 8:32-35; 1 Pet 2:22-25), and the idea must have come from *somewhere* (cf. Matt 8:17; 12:18-21; Mark 9:12; 10:45 [//Matt 20:28]; Luke 22:37). In any case, for early Christians, the image of the peaceful and humble king in Zechariah 9:9-10 was the perfect representation of Jesus.

In sharp contrast to this peaceful vision, but in continuity with older visions of divine kingship (cf. Nah 1:2-11; Hab 3:1-19; Zeph 1:2-18), 9:11-17 describes the LORD as a blood-soaked warrior. The exiles are gathered not so that God can guard them in peace (9:8; cf. 2:10-17 [6-13]) but so that God can muster them as an army. The expression "the blood of the covenant" appears only in Zechariah 9:11 and Exodus 24:8, where Moses sprinkles the people with the blood of their offering at Sinai, sealing their promise to obey God's *torah.* Here as there, God has delivered Israel from bondage and oppression, but will now lead them into times of trial and conflict. Far from banishing or breaking the bow from Judah and Ephraim (9:10), the LORD says,

> For I have bent Judah as my bow;
> I have made Ephraim its arrow.
> I will arouse your sons, O Zion,
> against your sons, O Greece,
> and wield you like a warrior's sword (9:13).

The mention of Greece as an enemy has sometimes suggested to the readers of Zechariah a very late date for this material, from the time of Alexander (331–323 BCE) or later still, from the Greek occupation and domination of Israel under Antiochus IV Epiphanes described in Daniel (175–163 BCE; cf. the discussion in Nogalski 1993b, 214). We need not go so late as that, however, to account for the conflict in this passage. More likely, this expansion dates to the emergence of Greece as a power in conflict with Persia: perhaps from near the time of the battles of Marathon (490 BCE) and Salamis (480 BCE), at which Persia fared badly (so Meyers and Meyers 1993; Petersen 1995, 3–5; Cook 2011).

The image of God as the divine warrior (cf. the discussions of Nah 1:2-11 and Hab 3:1-19) is particularly prominent in 9:14-17. In 9:14, the LORD wields the weapons of wind and storm, as in Israel's most ancient songs (cf. Exod 15:1-18 and Judg 5:1-31). The NRSV of 9:15 has, "they shall devour and tread down the slingers; they shall drink their blood like wine, and be full like a bowl, drenched like the corners of the altar," reading the Hebrew *khamu* ("they roar") as *damo* ("his blood"), with some Greek manuscripts. This reading calls to mind images elsewhere of wine as blood, and the winepress as judgment (e.g., Isa 49:26; 63:1-6; and Joel 4:13 [3:13]; cf. Petersen 1995, 54–55; O'Brien 2004, 238). It is not clear, however, that this reading is correct. *Targum Nebi'im* presents a broad paraphrase describing carousing over the spoils of victory, making it difficult to say precisely what Hebrew original it presumes, but the majority of Greek texts, as well as the Latin Vulgate, do not have "blood" in this verse. They read, much like *Tg. Neb.*, as though what is described is a raucous feast, not a bloodthirsty one (so Meyers and Meyers 1993, 154–55). If this is so, then this passage deals with the transformation of another image encountered earlier in the Twelve: the cup, and drunkenness, associated with military conquest. But while in Nahum 3:11 and Habakkuk 2:15-16 the cup is a metaphor for the shame of military defeat (cf. Isa 51:17-23; Jer 25:15-29; 49:12; 51:7; Ezek 23:32-34), Zechariah 9:15 seems to present this carousing positively—as a celebration of victory. This reading appears all the more likely given the celebration of fertile abundance in 9:17: "Grain shall make the young men flourish, / and new wine the young women."

Finally, for the first time in these chapters, an image that will recur again and again is raised—the notion of the king as shepherd:

> On that day the LORD their God will save them
> for they are the flock of his people;
> for like the jewels of a crown
> they shall shine on his land (9:16).

Here as elsewhere in the Twelve, "that day" is the day of the LORD, when the world is judged, God's people are delivered, and God's reign is at last fully realized (cf. Zeph 1:10). The expression "the flock of his people" (Heb., *tson 'ammo*) calls to mind an editorial note in the MT of Ezekiel 34:31, reflected also in the late expansion of the book at 36:38: *tson 'adam*, or "flock of people" (Tuell 2012, 258, 261). This connection will become important in subsequent chapters, which build on the metaphor of the shepherd in Ezekiel 34. This verse also, of course, calls to mind the sign-act of the crowns in Zechariah 6:9-15, applying that image to the kingdom that is to come.

The LORD as shepherd (10:1-11:3). In the MT, this unit is divided into two parts, 10:3-12 (breaking at the clear indication of the end of a divine speech; the expression *ne'um Yhwh* ["says the LORD"]; the scribes grouped the first two verses of the chapter with the previous unit) and 11:1-3 (a short poem continuing the theme of judgment in 10:1-12). While 10:1 continues the theme of agricultural abundance in 9:17, its point is quite distinct: rather than trusting the LORD, "who gives the showers of rain to you [Heb., 'them'], the vegetation of the field to everyone" (10:1), the people have placed their trust in false guides:

> For the teraphim utter nonsense,
> and the diviners see lies;
> the dreamers tell false dreams,
> and give empty consolation (10:2).

Elsewhere in Scripture, the *teraphim* are household gods (e.g., see Gen 31:19, 34-35; Judg 17:5; 18:14-20). Ezekiel 21:21 describes the Babylonian king Nebuchadrezzar using *teraphim* as a means of divination, much as we find in Zechariah 10:2. Babylonian texts describe rituals for "opening the mouth" of an idol so that it could serve as a means of communion with the god (Hurowitz 2003), but do not mention the use of images for divination. First Samuel 15:23, however, parallels "divination" with "idolatry" (Heb., *teraphim*), suggesting that these idols were used for fortunetelling in Israel, perhaps reflecting Canaanite practice. The Twelve describes this use of the *teraphim* not only in Zechariah 10:2 but also in Hosea 3:4.

Israel's trust in false spiritual guides is ascribed to lack of leadership: "the people wander like sheep; they suffer for lack of a shepherd" (10:2). Therefore, the LORD declares, "My anger is hot against the shepherds, / and I will punish the leaders; / for the LORD of hosts cares for his flock, the house of Judah" (10:3). This condemnation of Israel's current leaders features elsewhere in the final form of Zechariah 9–14 (cf. 11:4-17; 13:7-9; so Redditt 2008b, 79). Zechariah 10:2 may be the source for Matthew 9:36// Mark 6:34, which also speak of people like sheep wandering without a shepherd. It is more likely, however, that those Gospel texts, like 10:2, allude to Ezekiel 34:8, which is in turn derived from the oracle of Micaiah ben Imlah concerning the fate of Ahab and the armies of Israel: "I saw all Israel scattered on the mountains, like sheep that have no shepherd, and the LORD said, 'These have no master; let each one go home in peace'" (1 Kgs 22:17//2 Chr 18:16). Parallels to Ezekiel 34, which both condemns the false shepherds of Israel's past and affirms the LORD as Israel's true shepherd, will become particularly evident in Zechariah 11:4-17. Already in this one verse, however, we find not only the accusation that Israel's "shepherds" have left their people leaderless, and the affirmation that God will shepherd Judah, but also reference to God judging some of the flock as well as their shepherds. The NRSV "the leaders" (following *Tg. Neb.*, which reads *shiltonaya'*, "the rulers") is in Hebrew *ha'atudim* ("he-goats"); similarly, in Ezekiel 34:16, God judges the fat sheep—evidently, members of Jerusalem's noble and wealthy families—for their abuse of their fellows, as well as judging their shepherds. Christian readers may think of Matthew 25:31-46, where in Jesus' parable of the last judgment the Son of Man divides the people "as a shepherd separates the sheep from the goats" (Matt 25:32).

God's care for God's flock, however, involves not green pastures and still waters (Ps 23; Ezek 34:11-15) but training for battle: indeed, Petersen reads that God "musters" God's flock (Petersen 1995, 68–69)! A series of martial metaphors depict Judah as a "proud war-horse" (10:3; contrast 9:9-10), and as the source of tent-peg (10:4; possibly a reference to the battle camp, but cf. Judg 4:21-22; 5:26), battle bow (10:4; cf. 9:13-14, and contrast 9:10, where the same expression, *qeshet milkhamah*, is used), and "every commander" (10:4; note that the word *nogesh*, here evidently used positively for battle leaders, is in 9:8 used for Judah's oppressors). The expression "cornerstone" (Heb., *pinnah*) in 10:4 seems at first out of place, but this expression is used elsewhere for human leaders (so Petersen 1995, 68–69; cf. Judg 20:2; 1 Sam 14:38; Isa 19:13). That seems the point here as well: the "cornerstone" (or perhaps "strong tower") would be the future king, under the LORD's guidance (cf. *Tg. Neb.*, which reads "the king"). Led by their king and empowered by their God, Judah will be victorious over every enemy (10:5).

As in 9:13, Zechariah 10:6 affirms that the LORD will restore not only the exiles of Judah but those of Israel as well:

> I will strengthen the house of Judah,
> and I will save the house of Joseph. . . .
> Then the people of Ephraim shall become like warriors,
> and their hearts shall be glad as with wine (10:6-7).

God brings the exiles home from Egypt and Assyria (10:10)—with reference to the northern kingdom in particular, destroyed and dispersed by the Assyrians. The message here alludes to Hosea 9:1-4, reversing the judgment there described (so Nogalski 2011, 919). These northern exiles are restored to their former homes: to "Gilead and to Lebanon" (10:10; cf. Nogalski 2011, 920–21). The restoration of the northern tribes is described as a new exodus (cf. the discussion of Hag 2:5): "They shall pass through the sea of distress, / and the waves of the sea shall be struck down, / and all the depths of the Nile dried up" (10:11).

While 11:1-3 is set apart, both by the scribal paragraphing and by explicit markers within the text (10:12 concludes with *ne'um Yhwh*, "says the LORD," a typical conclusion to prophetic oracles, and 11:4 opens with the messenger formula), it belongs thematically and stylistically with the poetry of 10:1-12 rather than the prose of 11:4-17. Judgment is pronounced on Lebanon and Bashan, which are cleared to make room for restored Israel (11:1-2), and on their kings, the "shepherds" whose "glory is despoiled" (11:3). This brief subunit makes multiple allusions to prophetic texts. The comparison of judgment to a forest fire recalls Ezekiel 21:1-5 (20:45-49), although here the fire strikes the forests of Lebanon to the north, not the forests of the south. The fall of the cedar of Lebanon (11:2) recalls the parables in Ezekiel 17:1-21 and 22-24, where the cedar represents kingship, and particularly 31:1-18, where the "cedar of Lebanon" (31:3) is Assyria. The "roar of the lions" recalls the motto in Amos 1:2 (cf. Joel 4:16 [3:16]). Just as in the eighth century God had willed the devastation of the north, so now God wills its restoration.

Sign-act of the shepherd (11:4-17). This is a literary sign-act (see the discussion of 6:9-15) in which the prophet assumes the role of "a shepherd of a flock doomed to slaughter" (11:4). That we are in another world from the one presumed in 10:1–11:3 is apparent, not only in the shift from poetry to prose but also in the radically shifting tone. Rather than a triumphal vision of victory under God's appointed ruler, this sign-act condemns the corruption of the current leaders (cf. 10:1-3; 13:7-9; Redditt 2008b, 79) and declares doom not only on Judah but also on the entire earth. In the MT, this unit is divided into three unequal paragraphs, 11:4-14 (breaking at the messenger formula in 11:15), 15-16, and 17—letting the poetry of this last verse stand on its own, in contrast to the prose both preceding and following (12:1-14).

The LORD appoints the prophet as a shepherd, representing the true owners of the flock (the "sheep merchants;" cf. 11:7), and relating to the other shepherds who are, like him, hired hands—though with no sense of loyalty to or responsibility for their charges (cf. Ezek 34:1-10; John 10:12-13). It is because of the rapacity of these false shepherds, who enrich themselves at the flock's expense (11:5), that the flock is "doomed to slaughter" (11:4, 7). Indeed, God has permitted this circumstance to come to pass:

> For I will no longer have pity on the inhabitants of the earth, says the LORD. I will cause them, every one, to fall each into the hand of a neighbor, and each into the hand of the king; and they shall devastate the earth, and I will deliver no one from their hand (11:6).

The wholesale, cosmic judgment described here is reminiscent of Zephaniah 1:2-3, 18. The false shepherds, under the oversight of "the king" (perhaps an imperial figure from Persia or Greece; cf. Ezek 38:2-3, where Gog is described as "the chief prince" [Heb., *nasi' ro'sh*], leading other princes into battle), are permitted to devastate the entire earth.

Now, in a new aspect of the sign-act (11:7-14), the prophet brings forth two staves, with which presumably to shepherd the flock (cf. Ps 23:4), symbolically named Favor (*no'am*) and Unity (*khobelim*). At this point, the reader is bound to recall another sign-act in Ezekiel, the sign of the two sticks (37:15-17), where the sticks represent the northern and southern kingdoms, unified once more. Here, however, both Ezekiel's parable of the shepherds in Ezekiel 34 and the sign of the two sticks are deliberately subverted. Although the prophet at first appears to have come to rescue the flock from the wicked shepherds, and indeed deposes three of them (the "three" may have been known to the prophet's community but are unknown to us; Theodoret of Cyrus says that this represents Christ's deposition of Jewish prophets, priests, and kings; cf. Hill 2006, 263), he in the end permits the flock to perish: "So I said, 'I will not be your shepherd. What is to die, let it die; what is to be destroyed, let it be destroyed; and let those that are left devour the flesh of one another!'" (11:9).

As for the two staves, rather than (as in Ezekiel's sign) being brought together as one, they both are broken. The snapping of the staff Favor indicates the end of God's "covenant with all the peoples" (11:10). Perhaps this is a reference to the Noachic covenant with all of Noah's descendants (hence, all humanity), wherein God had promised to preserve the world in perpetuity (Gen 9:8-17). The breaking of the staff Favor in the sight of "the sheep merchants" (heavenly beings charged with the world's oversight?) declares that covenant null and void, so that the world can now indeed be laid waste. Next the prophet breaks the staff Unity, "annulling the family ties between Judah and Israel" (11:14)—directly subverting Ezekiel's sign-act as well as the hopeful messages about the lost northern tribes in Zechariah 8:13; 9:10, 13 and 10:6–11:3 (Redditt 2008b, 79).

Zechariah 11:12-13 is loosely cited in Matthew 27:9-10, where it is ascribed to Jeremiah. Prompted by this identification, as well as by the evident distinctions between Zechariah 1–8 and 9–14, some scholars proposed early on that this chapter was older than the preceding chapters, coming from Jeremiah's time if not from Jeremiah himself (see the discussion in Nogalski 1993b, 213–14). Marvin Sweeney also argues that this unit is older than the remainder of Zechariah 9–14: "the first person account of the prophet's symbolic action concerning the shepherds in Zech 11:4-17, may well be derived from Zechariah" (Sweeney 2000, 566). Given the dark, explicitly apocalyptic tone of this material, however, in sharp contrast to the hopeful message of Haggai–Zechariah 1–8 (and indeed of other portions of Zech 9–14), it seems best to date this material later than, not earlier than, its broader context.

Once more, we must pursue allusions to earlier Scripture to understand what is going on in this passage. Having given up on his charges in disgust, the prophet asks his employers for his wages, if they see fit to pay him. The pay he is given—thirty shekels of silver—is a studied insult (*contra* Sweeney 2000, 681). In the oldest law code in Scripture, the Covenant Code in Exodus 20:22–23:33, thirty shekels of silver is the price paid to the slave owner when a slave is gored to death by an ox (Exod 21:32). By giving the prophet this wage, the owners of the flock indicate their contempt for the prophet and his labor—they treat him essentially as a slave, not a hired hand. He repays their contempt with contempt. Refusing to accept "this lordly price at which I was valued by them" (the sarcasm fairly drips!), the prophet gets rid of it, throwing the money, at the LORD's direction, "into the treasury in the house of the LORD" (11:13). The NRSV of Zechariah 11:13 follows the Syriac, which assumes the Hebrew *'otser* ("treasury"; cf. JPSV); the MT actually reads *yotser* ("potter"). The words sound similar, making the confusion readily understandable—particularly in a passage that is already fairly obscure! Marvin Sweeney argues for the MT, seeing here a reference to Zechariah 12:1, where the term *yotser* is a divine epithet, and reading, "throw the money to 'the creator'" (Sweeney 2000, 681). *Targum Nebi'im* makes sense of the passage by entirely reconstructing it: misunderstanding the sarcasm, it assumes that the reference to a "lordly price" describes a high temple official, into whose office the prophet places a written account of the shepherds' misdeeds. The LXX understands that the prophet's action is a demonstration of contempt but assumes that the reference to the potter means that he threw the silver into a pottery kiln or furnace (hence the Greek *choneuterion*, or smelting furnace).

The purpose to which Matthew sets this passage, as well as his attribution of the text to Jeremiah, requires careful consideration. His tradition tells him that Judas had betrayed Jesus for money (Mark 14:10-11). Further, Matthew and Luke both have a tradition connecting the money Judas was given for this betrayal to a field called Hakeldama, or the Field of Blood—although they account for that connection, and that name, in very different ways (cf. Matt 27:3-10; Acts 1:18-20). Matthew first of all relates the amount the religious leaders pay Judas to Zechariah's thirty silver shekels (Matt 26:15). Then, he turns on the one hand to the Hebrew reading *yotser* ("potter") in

Zechariah 11:13 and on the other to the idea of purchasing a field. Both of these images find clear resonances with the book of Jeremiah, where the prophet both goes to a potter's house at the LORD's direction (Jer 18:1-3; cf. 19:1-13) and also buys a field (Jer 32:1-15)—placing the deed, for good measure, in a pottery jar (32:14)!

Weaving this all together, Matthew presents a narrative involving Judas's attempt to return the blood money, throwing the spurned coins into the temple (as in Zech 11:13), his subsequent suicide, and the priests' use of the money to purchase a potter's field, which is called (as it was purchased with blood money) Hakeldama (Matt 27:3-8). Then, for the fourteenth and final time in his Gospel, Matthew relates an event in Jesus' life to a Scripture reference:

> Then was fulfilled what had been spoken through the prophet Jeremiah, "And they took the thirty pieces of silver, the price of the one on whom a price had been set, on whom some of the people of Israel had set a price, and they gave them for the potter's field, as the Lord commanded me" (Matt 27:9-10).

As with Matthew's literal rendition of Zechariah 9:9, it is unlikely that this attribution is a simple mistake—particularly as the alleged "quotation" is actually not a quote at all, but a web of complex allusions. These two verses capture elements from Exodus 21:32, Zechariah 11:13, and Jeremiah 32. By ascribing the whole to Jeremiah, Matthew calls to mind the allusions to the potter's house in Jeremiah 18 and also accomplishes another implicit purpose. In Matthew's account of Peter's confession at Caesarea Philippi, Jesus is said to be not simply "one of the prophets" (cf. Mark 9:28) but specifically the prophet Jeremiah (Matt 16:14). Quite likely, in this suffering, sorrowful prophet, Matthew found a precursor of the Christ.

In the final form of Zechariah, 11:15-16 is in sequence with the remainder of the chapter, presenting yet another step in this complex literary sign-act. Once more, the prophet takes up his rod and staff, "the implements of a worthless shepherd" (11:15). But now, the focus is on a *single* worthless shepherd, not many. Once more the LORD raises up the wicked shepherd, but this time, rather than permitting his abuses, God condemns them. The poetic oracle in 11:17 declares the consequences of this shepherd's wanton cruelty:

> Oh, my worthless shepherd,
> who deserts the flock!
> May the sword strike his arm

and his right eye!
Let his arm be completely withered,
his right eye utterly blinded!

Intriguingly, Theodoret of Cyrus is aware of a tradition identifying the "worthless shepherd" as Antiochus IV Epiphanes. Although he prefers to see 11:17 as a prediction of the "Lawless One" in 2 Thessalonians 2:8-9, Theodoret acknowledges that, "since the one is a type of the other," either interpretation is fitting (Hill 2006, 266). Actually, the identification of the "worthless shepherd" is less important than the evident shift in these verses from the casual violence and utter pessimism of the sign-act back to the hopeful tone of the earlier material. Quite likely, the editors have added this section in an attempt to reconcile 11:4-14 with the preceding material.

Second Oracle (12–14)

Jerusalem, Judah, and the house of David (12:1–13:1). As in 9:1, this second major section of Zechariah 9–14 is given the title *massa'* ("oracle"), and opens with "The word of the Lord." But this time, rather than a target against which the word is directed, the text describes the subject of this word: *'al-Yisra'el*, "concerning Israel." This is odd, as in the following oracle, the focus is on Judah and Jerusalem, not on Israel. Likely, as Rex Mason observes, the editors of Zechariah are using the term as the Chronicler often does, to refer to Judah and Benjamin (Mason 2003, 133; cf. Tuell 2001, 155–59). This second oracle, as we have seen, can be understood as falling into three parts, mostly corresponding with the chapter divisions (12:1–13:1; 13:2-9; 14:1-21). An overarching structure is also evident, however, tying the whole collection together, based on the recurring expression *bayyom hahu'*: "On that day" (cf. 12:3, 4, 6, 8, 9, 11; 13:1, 2, 4; 14:4, 6, 8, 9, 13, 20, 21). As "that day" is evidently the day of the Lord (cf. 9:16; Meyers and Meyers 1993, 316–17), the concentration of this expression in these three chapters (elsewhere in Zechariah, it occurs at 2:15 [11]; 3:10; 6:10; 9:16; and 11:11) is another indication of the eschatological (that is, relating to the end times), and indeed increasingly apocalyptic, tone and tenor of this material.

The scribes divide Zechariah 12 into three parts: the heading in 12:1, 2-6 (a first-person speech from the Lord), and 7-14 (closing before "On that day . . ." in 13:1). A case can be made, however, for adding 13:1 to this unit. The expressions "house of David" and "inhabitants of Jerusalem" appear together in the Hebrew Bible only in 12:7-8, 10 and 13:1. Likely, then, 13:1 belongs with the preceding unit, rather than the following, which deals with the prophets rather than the nobility. The overarching subjects are the city of Jerusalem, the clans of Judah, and the royal house of David. In 12:2-9, the theme is God's reestablishment and defense of Jerusalem, particularly of David's house and tribe (cf. Zech 12:7-9; Redditt 2008b, 78). But in 12:10-14 there is a curious change of theme, as the tone shifts from exaltation to mourning. Rather than, as in 12:2-9, granting Jerusalem and its leaders strength to prevail over their enemies (12:5), God gives them "a spirit of compassion and supplication . . . so that, when they look on the one whom they have pierced, they shall mourn for him" (12:10). This somber mood extends into the following chapter, which, like the sign-act of the shepherds (11:4-17), pronounces judgment on shepherd and sheep alike. This unit, however, ends with the cleansing of "the house of David and the inhabitants of Jerusalem" (13:1), completing the process begun by the pouring out of God's spirit in 12:10.

The heading in Zechariah 12:1 exalts God as creator, using language drawn from Deutero-Isaiah and from Genesis. While the phrase *noteh shamayim* ("who stretched out the heavens") in many places expresses God's glory both as creator (Jer 12:10//51:15; Ps 104:2; Job 9:8) and as divine warrior (2 Sam 22:10//Ps 18:10; Ps 144:5), the accompanying expression *weyosek 'erets* ("and [who] founded the earth") occurs elsewhere only in Isaiah 51:13. In Scripture, the combination of these two epithets (God as creator of heaven and of earth) with the creation of humanity is found only in Zechariah 9–14 and Deutero-Isaiah (42:5; 44:24; 45:12; 51:13). Christine Mitchell observes, however, a similar expression in Persian royal inscriptions, from the time of Darius I (by whose reign Haggai and Zechariah date their oracles) to Artaxerxes III (425–338 BCE):

> A great god is Ahuramazda,
> Who established this earth,
> Who established that sky,
> Who established humanity. (trans. Mitchell [2014, 305])

The order is not the same, as the Old Persian inscriptions typically begin with earth, not heaven; Mitchell proposes, however, that this shift emphasizes the distinction between Ahuramazda and the LORD (Mitchell 2014, 308 n. 7). Further, while the Persian formula goes on to emphasize the establishment of order and peace through kingship, in Zechariah 12 the following material depicts chaos and dissolution—the abolition of the Persian order and the establishment of the LORD's kingdom (Mitchell 2014, 307–308). This study will have more to say concerning the influence of Deutero-Isaiah on the likewise anonymous writers we encounter in Zechariah 9–14. For now, however, 12:1 recalls the anonymous prophet of the exile's confidence that the creator God would deliver the exiles from Babylon. The LORD had in fact defeated that enemy, but the exiles had not all returned, and Jerusalem's full glory had not yet been restored (cf. Zech 1:12-17). The following verses predict that full victory.

Before turning to those verses, however, one should note that Zechariah 12:1 also alludes to the creation of humanity in Genesis 2:4b-7, which likewise combines God's creation of earth and sky with God's creation of humanity. There as here, the word used for the LORD's creative activity is the verb *yatsar* ("form")—a word elsewhere used for what potters do. In Genesis 2:7, the LORD God forms the human "from the dust of the ground" ("dust" is not the best translation; actually, the LORD uses the moistened topsoil [cf. Gen 2:4b-6]), making the image of God as potter particularly apt. But Zechariah 12:1 says that the LORD "formed the human spirit within" (Heb., *ruakh-'adam beqirbo*; cf. O'Brien 2004, 258). This translation could lend itself to a dualistic interpretation of the spirit placed within and animating the body (so Ambrose, *On the Holy Spirit* 2.4.56; Augustine, *On Genesis Against the Manicheans*, 2.8.11; cited in Ferreiro 2003, 271–72), but the Hebrew does not presume this notion. The JPSV better renders this phrase, "created man's breath [the basic meaning of *ruakh*] within him." Just so, in Genesis 2:7, the LORD "breathed into his nostrils the breath [Heb., *neshamah*, not *ruakh*] of life." The point, in each context, is that the cosmic God of earth and sky is also the personal God who gives life to humanity.

Zechariah 12:2-6 is the divine speech introduced by 12:1. Although the NRSV translates "Thus says the LORD," this is not the messenger formula *koh 'amar Yhwh* (cf. the discussion of that formula in Nah 1:12, and in "Haggai and Zechariah 1–8"), but the oracular formula *ne'um Yhwh*, commonly used to conclude a prophetic pronouncement. Here, however, it announces a divine address. Although the enemy Babylon had been defeated long before (cf. Zech 2:6-13), new enemies had arisen in its place (Redditt 2008b, 79). But whoever those enemies might be, their defeat is sure.

Much as in 10:3-5, a series of metaphors describes Jerusalem's victory. First, the LORD declares, "I am about to make Jerusalem a cup of reeling" (12:2). Drunkenness is used elsewhere for the shame of military defeat (cf. the discussion of Nah 3:11), especially in Habakkuk 2:16, where this same verb, *ra'al* ("reel, stagger"), occurs. In Zechariah 12:2, Jerusalem is the cup, and the shame is visited on those who attempt to take it. Among those involved in this siege, curiously, are people from Judah (so MT, *Tg. Neb.*, and the Vulgate; cf. Hanson 1979, 361–62; Towner 2006, 1280). The LXX understands Judah to be besieged as well (so JPSV, Meyers and Meyers 1993,

307, 316; Petersen 1995, 107; Nogalski 2011, 946), which does fit better with the remainder of the divine speech (cf. 12:7). As we will see, however, this picture of a community at odds with itself is consistent with 12:10–13:1, where at least some in Judah have cause to mourn "the one whom they have pierced" (12:10). As this study has already shown, Zechariah 9–14 is not a unified text: in the final form of this book, earlier, optimistic passages are juxtaposed with later, pessimistic ones, culminating in the radical pessimism of apocalypse, wherein resolution can only be found beyond history, in the future God alone can inaugurate.

The next metaphor, in 12:3, describes Jerusalem as "a heavy stone for all the peoples; all who lift it shall grievously hurt themselves." This recalls the "cornerstone" in 10:4, although here it is Jerusalem itself, and not its king, that is so described. The prophet uses the stone as a threat, rather than an image of solidity and security, much as in Isaiah 8:14, where the LORD becomes "a stone one strikes against; for both houses of Israel he will become a rock one stumbles over—a trap and a snare for the inhabitants of Jerusalem" (cf. 1 Pet 2:8). Of course, in Zechariah *Jerusalem* is the stone, and the threat is directed not inward but outward. This transformation of Jerusalem is accomplished "[o]n that day," when "all the nations of the earth shall come together against it"—an image reminiscent of Ezekiel's Gog oracles (Ezek 38–39; cf. Zech 11:6). The final battle between the nations of the earth and the people of God becomes a major feature of the biblical apocalypses (cf. Dan 12:1; Rev 20:7-10). Jerusalem is a trap for the unwary, hostile nations—a cup that incapacitates all who try to drink it, and a stone that crushes all who attempt to lift it.

The next two verses abandon metaphor for a straightforward image of military assault, although with a tinge of the miraculous. God, who keeps a "watchful eye" on Judah (12:4; cf. 2:12 [8]; 3:9; 4:10), will blind and panic the horses of the enemy (12:4; cf. 10:3) and madden their riders (12:4; cf. Deut 28:28). The result will be that Judah's clans will recognize "The inhabitants of Jerusalem have strength through the LORD of hosts, their God" (12:5; cf. 4:6).

The divine speech concludes, however, with an astonishing metaphor: "On that day I will make the clans of Judah like a blazing pot on a pile of wood, like a flaming torch among sheaves" (12:6). The image certainly derives from the parable of the cooking pot in Ezekiel 24:1-14 (cf. Ezek 11:3; Jer 1:13-17). But while in Ezekiel the red-hot pot left too long on the fire is an image of Jerusalem's ineradicable corruption and inevitable doom (cf. Tuell 2012, 160–62; 165–66), in Zechariah the blazing pot of Judah becomes a torch, setting a fire of destruction among its enemies all around.

Much as in 2:5-9 (1-5) and 11:7-14, Zechariah subverts an image used by Ezekiel and turns it to a different, indeed an opposite, end (a literary feat at which Ezekiel was himself adept; e.g., 11:3; 15:1-8; 19:1-9). Meanwhile, in the city, all is secure: "Jerusalem shall again be inhabited in its place, in Jerusalem" (12:6). While the LXX has only one mention of "Jerusalem" here, it seems likely that this repetition is original, and not a scribal error—driving home the solidity and stability of the city as, once more, thriving and fully occupied.

The positive emphasis on Jerusalem, and on Judah in particular, continues in the following verses: indeed, "the LORD will give victory to the tents of Judah first [!], that the glory of the house of David and the glory of the inhabitants of Jerusalem may not be exalted over that of Judah" (12:7; contrast 12:2). Added to this now, however, is explicit reference to the royal house of David. In 12:8, David is used as a metaphor: due to God's protective shield around Jerusalem (cf. 2:5), "the feeblest among them on that day shall be like David." This democratizing metaphor, using David as an image for the people, is found in Deutero-Isaiah, in the one reference that exilic prophet made to David (Isa 55:3-5). But then, Zechariah 12:8 goes on to avow, "the house of David shall be like God, like the angel of the LORD at their head" (12:8; for the angel of the LORD, cf. 1:11-12). God's own power and authority guarantees this superhuman invincibility (cf. 12:5); returning to divine speech, 12:9 affirms, "And on that day I will seek to destroy all the nations that come against Jerusalem."

From this height of power and victory, the tone shifts sharply in 12:10–13:1, from congratulation of Jerusalem and the house of David to criticism, from exaltation to penitence. The way to this shift has been prepared, in a sense, by the very imagery selected by the writers of 12:2-9. Recall that in each case, these images (the cup, the stone, the burning pot), while turned to positive ends in this chapter, are used elsewhere as images of destruction and judgment. Thus, 12:10 uses a positive image in a negative sense—or at least in a mournful, penitential one. God pours out God's spirit, much as in Joel 3:1-2 (2:28-29). But rather than a spirit of prophecy poured out on all people—and in clear contrast to the strength of God for victory poured out on Jerusalem, Judah, and the house of David in 12:5, 8—God pours out "a spirit of compassion and supplication on the house of David and the inhabitants of Jerusalem" (12:10). This spirit sufficiently softens their hearts so that "when they look on the one whom they have pierced, they shall mourn for him, as one mourns for an only child, and weep bitterly over him, as one weeps over a firstborn."

The MT actually reads *'elay 'eth 'asher-daqaru* ("to *me* whom they have pierced"), which the LXX *epiblepsontai pros me anth' on katorchesanto* ("they shall look *to me* because they mocked"[?]; the Greek texts of Aquila, Symmachus, and Theodotion all read *exekentesan*, "pierced") and the Vulgate also assume; hence the KJV "they shall look upon me whom they have pierced." JPSV reads "they shall lament to me about those who are slain" (cf. Meyers and Meyers 1993, 336–37)—a possible, if awkward, reading. The third person forms used later in the verse ("mourn for *him* . . . weep over *him*") suggest that *'elay* should read *'elaw* ("to him")—a common scribal error (cf. Hanson 1979, 356–57; Petersen 1995, 106; 108). John 19:37, which quotes Zechariah 12:10 with reference to Jesus' side pierced by a spear, renders the text as *hopsontai eis hon exekentesan*, "they shall look on *the one* whom they have pierced," which seems to be the form of the saying usually cited by early Christian writers (cf. Ferreiro 2003, 271–73; but cf. Theodoret of Cyrus [Hill 2006, 269], who read, "They will look on me, on the one they have pierced").

If we emend the text with the NRSV to read, "on the *one* whom they have pierced," the next question becomes, who might this be? Paul Hanson, who understands Zechariah 9–14 to describe a conflict between the religious and secular leaders of Jerusalem and a sectarian group he identifies with "the clans of Judah" (Hanson 1979, 363–65), proposes that the "pierced one" represents the oppressed out-group, which understood itself in terms of Deutero-Isaiah's Suffering Servant (Hanson 1979, 365–66; cf. LaCocque 1998, 402). The connection with Isaiah 53 in particular is alleged, in large measure, because both figures are said to be pierced: the Servant in 53:5 ("he was wounded [Heb., *mekholal*, "pierced"] for our transgressions"), the unnamed "pierced one" (Heb., *'asher-daqaru*, "whom they have pierced") in Zechariah 12:10. As Rex Mason observes, however, the suffering of the "pierced one" is not vicarious in Zechariah 12:10, at least not in the way that we see in Isaiah 53. Instead,

> the weeping over the "one they have pierced" (whoever that may be) is the result and consequence of that regeneration by Yahweh. It is not its cause. . . . It is not by contemplating his sufferings that they are to be saved. They contemplate his sufferings with grief because they have been saved. (Mason 2003, 164)

If the MT is correct, as seems likely from the textual evidence, the identity of the pierced one is plain: after all, it is the LORD who says, "when they look on me whom they have pierced." Incredible as it seems, this passage refers to an assault upon God by Jerusalem's leaders (so LaCocque 1998, 410–12)—perhaps through massive disrespect or disregard, or perhaps by oppressing "his true spokesmen keeping alight the flame of genuine faith" (Mason 2003, 164). There is precedent for this in Zechariah 6:8, where those who assault Judah are regarded as though they had assaulted God. We might also look to other instances from postexilic literature condemning the leadership, particularly the priesthood, of Jerusalem for horrific offenses against God (e.g., Isa 65:1-7; Mal 1:6–2:3). No wonder the people of Jerusalem and their leaders are called to mourn!

From early on, Christian readers found in Zechariah 12:10 a foreshadowing of Jesus' suffering and death. In addition to John 19:37, which quotes this passage with reference to Jesus' side pierced by a Roman spear, Revelation 1:7 describes the exalted, returning Christ as seen by everyone on earth:

> Look! He is coming with the clouds;
> And every eye will see him,
> even those who pierced him,
> and on his account all the tribes of the earth will wail.

This follows the reading of the LXX of Zechariah 12:12, *kai kopsetai he ge kata phulas* ("the earth shall mourn by tribe"). The early Christian apologist Justin Martyr read Zechariah 12:10 instead as referring specifically to the Jews, who looking on "him whom they have pierced . . . shall say, 'Why, O Lord, have you made us to err from your way? The glory which our fathers blessed has for us been turned into shame" (*First Apology* 52, cited by Ferreiro 2003, 271). Indeed, Hippolytus describes those who crucified Jesus, whom he identifies as "the people of the Hebrews," wailing when they see "him whom they have pierced," and repenting—but too late, as they have already been consigned to hell (*On the End of the World* 40, cited by Ferreiro 2003, 273). No contemporary Christian can read such passages without shame. But while repudiating the anti-Semitism of these writers, we can still learn from them. By identifying the "pierced one" with Jesus, whom they certainly regarded as divine, these early Christian exegetes recognized that God is the offended party in this verse. Jerusalem and its leaders have in some way affronted, or even assaulted, God. In Zechariah 12:10 and following, however, God's response is not to seek vengeance but to pour out God's spirit, and so to bring them to sorrow, remorse, repentance—and, ultimately, cleansing (13:1).

The reference in 12:10 to mourning "as one mourns for an only child" (Heb., *hayyakhid*) recalls other texts depicting an extremity of grief (Jer 6:26;

Amos 8:10), just as the reference to the firstborn (*habbekor*) recalls the grim story of the tenth plague in Exodus 12:29-32, and the "loud cry in Egypt" when the deaths of the firstborn were discovered. Genesis 22, where Abraham is commanded to give up "your son, your only son [*yekhideka*] Isaac, whom you love" (Gen 22:2; cf. also Judg 11:34), may also be in the background, particularly if, as the Chronicler records, Moriah is identified with Zion (2 Chr 3:1; cf. Gen 22:2). God is not to be trifled with.

In 12:11, Jerusalem's mourning is said to be "as great as the mourning for Hadad-rimmon in the plain of Megiddo." This may refer to rituals of mourning for a fertility god, whose "death" was mourned every winter and whose "rebirth" would be celebrated every spring (Hanson 1979, 366; LaCocque 1998, 413; Greenfield 1999, 380–81). Ezekiel 8:14 mentions women at the north gate of the temple "sitting there weeping for Tammuz," and the epic of Gilgamesh mentions a season of mourning decreed for this Babylonian fertility god (Speiser 1969, 84). Perhaps Zechariah 12:11 refers to a similar rite, performed for the Canaanite deity Baal-Hadad (called "Rimmon" in Syria; cf. 2 Kgs 5:18). We have no evidence, however, either for such a ritual or for the combination of divine names in the form "Hadad-Rimmon" (cf. Nogalski 2011, 951–52). *Targum Nebi'im* suggests another possibility; it reads that the mourning in Jerusalem on that day will be "like the mourning for Ahab son of Omri . . . and like the mourning for Josiah son of Amon." King Ahab fell at Ramoth-gilead, not at Megiddo (cf. 1 Kgs 22:29-40), but the writer of *Tg. Neb.* here conjectures that his killer was an Aramean named "Hadad son of Tabrimmon." Josiah, however, *did* die on the plains of Megiddo, in a battle against the armies of Pharaoh Neco (cf. 2 Kgs 23:28-30). Perhaps Hadad-Rimmon is the name of the place where Josiah died. According to the Chronicler, "All Judah and Jerusalem mourned for Josiah. . . . and all the singing men and singing women have spoken of Josiah in their laments to this day. They made these a custom in Israel" (2 Chr 35:24-25). Since a custom relating to mourning for Josiah is attested, it is perhaps more likely that this is the reference in Zechariah 12:11 (Towner 2006, 1281). But whether the passage describes a Canaanite custom of mourning for a god, or a Judean custom of mourning for a king, the point is the *intensity* of their grieving, which will be matched on that day by the grieving of Jerusalem.

Although the whole land is called to join in mourning (12:12, 14), the divisions of the mourners involve the political and religious leadership of Israel in particular (Redditt 2008b, 79). Four groups are mentioned, representing the nobility ("the family of the house of David," 12:12), the prophets ("the family of the house of Nathan," 12:12; for Nathan's role as David's prophet, cf. 2 Sam 7:1-17//1 Chr 17:1-15), the priests ("the house of Levi," 12:13; cf. Mal 2:4-9), and the Levites ("the family of the Shimeites," 12:13; cf. 1 Chr 6:2, 27; 23:7, 10). As such, the social order envisioned resembles the one presupposed by the Chronicler more than the twofold leadership envisioned in Zechariah 6:9-15.

In a sense, these verses reflect John Wesley's description of the threefold action of God's grace (Outler 1964, 365–66). First, God's prevenient grace leads us to faith and repentance. Jerusalem mourns its sin because the LORD first pours out "a spirit of compassion and supplication on the house of David and the inhabitants of Jerusalem" (12:10), enabling that response. Then, God's justifying grace brings us to repentance and the forgiveness of sins: the intense grief depicted in 12:10-14. Finally, Zechariah 13:1 depicts God's sanctifying grace. On behalf of the nobility and people of Jerusalem, God will open a fountain "to cleanse them from sin and impurity." In all of this, God is the primary actor; the people act in response to what God is doing or has already done.

Just as the spirit was poured out specifically on "the house of David and the inhabitants of Jerusalem" in 12:10, so it is for these groups specifically that God opens a fountain for cleansing (13:1). Intriguingly, although the prophets and priests (the "house of Nathan" [12:12] and the "house of Levi" [12:13]) join in mourning, nothing is said of their cleansing. The following unit (13:2-6), indeed, decrees further judgment on these very groups.

"Strike the shepherd, that the sheep may be scattered" (13:2-9). The scribes divide this chapter into two parts, 13:1-6 and 7-9. The prose in 13:1-6 presents three "on that day" statements (13:1, 2, 4; cf. 12:3). The first, concerning the house of David and the people of Jerusalem (13:1), is best read in connection with the previous unit. The second, 13:2-3, concerns the religious leadership, particularly the prophets, while the third, 13:4-6, condemns the prophets alone (cf. 12:12; Redditt 2008b, 79). Zechariah 13:7-9 is poetry, not prose, and returns to the apocalyptic imagery of widespread destruction ("the whole land," 13:8) in 11:4-14. Both 13:2-6 and 7-9 are divine speeches ("says the LORD of hosts," 13:2, 7; cf. 12:1), further supporting the decision in this study to deal with 13:2-9 as a broad unit, presented (following the MT) in two parts.

Zechariah 13:2 declares that the LORD of hosts "will cut off the names of the idols from the land, so that they shall be remembered no more." While reminiscent of Ezekiel's polemic against idolatry (e.g., 11:18; 20:32, 39), this approach is even more radical—not only the idols themselves but even their very names and memory will be abolished, an act that only God can accomplish. Nothing is said of the priestly leadership of Jerusalem, although they certainly would have been viewed as complicit in this idolatry (cf. Ezek 8:16-18; Isa 65:1-7). The prophets, however, are condemned specifically and forcefully: "I will remove from the land the prophets and the unclean spirit" (13:2). The expression *ruakh hattuma'ah* ("unclean spirit"; Greek *to pneuma to akatharton*) is found nowhere else in the Old Testament, and the noun *tuma'ah* ("ritually unclean") appears in the prophets only in Ezekiel (22:15; 24:11, 13; 26:17, 25, 29; 39:24) and in this verse of Zechariah. In the New Testament, Mark (1:26-27; 3:11; 5:8, 13; 6:7; 9:25) and Luke (8:29; 9:42) use the LXX formulation "unclean spirit" to refer to demons. It is more likely, however, that Zechariah 13:2 has in mind the story of Micaiah ben Imlah, where a spirit is sent from the LORD to act as "a lying spirit in the mouth of [Ahab's] prophets" (1 Kgs 22:19-23; cf. Meyers and Meyers 1993, 372–73). Implicitly, this text declares, the prophets of Jerusalem have been speaking the word of such a lying spirit—but no longer. The prophet and the "unclean spirit" alike will be barred on that day.

The following verses continue this intense rejection of prophecy. Should any ever again dare to speak as prophets, their own father and mother shall condemn them: "You shall not live, for you speak lies in the name of the LORD" (13:3; cf. Ezek 13, where male [13:8] and female [13:19] prophets alike are condemned for lying in God's name). Indeed, the prophets' own parents "shall pierce them through [Heb., *deqaruhu*; cf. 12:10] when they prophesy" (Zech 13:3). "On that day," these writers declare, "the prophets shall be ashamed, every one, of their visions [!]" (12:4; cf. Zech 1–8, in which vision reports are primary). Even characteristic prophetic dress (the "hairy mantle" [13:4] of the Elijah/Elisha cycle; cf. 1 Kgs 19:13, 19; 2 Kgs 2:8, 13-14) will be eschewed, as the erstwhile prophets declare themselves to be simple farmers, saying "I am no prophet" (13:5)—an astonishing twist on Amos's well-known declaration (Amos 6:14).

The extent and vehemence of this rejection of prophecy is certainly surprising, particularly in a prophetic book! Indeed, the LXX translators, uncomfortable with this condemnation of all prophets and prophecy, render the Hebrew *nebi'im* ("prophets") in Zechariah 13:2 as *pseudoprophetas*, or "*false* prophets." The Greek translators use this term multiple times in the LXX of Jeremiah, where MT has simply "prophet" (6:13; 33:7, 8, 11, 16 [26:7, 8, 11, 16]; 34:9 [27:9]; 35:1 [28:1]; 36:1, 8 [29:1, 8]); elsewhere, Josephus (*Ant* 8.7.1; 10.7.3) and Philo (*Spec* 3.8) also use *pseudoprophetes*, although both of them could have adopted this term from the LXX. In the New Testament, the emergence of false prophets is a sign of last days (e.g., Matt 24:24//Mk 13:22; 1 John 4:1; Rev 16:13; 19:29; 20:10), an idea likely dependent on the LXX of Zechariah 13:2. But the Hebrew text of Zechariah 13 has no such qualifier: not *false* prophecy, but *all* prophecy, is condemned.

A likely reason for this wholesale condemnation of prophecy may be revealed by 13:3, where the erstwhile prophets' own parents "pierce them [the MT reads "pierce him," *deqaruhu*] through." Indeed, stab wounds become "on that day" a marker of those who had formerly been called prophets—although they try to explain these scars away as accidental wounds "received in the house of my friends" (13:6). This same term (*daqar*) was used in 12:10 for the one "whom they have pierced" (*'asher-daqaru*). Perhaps, as Paul Hanson (1979, 365–66) and Rex Mason (2003, 164) propose, the offense described in 12:10 involved the persecution of the group responsible for 13:2-6, where the same treatment is visited on their erstwhile persecutors.

One way of thinking through this conflict comes from the work of Hanson (1979) and S. Dean McBride, Jr. (2000, 35; 2009), who argue that postexilic society was sharply divided between the people who had remained in the land during the fifty-odd years of the Babylonian exile and the returning descendants of the exiled nobility. The religious leaders of the people of the land were the Levites, left behind (as Jeremiah was) when the Zadokite priests of the Jerusalem temple (such as Ezekiel) were taken away into exile. Zadokite priests, such as Joshua, led the returning exiles (cf. Hag 1:1, 12, 14; 2:2, 4; Zech 3:1-10; 6:9-15).

While the Levites turned to Deutero-Isaiah for inspiration, basing their own program for the restoration of Judah on his vision (cf. Isa 60–62; so Hanson 1975, 44–45; McBride 2000, 35; cf. Steck 1989, 368), the Zadokite program was woven into the temple vision of Ezekiel 40–48 (Hanson 1975, 71; Tuell 1992, 13–14; 175–78; 2012). The Zadokite and Levite parties had a great deal in common, then: both groups were priestly parties interested in the temple, both appealed to prophetic witnesses, and both made recourse to visions and visionaries. The more exclusive Zadokite program (contrast Ezek 44:1-14 and Isa 56:1-8) of the returnees had the support of the Persian state, however, so at least in the short term its victory was assured (cf. Tuell 2005).

The rejected Levites, whose anonymous voices we hear in Trito-Isaiah, in Malachi, and in some of the material collected in Zechariah 9–14, became the loyal opposition. Their opponents in the religious hierarchy established by the returning *golah* Jews would have included particularly the prophetic group represented by Haggai–Zechariah 1–8 and Ezekiel 40–48. The invective in Zechariah 13:2-6 is likely directed against these official prophets—the central intermediaries of the postexilic period, to use Robert Wilson's terms (Wilson 1980, 83–84; cf. "Habakkuk and Nahum," above).

The poem in 13:7-9 turns from the prophets back to the king. Rather than promising victory (12:1-9) or offering forgiveness (12:10–13:1), however, this poem declares that the king, and his city, will fall. The poem opens with a summons to the sword: "'Awake, O sword, against my shepherd, / against the man who is my associate,' says the LORD of hosts" (13:7). This opening recalls Ezekiel's song of the sword (21:13-22 [8-17]), where the sword personified represents warfare and devastation coming against Jerusalem. Here the sword is directed "against my shepherd"—clearly, the Davidic king (so *Tg. Neb.*). But while before this in Zechariah 9–14 "shepherd" has been a negative image for earthly kings (cf. 10:3-5; 11:4-17), here the LORD of hosts calls him not only "*my* shepherd" but also *'amithi*: "my associate" in the NRSV. Elsewhere, *'amith* occurs only in Leviticus, where this term refers to a fellow Israelite (e.g., Lev 5:21; 10:17; hence the LXX *polite*, "citizen"); the NRSV often renders it as "neighbor" (note that *Tg. Neb.* has "his [that is, the king's] companion"). In short, the coming destruction is not described as a judgment on the shepherd (*contra* Redditt 2008b, 79) but as a test (cf. 13:9). Similarly, in Ezekiel 38–39, the advance of Gog is not a punishment but a demonstration of divine power (cf. 38:16; 39:7-8; see also Rev 20:7-10). The emergence of trouble just when all seems to be going well is a common human experience, and a warning against complacency. What Jim Durlesser writes concerning Ezekiel 38–39 could also be said concerning Zechariah 13:7-9: "The message . . . is that sin, oppression, and the brutality of war are not vanquished without significant effort, and that we ought not become lax or over-confident" (Durlesser 1995, 34).

The difficult times to come are described again using the "sheep without a shepherd" image (cf. Zech 10:2). But this time, the sheep are not bereft because their shepherd is irresponsible or cruel, but because God has ordered him removed: "Strike the shepherd, that the sheep may be scattered; / I will turn my hand against the little ones" (13:7). In Mark and Matthew (Matt 26:31//Mark 14:27), Jesus quotes this passage to predict the disciples' flight: "You will all become deserters; for it is written, 'I will strike the shepherd, and the sheep will be scattered'" (Mark 14:27). Paul Redditt proposes that 13:7 refers to an inversion of Zechariah 2:6-13; 6:8: after gathering in the exiles, the LORD now scatters them again (Redditt 2008b, 79). But whether the scattering is literal or metaphorical, two points seem evident: first, that this is the LORD's doing, and second, that it is done despite the king being God's own choice, even God's friend.

Why, then, does God remove the people's shepherd, throw them into disarray, and even strike out against the weakest of them, cutting off two thirds of the population (13:8)? It is done, God declares, to "refine them as one refines silver, / and test them as gold is tested" (13:9). In the Hebrew Bible, the smelting furnace is always a metaphor for severe trial (cf. Prov 17:3; 27:21; Isa 48:10; Ezek 22:17-22; in Deut 4:20; 1 Kgs 8:51; and Jer 11:4, this metaphor is used for Israel's bondage in Egypt). Just as the furnace melts the raw ore so that the dross can be skimmed off, leaving the pure metal, so fiery trials purify and strengthen those who endure them faithfully (cf. Mal 3:2-3). Indeed, the LORD declares that such will be the result of *this* trial: the people will call upon the LORD, and the LORD will answer; once more, they will declare themselves to be God's people, and the LORD to be their God (13:9; cf. 8:8).

Here as elsewhere (cf. 2:5-9 [1-5]; 11:7-14; 12:6), the community of Zechariah is taking an image from Ezekiel (here, Ezek 22:17-22) and inverting it. In this case, however, Ezekiel used the image of the smelter to declare Jerusalem dross, not silver, which could *not* be refined. Inverting Ezekiel's image, then, restores this metaphor to its customary meaning.

What are we to do with this difficult metaphor? Although the verb for testing is different (not, as in Zech 13:9, *tsaraph* ["burn, smelt"] or *bakhan* ["test, try"], but *nasah* ["test"]), the reader is bound to think of Genesis 22, where God tests Abraham. Regarding that passage, Ellen Davis observes, "But the all-important question is, what is God testing him for? It seems to me that the point of the test is not in fact whether Abraham will obey, but the somewhat different question, can Abraham trust God?" (Davis 2014). Perhaps, in Zechariah 13:1-9 as well, this is the point of the test: as God indeed says of those who come through this trial, "They will call on my name, and I will answer them" (13:9). The New Testament book of James, while also affirming that spiritual growth comes through suffering, gets at this issue differently. James rejects the notion that God *sends* trials: "No one, when tempted, should say, 'I am tempted of God'; for God cannot be tempted by evil and he himself tempts no one" (Jas 1:13). Instead, as the source of "every perfect gift" (1:17), God empowers us to triumph over trials, so that, having "stood the test," we might "receive the crown of life that the Lord has promised to those who love him" (1:12). Pragmatically, one might say that from the perspective of the worshiper, it makes no difference whether God sends trials or not—hard times come, in any case. The question is whether we will be broken by them, or learn through them to trust that, when we call upon the LORD, the LORD will answer.

The day of the LORD (14:1-21). The scribes construed Zechariah 14 as a single paragraph, with no subunits. In comparison with earlier chapters in Zechariah 9–14, which as this commentary has shown typically feature multiple levels of composition, a remarkable unity of style and theme indeed characterizes this chapter. Earlier chapters in Zechariah 9–14 involved mingled poetry and prose; this chapter, however, is all prose. Apocalyptic themes and images used in later apocalypses have recurred throughout this book, and especially in these final six chapters; Zechariah 14, however, is a full-blown apocalypse (Hanson 1979, 369–72). The expression *bayyom hahu'*, "on that day," recurs throughout this second oracle (cf. 12:3, 4, 6, 8, 9, 11; 13:1, 2, 4); the highest concentration of these formulae occurs, however, in this final chapter (14:4, 6, 8, 9, 13, 20, 21). This study will consider the chapter in eight sections, marked off by these seven statements concerning the day of the LORD.

Zechariah 14:1-3 describes in stark prose the destruction depicted metaphorically in 13:7-9. The day elsewhere called simply "that day" is here defined: "a day is coming for the LORD" (14:1). As in 12:2, God gathers "all the nations against Jerusalem in battle" (14:2; cf. Ezek 38–39). Jerusalem again experiences all the horrors of a city reduced by siege: plunder, rape, and exile (cf. Nah 2–3). But at the moment when all seems lost, the LORD intervenes: "Then the LORD will go forth and fight against those nations as when he fights on a day of battle" (14:3; cf. Dan 12:1).

The divine warrior stands astride the Mount of Olives, which splits in two (14:4-5; cf. Nah 1:5; Hab 3:10), forming a new valley called *gey'-haray*, "the valley of my mountains" (the NRSV has "the LORD's mountain," but LXX also has the plural). This may recall Zechariah's eighth vision (6:1-8), where the four chariots come "out from between two mountains—mountains of bronze" (6:1). The earthquake that splits the Mount of Olives is compared to "the earthquake in the days of King Uzziah of Judah" (cf. Amos 1:1): a significant quake that left archaeological traces on Strata VI at Hazor, dating to the mid-eighth century (cf. Achtemeier 1996, 170). Through this new valley, Jerusalem's population escapes "to Azal" (an unknown place name, but all the versions agree on it). Once the population is safe, "Then the LORD my God will come; and all the holy ones with him" (14:5). The title "the LORD my God," while fairly common in the Psalms (11 times), appears only seven times in the prophetic books: once each in Isaiah (25:1) and Jeremiah (31:18), and in the Twelve once in Jonah (2:7[6]; significantly, in a psalm), once in Habakkuk (1:12), and *three times* in Zechariah 9–14 (11:4; 13:9; 14:5). As all three Zechariah references occur in material dealing with the destruction of Jerusalem or its king, we likely find here evidence for a common stratum, a late, apocalyptic portion of this material. The "holy ones" are likely heavenly beings (cf. Job 5:1; 15:15), the LORD's cohort (cf. Hab 3:5), following their leader into battle.

Not only the geography of Judah's hill country but also the very structure of the cosmos itself is changed as the LORD goes into battle (14:6-7). It is difficult to visualize the "singular day" (Petersen's translation of *yom-'ekhad,* literally, "one day," in 14:7 [1995, 133]; NRSV has "continuous day") that these verses describe, a day of which the LORD alone truly knows (14:8). First, while 14:7 describes light even at nighttime, 14:6 states, *lo'-yihyeh 'or*: "there will be *no* light"! Although the NRSV does not include this phrase, there is no valid textual reason to exclude it—all the versions assume it. Perhaps the best way to read this phrase is with reference to Genesis 1:3: "Then God said, 'Let there be light'" (Heb., *yehi 'or*). Much as Zephaniah 1:2-3 moves backwards through the creation account in Genesis 1:20-31 to depict God's judgment as un-creation, so Zechariah 14:6 inverts the first creative act of God, so undoing the order that God's creation establishes—particularly, the reliable sequence of day and night (cf. Gen 1:4-5). This in turn undoes the regular sequence of the seasons (cf. Gen 1:14-19). While the MT of 14:6 is garbled (not surprisingly—it is difficult for a scribe to copy a baffling text faithfully), the versions enable us to reconstruct a text meaning "there shall not be either cold or frost" (so Petersen 1995, 136). Other passages also describe the collapse of the natural order at the end of time (e.g., Joel 3:3-4 [2:30-31], quoted in Mark 13:24-25). The continual light in 14:7 may also reflect Isaiah 60:19-20, where the "everlasting light" of the LORD's glory replaces the sun and moon (so Petersen 1995, 145; cf. Rev 21:23). If so, then these verses express not only the chaos of natural order undone but also the promise of God's continual presence with God's people, to the end of time and beyond (cf. Matt 28:20; Rev 22:12-13).

Zechariah 14:8 continues the theme of a seasonless year, with free-flowing water year round: "On that day living waters shall flow out from Jerusalem, half of them to the eastern sea and half of them to the western sea; it shall continue in summer as in winter." The idea of Zion as a source of waters also appears in 13:1, and features elsewhere in Scripture (e.g., Isa 8:6; Ezek 47:1-12; Joel 4:18 [3:18]; Ps 46:5 [4]). The dual rivers in 14:8, flowing east to the Dead Sea and west to the Mediterranean, may reflect the description of the Canaanite god 'El's dwelling, said to lie "at the source of twin rivers, by the pools of the double-deep" (*CTA* 4.4.21-22; note that in Ezek 47:9, the MT has *nakhalayim*: "*two* rivers"), as well as Eden, the well-watered garden of God (Gen 2:8-17). If Zion is identified with Eden here (cf. Ezek 28:13-14; Tuell 2000), then the two rivers are likely the Pishon and the Gihon from Genesis 2:10-14, flowing from Zion/Eden east and west as the Tigris and Euphrates flow north to south. As in Ezekiel 47:1-12, this Edenic imagery expresses the blessing wrought by the presence of God (cf. Hag 2:18-19). Further, as in Revelation 22:1-7, the restoration of the garden of Eden at the end of time brings reality full circle (cf. Frye 1982, 169)—a major apocalyptic theme (cf. Gunkel 1895).

After God's victory over every enemy, "the LORD will become king over all the earth" (14:9; cf. Pss 47; 93; 95–99). Paul Hanson sees this acclamation of divine kingship as the climax of the old Divine Warrior myth, here reclaimed in apocalyptic dress (Hanson 1979, 371–72; cf. McBride 2014). Christian readers may think of 1 Corinthians 15:23-28, where Jesus, having at last triumphed over "every ruler and every authority and power" (1 Cor 15:24), yields up his kingdom to God at the end of time, "so that God may be all in all" (1 Cor 15:28). Zechariah 14:9 ties the acclamation of God's kingship to the uniqueness of God's name: "on that day the LORD will be one and his name one" (Heb., *Yhwh 'ekhad weshem 'ekhad*). The close similarity to Deuteronomy 6:4—*Shema' Yisra'el Yhwh 'elohenu Yhwh 'ekhad* ("Hear, O Israel: The LORD is our God, the LORD alone")—is surely no accident. As McBride observes, the point of this ancient confession is not monotheism in some abstract philosophical sense.

> The verse was read as an oath of allegiance to the suzerainty of Yahweh alone. Rather than proclaiming God's unity, it [the *Shema*] effected the unity, the corporate identity of those bound into his kingdom, setting them free from the lesser political dominions of the world. (McBride 1973, 278)

On the day of the LORD, the exclusive worship of the unique God, to which God's people are called throughout Scripture, is fully realized at last.

In an intriguing inversion of the image in Isaiah 2:2-4//Micah 4:1-3, rather than Zion being elevated as "the highest of the mountains," the land all around Zion is flattened to a plain, "but Jerusalem shall remain aloft" (14:10). The exalted city is filled with people and given a promise: "never again shall it be doomed to destruction; Jerusalem shall abide in security" (14:11). That security is guaranteed by a final death blow to the nations—a plague that rots the flesh of "all the peoples that wage war against Jerusalem" (14:12).

Zechariah 14:13-19 further describes the final victory of the LORD and its consequences for the nations. Panic-stricken, Jerusalem's enemies will turn on one another (14:13; cf. 2 Chr 20:23-24; Ezek 38:21). The NRSV rendering, "even Judah will fight at Jerusalem," reflects the ambiguity of the Hebrew in 14:14 (Meyer and Meyers 1993, 458). Does this mean that Judah will fight *for* Jerusalem (cf. JPSV; so O'Brien 2004, 279) or that Judah too is in the siege *against* Jerusalem (cf. the discussion of 12:2)? As Zechariah 9–14 certainly does describe a division within the people—a common feature of apocalypses, which often distinguish between the true believers and the untrue (e.g., 1 QM 2:1-6; Rev 13:11-15; cf. Matt 28:17)—it seems most likely that Judah here is numbered among the nations assaulting the city, or at least presented in distinction from it (Petersen 1995, 153–54). Jerusalem then plunders the defeated nations (cf. Exod 12:33-36; Ezek 39:9-10; 2 Chr 20:25), who will never again be able to mount an attack on Jerusalem; the plague strikes their "horses, the mules, the camels, the donkeys, and whatever animals may be in those camps" (14:15), destroying their military capability entirely.

Yet despite the sweeping devastation of plague and war, the enemies of Jerusalem are not utterly destroyed: "all who survive of the nations that have come against Jerusalem shall go up year after year to worship the King, the LORD of hosts, and to keep the festival of booths" (14:16). Similarly in the book of Revelation, even after the last judgment sees all the enemies of God's people (including Death and Hades) "thrown into the lake of fire" (Rev 20:11-15), John can still somehow say of the New Jerusalem, "The nations will walk by its light, and the kings of the earth will bring their glory into it. . . . People will bring into it the glory and the honor of the nations" (Rev 21:24-26). God's ultimate purpose is not destruction but transformation. In Zechariah 14:17-19, the nations do not necessarily come willingly—the threat of drought and plague coerces their participation, and particularly the participation of Egypt (14:18-19; for Egypt as a symbol of foreign oppression, cf. Hos 11:5; Zech 10:10-11)! Still, come they do, every year at *Sukkot,* the Festival of Booths. This autumn pilgrim feast, the most important of the festivals according to many biblical traditions (e.g., 1 Kgs 8:2; Isa 30:29; Ezek 45:25; Neh 8:14; John 7:2, which refer to the *Sukkot* as "*the* feast"), is an appropriate time for the nations to come to Jerusalem, as it is also the time set for the reading and remembrance of the Law of Moses (Deut 31:10-11; Neh 8:13-18). The nations join the faithful of Israel in proclaiming fealty to the LORD and faithfulness to God's commandments.

Meanwhile, in Jerusalem, *everything* is holy, not just in the temple precincts but throughout the city. Every cooking pot in Judah and Jerusalem is fit "to boil the flesh of the sacrifice" (14:21; cf. Lev 6:24-30; 22:1-7, 10-16; contrast Hag 2:10-12). Even the harness bells of horses in Jerusalem are engraved, "Holy to the LORD" (14:20)! This democratization of holiness is reminiscent of the Holiness Code (Lev 17–26), but while that document sought to make all Israel holy through a heightened sense of purity and impurity extended to each Israelite ("You shall be holy, for I the LORD your

God am holy," Lev 19:2), here that sanctity is granted by an act of God. The conclusion of this series of "on that day" statements pertains to the expulsion of the *kena'ani* (literally, "the Canaanites") from "the house of the LORD of hosts" (14:21). Since this chapter has already emphasized, on the one hand, the extension of temple holiness to the entire city (14:20-21) and, on the other, has stipulated the presence of foreigners in the city, at least on *Sukkot* (14:16-19), the exclusion of the Canaanites seems odd. Likely, as in Zephaniah 1:11, we should understand "Canaanites" here to mean "merchants" (cf. Hos 12:8; Prov 31:24; Job 41:6; as well as *kin'an*, meaning "tradesman," in Isa 23:8). Christian readers are likely to think of Jesus cleansing the temple, an incident recounted in all four Gospels (Matt 21:12-16; Mark 11:15-17; Luke 19:45-46; John 2:13-17). Clearly Jesus too regarded the conduct of trade as inappropriate in the temple precincts. For Jesus as for the writers of the apocalypse in Zech 14, God's presence is not a commodity that we can control, but a power that transforms our lives and our world.

Malachi

Reading Malachi

It is something of a truism that history is written by the winners. The story of the past is told from the "top"—from the perspective of the dominant majority, or of the wealthy and powerful minority. Until quite recently, that has meant that women, or racial minorities, or homosexual persons, or the poor were invisible in such histories, their contributions largely unsung. Today, this historical myopia is broadly challenged, but still, uncovering those hidden, forgotten, or even actively suppressed stories is a difficult enterprise. The Bible is no exception to this rule. Indeed, some have noted that the very fact that Scripture is *written* means that it was produced by and for literate cultural elites (so Carr 2005, 8–10).

Despite the general bias toward power and privilege in ancient texts, however, the Bible does preserve the perspectives of at least some persons from the social periphery. Feminist critics have revealed the masculine bias frequently assumed by the Bible's interpreters and uncovered ignored indications of the lives of women in ancient Israelite society (Meyers 2014). Books highly critical of the elites, such as Habakkuk and Zephaniah, survive. We also find other voices preserved in Scripture, from people whose identities are hidden and whose names we do not know.

"Malachi" does not follow the usual form for Hebrew names. We might expect something like "Malachiah" ("the Lord's messenger"[?]; cf. the names "Zephaniah" and "Zechariah"). But "Malachi" (Heb., *Mal'aki*) means simply "*my* messenger"—a very unlikely name for any parent to give a child (Scalise 2009, 320)! Probably, this designation for the book was taken by its editors from Malachi 3:1: "See, I am sending my messenger (*mal'aki*) to prepare the way before me, and the Lord whom you seek will suddenly come to his temple." This book presents itself as the oracles of that messenger, sent to proclaim the Lord's coming. Like Deutero- and Trito-Isaiah, the prophet whose voice we hear in the book of Malachi is anonymous. Particularly like Trito-Isaiah, and strikingly unlike Haggai–Zechariah 1–8, Malachi reflects the position of an out-group, opposed to the temple hierarchy of the returnees from exile (1:6-10; 2:1-3). In this book, we have a view of postexilic history from the perspective not of the "winners" but of the losers.

Authorship, Date, and Setting

Scholars have long noted that the titles at Zechariah 9:1; 12:1 and Malachi 1:1 are similar. In the Hebrew, all three begin with *massa' dabar Yhwh* ("An oracle: the word of the LORD"). This suggests a relationship among Zechariah 9–11 and 12–14 and the book of Malachi. Indeed, David Petersen argues that Malachi only came to be regarded as a book at a late stage, so that the collection of which it is a part could be designated "the Book of the *Twelve*." One should rather, he proposes, read this as the last of three *massa'ot* appended to Zechariah 1–8 (Petersen 1995, 1–3). The titles are not identical, however. In Zechariah 9:1 the word of the LORD is directed against the nations listed in Zechariah 9:1-8. In Zechariah 12:1, the *subject* of that word is defined: i.e., Israel. In Malachi, much as in Nahum and Habakkuk, the word is conveyed to and through a messenger (cf. Nah 1:1; Hab 1:1). Further, Malachi 1 shares a common vocabulary with Zechariah 7–8: for example, the expression *khalah* with *panim* (NRSV "entreat/implore the favor of"; literally, "entreat the face of") occurs in both Zechariah 7:2; 8:21-22 and Malachi 1:9; elsewhere in the Prophets, it is found only in Jeremiah 26:19. James Nogalski therefore proposes that these chapters were originally in sequence, linked by catchwords (Nogalski 1993b, 187 n. 21, 197–200), so that the addition of Malachi precedes the insertion of Zechariah 9–14. As Malachi does not reflect the later apocalyptic themes of Zechariah 9–14, its content confirms what these more formal features imply. Rather than Malachi being the third *massa'* tacked onto Zechariah, cut loose secondarily to become the twelfth "minor prophet," it is more likely that the designation of Malachi as a *massa'* prompted that designation for the two later collections in Zechariah 9–14 (Nogalski 1993b, 188–89).

Like Nahum and Habakkuk, Malachi contains no dates. Still, it seems most likely, given its consistent placement at the end of the Twelve, that Malachi comes, like Haggai and Zechariah, from the time of the Judean Restoration in the early Persian period (cf. the "Introduction"). A common setting may be indicated by the use of the title "LORD of hosts" (Heb., *Yhwh tseba'oth*; cf. the discussion of this title in Nah 3:5, above), which appears fourteen times in Haggai, fifty-three times in Zechariah, and twenty-four times in Malachi. From Malachi's scathing criticisms of temple worship (see

Mal 1:6-14), the temple must have been rebuilt by the time this book was written; therefore, Malachi must be dated somewhat after Haggai–Zechariah 1–8. Malachi does not seem to know about the reforms established by Ezra or Nehemiah, however, or about Ezra's Torah (Ezra 7:11-28). This suggests that the book of Malachi was likely written between 515 and 458 BCE.

As this commentary has already observed, the time after the return from exile was a time of serious conflict within the Judean community, between the returning exiles and the people who had remained in the land. In this conflict, Haggai–Zechariah 1–8, Ezek 40–48, and later Ezra–Nehemiah reflect the positions of the returnees and their priestly leaders, the descendants of Zadok. Malachi, like portions of Zechariah 9–14 and Trito-Isaiah, represents the viewpoint of the people in the land, led by Levitical priests (cf. Mal 2:4-9) who were not Zadokites (Hanson 1979, 263–64; McBride 2000, 35).

To understand these tensions, one needs to go back to a much earlier stage in Israel's history. When David first established Jerusalem as his capital, he appointed *two* high priests for the LORD's shrine (2 Sam 20:25): Abiathar, who belonged to a northern Levitical family, and Zadok, who represented southern priestly claims. In this way, both the southern and northern tribes had their priestly representatives in Jerusalem. This practice ended when David died and Solomon became king. Abiathar had supported Adonijah, Solomon's rival for the throne; so Solomon exiled him to Anathoth (1 Kgs 2:26-27), and Zadok became the sole high priest. For nearly four hundred years, the descendants of Zadok, called the Zadokites, would remain in control of the Jerusalem temple. The Levites, though largely denied the rights of sacrifice and leadership in worship at both the northern shrines and in Jerusalem, continued to teach and to preserve their traditions; the northern traditions in Torah and the book of Deuteronomy particularly reflect Levitical ideals. When Jerusalem fell in 587 BCE, the Zadokites, as the priestly house loyal to the Davidic kings, were taken away into exile, while the old northern Levitical families were left in place.

Certainly, worship continued in the land after the Zadokites' departure. The entire book of Lamentations seems to presuppose worship on the site of the ruined temple. This worship evidently did not involve blood sacrifice, as the altar had been destroyed and the sacrificial priests, the Zadokites, were gone (cf. Ezek 40:45-46), but other Levitical priests remained to teach and lead worship. Jeremiah 41:4-5 describes eighty men "from Shechem and Shiloh and Samaria" coming to the temple site with "grain offerings and incense." Intriguingly, Malachi contrasts the corrupt cult of the rebuilt temple with "incense offered in my name, and a pure offering" made outside of the temple "in every place" (Mal 1:11), perhaps with reference to these Levitical services.

With the end of the exile, the returning Zadokite priests took control of worship in the rebuilt temple and rejected the claims of the Levitical priests in the land, denying them any role in the restored temple (cf. Ezra 4:1-3). Preference for the Zadokites is apparent in Haggai (Hag 1:1, 12-15; 2:2, 4) and in Zechariah 1–8 (3:1-10; 4:1-14; 6:9-15). If the interpretation this commentary proposes for Haggai's request for a *torah* from the priests (Hag 2:10-19) is correct, Haggai also rejects non-Zadokite priestly claims. Ezekiel 44:9-16, likely written around this time, explicitly denies the title "priest" to Levites, and recognizes the priestly status of Zadokites alone (Tuell 2005, 187–91). Meanwhile, Isaiah 56:1-8 affirms a more inclusive view toward priesthood (Tuell 2005, 192–95), while Isaiah 65:1-7 and 66:1-4 sharply condemn the priesthood and liturgy of the restored temple (Hanson 1979, 146–50; 178–86). It is in this light that we need to view Malachi's angry critique of priesthood and worship in the restored temple.

Structure

Even a swift reading reveals a distinctive, recurring pattern in the book of Malachi. Again and again, a prophetic statement (e.g., "I have loved you, says the LORD," 1:2) elicits a question from Malachi's audience (e.g., "But you say, 'How have you loved us?'" 1:2; note that these questions are not the actual words of the community but rather what Malachi imagines them to think), or from God. The question then prompts a response (e.g., God's promise to restore the nation and destroy its enemy Edom in 1:2-5). While this pattern is not followed in a lock-step fashion (there is no opening statement in 2:10-16, and in 3:6-12 there are multiple questions), it recurs with sufficient force to shape the book around a series of arguments. This contentious style suggests to many a literary form sometimes called the disputation speech (Nogalski 1993b, 182) although Petersen prefers the term "diatribe," from Greek rhetoric (1995, 31-32), and O'Brien prefers the Hebrew concept *rib*, or covenant lawsuit (1988, 79–80; cf. Achtemeier 1986, 171–72). In any case, based on this repeated pattern, most interpreters of the book agree on a structure: a superscription (1:1) followed by six speeches (1:2-5; 1:6–2:9; 2:10-16; 2:17–3:5; 3:6-12, 13-21 [3:13–4:3]) and a conclusion (3:22-24 [4:4-6]; so Mason 1977, 136; Nogalski 1993b, 182–83; Petersen 1995, vi; O'Brien 2004, 286). Marvin Sweeney's structure varies slightly, identifying the fourth and fifth speeches as 2:17–3:7 and 3:8-12 (2000, 739, 742), and the sixth speech as including the conclusion (2000, 744). The Masoretes also divide Malachi into eight parts, which sometimes coincide with the breaks identified by modern readers but often do not: 1:1-13; 1:14–2:9; 2:10-12, 13-16; 2:17–3:12, 3:13-18, 19-21 (4:1-3), 22-24 (4:4-6). This commentary will follow the broadly accepted division into six speeches with an editorial superscription and conclusion. It will also note places where the scribal paragraphing urges reading across units, and places where it points to subdivisions within longer speeches.

Malachi as the Conclusion to the Book of the Twelve, the *Nebi'im*, and the Christian Old Testament

Malachi, like Nahum and Habakkuk, is designated a *massa'* ("oracle"; cf. Mal 1:1, and the discussions of Nah 1:1 and Hab 1:1 in context). This designation both opens and closes the latter half of the Twelve, thus uniting the six books this study considers. But one can read Malachi as the "end bracket" of much larger collections as well. As the Introduction to this commentary observes, ancient tradition sees the Book of the Twelve as opening with Hosea and closing with Malachi (e.g., *b. Baba Bathra* 14b). One can draw broad parallels between these first and last books in the Twelve: both come from Levitical circles, and both use the metaphor of marriage and divorce to describe the relationship between God and Israel (cf. Hos 1–2; Mal 2:10-16; so O'Brien 1988, 66–69). One can identify more specific links, however. John D. W. Watts observes that Hosea 3:1 (cf. 11:1 and 14:5 [4]) and Malachi 1:2 and 2:11 are the only mentions of God's love for Israel in the Twelve. He therefore argues that Hosea 1–3 and Malachi form a literary frame around the Twelve, emphasizing God's love (Watts 2000b, 212). One should observe that Zephaniah 3:17 also touches on this theme, though the noun *'ahabah* ("love") is used, not the verb *'ahab* ("he loves") found in Hosea and Malachi. In the final form of the Twelve, then, God's love for Israel opens, centers, and closes the entire collection.

Canonically, Malachi also appears at the close of the *Nebi'im*, or the Prophets, the second part of the Jewish canon, placed between the *Torah* (Law) and *Kethubim* (Writings). The *Nebi'im* opens in Joshua with explicit reference to the Mosaic Torah: "Only be strong and very courageous, being careful to act in accordance with all the law [Heb., *torah*] that my servant Moses commanded you; do not turn from it to the right hand or to the left, so that you may be successful wherever you go" (Josh 1:7). Similarly, the editorial conclusion at Malachi 3:22 (4:4) reads, "Remember the teaching [Heb., *torah*] of my servant Moses, the statutes and ordinances that I commanded him at Horeb for all Israel." In this way, the *Nebi'im* begins and ends with reference back to Torah (so also Childs 1978, 51–52).

Of course, in the Christian canon, Malachi's placement both at the end of the Twelve and at the end of the Prophets also means that this book comes at the end of the Old Testament. In that position, the concluding words regarding the promise of Elijah (Mal 3:23-24[4:5-6]) point forward to the ministry of John the Baptist (Matt 3:1-12), of whom Jesus says, "For all the prophets and the law prophesied until John came; and if you are willing to accept it, he is Elijah who is to come" (Matt 11:13-14). In the Christian Bible, Malachi serves as the pivot point of the canon, joining the Old Testament to the New (cf. Towner 2006, 1284).

Commentary

Superscription (1:1)

The use of the title *massa'* ("An oracle") at the beginning of this book recalls the use of the same title in Nahum 1:1 and Habakkuk 1:1. Here as there, this title characterizes what will follow as a message of judgment. But while the target of the judgment in Nahum and in the final form of Habakkuk is a foreign nation (Assyria in Nahum; Babylon in Habakkuk), the judgment here is spoken to Israel.

The judgment comes *beyad mal'aki*: literally, "by the hand of my messenger/Malachi," a complexity concealed by the NRSV translation "by Malachi" (for the likelihood that "Malachi" is a pseudonym, see "Reading Malachi," above). Among the Twelve, only Haggai 1:1, 3; 2:1 and Malachi 1:1 state that the word of the LORD comes "by the hand of" the prophet (see the discussion of Hag 1:1). Torah uses this expression, which emphasizes the role of the prophet as intermediary (cf. Petersen 1984, 45), for Moses (Exod 9:35; Lev 10:11; Num 16:40; 27:23). While in the Deuteronomistic History, the word of the LORD comes "by the hand" of a specific prophet (Ahijah the Shilonite in 1 Kgs 12:15; 14:18; 15:29; Jehu son of Hanani in 1 Kgs 16:7, 10; Joshua in 1 Kgs 16:34; Elijah in 1 Kgs 17:16; 2 Kgs 9:36; 10:10; Jonah in 2 Kgs 14:25) or of "his servants the prophets" (2 Kgs 21:10; 22:4) twelve times. The use of this expression at the beginning of Malachi heightens the book's Levitical links to Moses and to Deuteronomy, and stands in counterpoise to the explicit mention of the Torah of Moses, "commanded him at Horeb for all Israel," at its conclusion (3:22 [4:4]; cf. Deut 4:10, 15; 5:2).

First Disputation: "How have you loved us?" (1:2-5)

Malachi opens with a forthright declaration of God's love: "I have loved you, says the LORD" (1:2). First-person declarations of God's love are not common in the Old Testament. Apart from this passage, only in Isaiah 43:4; Jeremiah 31:3; and Hosea 11:1; 14:4 does God tell someone, "I love you" (cf. Wisdom's declaration of love for those who love her in Prov 8:17). The parallels with Hosea are particularly striking, as Hosea opens the Book of the Twelve just as Malachi closes it (see the discussion above). The "you" is plural in Hebrew, indicating that God is addressing the whole people collectively. The people respond by asking for proof of God's love. Curiously, God demonstrates love for Israel by utterly devastating Edom.

Edom was a minor kingdom located south of Judah and southwest of Moab. Some texts regard Edom positively. Deuteronomy 23:8 permits Edomites to be included in the worshiping congregation after living among the people of Israel for three generations. Edom was also respected as a place of ancient wisdom (Job 1:1; 2:11; Jer 49:7; Obad 8). According to archaeologist Ephraim Stern (1982, 253), the Kedarite Arabs had already decimated Edom by the Babylonian period, forcing its people into the Negeb and the highlands of southern Judea; certainly, then, Edom would have been desolate in Malachi's time (as Mal 1:3 records). In Malachi, however, God not only declares, "I have made his hill country a desolation" (1:3), but also promises to defeat any future attempt to rebuild "until they are called the wicked country, the people with whom the LORD is angry forever" (1:4).

What reason could there be for this unrelenting hostility? Elsewhere, Edom is condemned for looting Jerusalem after its fall to Babylon (e.g., Ps 137:7; Lam 4:21-22; Obad 11-14). In Malachi, however, the reason given for God's hatred of Edom relates not to events in relatively recent history but to Israel's own mythic origins: "Is not Esau Jacob's brother? says the LORD. Yet I have loved Jacob but I have hated Esau" (1:2-3; cf. Gen 25:19-26). The apostle Paul uses this disturbing declaration in Romans 9:13 as part of a larger argument concerning the salvation of Israel (Rom 9–11). Since apart from God's deliverance no one could be saved, Paul argues, God cannot be called unjust, even if God is arbitrary (although ultimately, Paul denies that God *is* arbitrary, and asserts God's faithfulness; cf. Rom 11:26-27).

According to ancient tradition, the Edomites were the descendants of Isaac's eldest son Esau (also called Edom; see Gen 25:25, 30 and the genealogies in 36:1-43), while Israel was descended from Esau's twin brother Jacob (also called Israel; see Gen 32:22-32). Malachi 1:2-5 recalls that tradition and also sounds themes from Ezekiel 35:1-15, an oracle against Mount Seir (another name for Edom; note in particular the use of the word "desolation" [Heb., *shemamah*] in Mal 1:3 and Ezek 35:3, 4, 7, 9, 14, 15). Ezekiel ascribes Edom's hostility toward Judah to "an ancient enmity" (Heb., *'ebat 'olam*). In Genesis, that "ancient enmity" between Edom and Israel begins in the womb (Gen 25:22-23), and continues through their childhood and youth. When Jacob by trickery steals the deathbed blessing their father had intended for Esau, Isaac pronounces over his eldest son the only "blessing" he has left to give:

> By your sword you shall live,
> and you shall serve your brother;
> but when you break loose,
> you shall break his yoke from your neck (Gen 27:40).

Although Genesis 33:1-17 describes the reconciliation of the two brothers, Ezekiel declares that Edom's relentless pursuit of vengeance had turned it from a blood relation of Israel to a blood enemy (Ezek 35:6), doomed to total destruction.

Another likely parallel to Malachi 1:2-5 is Obadiah, which also alludes to the Jacob and Esau story (Obad 10), and where Edom represents of all the nations arrayed against Jerusalem (Obad 15-16; cf. Zech 14:1-3). So too Malachi states that witnessing Edom's desolation will prompt Israel to acclaim God's lordship over the nations: "Great is the LORD beyond the borders of Israel!" (1:5). These verses seem, in short, to relate more to the broader context of the Twelve than to the concerns of Malachi specifically (Nogalski 1993b, 192–94), making it likely that 1:2-5 is part of the editing of this book as the conclusion to the Twelve. Indeed, the use of the divine name *Yhwh* ("the LORD") in 1:2-5 rather than *Yhwh tseba'oth* ("the LORD of hosts"), as is more typical of Malachi, is suggestive. Still, the scribal paragraphing does not break until after the dual indications of divine speech in 1:13, and so incorporates this opening unit into the following disputation. This suggests that the scribes regarded God's declaration of love for Israel to be an integral part of the book, and particularly of the dispute about divine honor that follows (1:6–2:9).

Second Disputation: "How have we despised your name?" (1:6–2:9)

The second disputation opens with a commonplace aphorism reminiscent of Proverbs: "A son honors his father, and servants honor their master" (1:6). By extension, surely God, who is both like and yet greater than father (cf. Mal 2:10; Pss 68:6 [5]; 89:27 [26]) or master (cf. Ps 123:2), deserves honor, and surely priests ought to be expected to show that honor more than anyone. Yet, the LORD of hosts says, rather than showing God honor, the priests "despise my name" (1:6), prompting the priests to ask how they have done so (1:6-7).

As this study already has observed (see "The Early Persian Period" in the introduction to Haggai), the Jerusalem temple in the Persian period was supported by the Persian state, money from the tribute of the province being used to fund the sacrificial service of the temple (Ezra 6:6-12; Ezek 45:13-17; cf. Tuell 1992, 109–10). Animals offered for sacrifice were supposed to be *tamim*: "perfect, without blemish" (e.g., Lev 1:3, 10; 3:1, 6; 5:15, 18). Malachi accuses the Zadokite priests of using the money they were given to buy substandard animals, and presumably pocketing the rest (Mal 1:6-8)! For Malachi, the disrespect their actions show toward God is a far more serious offense than their defrauding of the Persian bureaucracy (1:8). Far from being "holier than thou" (cf. Isa 65:5), the priests of the restored temple have shown themselves to be hopelessly defiled, to the extent that God calls for an end to the sacrificial liturgy: "Oh, that someone among you would shut the temple doors [so *Tg. Neb.*; MT and LXX simply have "doors"], so that you would not kindle fire on my altar in vain!" (1:10; cf. 2 Chr 28:24; 29:3; Ps 24:7, 9). Indeed, the LORD of hosts says, "I will not accept an offering from your hands" (1:10).

In contrast to the unacceptable sacrifices of the rebuilt temple, Malachi speaks of other offerings: "For from the rising of the sun to its setting my name is great among the nations, and in every place incense is offered to my name, and a pure offering; for my name is great among the nations, says the LORD of hosts" (1:11). This openness to the nations stands in contrast to the first disputation, but in continuity with texts such as Zechariah 14:16 or Isaiah 66:19-21. The incense offerings in Malachi 1:11 recall Jeremiah 41:5, where eighty men "from Shechem and Shiloh and Samaria" come to the site of the ruined temple with "grain offerings and incense." Different terms for "incense" are used: the unique Hebrew *muqtar* in Mal 1:11 (but compare the terms for "incense altar" in Exod 30:1 [*miqtar*] and 2 Chr 30:14 [*miqatteret*], and for "censer" in Ezek 8:11 and 2 Chr 26:19 [*miqteret*]) versus the common term *lebonah* in Jer 41:5 (e.g., Exod 30:4; Lev 2:1-2; Isa 43:23). Still, both likely refer to Levitical services in the land, performed in the absence of the Zadokite priests. By comparison, the Jerusalem priests serve their God polluted food (1:13; cf. Ezek 44:7). Although the MT of 1:13 reads *wehippakhetem 'otho*, "you sniff at it"—presumably, the offerings presented to the LORD (this is the reading assumed by the LXX and *Tg. Neb.*)—the NRSV reads "you sniff at *me*," following rabbinic sources that treat this passage as a *Tiqqune sopherim*—that is, a scribal emendation to preserve divine honor (Gelston 2010, 150*; cf. Hab 1:12; Zech 2:12 [8]). Since priestly contempt for the LORD of hosts is the point of this disputation, this reading is certainly possible, and even likely.

The effect of this corruption, Malachi states, is that the entire liturgy has been cursed. A curse is pronounced on any worshiper who is complicit in the priests' fraud (1:14; note that this verse opens the second paragraph in the MT, 1:14–2:9). Indeed, the LORD declares, "If you will not listen, if you will not lay it to heart to give glory to my name, says the LORD of hosts, then I will send the curse on you and I will curse your blessings; indeed I have already cursed them, because you do not lay it to heart" (2:2). Blessing the people is one of the fundamental tasks of the priesthood (cf. Lev 9:22-23; Num 6:22-27; Deut 10:8; 21:5; 1 Chr 23:13; 2 Chr 30:27). Yet Malachi in essence says to his audience, "Do not let these people bless you! Their blessings are curses!" Malachi vividly portrays God's rejection of the priests in a potent image: "I will rebuke your offspring, and spread dung on your faces, the dung of your offerings" (2:3). As dung is ritually unclean (Exod 29:14; Lev 4:11; 8:17; 16:27; Num 19:5; cf. Ezek 4:9-17), this action not only shows contempt and loathing for the priests but also renders them ritually defiled. The NRSV of 2:3 follows LXX and the Syriac, and reads "I will put you out of my presence," which would surely be the inevitable result of the defilement this verse describes. The MT, however, reads *wenasa' 'ethkem 'elaw* ("and he will bear you to it"; cf. KJV), which is meaningful. The "it," here, is presumably the dung, so the point of the Hebrew could be either that the LORD of hosts will bear the priests to the dungheap (so JPSV) or a warning to Malachi's audience that the *priest* will bear *them* to the dungheap—undergirding the warning concerning the defiled priests in 1:14–2:2.

In place of the exclusive claims of these discredited Zadokites, Malachi calls for a return to "my covenant with Levi" (2:4, 8; cf. Jer 33:21-22)—in contrast, presumably, with the covenant with Phineas (Num 25:12), also called "my covenant of peace" (Heb., *shalom*; cf. Mal 2:5, which calls the covenant with Levi a "covenant of life and well-being [also *shalom*]"). While that covenant had been with a single Levitical family, extending from Aaron through Eleazar to Phineas and ultimately to Zadok (1 Chr 6:1-15, 50-53; cf. Cross 1973, 210), the covenant with Levi presumes that *all* Levites are given the opportunity to serve as priests (so Deut 18:1). According to this covenant, priests are called to lives of reverence (2:5). They are to be men of "integrity and uprightness" (2:6), who by their teaching will lead Israel to the truth (2:6-7; for the obligation of priests to teach, cf., e.g., Lev 10:10-11; Deut 33:8-10; 2 Kgs 17:27-28; 2 Chr 15:3; Ezek 44:23-24; Hos 4:6). The true priest, Malachi pronounces, "is the messenger [Heb., *mal'ak*!] of the LORD of hosts" (2:7). The priests in the restored temple, however, have "corrupted the covenant of Levi" (2:8). Although their false instruction and poor example have led the people into error, the priesthood remains closed and exclusive: "you have not kept my ways but have shown partiality in your instruction" (2:9; literally, "you have lifted up the face;" for this expression for showing favor or partiality, cf., e.g., Gen 19:21; Ps 4:7 [6]). In contrast to this partiality, Malachi calls for an openness and inclusivity in the priesthood (cf. Isa 56:1-8), including all Levites.

Third Disputation: "Why are we faithless to one another?" (2:10-16)

The scribes divide these verses into two paragraphs, 2:10-12 and 13-16. To be sure, it is possible to read these sections as two different disputations, the first involving marriage to "the daughter of a foreign god" (2:11), the second divorce from "the wife of your youth" (2:14). These offenses are clearly interrelated, however. The first offense results in God both denying legal recourse and intercession to the offenders (reading Heb., *'er we'oneh* [NRSV "witness or answer"] as two terms for legal representation, following O'Brien 1990, 69–72) and refusing sacrificial offerings on their behalf (2:12). When the people tearfully ask why their sacrifices are no longer accepted on God's altar (2:13-14), however, the answer is, "Because the LORD was a witness between you and the wife of your youth, to whom you have been faithless" (2:14). It is best then to treat 2:10-16 as a unit and to understand Judah's "marriage" and "divorce" as interrelated, or even as two different aspects of the same problem: Judah's faithlessness.

The third disputation opens not with a statement from God but with three questions from the prophet. The first two questions recall the proverbial statement concerning God as father in 1:6: is God indeed the one father and creator of all? The third question assumes that the answer to the first two is yes. Since those who have the same father are family, joined by bonds of kinship, "Why then are we faithless to one another, profaning the covenant of our ancestors?" (2:10). Following on the emphasis on the covenant with Levi in 2:4, and the condemnation of partiality in 2:9, one could think that the topic here is still priesthood. Malachi 2:11 speaks of *Judah*, however, not Levi, so that the offenses described in the following verses are committed by all the people in Judah, not by the priests alone. Even so, 2:10-16 continues to address false worship—specifically, idolatry (with O'Brien 1990 and 2004, Petersen 1995, Nogalski 2011).

Most readers of Malachi have understood the problem addressed in 2:10-16 to be marriages to wealthy foreign women ("the daughter of a foreign god," 2:11), and the divorce of native Israelite wives ("the wife of your youth," 2:14) to make those marriages possible (e.g., Orelli 1893, 394–98; Achtemeier 1986, 182–83; Towner 1993, 1284; Schuller 1996, 864–67; Hanson 2000, 685; Sweeney 200, 731–39; Scalise 2009, 344–45)—a reading consonant with early Christian approaches to the passage (e.g., Jerome, *Jov.* 1:10; Tertullian, *Marc.* 4:34; Hill 2006, 285–87). Indeed W. Sibley Towner calls 2:16 ("I hate divorce, says the LORD, the God of Israel") "the strongest condemnation of divorce expressed anywhere in the Hebrew Bible" (Towner 1993, 1430). Since foreign marriages are also condemned in Ezra 9:1–10:44, this passage is often used to date Malachi to the time of Ezra's reforms.

This consensus faces numerous problems, however. First, nowhere else is a foreign woman called *bat-'el nekar* ("daughter of a foreign god," 2:11). The versions are of little help in deciphering this phrase. While the Vulgate simply renders the MT literally into Latin, *Tg. Neb.* drops the reference to a deity and condemns "taking as his wife a daughter of the [presumably foreign] people," and LXX drops mention of the daughter and condemns caring for a foreign god; both the Aramaic and Greek versions seem to assume the text of MT and attempt to explain it. As Julia O'Brien observes, "daughter of a foreign god" more naturally describes a goddess than an idol-worshiping woman (O'Brien 1990, 67–68; cf. Nogalski 2011, 1033–34). Indeed, Petersen proposes emending *'asher 'aheb* in 2:11 (from the clause "the sanctuary of the Lord, *which he loves*") to *'Asherah 'aheb* ("He [i.e., Judah] loved Asherah" [a major Canaanite goddess; e.g., 1 Kgs 15:13//2 Chr 15:16; 2 Kgs 21:7; cf. Deut 12:3, where "sacred poles" is, in Heb., *'asherim*]; Petersen 1995, 194). While there is no basis for such an emendation, the broader context supports reading 2:10-16 as involving false worship, not matrimony. The sin condemned profanes "the sanctuary of the Lord, which he loves" (2:11), with the result that the sacrifices of the people are no longer accepted on God's altar (2:12-13). Cultic language recurs throughout the unit (cf. O'Brien 1990, 67–69; Schuller 1996, 864): Judah is condemned for profanation (Heb., *khalal*; 2:10, 11), faithlessness (Heb., *bagad*; 2:10, 11, 14, 15, 16; cf. Hos 5:7; 6:7), and committing an abomination (Heb., *to'ebah*; 2:11). The term *to'ebah* is particularly interesting, as it is used in Deuteronomy (e.g., Deut 7:25-26; 18:9-12; 27:15), Kings (1 Kgs 14:24; 2 Kgs 16:3; 21:2, 11; 23:13), and Ezekiel (43 times; e.g., Ezek 5:9-11; 9:4; 16:50) for idolatry.

Another problem with the marriage interpretation in 2:10-16 is the description of "the wife of your youth" as "your wife by covenant" (Heb., *'eshet beriteka*) in 2:14. Marriage is not described as a *berit* ("covenant") anywhere else in the Hebrew Bible (O'Brien 1990, 68)—at least, no *human* marriage is so described. The exception that proves the rule is Ezekiel 16:60, where the Lord, addressing Jerusalem as an unfaithful spouse, affirms that once its time of punishment is past, "I will remember my covenant with you in the days of your youth [!], and I will establish with you an everlasting covenant" (cf. Mal 2:14-15; so O'Brien 2004, 300). Quite likely, as in Ezekiel 16 and Hosea 1–2, Malachi 2:10-16 uses marriage as a metaphor for the relationship between God and God's people, so that idolatry becomes adultery (cf. the discussion of Nah 3).

In those earlier texts, however, the male *Yhwh* was wedded to the female Jerusalem, or Israel. Here, male Judah has betrayed "the wife of your youth" for a goddess. While Scripture can imagine the LORD in feminine terms (cf. Hos 11:1-9; Ps 22:9; 123:2), that is not the case here, as the LORD is "a witness between you and the wife of your youth" (2:14). The forsaken bride may be the temple, though the term used in 2:11 for the shrine (Heb., *qodesh*, "holy [place]") is masculine, and Malachi is in any case at best ambivalent toward the temple. Perhaps the reference is, more abstractly, to the life of faith and commitment abandoned by Judah in its idolatry (cf. 2:5-7; 3:5), a life that was expected to bear fruit in righteousness (i.e., "divine seed" [Heb., *zera' 'elohim*] in 2:15; still thinking of actual marriages, NRSV has "Godly offspring").

A final problem with reading 2:10-16 as regarding actual (as opposed to metaphorical) marriage and divorce is 2:16, "For I hate divorce, says the LORD the God of Israel." The MT reads *ki-sane' shalakh* ("For he hates divorce"), but the form of this verse attested in the Dead Sea scrolls at Qumran is *ky 'm snth shlkh*: "But if you hate her, then divorce" (4QXIIa). *Targum Nebi'im*, which has *'arey 'im senet lah patrah* ("For if you hate her, you shall divorce her"), reflects that alternate reading. So does the LXX, though a bit more cryptically, as well as the Vulgate. Despite the broad attestation for this alternate reading, it is unlikely to be the original, as it conflicts with the emphasis on faithfulness and commitment in both the broader context of 2:10-16 and in the remainder of the verse in which it appears. Further, it is far more likely that this alternate reading attempts to deal with the difficult text in the MT of 2:16 than that the MT resulted from deliberate alteration or scribal error.

The difficulty in this sentence lies not in its wording, grammar, or syntax, which are clear, but in its meaning. Everywhere else in the Hebrew Bible, divorce is accepted, with no shame implied to the woman who is divorced (nothing is ever said of wives divorcing their husbands). The divorced daughter of a priest can return to her father's house and eat from the offerings restricted to the priests and their families (Lev 22:13), and oaths sworn by divorced women have legal standing (Num 30:9). While a priest may not marry a divorced woman (Lev 21:7, 13-14; Ezek 44:22), this restriction on priestly marriages clearly implies that other Israelite men could marry divorced women. The law concerning divorce (Deut 24:1-4) assumes this, though it places a restriction on remarriage: a woman who has remarried since her husband divorced her cannot return to her first husband. The prophets use this law metaphorically, to condemn Israel for worshiping other gods and then thinking that they could return to the Lord as though nothing had happened (cf. Isa 50:1; Jer 3:1, 8).

Although we can imagine that divorce was intended to be rare, the exception to the rule, the Old Testament never states the acceptable grounds for divorce. Deuteronomy 24:1 only says that a man can divorce his wife if he finds "something objectionable about her." The Hebrew word translated "something objectionable" in the NRSV is *'erwah* (cf. the discussion of Nah 3:5): literally, "nakedness" or "something shameful." Since the law does not clearly specify the conditions under which divorce is permissible, the sages debated the issue intensely. The alternate reading for Malachi 2:16 in 4QXIIa, reflected in the versions of this passage, sounds very like the teaching of Jesus ben Sirach: "Do you have a wife who pleases you? Do not divorce her; but do not trust yourself to one whom you detest" (Sir 7:26). Ben Sirach infers that, while a good marriage is cause for celebration and lifelong commitment, incompatibility is sufficient grounds for divorce. Somewhat similarly, in the Mishnah (*b Gittin* 90a), Rabbi Hillel declares that even bad cooking is sufficient grounds for divorce—meaning, evidently, that a marriage can be dissolved for any reason whatsoever. Rabbi Shammai, on the other hand, insists that serious reasons are required for divorce. Jesus' teaching, permitting divorce only in cases of adultery (cf. Matt 5:31-32; 19:9), reflects the more hardline approach of Shammai.

In the context of the Hebrew Bible, then, Malachi 2:16 is anomalous if applied to actual divorce. This anomaly accounts for the alternate reading represented in 4QXIIa and the versions, which is more in keeping with the whole of Scripture. But if this verse concerns metaphorical divorce, then there is no anomaly. The point of the passage then would be that God calls Judah to covenant faithfulness without wavering.

If the problem addressed in this disputation is idolatry, how does that sin involve faithlessness "to one another" (2:10)? Surely, if the problem addressed in 2:10-16 continues to be (as in 1:6–2:9) corrupt worship, that is an issue between Judah and God, its father and creator, rather than among the people. As David Petersen observes (1995, 196), however, the emphasis on God's people having one father and one creator in 2:10 surely means that "they too should be one, that is to say, a people who keep covenantal faith with one another and who venerate one deity." While the NRSV emends the MT in 2:15 and interprets the Hebrew word *'ekhad* ("one") in this verse as referring to the one God, the Hebrew is meaningful as it stands, and the "one" may refer to *Judah*, bound as one to the covenant faith ("the wife of your youth") as husband and wife "become one flesh" in Genesis 2:24. The verse would then read, "And did he not make *them* one and the remnant of his spirit?" (with Nogalski 2011, 1038). Christian readers may think of Paul's description of the church as the body of Christ (1 Cor 12:12-31), or of Jesus' prayer for the church in John 17:20, "that they may all be one." In Malachi, the oneness of God's people requires their faithfulness to the "covenant of our ancestors" (2:10; literally, "the covenant of our fathers"). Petersen observes that this expression refers particularly to the Sinai covenant as set forth in Deuteronomic traditions (cf. Deut 4:30-31; 29:24-25; Jer 34:13-14), and all that it entails (Petersen 1995, 197). The fundamental ground of that covenant, however, is Israel's sole allegiance to the one God (Deut 6:4-5). Without right worship, there is no community.

Fourth Disputation: "Where is the God of justice?" (2:17–3:5)

The fourth disputation opens with a statement from the prophet: "You have wearied the LORD with your words," prompting the immediate question, "How have we wearied him?" (2:17). The Hebrew verb translated "weary" (*yaga'*) occurs twenty-six times in Scripture; in the Twelve, only in Malachi 2:17 (twice) and in Habakkuk 2:13. It is, however, typical of Deutero-Isaiah, appearing in those chapters nine times (40:28, 30, 31; 43:22, 23, 24; 47:12, 15; 49:4; cf., in Trito-Isaiah, 57:10; 62:8; 65:23). The causative form of the verb used in Malachi 2:17 ("to *make* [someone] weary") appears elsewhere only in Isaiah 43:23-24: first, in reference to sacrifices not offered during the exile ("I have not burdened you with offerings, or wearied you with frankincense," Isa 43:23); then, in acknowledgment of Israel's need for propitiation despite the loss of sacrifices: "you have burdened me with your sins; you have wearied me with your iniquities" (Isa 43:24). Knowing that they have wearied the LORD with their sins and iniquities, the exiles may fear that God is weary of *them*, and does not or cannot hear their cries. The LORD, however, reassures them that, despite the loss of temple, altar, and priesthood, "I, I am He who blots out your transgressions for my own sake, and I will not remember your sins" (Isa. 43:25). In Malachi, of course, Judah once more has a temple, a priesthood, and a functioning sacrificial cult. Yet, according to the prophet, *they* have wearied the LORD with their bland, cynical indifference. Far from being moved to repentance and change by the prophet's call to reform, the people say, "All who do evil are good in the sight of the LORD, and he delights in them," or ask, "Where is the God of justice?" (2:17). In other words, Malachi's community believes either that God doesn't see what they do or that God doesn't care.

Malachi gives assurance that these questions and doubts are about to be addressed, for "the LORD whom you seek will suddenly come to his temple" (3:1). Those who piously claim to delight in God's covenant (3:1) will soon have the opportunity to express their gratitude personally! Although the actual phrase is not used, Malachi clearly proclaims the imminent arrival of the day of the LORD (so Nogalski 2011, 1047, who sees the focus of the remainder of the book to be "the coming day of YHWH"; for "the day of the LORD," cf. the discussion of Nah 1:8).

Actually, Malachi proclaims the advent not only of the LORD but also of the LORD's messenger. It is unclear in the following verses whether the coming cleansing is to be carried out by that messenger or by the LORD, though given the pattern elsewhere in the Twelve, the latter seems more likely. As we have seen, "my messenger" is in Hebrew *mal'aki*. The term *mal'ak* appears twenty-six times in the Twelve, although twenty of those occurrences are in Zechariah (19 times in Zech 1–8, once in 12:8). In Zechariah and in Hosea 12:4, *mal'ak* refers to a supernatural being (our word "angel" comes from the Greek *angelos*, which also means "messenger," used in LXX to translate *mal'ak*). In Nahum 2:13, it refers to human messengers. The prophet Haggai is called *mal'ak Yhwh* ("the messenger of the LORD") in Haggai 1:13. In Malachi, *mal'ak* appears in the superscription (Mal 1:1), where Malachi/*mal'aki* is the one through whom this *massa'* is communicated; in 2:7, where the priest is called "the messenger of the LORD of hosts"; and twice in 3:1. It seems most likely then that 3:1 also has a human messenger in mind, probably the prophet who speaks for God in this book. But already within the editing of Malachi, we can see the beginning of a series of progressive reflections on this enigmatic figure. In the conclusion to this book (cf. 3:23 [4:5]), the prophetic forerunner of the day of the LORD has become Elijah, who was taken alive into the heavens in a chariot of fire (2 Kgs 2:11) and so can be called upon for this task. In Christian Scripture, Jesus is the one who comes to cleanse his people from their sins (Mal 3:2-3), and John the Baptist becomes the "messenger" sent to proclaim Jesus' coming (see the quotes of Mal 3:1 at Matt 11:10; Mark 1:2; Luke 1:76; 7:27), and "Elijah who is to come" (Matt 11:14; cf. Matt 17:10-11; Mark 9:11-12; Luke 1:17).

The ambivalence in Malachi 3 concerning the actions of the messenger and the LORD, however, continued to yield conflicting interpretations in Christian readings. For example, Augustine on the one hand describes John the Baptist as the messenger in 3:1 (*Tra. Ev. Jo.* 14.10.1), and on the other understands Jesus to be the "angel" (i.e., "messenger") of both Malachi 2:7 and 3:1—indeed, according to Augustine, Malachi 3:1-2 relates both to Christ's first coming (reading the LORD coming to his temple as a reference to the incarnation; cf. Matt 26:59-61; Mark 14:55-59; John 2:19-21) and his second ("Who can endure the day of his coming?" Mal 3:2; cf. *Civ.* 18:35; 20:25). It is little wonder, then, that Charles Jennens used Malachi

3:1-3 (in continuity with Hag 2:6-7) in the libretto for the Christmas section of George Handel's famous oratorio *The Messiah*. Likewise, in the Revised Common Lectionary, Malachi 3:1-4 is read every year in Epiphany, at Candlemas or the Presentation of the Lord (commemorating Jesus' presentation at the temple, cf. Luke 2:22-40), and is also the Old Testament reading for the Second Sunday of Advent, Year C, matched on the one hand with readings from Luke concerning John the Baptist (Luke 1:68-79; 3:1-6) and on the other with Paul's prayer in Philippians 1:3-11 "that in the day of Christ [Paul's transformation of "the day of the LORD"] you may be pure and blameless" (Phil 1:10).

The announcement of the LORD's coming would be good news, if as they claim, Malachi's people indeed seek the LORD (3:1, cf. 1 Chr 28:9) and if they truly delight in God's covenant (3:1; cf. 2:4, 8, 10, 14)—but of course, they do not. The reader is clued to this by the use of the word *pitо̄m* ("suddenly"), which is used for calamitous surprises: ambush, destruction, and sudden death (e.g., Num 6:9; Josh 11:7; Jer 4:20). One is reminded of Amos exhorting the people of Israel, "Alas for you who desire the day of the LORD! / Why do you want the day of the LORD? / It is darkness, not light" (Amos 5:18). For the corrupt temple establishment, then, the announcement of the LORD's appearing is anything but good news! "For he is like a refiner's fire and like fullers' soap," Malachi says; "he will sit as a refiner and purifier of silver, and he will purify the descendants of Levi and refine them like gold and silver, until they present offerings to the LORD in righteousness" (Mal 3:2b-3; perhaps better translated simply as "right offerings"). The image of the smelting furnace, as this study has already observed (cf. the discussion of Zech 13:9), is typically used in Scripture as a metaphor for trials that make one stronger and one's commitments clearer. The metaphor of launderers and soap is used by Jeremiah as well, who cries, "O Jerusalem, wash your heart clean of wickedness so that you may be saved" (Jer 4:14), but who also uses this same image to underline the people's ineradicable guilt: "Though you wash yourself with lye / and use much soap, / the stain of your guilt is still before me, / says the Lord GOD." In Psalm 51:4 (2), the Psalmist pleads for God to "Wash me thoroughly from my iniquity, / and cleanse me from my sin" (cf. Ps 51:9 [7]). As Malachi also recognizes, only God can cleanse the stain of sin. Once purified and cleansed by God in the coming trials, the priesthood will at last present right offerings to the LORD, restoring Judah and Jerusalem to a right relationship with God (3:4).

As in 2:4-9, Malachi contrasts the lives God intended "the descendants of Levi" to lead with the lifestyle they in fact follow and model for their congregation. In 3:5, God accuses the priests of sorcery (Heb., *kiseph*): an accusation raised against foreign Babylon (Isa 47:9-11) and Nineveh (Nah 3:4), and reminiscent of the strange rites that Trito-Isaiah accuses the priests of practicing (cf. Isa 65:3-5). Otherwise, the offenses detailed in this verse involve right living rather than right worship: coming from the Decalogue (adultery and swearing falsely) and from the prophetic witness elsewhere condemning injustice toward the poor and marginalized (e.g., Zech 7:9-10). Now that God's imminent judgment on these offenses has been announced, no one guilty of the acts of social injustice and false worship described in this verse can claim ignorance as a defense.

Fifth Disputation: "How shall we return?" (3:6-12)

The MT combines the fourth and fifth disputations into a single paragraph. The beginning of the fifth disputation is somewhat vague: the divine statement and question in 3:6-7 are followed not by a response but by yet another question (3:8; note that Sweeney [2000, 739, 742] extends the fourth disputation to 3:7 and begins the fifth at 3:8). Although 3:5 closes with *'amar Yhwh tseba'ot* ("says the LORD of hosts"), a fairly definite marker of the end of a unit, reading across these two units makes the injunction to pay the tithe in 3:6-12 a practical, concrete response to the failure evident in 2:17–3:5.

Having considered what has gone wrong in Judah's worship, Malachi now proposes a way to set things right. First, he observes, there is hope for Judah, since God does not change (Mal 3:6). Indeed, the survival of Israel through the generations has been due to God's faithfulness, despite Israel's faithlessness. If the day of the LORD is to be a blessing rather than a terror, however, circumstances must change: "Return to me, and I will return to you, says the LORD of hosts" (Mal 3:7; cf. Zech 1:3).

In keeping with the pattern this study has witnessed throughout Malachi, this divine statement is followed by a question from the community: "How shall we return?" (Mal 3:7). But instead of answering the question, the prophet seems to introduce another issue: the people are guilty of robbing God by withholding their tithe (Mal 3:8-9). As this theme develops, however, it is clear that this *is* the answer to their question. If the people are serious about returning to God, they must demonstrate that seriousness by a real, tangible commitment of their resources.

The tithe (Heb., *ma'aser*, "one-tenth") is solidly rooted in all of Israel's legal traditions. Leviticus 27:30 declares that "All tithes of the land, whether from the seed of the ground or the fruit of the tree, are the LORD's; they are holy to the LORD." As Malachi also states, the tithe is not a gift to God from the worshiper: it is God's own property. To keep the tithe is to be guilty of theft from God! Numbers 18:21 declares that the tithe is to be given to the Levites, who have no lands of their own (cf. Num 35:1-8; Josh 21:1-42); the stress on the tithe, then, once more reflects the Levitical leanings of our anonymous prophet. Deuteronomy 14:28-29 sets aside the tithe from every third year not only for the Levites but also for the support of widows, orphans, and foreigners living in the land. This trio is frequently mentioned in biblical calls for justice, as these are all persons likely to fall through the cracks of a clan-based culture: the widow, without the support of a husband; the orphan, without parents to safeguard her or his future; the *ger*, or landless foreigner, living in the land without legal protections (e.g., Exod 22:21-24; Deut 10:18-19; Zech 7:10; Mal 3:5). In Malachi's day, failure to pay the tithe would have meant that these needy people were forced into starvation. In our own time, such persons continue to be in jeopardy, particularly the immigrants who cross our borders at great risk, seeking a better life for themselves and their children. Malachi's word to his community speaks prophetically to ours as well: those who truly wish to return to God will care for the least by paying the tithe.

Although Malachi 3:6-12 is not part of the common lectionary, it is probably familiar to many readers as a favorite preaching passage for stewardship sermons. Certainly Malachi's challenge to his audience is an appropriate challenge to contemporary worshipers as well. Genuine faith calls for genuine commitment of our time and resources. Indeed, Malachi declares that God will respond to our generosity with generosity: "put me to the test, says the LORD of hosts; see if I will not open the windows of heaven for you and pour down for you an overflowing blessing" (3:10). We must be careful here: Malachi is certainly not advocating some spiritual get-rich-quick scheme. God will not be reduced to a means to our own ends. Rather, just as Haggai declared that the fertility of the land was inextricably linked to God's presence in the temple (cf. Hag 1:3-11; 2:15-19), so Malachi affirms that only when what belongs to God has been given to God can God's blessings once more be felt in the land.

Sixth Disputation: "What do we profit by keeping his command?" (3:13-21 [3:13–4:3])

The MT divides this unit in two parts, 3:13-18 and 19-21 (4:1-3). Intriguingly, the Christian Old Testament also breaks at this same point, beginning a new chapter. There is some warrant for breaking here: 3:19-21 (4:1-3) presents a description of the day of the LORD as cosmic devastation, strongly reminiscent of Zephaniah 1:2-3, 14-18. In the Revised Common Lectionary, Malachi 3:19-20a (4:1-2a)—the second reading from Malachi in the lectionary (cf. Mal 3:1-4)—is the Old Testament lection for Proper 28 (33) in the season after Pentecost, Year C. Breaking at this point, however, misses the connection with the divine judgment described in 3:16-18, where God distinguishes clearly "between the righteous and the wicked, between one who serves God and one who does not serve him" (3:18). With regard to the final form of Malachi, it is best to keep these depictions of final judgment in Malachi together in a single unit. As we will see, however, the sense of the scribes and of the editors of Christian Scripture that a break occurs after 3:18 may guide the reader into a deeper understanding of Malachi's composition.

After his discussion of paying the tithe as the way back to right relationship with God, Malachi returns to the cynicism of the people. This final disputation begins once more with a divine statement ("You have spoken harsh words against me, says the LORD," 3:13; cf. 2:17), prompting the question, "How have we spoken against you?" The response is scathing. This community, Malachi claims, has said, "It is vain to serve the LORD. What do we profit by keeping his command or by going about as mourners before the LORD of hosts?" (3:14). The word rendered "vain" in the NRSV, Hebrew *shawe'*, is used in the Decalogue in the commandment forbidding misuse of the LORD's name (cf. Exod 20:7; Deut 5:11). These people have no respect for God at all. Apparently, the tithe has not been paid because they have spent the money on themselves—and why not? Why should they do without the finer things—"go about as mourners"—in order to obey the commands of a God they do not honor? Further, the people say, how they live does not seem to matter anymore. Evildoers are not judged, the arrogant prosper, and God does nothing (3:15; cf. 2:17). Why, then, should they even try to do good? These questions concerning God's justice did not originate with Malachi's community and certainly do not end with them. Similar questions were raised by Habakkuk (Hab 1:1-4, 13-17), and are still raised today. In every age, the wicked seem to prosper, while the righteous all too often suffer. What, then, is the point of a life of faith? Where is the profit?

Malachi's answer is, really, no answer at all. Instead, he says, "Then those who revered the LORD spoke with one another" (3:16). The quiet conversation of the faithful, in contrast to the strident questions of the faithless, gains the attention of God, and it is those persons, "who revered the LORD and thought on his name," to whom God responds. How one understands the nature of God's response depends on the translation of Malachi 3:16, and particularly the meaning of the enigmatic "book of remembrance" (Heb., *sepher zikaron*) in this verse.

Many interpreters understand the book of remembrance as a supernatural book (e.g., Exod 32:32-33; Ps 40: 8 [7]; Dan 12:1; cf. Rev 20:12) in which the deeds of the righteous are recorded (e.g., Towner 2006, 1287–88;

Achtemeier 1986, 194–95). There are two other references to a book of remembrance in Scripture, however. The first is mentioned in Exodus 17:14, where following the defeat of Amalek, the LORD instructs Moses, "Write this as a reminder in a book [*zikaron bassepher*]" (cf. Scalise 2009, 359). Here, the book is intended to remind Joshua in the future of Amalek's perfidy. The second is in Esther 6:1, where King Xerxes, having a bout of insomnia, orders that "the book of records" (*sepher hazzikronot*) be read to him. This book is also called "the annals" (Heb., *dibre hayyamim*, literally "the words of the days"; in the Hebrew Bible, this is the title of Chronicles)—likely "a record of events from the king's reign" (Nogalski 2011, 1062). As neither of these books is of heavenly origin, it seems probable that Malachi's, too, is an ordinary book.

Once one recognizes that Malachi's "book of remembrance" is likely an actual book, features of the syntax of this verse, often overlooked, become apparent. The NRSV reads, "a book of remembrance was written before him of those who revered the LORD" (3:16; following *Tg. Neb.*). The Hebrew reads, however, not "of" but "for" (the Hebrew preposition *le*; cf. LXX). In short: God causes a book to be written *for* the faithful (Nogalski 2011, 1062–65). This book will offer them reassurance: "They shall be mine, says the LORD of hosts, my special possession on the day when I act, and I will spare them as parents spare their children who serve them" (Mal 3:17). The book of remembrance will also make very clear, despite the cynicism of Malachi's community, that commitment to God *does* matter, by demonstrating "the difference between the righteous and the wicked, between one who serves God and one who does not serve him" (3:18).

While 3:16-18 is integrated into the final form of the book, the abrupt shift at 3:16, as well as the sense of the Masoretes and of the editors of the Christian Old Testament that there is a break after 3:18, strongly suggest that these verses were not originally part of the book (Nogalski 2011, 1065–66). Indeed, while 3:15 speaks of the arrogant (Heb., *zedim*) and evildoers (*'ose rishah*) escaping any penalty, 3:19 (4:1) pronounces God's punishment upon these very groups: "See, the day is coming, burning like an oven, when all the arrogant [*zedim*] and all evildoers [*'ose rishah*] will be stubble; the day that comes shall burn them up, says the LORD of hosts." Likely, then, the description of the day of the LORD in 3:19-21 (4:1-3) originally followed on 3:15, providing an immediate answer to the question posed. The editors of the Twelve have inserted 3:16-18 to stress that God has caused a book to be written, to provide comfort to the faithful and assurance of God's justice. Quite likely, that book is the Book of the Twelve (with Nogalski 1993b, 206–10; 2011, 1073–75). As was noted in the Introduction to this commentary, ben Sirach declares that the Twelve "comforted the people of Jacob and delivered them with confident hope" (Sir 49:10), which is a fair summation of the purpose for Malachi's "book of remembrance" (Nogalski 1993b, 209). By relating God's faithfulness, for good and ill, from the time of Assyria through the Babylonian exile up to the time of reconstruction under Persian rule, the Twelve provides confidence for the future completion of God's design on the coming day of the LORD.

That day, as described in Malachi 3:19-21 (4:1-3), is not only a day of fiery judgment for the wicked but also a day of renewal and blessing for the faithful, "who revere my name" (3:20 [4:2]; recall the use of *shawe'* in 3:14). The faithful are not only rejuvenated (3:20 [4:2]); they are also called to participate in God's victory: "you shall tread down the wicked, for they will be ashes under the soles of your feet, on the day when I act, says the LORD of hosts" (3:21 [4:3]; cf. Zech 10:3-6; 12:1-9). The LORD is described as "the sun of righteousness," who shall rise "with healing in its [LXX has "his" (cf. KJV), but MT and *Tg. Neb.* have "her," perhaps with reference to "righteousness," which is feminine in Hebrew] wings" (4:2). Christian readers will think immediately of the third stanza of Charles Wesley's 1739 Christmas carol "Hark! the Herald Angels Sing":

> Hail the heav'n-born Prince of Peace!
> Hail the Sun of Righteousness!
> Light and life to all he brings,
> Risen with healing in his wings.

Solar images for the LORD are, as this study has discussed, fairly common in Scripture (cf. the discussion of Zech 6:1-8). The Egyptian sun disc, often combined with a winged scarab, was a widespread symbol in the ancient Middle East, even incorporated into the royal seals of Judean kings (cf. Tushingham 1970 and 1971, Lance 1971). Indeed, a modification of the winged solar disc appears with Persian king Darius's inscription at Behistun, at his palace at Persepolis (cf. Frye 1963, figs. 30 and 67), and above the door of his tomb (Boyce 1984, 290); Richard Frye proposed that it is meant to be an iconographic representation of the Persian god Ahuramazda (Frye 1963). In Malachi, the image represents a positive, beneficent counter to the destructive image of the day of the LORD "burning like an oven" (4:1): the sunrise of that day, representing the coming of the LORD, not only burns but also heals.

Conclusion (3:22-24 [4:4-6])

The Masoretes treat the conclusion as a single paragraph. Many interpreters, however, have recognized two stages in this conclusion. The first, 3:22 (4:4), seems intended as a conclusion not only to Malachi but also to the Prophets as a whole (Mason 1977, 159–60; Childs 1978, 51–52; Nogalski 1993b, 185). In its final form, the *Nebi'im* opens and closes with reference to Moses, the servant of the LORD (cf. Josh 1:7 and Mal 3:22 [4:4]) and to Moses' *Torah* (cf. Josh 1:7 and Mal 3:22 [4:4]; NRSV translates *torah* in the Mal passage as "teaching"). Both the language of this verse, strongly reminiscent of Deuteronomy, and the reference to the mountain where the Law was revealed as Horeb suggest that this verse comes from Levitical circles, likely related to those that informed the anonymous prophet we hear in Malachi.

If the first conclusion to Malachi calls to mind the Law, the second calls to mind the Prophets, in the person of the quintessential prophet Elijah (cf. Zech 13:4). As this study observed above, the second ending to Malachi represents a further development in the role of *malaki* ("my messenger") in Malachi 3:1. As the identification of John the Baptist with Elijah demonstrates (the discussion of Mal 3:1, above), the notion of Elijah as forerunner of the Messiah, likely derived from Malachi, is quite old. Doubtless influenced by this passage, Jewish tradition came to regard Elijah as continuing to visit the earth and teach (e.g., *b Shab* 13a and b; *b 'Eruv* 43b; *b Sanh* 113a). Still today, whenever the Passover is celebrated, a cup of wine is poured for Elijah, a door is opened, and the family stands, prepared to welcome him as a guest. Whenever the ritual of circumcision (*bris*) is performed, a chair is placed and left empty for Elijah.

In Malachi 3:23-24 (4:5-6), however, Elijah comes not to prepare the way for the Messiah but to prepare the community for "the great and terrible day of the LORD" (3:23 [4:5]). He does this by teaching and persuasion, much as "Malachi" has done throughout this book. Just as the second and third disputations began with familial imagery (cf. Mal 1:6; 2:10), so the book ends by describing Elijah's mission as one of reconciling families: "He will turn the hearts of parents to their children and the hearts of children to their parents" (3:24 [4:6]; the Hebrew has literally, "the heart of fathers to sons and the heart of sons to their fathers").

The book ends with a stern warning: should there be no reconciliation, God will come "and strike the land with a curse" (3:24 [4:6]). The Hebrew word rendered "curse" in the NRSV is *kherem*, or the ban—often connected elsewhere with holy war, where the enemy is utterly destroyed as a kind of whole offering to God (1 Kgs 20:28; Jer 6:11). But this cannot be the intention of *kherem* everywhere that the term appears. For example, Deut

7:2 orders that the inhabitants of the land be *hakharem takharim*, that is, "certainly (or completely) placed under the ban" (the NRSV reads "utterly destroyed"), yet Deut 7:3 forbids intermarriage—difficult to understand if the intent of the text is genocide (cf. Creach 2013, 108)! Drawing on Origen's allegorical reading of the ban as depicting the believer's spiritual struggle with sin ("within us are the Canaanites; within us are the Perizzites; here [within] are the Jebusites," *Hom. Josh.*, 34; cited in Creach 2013, 102), Jerome Creach suggests that *kherem* came to be sublimated or spiritualized, so that what had once been a "reprehensible practice . . . close to 'ethnic cleansing,' was transformed into a metaphor of spiritual purity" (Creach 2013, 108). Perhaps in the conclusion of Malachi as well, the ban is a metaphor for spiritual purgation. While in Malachi 3:19 (4:1), the fires of the day of the LORD seem purely destructive to "the arrogant and all evildoers," in Malachi 3:2-4, they are fires of purgation, intended to "purify the descendants of Levi" (3:3). Similarly, in Zechariah 14:16-19 the nations that had seemed to be utterly destroyed somehow turn up in the world to come as guests at the Feast of Booths. Ehud ben Zvi notes that in Jewish liturgy, when Malachi is read, 3:23 (4:5) is repeated at the end of the book, "so as to conclude the public reading on a strong, hopeful note, rather than the threat of the final phrase" (ben Zvi 2004, 1274). Perhaps this custom grasps the true intent both of Malachi and of the Book of the Twelve as a whole. God comes in the end, not to curse but to bless.

Bibliography

Achtemeier, Elizabeth. 1986. *Nahum–Malachi.* IBC. Louisville: John Knox.

———. 1996. *Minor Prophets I.* NIBCOT 17. Peabody MA: Hendrickson.

Ackroyd, Peter. 1952. "The Book of Haggai and Zechariah I-VIII," *JJS* 3:155–56.

———. 1996. "Haggai, the Book of." In *HBD*, 396–97.

Albertz, Rainer. 2003. "Exile as Purification: Reconstructing the 'Book of the Four.'" In *Thematic Threads in the Book of the Twelve*, 232–251. BZAW 325. Berlin: De Gruyter.

Albright, William Foxwell. 1950. "The Psalm of Habakkuk." In *Studies in Old Testament Prophecy*, 1–18. Ed. H. H. Rowley. Edinburgh: T. & T. Clark.

Andersen, Francis I. 2001. *Habakkuk.* AB 25. New York: Doubleday.

Andersen, Francis I. and David Noel Freedman. 1988. *Amos.* AB 24a. New York: Doubleday.

Barth, Karl. 2002. *Prayer.* 50th anniversary edition. Ed. Don E. Saliers; trans. Sara F. Terrien. Louisville: Westminster John Knox.

Bass, Diana Butler. 2012. *Christianity After Religion: The End of Church and the Birth of a New Spiritual Awakening.* New York: HarperOne.

Bell, Rob. 2011. *Love Wins: A Book about Heaven, Hell, and the Fate of Every Person Who Ever Lived.* New York: HarperOne.

ben Zvi, Ehud. 1991. *A Historical-Critical Study of the Book of Zephaniah.* BZAW 198. Berlin: de Gruyter.

———. 1996. "Twelve Prophetic Books or 'The Twelve': A Few Preliminary Considerations." In *Forming Prophetic Literature: Essays on Isaiah and the Twelve in Honor of John D. W. Watts*, 125–56. JSOTSup 235. Sheffield: Sheffield Academic.

———. 2004. "Introduction and Footnotes to Malachi." In *JSB*, 1268–74.

Bennett, Robert. 1996. "The Book of Zephaniah: Introduction, Commentary, and Reflections." *NIB* 7, 657–704.

Berlin, Adele. 1994. *Zephaniah.* AB 25a. New York: Doubleday.

Beuken, W. A. M. 1967. *Haggai-Sacharia 1–8: Studien zur Überlieferungsgeschichte der Frühnachexilischen Prophetie.* Assen: Van Gorcum.

Biddle, Mark E. 1991. "The Figure of Lady Jerusalem: Identification, Deification, and Personification of Cities in the Ancient Near East." In *The Biblical Canon in Comparative Perspective: Scripture in Context IV*, 173–94. ANETS 11. Lewiston: Mellen.

Blenkinsopp, Joseph. 1987. "The Mission of Udjahorresnet and Those of Ezra and Nehemiah." *JBL* 106:409–21.

Block, Daniel. 1998. *The Book of Ezekiel: Chapters 25–48.* NICOT. Grand Rapids MI: Eerdmans.

Boda, Mark. 2008. "*Hoy, hoy*: The Prophetic Origins of the Babylonian Tradition in Zechariah 2:10-17." In *Tradition in Transition: Haggai and Zechariah 1–8 in the Trajectory of Hebrew Theology*, 171–90. New York: T & T Clark.

Boyce, Mary. 1984. "Persian Religion in the Achemenid Age." In *CHJ* 1, 279–307. Cambridge: Cambridge University.

Brettler, Marc Zvi. 2004. "Introduction to Nevi'im." In *JSB*, 451–61.

Brown, William P. 1996. *Obadiah through Malachi.* WBC. Louisville: Westminster John Knox.

Bucur, Bogdan G. and Elijah N. Mueller. 2011. "Gregory Nazianzen's Reading of Habakkuk 3:2 and Its Reception: A Lesson from Byzantine Scripture Exegesis." *Pro Ecclesia* 20:86–103.

Budde, Karl. 1921. "Eine folgenschwere Redaktion des Zwölfprophetenbuchs." *ZAW* 39:218–29.

Carr, David M. 1996. *Reading the Fractures of Genesis: Historical and Literary Approaches.* Louisville: Westminster John Knox.

———. 2005. *Writing on the Tablet of the Heart: Origins of Scripture and Literature.* Oxford: Oxford University.

Childs, Brevard S. 1978. "The Canonical Shape of the Prophetic Literature." *Int* 32:46–55.

———. 1979. *Introduction to the Old Testament as Scripture.* Philadelphia: Fortress Press.

Christensen, Duane L. 1986. "Josephus and the Twenty-Two Book Canon of Sacred Scripture," *JETS* 29:37–46.

———. 1996. "Nahum, the Book of." In *HBD*, 731–32.

———. 2009. *Nahum.* AB 24f. New Haven: Yale University.

Cook, Stephen L. 1995. *Prophecy and Apocalypticism: The Postexilic Social Setting.* Minneapolis: Fortress.

———. 2003. *The Apocalyptic Literature.* IBT. Nashville: Abingdon.

———. 2010. "Haggai," "Zechariah," and "Malachi" in *The New Interpreter's Bible One-Volume Commentary*, ed. Beverly Roberts Gaventa and David Peterson, 529–39. Nashville: Abingdon.

———. 2011. "Haggai," "Zechariah," and "Malachi," in *The Oxford Encyclopedia of the Books of the Bible* 1, 357–61; 2, 34–41; 465–71. New York: Oxford University.

Cooperman, Alan et al. 2015. "America's Changing Religious Landscape: Christians Decline Sharply as Share of Population; Unaffiliated and Other Faiths Continue to Grow." *The Pew Forum on Religion and Public Life.* http://www.pewforum.org/files/2015/05/RLS-08-26-full-report.pdf.

Cowley, Arthur. 1923. *Aramaic Papyri of the Fifth Century B.C.* Oxford: Clarendon.

Clements, R. E. 1986. "The Chronology of Redaction in Ezekiel 1–24." In *Ezekiel and His Book: Textual and Literary Criticism and their Interrelation.* BETL 74. Leuven: Leuven University.

Creach, Jerome. 2013. *Violence in Scripture.* IRUSC. Louisville: Westminster John Knox.

Crenshaw, James L. 1998. *Old Testament Wisdom: An Introduction*, Revised and Enlarged. Louisville: Westminster John Knox.

Cross, Frank Moore. 1975. "A Reconstruction of the Judean Restoration." *Int* 29:187–201.

———. 1973. *Canaanite Myth and Hebrew Epic.* Cambridge: Harvard University.

Dahood, Mitchell. 1965. *Psalms I: 1–50.* AB 16. Garden City NY: Doubleday.

Davis, Ellen. 1989. *Swallowing the Scroll: Textuality and the Dynamics of Discourse in Ezekiel's Prophecy.* JSOTSup 78. Sheffield: Almond.

———. 2014. "Abraham and the Origins of Intercessory Prayer." 2014 Schaff Lectures, Pittsburgh Theological Seminary, Pittsburgh.

del Olmo Lete, G. 1999. "DEBER." In *DDD*, 231–32. Leiden: Brill.

Delitzsch, Franz. 1873. *Biblical Commentary on the Psalms.* CFTL 4:29. Edinburgh: T. & T. Clark.

De Roche, Michael. 1980. "Zephaniah 1:2-3: The 'Sweeping' of Creation." *VT* 30:104–109.

Dick, Michael B. 2006. "The Neo-Assyrian Royal Lion Hunt and Yahweh's Answer to Job." *JBL* 125:243–70.

Duguid, Iain. 1994. *Ezekiel and the Leaders of Israel.* VTSup 56; Leiden: Brill.

Duhm, Bernhard.1906. *Das Buch Habakuk: Text, übersetzung und erklärung.* Tübingen: J. C. B. Mohr.

Dunn, James D. G. 1988. *Romans 1–8.* WBC 38A. Dallas: Word.

Durlesser, Jim. 1995. "A Study of Apocalyptic Literature in the Old Testament." In *Approaching the New Millennium: Student Book*, 33–38. Nashville: United Methodist Publishing House.

Ego, Beate. 2003. "The Repentance of Nineveh in the Story of Jonah and Nahum's Prophecy of the City's Destruction—A Coherent Reading of the Book of the Twelve as Reflected in the Aggadah." In *Thematic Threads in the Book of the Twelve*, 155–64. BZAW 325; Berlin: de Gruyter.

Eichrodt, Walther. 1970. *Ezekiel.* Trans. Cosslett Quin. OTL. Philadelphia: Westminster.

Eliade, Mircae. 1974. *The Myth of the Eternal Return, or Cosmos and History.* Princeton: Princeton University.

Fabry, Heinz-Josef. 2006. *Nahum*. HTKAT. Freiburg: Herder.

Ferreiro, Alberto, ed. 2003. *The Twelve Prophets. ACCS* 14. Downers Grove IL: Intervarsity.

Fitzgerald, Aloysius. 1972. "The Mythological Background for the Presentation of Jerusalem as a Queen and False Worship as Adultery in the OT." *CBQ* 34:403–16.

Floyd, Michael H. 1994. "The Chimerical Acrostic of Nahum 1:2-10." *JBL* 113:421–37.

———. 2000. *The Minor Prophets, Part 2*. FOTL 22. Grand Rapids, MI: Eerdmans.

———. 2002. "The *massa'* as a Type of Prophetic Book." *JBL* 121:401–22.

Freedman, David N. 1961. "The Chronicler's Purpose," *CBQ* 23:436–42.

Friebel, Kelvin G. 1999. *Jeremiah's and Ezekiel's Sign-Acts: Rhetorical Nonverbal Communication*. JSOTSup 283. Sheffield: Sheffield Academic.

Frye, Northrop. 1982. *The Great Code: The Bible and Literature*. San Diego: Harcourt Brace Jovanovich.

Frye, Richard N. 1963. *The Heritage of Persia*. New York: The New American Library.

Fuller, Russell E. 1997. "The Twelve." In *DJD* 15. 10, 221–318; Plates 76–82. Oxford: Clarendon.

García-Treto, Francisco O. 1996. "The Book of Nahum: Introduction, Commentary, and Reflections." In *NIB* 7, 591–619.

Gelston, Anthony, ed. 2010. *Biblia Hebraica Quinta, Fascicle 13: The Twelve Minor Prophets*. Stuttgart: Deutsche Bibleschaft.

Gevaryahu, Haim M. I. 1975. "Biblical Colophons: A Source for the 'Biography' of Authors, Texts, and Books." In *Congress Volume: Edinburgh 1974*, 42–59. Ed. G. W. Anderson et al. *VTSup* 28. Leiden: E. J. Brill.

Gifford, Paul. 2007. "Expecting Miracles: The Prosperity Gospel in Africa." In *Christian Century*. http://www.christiancentury.org/article/2007-07/expecting-miracles-0.

Goldingay, John and Pamela J. Scalise. 2009. *Minor Prophets II*. NIBCOT 18. Peabody MA: Hendrickson.

Good, Edwin M. 1959. "The Barberini Greek Version of Habakkuk III." *VT* 9:11–30.

Goodenough, Erwin R. 1953–68. *Jewish Symbols in the Greco-Roman Period.* Bollingen 37. Princeton: Princeton University.

Gowan, Donald E. 1976. *The Triumph of Faith in Habakkuk.* Atlanta: John Knox Press.

Grayson, A. Kirk. 1975. *Assyrian and Babylonian Chronicles.* TCS. Locust Valley NY: Augustin.

Greenberg, Moshe. 1984. "The Design and Themes of Ezekiel's Program of Restoration." *Int* 38:181–208.

Greenfield, J. C. 1999. "HADAD." In *DDD,* 377–82.

Gunkel, Hermann. 1895. *Schöpfung und Chaos in Urzeit und Endzeit: eine religionsgeschichtliche Untersuchung über Gen 1 und Ap Joh 12.* Göttingen: Vandenhoeck und Ruprecht.

———. 1906. "Die israelitische Literatur." In *Die orientalischen Literaturen.* Ed. Erich Schmidt et al. Die Kultur der Gegenwart 1, 7. Berlin: B. G. Teubner.

Haak, Robert D. 1992. *Habakkuk. VTSup* 44. Leiden: E. J. Brill.

Hahn, Scott W. 2012. *The Kingdom of God as Liturgical Empire: A Theological Commentary on 1–2 Chronicles.* Grand Rapids MI: Baker.

Hallaschka, Martin. 2010. *Haggai und Sacharja 1–8: Eine redaktionsgeschichtliche Untersuchung.* BZAW 411. Berlin: de Gruyter.

Hanson, Paul. 1976a. "Apocalypticism." In *IDBSup.*

———. 1976b. "Zechariah, Book of." In *IDBSup.*

———. 1979. *The Dawn of Apocalyptic: The Historical and Sociological Roots of Jewish Apocalyptic Eschatology.* Philadelphia: Fortress.

———. 1996. "Zechariah, Book of." In *HBD,* 1239–40.

———. 2000. "Malachi." In *HBC,* 683–86.

Hays, Richard B. 2002. *The Faith of Jesus Christ: The Narrative Substructure of Galatians 3:1–4:11.* 2nd ed. Grand Rapids: Eerdmans.

Heschel, Abraham. 1975. *The Prophets,* Volume 2. New York, Harper and Row (reprint of *The Prophets.* New York: Harper and Row, 1962).

Hiebert, Theodore. 1986. *God of My Victory: The Ancient Hymn in Habakkuk 3*. HSM 38. Atlanta: Scholars.

———. 1996. "The Book of Habakkuk: Introduction, Commentary, and Reflections." *NIB* 7, 622–55.

Hill, Robert Charles, ed. 2006. *Theodoret of Cyrus: Commentary on the Twelve Prophets*. Brookline: Holy Cross.

Holladay, John S. 1970. "Assyrian Statecraft and the Prophets of Israel." *HTR* 634:29–51.

Horn, Siegfried and P. Kyle McCarter. 1999. "The Divided Monarchy: The Kingdoms of Israel and Judah." In *Ancient Israel*. Washington, D.C.: Biblical Archaeology Society.

House, Paul R. 1990. *The Unity of the Book of the Twelve*. JSOTSup 97; Bible and Lit Series 27. Decatur GA: Almond.

Hurowitz, Victor. 2003. "The Mesopotamian God Image, from Womb to Tomb," *JAOS* 123:147–57.

Hurvitz, Avi. 1982. *A Linguistic Study of the Relationship between the Priestly Source and the Book of Ezekiel: A New Approach to an Old Problem*. CahRB 20. Paris: J. Gabalda.

Japhet, Sara. 1993. *I & II Chronicles*. OTL. Louisville: Westminster/John Knox.

Jeremias, Jörg. 1970. *Kultprophetie und Gerichtsverkündigung in der späten Königszeit Israels*. WMANT 35. Neukirchen-Vluyn: Neukirchener Verlag.

Jewett, Robert. 2007. *Romans*. Hermeneia. Minneapolis: Fortress.

Jones, Barry Alan. 1995. *The Formation of the Book of the Twelve: A Study in Text and Canon*. SBLDS 149. Atlanta: Scholars.

Kamrat, Yural. 2007. "Nineveh, History." In *EncJud* 15, 271. Jerusalem: Keter.

Kent, Roland. 1934. "More Old Persian Inscriptions." *JAOS* 54:34–52.

Klostermann, August. 1896. *Geschichte des Volkes Israel bis zur Restauration unter Esra und Nehemia*. München: C. H. Beck.

Knoppers, Gary N. 2004. *I Chronicles 10–29*. AB 12a. New York: Doubleday.

Koch, Klaus. 1987. "Is Daniel Also Among the Prophets?" In *Interpreting the Prophets*, 237–48. Philadelphia: Fortress.

Konkel, Michael. 2001. *Architektonik des Heiligen: Studien zur zweiten Templelvision Ezechiels [Ez 40–48]*. BBB 129. Bodenheim: Philo.

LaCocque, André. 1998. "*Et aspicient ad me quem confixerunt*." In *Thinking Biblically: Exegetical and Hermeneutical Studies*, 401–21. Chicago: University of Chicago.

Lance, H. Darrell. 1971. "The Royal Stamps and the Kingdom of Josiah." *HTR* 64:315–32.

Levenson, Jon. 1984. "The Temple and the World." *JR* 64:275–98.

Lewis, C. S. 1960. *The Screwtape Letters*. New York: Macmillan.

———. 1962, 1976. *The Problem of Pain*. New York: Macmillan.

Lichtheim, Miriam. 1973–80. *Ancient Egyptian Literature*. Berkeley: University of California.

Limburg, James. 1988. *Hosea–Micah*. IBC. Atlanta: John Knox.

Lugo, Luis et al. 2012. "'Nones' on the Rise: One-in-Five Adults Have No Religious Affiliation." *The Pew Forum on Religion and Public Life*. http://www.pewforum.org/uploadedFiles/Topics/Religious_Affiliation/Unaffiliated/NonesOnTheRise-full.pdf.

McBride, S. Dean. 1973. "The Yoke of the Kingdom: An Exposition of Deuteronomy 6:4–5," *Int* 27:273–306.

———. 2000. "Biblical Literature In Its Historical Context: The Old Testament." In *HBC*, 28–38.

———. 2009. "Jeremiah and the Levitical Priests of Anathoth." In *Thus Says the Lord: Essays on the Former and Latter Prophets in Honor of Robert R. Wilson*, 179–96. LHB/OTS 502. London: T. & T. Clark.

———. 2014. "The Name Above All Others: Denominating Divine Providence and Presence in Biblical Traditions." 2014 Sprunt Lectures. Union Presbyterian Seminary, Richmond.

Masalha, Nur. 2009. "60 Years after the Nakba: Historical Truth, Collective Memory and Ethical Obligations." *Kyoto Bulletin of Islamic Area Studies* 3–1:37–88.

Mason, Rex. 1977. *The Books of Haggai, Zechariah and Malachi*. Cambridge: Cambridge University.

———. 2003. "The Use of Earlier Biblical Material in Zechariah 9–14: A Study in Inner Biblical Exegesis." In *Bringing Out the Treasure: Inner Biblical Allusion in Zechariah 9–14*, 2–208. JSOTSup 370. New York: Sheffield Academic.

Mazar, Benjamin. 1957. "The Tobiads." *IEJ* 7: 137–45; 229–38.

Meek, Theophile. 1969. "The Code of Hammurabi." In *ANET*, 163–80. Princeton: Princeton University.

Mettinger, Tryggve N. D. 1982. *The Dethronement of Sabaoth: Studies in the Shem and Kabod Theologies.* ConBOT 18. Lund: C. W. K. Gleerup.

Meyers, Carol L. 2014. "Was Ancient Israel a Patriarchal Society?" *JBL* 133:8–27.

Meyers, Carol L. and Eric M. 1987. *Haggai, Zechariah 1–8.* AB 25b. Garden City NY: Doubleday.

———. 1993. *Zechariah 9–14.* AB 25c. Garden City NY: Doubleday.

Meyers, Eric M. 1987. "The Persian Period and the Judean Restoration: From Zerubbabel to Nehemiah." In *Ancient Israelite Religion*, 509–21. Philadelphia: Fortress.

Miles, Jack. 1995. *God: A Biography.* New York: Knopf.

Mitchell, Christine. 2014. "A Note on the Creation Formula in Zech 12:1-8; Isa 42:5-6; and Old Persian Inscriptions." *JBL* 133:305–308.

Negev, Avraham, ed. 1986. *The Archaeological Encyclopedia of the Holy Land.* New York: Thomas Nelson.

Neihr, Herbert. 1999. "HOST OF HEAVEN." In *DDD*, 428–30.

Newport, Frank. 2013. "Most Americans Say Religion Is Losing Influence in U.S." *Gallup.com.* http://www.gallup.com/poll/162803/americans-say-religion-losing-influence.aspx.

Nogalski, James. 1993a. *Literary Precursors of the Book of the Twelve.* BZAW 217. Berlin: de Gruyter.

———. 1993b. *Redactional Processes in the Book of the Twelve.* BZAW 218. Berlin: de Gruyter.

———. 2003. "The Day(s) of YHWH in the Book of the Twelve." In *Thematic Threads*, 192–213.

———. 2011a. *The Book of the Twelve: Hosea–Jonah*. SHBC. Macon GA: Smyth & Helwys.

———. 2011b. *The Book of the Twelve: Micah–Malachi*. SHBC. Macon GA: Smyth & Helwys.

O'Brien, Julia. 1990. *Priest and Levite in Malachi*. SBLDS 121. Atlanta: Scholars.

———. 2004. *Nahum, Habakkuk, Zephaniah, Haggai, Zechariah, Malachi*. AOTC. Nashville: Abingdon.

———. 2007. "Nahum-Habakkuk-Zephaniah: Reading the 'Former Prophets' in the Persian Period." *Int* 61:168–83.

Odell, Margaret S. 2000. "Zephaniah." In *HBC*, 671–74.

———. 2005. *Ezekiel*. SHBC. Macon GA: Smyth & Helwys.

Oppenheim, A. Leo. 1969. "Babylonian and Assyrian Historical Texts." In *ANET*, 265–318.

Orelli, Conrad von. 1893. *The Twelve Minor Prophets*. Edinburgh: T. & T. Clark.

Outler, Albert C. 1964. *John Wesley*. LPT. New York: Oxford University.

Pajunen, Mika S. and Hanne von Weissenberg. 2015. "The Book of Malachi, Manuscript 4Q76 (4QXII), and the Formation of the 'Book of the Twelve.'" *JBL* 134: 731–51.

Parker, Theodore. 1879. "Of Justice and the Conscience." In *The Collected Works of Theodore Parker* 2, 37–57. London: Trubner.

Patton, Corrine. 2000. "'Should Our Sister Be Treated Like a Whore?' A Response to Feminist Critiques of Ezekiel 23." In *The Book of Ezekiel: Theological and Anthropological Perspectives*, 221–38. SBLSymS. Atlanta: Society of Biblical Literature.

Perdue, Leo G. and Robert Wilson. 2006. "Introduction and Notes on Jeremiah." In *HSB*, 998–1084.

Perry, Alex. 2010. "Retiring from Public Life, Desmond Tutu Reflects on Good and Evil." *Time.com*. http://www.time.com/time/world/article/0,8599,2023562,00.html#ixzz18gMfN9xL.

Petersen, David L. 1984. *Haggai and Zechariah 1–8*. OTL. Philadelphia: Westminster.

———. 1995. *Zechariah 9–14 and Malachi.* OTL. Louisville: Westminster John Knox.

———. 2000. "Zechariah," *HBC*, 677–82.

Polzin, Robert. 1976. *Late Biblical Hebrew: Toward an Historical Typology of Biblical Hebrew Prose.* HSM 12. Missoula MT: Scholars.

Puech, Emile. 1999. "MILCOM." In *DDD*, 575–76.

Redditt, Paul L. 1992. "Zerubbabel, Joshua, and the Night Visions of Zechariah." *CBQ* 54:249–59.

———. 1995. *Haggai, Zechariah and Malachi.* Grand Rapids MI: Eerdmans.

———. 2008a. *Introduction to the Prophets.* Grand Rapids MI: Eerdmans.

———. 2008b. "The King in Haggai–Zechariah 1–8 and the Book of the Twelve." In *Tradition in Transition,* 56–82. New York: T & T Clark.

Rendtorff, Rolf. 2000. "How to Read the Book of the Twelve as a Theological Unity." In *Reading and Hearing the Book of the Twelve*, 75–87. SBLSymS 15. Atlanta: Society of Biblical Literature.

Renz, Thomas. 2009. "A Perfectly Broken Acrostic in Nahum 1?" *JHebS* 9:2–26.

Richards, Kent Harold. 2006. "Introduction and Notes on Habakkuk." *HSB*, 1254–58.

Roberts, J.J.M. 1979. "A Christian Perspective on Prophetic Prediction." *Int* 33: 240–53.

———. 1991. *Nahum, Habakkuk, and Zephaniah.* OTL. Louisville: Westminster/John Knox.

———. 2005. "Bearers of the Polity: Isaiah of Jerusalem's View of the Eighth-Century Judean Society." In *Constituting the Community: Studies on the Polity of Ancient Israel in Honor of S. Dean McBride, Jr.*, 145–52. Winona Lake IN: Eisenbrauns.

Roberston, O. Palmer. 1990. *The Books of Nahum, Habakkuk, and Zephaniah.* NICOT. Grand Rapids MI: Eerdmans.

Rom-Shiloni, Dalit. 2005. "Ezekiel as the Voice of the Exiles and Constructor of Exilic Ideology," *HUCA* 76:1–46.

Roof, Wade Clark. 1993. *A Generation of Seekers: The Spiritual Journeys of the Baby Boom Generation.* San Francisco: HarperSan Francisco.

Roux, Georges. 1980. *Ancient Iraq.* Harmondsworth: Penguin.

Rudolph, Wilhelm. 1975. *Micha-Nahum-Habakuk-Zephanja.* KAT 13.3. Gütersloh: Gütersloher Verlagshaus Gerd Mohn.

Sabottka, Liuder. 1972. *Zephanja: Versucht einer Neuübersetung mit philologischem Kommentar.* BibOr 25. Rome: Biblical Institute.

Sacks, Oliver. 1970. *Migraine: The Evolution of a Common Disorder.* Berkeley: University of California.

———. 2012. *Hallucinations.* New York: Knopf.

Sasson, Jack M. 1990. *Jonah.* AB 24b. New York: Doubleday.

Schart, Aaron. 1998. *Die Entstehung des Zwölfprophetenbuchs: Neubearbeietungen von Amos im Rahmen schriftenübergreifender Redaktionsprozesse.* BZAW 260. Berlin: de Gruyter.

Schniedewind, William M. 1995. *The Word of God in Transition: From Prophet to Exegete in the Second Temple Period.* JSOTSup 197. Sheffield: Sheffield Academic.

———. 2004. *How the Bible Became a Book: The Textualization of Ancient Israel.* Cambridge: Cambridge University.

Schuller, Eileen. 1996. "Malachi." In *NIB* 7, 841–77.

Seifrid, Mark A. 2007. "Romans." In *Commentary of the New Testament Use of the Old Testament,* 607–94. Eds. G. K. Beale and D. A. Carson. Grand Rapids MI: Baker.

Sellin, Ernst. 1930. *Das Zwölfprophetenbuch überstetz und eklärt.* Second and third revised edition, Zweite Hälfte: *Nahum-Maleachi.* KAT. Leipzig: A. Deichersche.

Setel, T. Drorah. 1985. "Prophets and Pornography: Female Sexual Imagery in Hosea." In *Feminist Interpretation of the Bible,* 86–95. Philadelphia: Westminster.

Seux, Marie-Joseph. 1981. "Shiggayon=shigu?" *In Mélanges bibliques et orietaux en l'honneur de M. Henri Cazelles,* 419–38. Ed. A. Caquot and M. Delcor, AOAT 12. Neukirchen-Vluyn: Butzton and Bercker Kevelaer.

Shuler, Philip L. 1996. "Zechariah." In *HBD,* 1238–39.

Skehan, Patrick William. 1965. "Broken Acrostic and Psalm 9." *CBQ* 27:1–5.

Smith, Mark S. 1990. *The Early History of God.* San Francisco: HarperCollins.

Smith-Christopher, Daniel. 1996. "The Additions to Daniel." In *NIB* 7, 155–94.

———. 2005. "Ezekiel in Abu Ghraib: Rereading Ezekiel 16:37–39 in the Context of Imperial Conquest." In *Ezekiel's Hierarchical World: Wrestling with a Tiered Reality*, 141–57. SBLSymS 20. Atlanta: Society of Biblical Literature.

Soll, Will. 1992. "Acrostic." In *ABD* 1, 58–60.

Sommer, Benjamin D. 1996. "Did Prophecy Cease? Evaluating a Reevaluation." *JBL* 115:31–47.

Speiser, E. A. 1969. "Epic of Gilgamesh." In *ANET*, 72–98.

Spiegelberg, Wilhelm. 1914. *Die sogenannte demotische Chronik des Pap. 215 der Bibliotheque Nationale zu Paris, nebst den auf der Ruckseite des Papyrus stehenden Texten.* Demotische Studien 7. Leipzig.

Spronk, Klaas. 1997. *Nahum.* HCOT. Kampen: Kok Pharos.

Stager, Lawrence E. 1991. "When Caananites and Philistines Ruled Ashkelon." *BAR* 17:24–37, 40–43.

Steck, Odil. 1989. "Tritojesaja im Jesajabuch," in *Le livre d'Isaïe: les oracles et leurs relectures unité et complexité de l'ouvrage.* BETL 81. Louvain: Leuven University.

———. 1991. *Der Abschluß der Prophetie im Alten Testament: Ein Versuch zur Frage der Vorgeschichte des Kanons.* B-TS 17. Neukirchen-Vluyn: Neukirchener Verlag.

Stern, Ephraim. 1982. *Material Culture in the Land of the Bible in the Persian Period 538–332.* Warminster: Aris and Phillips.

Suchocki, Marjorie. 2008. "A Plain Account of a Plain Account (of Christian Perfection): Perfection of Prayer and Persistence of Grace." 2008 Albright-Deering Lectures, Pittsburgh Theological Seminary, Pittsburgh.

Sweeney, Marvin. 2000. *The Twelve Prophets* 2. Berit Olam; Collegeville MN: Liturgical Press.

———. 2003a. *The Prophetic Literature.* IBT. Nashville: Abingdon.

———. 2003b. *Zephaniah.* Hermeneia. Minneapolis: Fortress.

Sykes, Seth. 2002. *Time and Space in Haggai–Zechariah 1–8: A Bakhtinian Analysis of a Prophetic Chronicle.* Studies in Biblical Literature 24. New York: Peter Lang.

Tappy, Ron, Marilyn Lundberg, P. Kyle McCarter, and Bruce Zuckerman. 2006. "An Abecedary of the Mid-Tenth Century B.C.E. from the Judaean Shephelah." *BASOR* 344:5–46.

Teresa, Mother. 2007. *Come Be My Light: The Private Writings of the "Saint of Calcutta."* Ed. Brian Kolodiejchuk. New York: Doubleday.

Timmer, Daniel C. 2010. "God and Nineveh, Jonah and Nahum: Odd Pairs and Coherence in the Twelve." Presented to the Society of Biblical Literature, Atlanta, GA.

Towner, W. Sibley. 2006. "Introduction and Footnotes to Zechariah" and "Introduction and Footnotes to Malachi." In *HSB*, 1269–83; 1284–88.

Trible, Phyllis. 1996. "The Book of Jonah: Introduction, Commentary, and Reflections." In *NIB* 7, 462–529.

Tuell, Steven S. 1991. "The Southern and Eastern Borders of Abar-Nahara." *BASOR* 284:51–57.

———. 1992. *The Law of the Temple in Ezekiel 40–48.* HSM 49; Atlanta: Scholars.

———. 2000. "The Rivers of Paradise: Ezek 47:1-12 and Gen 2:10-14," in *God Who Creates: Essays in Honor of W. Sibley Towner,* 171–89. Grand Rapids MI: Eerdmans.

———. 2001. *1 and 2 Chronicles.* IBC. Louisville: Westminster-John Knox.

———. 2003. "Haggai–Zechariah: Prophecy After the Manner of Ezekiel," in *Thematic Threads,* 273–91.

———. 2005. "The Priesthood of the 'Foreigner': Evidence of Competing Polities in Ezekiel 44:1-14 and Isaiah 56:1-8." In *Constituting the Community: Studies on the Polity of Ancient Israel in Honor of S. Dean McBride, Jr.,* 183–204. Winona Lake IN: Eisenbrauns.

———. 2011. "The Meaning of the Mark: New Light on Ezekiel 9 from the History of Interpretation." In *After Ezekiel: Essays on the Reception of a Difficult Prophet*, eds. Paul Joyce and Andrew Mein, 185–202. LHB/OTS 535. London: T&T Clark.

———. 2012. *Ezekiel*. UBC. Grand Rapids MI: Baker, (orig. NIBCOT 16; Peabody MA: Hendrickson, 2009).

Tushingham, A. Douglas. 1970–71. "A Royal Israelite Seal (?) and the Royal Jar Handle Stamps." *BASOR* 200:71–78 and 201:23–35.

Ussishkin, David. 1982. *The Conquest of Lachish by Sennacherib*. Tel Aviv: Institute of Archaeology.

Vanderhooft, David S. 2010. "The *tokakhat*, 'disputation,' of Habakkuk as a Contrarian Argument in the Book of the Twelve." Presented to the Society of Biblical Literature, Atlanta, GA.

Vanderkam, James. 2006. "Calendar." In *NIBD* 1.

Van Dijk-Hemmes, Fokkelien. 1996. "The Metaphorization of Woman in Prophetic Speech: An Analysis of Ezekiel 23." In *On Gendering Texts: Female and Male Voices in the Hebrew Bible*, 167–76. Leiden: Brill.

Vermes, Geza. 1995. *The Dead Sea Scrolls in English*, 4th ed. London: Penguin.

———. 2000. *An Introduction to the Complete Dead Sea Scrolls*. Minneapolis: Fortress.

Wallace, Charles Jr. 1997. *Susanna Wesley: The Complete Writings*. New York: Oxford University.

Waltke, Bruce K. 1991. "Superscripts, Postcripts, or Both." *JBL* 110: 583–96.

Watts, John D. W. 2000a. "Superscriptions and Incipits in the Book of the Twelve." In *Reading and Hearing*, 110–24.

———. 2000b. "A Frame for the Book of the Twelve: Hosea 1–3 and Malachi," in *Reading and Hearing*, 209–17.

Weis, Richard D. 1992. "Oracle." In *ABD* 5, 28–29.

Weissbach, Franz Heinrich. 1911. *Die Keilinschriften der Achämeniden*. VAB 3. Leipzig: J. C. Hinrichs.

Wesley, John. 1777. *A Plain Account of Christian Perfection.* Foundations of Faith. Orlando: Relevant, 2006 (original 1725; final revision 1777).

Wessels, Wilhelm J. 1998. "Nahum, An Uneasy Expression of Yahweh's Power." *OTE* 11: 615–28.

Williamson, H. G. M. 1982. *1 and 2 Chronicles.* NCBC. Grand Rapids MI: Eerdmans and London: Marshall, Morgan, and Scott.

Wilson, Robert. 1980. *Prophecy and Society in Ancient Israel.* Philadelphia: Fortress.

———. 2000. "Ezekiel." *HBC,* 583–622.

Wolfe, Rolland Emerson. 1933. *The Editing of the Book of the Twelve: A Study of Secondary Material in the Minor Prophets.* Ph.D. Dissertation, Harvard University.

Wolff, Hans Walter. 1951. *Haggai: Eine Auslegung;* BibS(N) 1. Neukirchen-Vluyn: Neukirchener Verlag.

———. 1988. *Haggai: A Commentary.* Trans. Margaret Kohl. Minneapolis: Augsburg.

Xella, P. 1999. "RESHEPH." In *DDD,* 700–703.

Yadin, Yigael. 1983. *The Temple Scroll, Volume 1: Introduction.* Jerusalem: Israel Exploration Society.

Zimmerli, Walther. 1979. "Vom Prophetenwort zum Prophetenbuch," *TLZ* 104: 481–96.

Index

Reading Judges

A Literary and Theological Commentary

Mark E. Biddle

Reading the Old Testament book of Judges presents a number of significant challenges related to social contexts, historical settings, and literary characteristics. Acknowledging and examining these difficulties provides a point of entry into the world of Judges and promises to enrich the reading experience. *978-1-57312-631-1 240 pages/pb* ***$32.00***

Reading Samuel

A Literary and Theological Commentary

Johanna W. H. van Wijk-Bos

Interpreted masterfully by pre-eminent Old Testament scholar Johanna W. H. van Wijk-Bos, the story of Samuel touches on a vast array of subjects that comprise the rich fabric of human life. The reader gains an inside look at royal intrigue, military campaigns, occult practices and the significance of religious objects of veneration.

978-1-57312-607-6 256 pages/pb ***$32.00***

Reading Job

A Literary and Theological Commentary

James L. Crenshaw

At issue in the Book of Job is a question with which most all of us struggle at some point in life, "Why do bad things happen to good people?" James Crenshaw has devoted his life to studying the disturbing matter of theodicy—divine justice—that troubles many people of faith.

978-1-57312-574-1 192 pages/pb ***$32.00***

Reading Ezekiel

A Literary and Theological Commentary

Marvin A. Sweeney

In this volume, biblical scholar Marvin A. Sweeney considers one of the most interesting and compelling books of the Hebrew Bible. Ezekiel is simultaneously one of the Bible's most difficult and perplexing books as it presents the visions and oracles of Ezekiel, a Judean priest and prophet exiled to Babylonia in the sixth century BCE. *978-1-57312-658-8 264 pages/pb* ***$32.00***